Peter Silu

The Design and Analysis of Parallel Algorithms

Selim G. Akl

Queen's University
Kingston, Ontario, Canada

Prentice Hall, Englewood Cliffs, New Jersey 07632

LIBRARY OF CONGRESS
Library of Congress Cataloging-in-Publication Data

Akl, Selim G.
    The design and analysis of parallel algorithms / by Selim G. Akl.
       p.   cm.
    Bibliography: p.
    Includes index.
    ISBN 0-13-200056-3
    1. Parallel programming (Computer science) 2. Algorithms.
    I. Title.
    QA76.6.A38 1989
    004'.35--dc19   88-25019
                                                           CIP

Editorial/production supervision,
  Ann Mohan
Cover design: Lundgren Graphics Ltd.
Manufacturing buyer: Mary Noonan

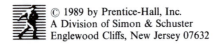 © 1989 by Prentice-Hall, Inc.
A Division of Simon & Schuster
Englewood Cliffs, New Jersey 07632

Printed in the United States of America
10 9 8 7 6 5 4 3 2 1

ISBN 0-13-200056-3

Prentice-Hall International (UK) Limited, *London*
Prentice-Hall of Australia Pty. Limited, *Sydney*
Prentice-Hall Canada Inc., *Toronto*
Prentice-Hall Hispanoamericana, S.A., *Mexico*
Prentice-Hall of India Private Limited, *New Delhi*
Prentice-Hall of Japan, Inc., *Tokyo*
Simon & Schuster Asia Pte. Ltd., *Singapore*
Editora Prentice-Hall do Brazil, Ltda., *Rio de Janeiro*

To Theo,
For making it worthwhile.

Contents

Preface

The need for ever faster computers has not ceased since the beginning of the computer era. Every new application seems to push existing computers to their limit. So far, computer manufacturers have kept up with the demand admirably well. In 1948, the electronic components used to build computers could switch from one state to another about 10,000 times every second. The switching time of this year's components is approximately 1/10,000,000,000th of a second. These figures mean that the number of operations a computer can do in one second has doubled, roughly every two years, over the past forty years. This is very impressive, but how long can it last? It is generally believed that the trend will remain until the end of this century. It may even be possible to maintain it a little longer by using optically based or even biologically based components. What happens after that?

If the current and contemplated applications of computers are any indication, our requirements in terms of computing speed will continue, at least at the same rate as in the past, well beyond the year 2000. Already, computers faster than any available today are needed to perform the enormous number of calculations involved in developing cures to mysterious diseases. They are essential to applications where the human ability to recognize complex visual and auditory patterns is to be simulated in real time. And they are indispensable if we are to realize many of humanity's dreams, ranging from reliable long-term weather forecasting to interplanetary travel and outer space exploration. It appears now that parallel processing is the way to achieve these desired computing speeds.

The overwhelming majority of computers in existence today, from the simplest to the most powerful, are conceptually very similar to one another. Their architecture and mode of operation follow, more or less, the same basic design principles formulated in the late 1940s and attributed to John von Neumann. The ingenious scenario is very simple and essentially goes as follows: A control unit fetches an instruction and its operands from a memory unit and sends them to a processing unit; there the instruction is executed and the result sent back to memory. This sequence of events is repeated for each instruction. There is only *one* unit of each kind, and only *one* instruction can be executed at a time.

With parallel processing the situation is entirely different. A parallel computer is one that consists of a collection of processing units, or *processors*, that cooperate to solve a problem by working simultaneously on different parts of that problem. The number of processors used can range from a few tens to several millions. As a result, the time required to solve the problem by a traditional uniprocessor computer is significantly reduced. This approach is attractive for a number of reasons. First, for many computational problems, the natural solution is a parallel one. Second, the cost and size of computer components have declined so sharply in recent years that parallel computers with a large number of processors have become feasible. And, third, it is possible in parallel processing to select the parallel architecture that is best suited to solve the problem or class of problems under consideration. Indeed, architects of parallel computers have the freedom to decide how many processors are to be used, how powerful these should be, what interconnection network links them to one another, whether they share a common memory, to what extent their operations are to be carried out synchronously, and a host of other issues. This wide range of choices has been reflected by the many theoretical models of parallel computation proposed as well as by the several parallel computers that were actually built.

Parallelism is sure to change the way we think about and use computers. It promises to put within our reach solutions to problems and frontiers of knowledge never dreamed of before. The rich variety of architectures will lead to the discovery of novel and more efficient solutions to both old and new problems. It is important therefore to ask: How do we solve problems on a parallel computer? The primary ingredient in solving a computational problem on any computer is the solution method, or *algorithm*. This book is about *algorithms for parallel computers*. It describes how to go about designing algorithms that exploit both the parallelism inherent in the problem and that available on the computer. It also shows how to analyze these algorithms in order to evaluate their speed and cost.

The computational problems studied in this book are grouped into three classes: (1) sorting, searching, and related problems; (2) combinatorial and numerical problems; and (3) problems arising in a number of application areas. These problems were chosen due to their fundamental nature. It is shown how a parallel algorithm is designed and analyzed to solve each problem. In some cases, several algorithms are presented that perform the same job, each on a different model of parallel computation. Examples are used as often as possible to illustrate the algorithms. Where necessary, a sequential algorithm is outlined for the problem at hand. Additional algorithms are briefly described in the Problems and Bibliographical Remarks sections. A list of references to other publications, where related problems and algorithms are treated, is provided at the end of each chapter.

The book may serve as a text for a graduate course on parallel algorithms. It was used at Queen's University for that purpose during the fall term of 1987. The class met for four hours every week over a period of twelve weeks. One of the four hours was devoted to student presentations of additional material, reference to which was found in the Bibliographical Remarks sections. The book should also be useful to computer scientists, engineers, and mathematicians who would like to learn about parallel models of computation and the design and analysis of parallel algorithms. It is assumed that the reader possesses the background normally provided by an undergraduate introductory course on the design and analysis of algorithms.

The most pleasant part of writing a book is when one finally gets a chance to thank those who helped make the task an enjoyable one. Four people deserve special credit: Ms. Irene LaFleche prepared the electronic version of the manuscript with her natural cheerfulness and unmistakable talent. The diagrams are the result of Mr. Mark Attisha's expertise, enthusiasm, and skill. Dr. Bruce Chalmers offered numerous trenchant and insightful comments on an early draft. Advice and assistance on matters big and small were provided generously by Mr. Thomas Bradshaw. I also wish to acknowledge the several helpful suggestions made by the students in my CISC-867 class at Queen's. The support provided by the staff of Prentice Hall at every stage is greatly appreciated

Finally, I am indebted to my wife, Karolina, and to my two children, Sophia and Theo, who participated in this project in more ways than I can mention. Theo, in particular, spent the first year of his life examining, from a vantage point, each word as it appeared on my writing pad.

Selim G. Akl
Kingston, Ontario

1

Introduction

1.1 THE NEED FOR PARALLEL COMPUTERS

A battery of satellites in outer space are collecting data at the rate of 10^{10} bits per second. The data represent information on the earth's weather, pollution, agriculture, and natural resources. In order for this information to be used in a timely fashion, it needs to be processed at a speed of at least 10^{13} operations per second.

Back on earth, a team of surgeons wish to view on a special display a reconstructed three-dimensional image of a patient's body in preparation for surgery. They need to be able to rotate the image at will, obtain a cross-sectional view of an organ, observe it in living detail, and then perform a simulated surgery while watching its effect, all without touching the patient. A minimum processing speed of 10^{15} operations per second would make this approach worthwhile.

The preceding two examples are representative of applications where tremendously fast computers are needed to process vast amounts of data or to perform a large number of calculations quickly (or at least within a reasonable length of time). Other such applications include aircraft testing, the development of new drugs, oil exploration, modeling fusion reactors, economic planning, cryptanalysis, managing large databases, astronomy, biomedical analysis, real-time speech recognition, robotics, and the solution of large systems of partial differential equations arising from numerical simulations in disciplines as diverse as seismology, aerodynamics, and atomic, nuclear, and plasma physics. No computer exists today that can deliver the processing speeds required by these applications. Even the so-called *supercomputers* peak at a few billion operations per second.

Over the past forty years dramatic increases in computing speed were achieved. Most of these were largely due to the use of inherently faster electronic components by computer manufacturers. As we went from relays to vacuum tubes to transistors and from small to medium to large and then to very large scale integration, we witnessed—often in amazement—the growth in size and range of the computational problems that we could solve.

Unfortunately, it is evident that this trend will soon come to an end. The limiting factor is a simple law of physics that gives the speed of light in vacuum. This speed is approximately equal to 3×10^8 meters per second. Now, assume that an electronic device can perform 10^{12} operations per second. Then it takes longer for a signal to travel between two such devices one-half of a millimeter apart than it takes for either of them to process it. In other words, all the gains in speed obtained by building superfast electronic components are lost while one component is waiting to receive some input from another one. Why then (one is compelled to ask) not put the two communicating components even closer together? Again, physics tells us that the reduction of distance between electronic devices reaches a point beyond which they begin to interact, thus reducing not only their speed but also their reliability.

It appears that the only way around this problem is to use *parallelism*. The idea here is that if several operations are performed simultaneously, then the time taken by a computation can be significantly reduced. This is a fairly intuitive notion, and one to which we are accustomed in any organized society. We know that several people of comparable skills can usually finish a job in a fraction of the time taken by one individual. From mail distribution to harvesting and from office to factory work, our everyday life offers numerous examples of parallelism through task sharing.

Even in the field of computing, the idea of parallelism is not entirely new and has taken many forms. Since the early days of information processing, people realized that it is greatly advantageous to have the various components of a computer do different things at the same time. Typically, while the central processing unit is doing calculations, input can be read from a magnetic tape and output produced on a line printer. In more advanced machines, there are several simple processors each specializing in a given computational task, such as operations on floating-point numbers, for example. Some of today's most powerful computers contain two or more processing units that share among themselves the jobs submitted for processing.

In each of the examples just mentioned, parallelism is exploited profitably, but nowhere near its promised power. Strictly speaking, none of the machines discussed is truly a parallel computer. In the modern paradigm that we are about to describe, however, the idea of parallel computing can realize its full potential. Here, our computational tool is a *parallel computer*, that is, a computer with many processing units, or *processors*. Given a problem to be solved, it is broken into a number of subproblems. All of these subproblems are now solved simultaneously, each on a different processor. The results are then combined to produce an answer to the original problem. This is a radical departure from the model of computation adopted for the past forty years in building computers—namely, the sequential uniprocessor machine.

Only during the last ten years has parallelism become truly attractive and a viable approach to the attainment of very high computational speeds. The declining cost of computer hardware has made it possible to assemble parallel machines with millions of processors. Inspired by the challenge, computer scientists began to study parallel computers both in theory and in practice. Empirical evidence provided by homegrown prototypes often came to support a large body of theoretical studies. And very recently, a number of commercial parallel computers have made their appearance on the market.

With the availability of the hardware, the most pressing question in parallel computing today is: How to program parallel computers to solve problems efficiently and in a practical and economically feasible way? As is the case in the sequential world, parallel computing requires algorithms, programming languages and compilers, as well as operating systems in order to actually perform a computation on the parallel hardware. All these ingredients of parallel computing are currently receiving a good deal of well-deserved attention from researchers.

This book is about one (and perhaps the most fundamental) aspect of parallelism, namely, *parallel algorithms*. A parallel algorithm is a solution method for a given problem destined to be performed on a parallel computer. In order to properly design such algorithms, one needs to have a clear understanding of the *model of computation* underlying the parallel computer.

1.2 MODELS OF COMPUTATION

Any computer, whether sequential or parallel, operates by executing instructions on data. A stream of instructions (the algorithm) tells the computer what to do at each step. A stream of data (the input to the algorithm) is affected by these instructions. Depending on whether there is one or several of these streams, we can distinguish among four classes of computers:

1. Single Instruction stream, Single Data stream (SISD)
2. Multiple Instruction stream, Single Data stream (MISD)
3. Single Instruction stream, Multiple Data stream (SIMD)
4. Multiple Instruction stream, Multiple Data stream (MIMD).

We now examine each of these classes in some detail. In the discussion that follows we shall not be concerned with input, output, or peripheral units that are available on every computer.

1.2.1 SISD Computers

A computer in this class consists of a single processing unit receiving a single stream of instructions that operate on a single stream of data, as shown in Fig. 1.1. At each step during the computation the control unit emits one instruction that operates on a datum obtained from the memory unit. Such an instruction may tell the processor, for

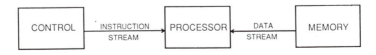

Figure 1.1   SISD computer.

example, to perform some arithmetic or logic operation on the datum and then put it back in memory.

The overwhelming majority of computers today adhere to this model invented by John von Neumann and his collaborators in the late 1940s. An algorithm for a computer in this class is said to be *sequential* (or *serial*).

Example 1.1

> In order to compute the sum of n numbers, the processor needs to gain access to the memory n consecutive times and each time receive one number. There are also $n - 1$ additions involved that are executed in sequence. Therefore, this computation requires on the order of n operations in total.   □

This example shows that algorithms for SISD computers do not contain any parallelism. The reason is obvious, there is only one processor! In order to obtain from a computer the kind of parallel operation defined earlier, it will need to have several processors. This is provided by the next three classes of computers, the classes of interest in this book. In each of these classes, a computer possesses N processors, where $N > 1$.

1.2.2 MISD Computers

Here, N processors each with its own control unit share a common memory unit where data reside, as shown in Fig. 1.2. There are N streams of instructions and one stream of data. At each step, one datum received from memory is operated upon by all the processors simultaneously, each according to the instruction it receives from its control. Thus, parallelism is achieved by letting the processors do different things at the same time on the same datum. This class of computers lends itself naturally to those computations requiring an input to be subjected to several operations, each receiving the input in its original form. Two such computations are now illustrated.

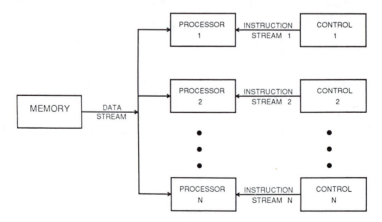

Figure 1.2   MISD computer.

Example 1.2

It is required to determine whether a given positive integer z has no divisors except 1 and itself. The obvious solution to this problem is to try all possible divisors of z: If none of these succeeds in dividing z, then z is said to be *prime*; otherwise z is said to be *composite*.

We can implement this solution as a parallel algorithm on an MISD computer. The idea is to split the job of testing potential divisors among processors. Assume that there are as many processors on the parallel computer as there are potential divisors of z. All processors take z as input, then each tries to divide it by its associated potential divisor and issues an appropriate output based on the result. Thus it is possible to determine in *one step* whether z is prime. More realistically, if there are fewer processors than potential divisors, then each processor can be given the job of testing a different subset of these divisors. In either case, a substantial speedup is obtained over a purely sequential implementation.

Although more efficient solutions to the problem of *primality testing* exist, we have chosen the simple one as it illustrates the point without the need for much mathematical sophistication.   □

Example 1.3

In many applications, we often need to determine to which of a number of classes does a given object belong. The object may be a mathematical one, where it is required to associate a number with one of several sets, each with its own properties. Or it may be a physical one: A robot scanning the deep-sea bed "sees" different objects that it has to recognize in order to distinguish among fish, rocks, algae, and so on. Typically, membership of the object is determined by subjecting it to a number of different tests.

The classification process can be done very quickly on an MISD computer with as many processors as there are classes. Each processor is associated with a class and can recognize members of that class through a computational test. Given an object to be classified, it is sent simultaneously to all processors where it is tested in parallel. The object belongs to the class associated with that processor that reports the success of its test. (Of course, it may be that the object does not belong to any of the classes tested for, in which case all processors report failure.) As in example 1.2, when fewer processors than classes are available, several tests are performed by each processor; here, however, in reporting success, a processor must also provide the class to which the object belongs.   □

The preceding examples show that the class of MISD computers could be extremely useful in many applications. It is also apparent that the kind of computations that can be carried out efficiently on these computers are of a rather specialized nature. For most applications, MISD computers would be rather awkward to use. Parallel computers that are more flexible, and hence suitable for a wide range of problems, are described in the next two sections.

1.2.3 SIMD Computers

In this class, a parallel computer consists of N identical processors, as shown in Fig. 1.3.

Each of the N processors possesses its own local memory where it can store both

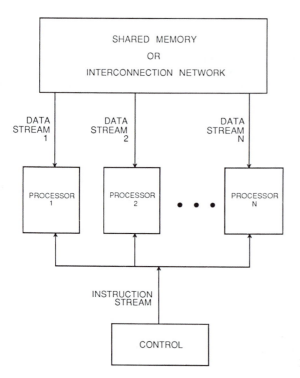

Figure 1.3 SIMD computer.

programs and data. All processors operate under the control of a single instruction stream issued by a central control unit. Equivalently, the N processors may be assumed to hold identical copies of a single program, each processor's copy being stored in its local memory. There are N data streams, one per processor.

The processors operate synchronously: At each step, all processors execute the same instruction, each on a different datum. The *instruction* could be a simple one (such as adding or comparing two numbers) or a complex one (such as merging two lists of numbers). Similarly, the *datum* may be simple (one number) or complex (several numbers). Sometimes, it may be necessary to have only a subset of the processors execute an instruction. This information can be encoded in the instruction itself, thereby telling a processor whether it should be *active* (and execute the instruction) or *inactive* (and wait for the next instruction). There is a mechanism, such as a global clock, that ensures lock-step operation. Thus processors that are inactive during an instruction or those that complete execution of the instruction before others may stay idle until the next instruction is issued. The time interval between two instructions may be fixed or may depend on the instruction being executed.

In most interesting problems that we wish to solve on an SIMD computer, it is desirable for the processors to be able to communicate among themselves during the computation in order to exchange data or intermediate results. This can be achieved in two ways, giving rise to two subclasses: SIMD computers where communication is through a *shared memory* and those where it is done via an *interconnection network*.

1.2.3.1 Shared-Memory (SM) SIMD Computers.   This class is also known in the literature as the Parallel Random-Access Machine (PRAM) model. Here, the N processors share a common memory that they use in the same way a group of people may use a bulletin board. When two processors wish to communicate, they do so through the shared memory. Say processor i wishes to pass a number to processor j. This is done in two steps. First, processor i writes the number in the shared memory at a given location known to processor j. Then, processor j reads the number from that location.

During the execution of a parallel algorithm, the N processors gain access to the shared memory for reading input data, for reading or writing intermediate results, and for writing final results. The basic model allows all processors to gain access to the shared memory simultaneously if the memory locations they are trying to read from or write into are different. However, the class of shared-memory SIMD computers can be further divided into four subclasses, according to whether two or more processors can gain access to the same memory location simultaneously:

(i) **Exclusive-Read, Exclusive-Write (EREW) SM SIMD Computers.**   Access to memory locations is exclusive. In other words, no two processors are allowed simultaneously to read from or write into the same memory location.

(ii) **Concurrent-Read, Exclusive-Write (CREW) SM SIMD Computers.** Multiple processors are allowed to read from the same memory location but the right to write is still exclusive: No two processors are allowed to write into the same location simultaneously.

(iii) **Exclusive-Read, Concurrent-Write (ERCW) SM SIMD Computers.** Multiple processors are allowed to write into the same memory location but read accesses remain exclusive.

(iv) **Concurrent-Read, Concurrent-Write (CRCW) SM SIMD Computers.** Both multiple-read and multiple-write privileges are granted.

Allowing multiple-read accesses to the same address in memory should in principle pose no problems (except perhaps some technological ones to be discussed later). Conceptually, each of the several processors reading from that location makes a copy of the location's contents and stores it in its own local memory.

With multiple-write accesses, however, difficulties arise. If several processors are attempting simultaneously to store (potentially different) data at a given address, which of them should succeed? In other words, there should be a deterministic way of specifying the contents of that address after the write operation. Several policies have been proposed to resolve such *write conflicts*, thus further subdividing classes (iii) and (iv). Some of these policies are

(a) the smallest-numbered processor is allowed to write, and access is denied to all other processors;

(b) all processors are allowed to write provided that the quantities they are attempting to store are equal, otherwise access is denied to all processors; and

(c) the sum of all quantities that the processors are attempting to write is stored.

A typical representative of the class of problems that can be solved on parallel computers of the SM SIMD family is given in the following example.

Example 1.4

Consider a very large computer file consisting of n distinct entries. We shall assume for simplicity that the file is not sorted in any order. (In fact, it may be the case that keeping the file sorted at all times is impossible or simply inefficient.) Now suppose that it is required to determine whether a given item x is present in the file in order to perform a standard database operation, such as *read, update,* or *delete.* On a conventional (i.e., SISD) computer, retrieving x requires n steps in the worst case where each step is a comparison between x and a file entry. The worst case clearly occurs when x is either equal to the last entry or not equal to any entry. On the average, of course, we expect to do a little better: If the file entries are distributed uniformly over a given range, then half as many steps are required to retrieve x.

The job can be done a lot faster on an **EREW SM SIMD** computer with N processors, where $N \leqslant n$. Let us denote the processors by $P_1, P_2, \ldots, P_N$.[1] To begin with, we need to let all the processors know the value of x. This can be done using an operation known as *broadcasting*:

1. P_1 reads x and communicates it to P_2.
2. Simultaneously, P_1 and P_2 communicate x to P_3 and P_4, respectively.
3. Simultaneously, P_1, P_2, P_3, and P_4 communicate x to P_5, P_6, P_7, and P_8, respectively,

and so on.

The process continues until all processors obtain x. As the number of processors that receive x doubles at each stage, broadcasting x to all N processors requires $\log N$ steps.[2] A formal statement of the broadcasting process is given in section 2.5.1.

Now the file to be searched for x is subdivided into subfiles that are searched simultaneously by the processors: P_1 searches the first n/N elements, P_2 searches the second n/N elements, and so on. Since all subfiles are of the same size, n/N steps are needed in the worst case to answer the query about x. In total, therefore, this parallel algorithm requires $\log N + n/N$ steps in the worst case. On the average, we can do better than that (as was done with the SISD computer): A location F holding a Boolean value can be set aside in the shared memory to signal that one of the processors has found the item searched for and, consequently, that all other processors should terminate their search. Initially, F is set to *false.* When a processor finds x in its subfile, it sets F to *true.* At every step of the search all processors check F to see if it is *true* and stop if this is the case. Unfortunately, this modification of the algorithm does not come for free: $\log N$ steps are needed to broadcast the value of F each time the processors need it. This leads to a total of $\log N + (n/N)\log N$ steps in the worst case. It is possible to improve this behavior by having the processors either check the value of F at every $(\log N)$th step, or broadcast it (once *true*) concurrently with the search process.

---

[1]Note that the indexing schemes used for processors in this chapter are for illustration only. Thus, for example, in subsequent chapters a set of N processors may be numbered 1 to N, or 0 to $N - 1$, whichever is more convenient.

[2]All logarithms in this book are to the base 2, unless otherwise indicated. If N is not a power of 2, then $\log N$ is always rounded to the next higher integer. Similarly, and unless otherwise stated, we shall assume that all real quantities—such as those arising from computing square roots and ratios—are rounded appropriately.

In order to truly exploit this early termination trick without increasing the worst-case running time, we need to use a more powerful model, namely, a CREW SM SIMD computer. Since concurrent-read operations are allowed, it takes one step for all processors to obtain x initially and one step for them to read F each time it is needed. This leads to a worst case of n/N steps.

Finally we note that an even more powerful model is needed if we remove the assumption made at the outset of this example that all entries in the file are distinct. Typically, the file may represent a textual database with hundreds of thousands of articles, each containing several thousand words. It may be necessary to search such a file for a given word x. In this case, more than one entry may be equal to x, and hence more than one processor may need to report success at the same time. This means that two or more processors will attempt to write into location F simultaneously, a situation that can only be handled by a CRCW SM SIMD computer. □

Simulating Multiple Accesses on an EREW Computer.   The EREW SM SIMD model of a parallel computer is unquestionably the weakest of the four subclasses of the shared-memory approach, as it restricts its access to a given address to one processor at a time. An algorithm for such a computer must be specifically designed to exclude any attempt by more than one processor to read from or write into the same location simultaneously. The model is sufficiently flexible, however, to allow the simulation of multiple accesses at the cost of either increasing the space and/or the time requirements of an algorithm.

Such a simulation may be desirable for one of two reasons:

1. The parallel computer available belongs to the EREW class and thus the only way to execute a CREW, ERCW, or CRCW algorithm is through simulation or
2. parallel computers of the CREW, ERCW, and CRCW models with a very large number of processors are technologically impossible to build at all. Indeed, the number of processors that can be simultaneously connected to a memory location is limited
   (i) not only by the physical size of the device used for that location,
   (ii) but also by the device's physical properties (such as voltage).

Therefore concurrent access to memory by an arbitrary number of processors may not be realizable in practice. Again in this case simulation is the only resort to implement an algorithm developed in theory to include multiple accesses.

(i) *N Multiple Accesses.*   Suppose that we want to run a parallel algorithm involving multiple accesses on an EREW SM SIMD computer with N processors $P_1, P_2, \ldots, P_N$. Suppose further that every multiple access means that *all N processors* are attempting to read from or write into the same memory location A. We can simulate multiple-read operations on an EREW computer using a *broadcast* procedure as explained in example 1.4. This way, A can be distributed to all processors in log N steps. Similarly, a procedure symmetrical to broadcasting can be used to handle multiple-write operations. Assume that the N processors are allowed to write in A simultaneously only if they are all attempting to store the same value. Let the value that P_i is attempting to write be denoted by a_i, $1 \leqslant i \leqslant N$. The procedure to store in A works as follows:

1. For $1 \leqslant i \leqslant N/2$, if a_i and $a_{i+N/2}$ are equal, then P_i sets a secondary variable b_i to *true*; otherwise b_i is set to *false*.

2. For $1 \leqslant i \leqslant N/4$, if b_i and $b_{i+N/4}$ are both *true* and $a_i = a_{i+N/4}$, then P_i sets b_i to *true*; otherwise b_i is set to *false*.

And so on. After $\log N$ steps, P_1 knows whether all the a_i are equal. If they are, it proceeds to store a_1 in A; otherwise no writing is allowed to take place. This *store* procedure is the subject of problem 2.13.

The preceding discussion indicates that multiple-read and multiple-write operations by all processors can be simulated on the EREW model. If every step of an algorithm involves multiple accesses of this sort, then in the worst case such a simulation increases the number of steps the algorithm requires by a factor of $\log N$.

(ii) *m out of N Multiple Accesses.*   We now turn to the more general case where a multiple read from or a multiple write into a memory location does not necessarily implicate all processors. In a typical algorithm, arbitrary subsets of processors may be each attempting to gain access to different locations, one location per subset. Clearly the procedures for broadcasting and storing described in (i) no longer work in this case. Another approach is needed in order to simulate such an algorithm on the EREW model with N processors. Say that the algorithm requires a total of M locations of shared memory. The idea here is to associate with each of the M locations another $2N - 2$ locations. Each of the M locations is thought of as the root of a binary tree with N leaves (the tree has depth $\log N$ and a total of $2N - 1$ nodes). The leaves of each tree are numbered 1 through N and each is associated with the processor with the same number.

When m processors, $m \leqslant N$, need to gain access to location A, they can put their requests at the leaves of the tree rooted at A. For a multiple read from location A, the requests trickle (along with the processors) up the tree until one processor reaches the root and reads from A. The value of A is then sent down the tree to all the processors that need it. Similarly, for a multiple-write operation, the processors "carry" the requests up the tree in the manner described in (i) for the *store* procedure. After $\log N$ steps one processor reaches the root and makes a decision about writing. Going up and down the tree of memory locations requires $2 \log N$ steps. The formal description of these simulations, known as *multiple broadcasting* and *multiple storing*, respectively, is the subject of section 3.4 and problem 3.33.

Therefore, the price paid for running a parallel algorithm with arbitrary multiple accesses is a $(2N - 2)$-fold increase in memory requirements. Furthermore, the number of steps is augmented by a factor on the order of $\log N$ in the worst case.

Feasibility of the Shared-Memory Model.   The SM SIMD computer is a fairly powerful model of computation, even in its weakest manifestation, the EREW subclass. Indeed, the model allows all available processors to gain access to the shared memory simultaneously. It is sometimes said that the model is unrealistic and no parallel computer based on that model can be built. The argument goes as follows. When one processor needs to gain access to a datum in memory, some circuitry is needed to create a path from that processor to the location in memory holding that datum. The cost of such circuitry is usually expressed as the number of logical gates required to decode the address provided by the processor. If the memory consists of M locations, then the cost of the decoding circuitry may be expressed as $f(M)$ for some cost function f. If N processors share that memory as in the SM SIMD model, then the cost of the decoding circuitry climbs to $N \times f(M)$. For large N and M this may lead to prohibitively large and expensive decoding circuitry between the processors and the memory.

There are many ways to mitigate this difficulty. All approaches inevitably lead to models weaker than the SM SIMD computer. Of course, any algorithm for the latter may be simulated on a weaker model at the cost of more space and/or computational steps. By contrast, any algorithm for a weaker model runs on the SM SIMD machine at no additional cost.

One way to reduce the cost of the decoding circuitry is to divide the shared memory into R blocks, say, of M/R locations each. There are $N + R$ two-way lines that allow any processor to gain access to any memory block at any time. However, no more than one processor can read from or write into a block simultaneously. This arrangement is shown in Fig. 1.4 for $N = 5$ and $R = 3$. The circles at the intersections of horizontal and vertical lines represent small (relatively inexpensive) switches. When

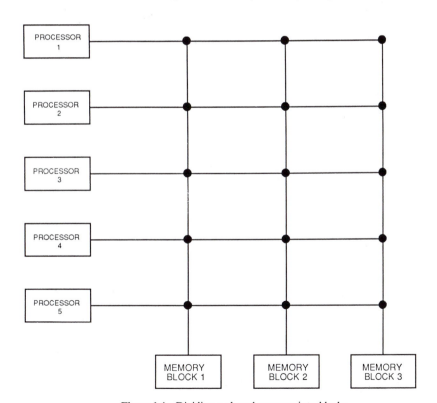

Figure 1.4   Dividing a shared memory into blocks.

the ith processor wishes to gain access to the jth memory block, it sends its request along the ith horizontal line to the jth switch, which then routes it down the jth vertical line to the jth memory block. Each memory block possesses one decoder circuit to determine which of the M/R locations is needed. Therefore, the total cost of decoding circuitry is $R \times f(M/R)$. To this we must add of course the cost of the $N \times R$ switches. Another approach to obtaining a weaker version of the SM SIMD is described in the next section.

1.2.3.2 Interconnection-Network SIMD Computers.   We concluded section 1.2.3.1 by showing how the SM SIMD model can be made more feasible by dividing the memory into blocks and making access to these blocks exclusive. It is natural to think of extending this idea to obtain a slightly more powerful model. Here the M locations of the shared memory are distributed among the N processors, each receiving M/N locations. In addition every pair of processors are connected by a two-way line. This arrangement is shown in Fig. 1.5 for $N = 5$. At any step during the computation, processor P_i can receive a datum from P_j and send another one to P_k (or to P_j). Consequently, each processor must contain

(i) a circuit of cost $f(N - 1)$ capable of decoding a $\log(N - 1)$-bit address—this allows the processor to select one of the other $N - 1$ processors for communicating; and

(ii) a circuit of cost $f(M/N)$ capable of decoding a $\log(M/N)$-bit address provided by another processor.

This model is therefore more powerful than the R-block shared memory, as it allows instantaneous communication between any pair of processors. Several pairs can thus communicate simultaneously (provided, of course, no more than one processor attempts to send data to or expects to receive data from another processor). Thus,

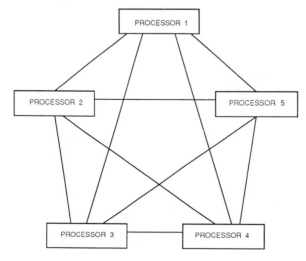

Figure 1.5 Fully interconnected set of processors.

potentially all processors can be busy communicating all the time, something that is not possible in the R-block shared memory when $N > R$. We now discuss a number of features of this model.

(i) Price.   The first question to ask is: What is the price paid to fully interconnect N processors? There are $N - 1$ lines leaving each processor for a total of $N(N - 1)/2$ lines. Clearly, such a network is too expensive, especially for large values of N. This is particularly true if we note that with N processors the best we can hope for is an N-fold reduction in the number of steps required by a sequential algorithm, as shown in section 1.3.1.3.

(ii) Feasibility.   Even if we could afford such a high price, the model is unrealistic in practice, again for large values of N. Indeed, there is a limit on the number of lines that can be connected to a processor, and that limit is dictated by the actual physical size of the processor itself.

(iii) Relation to SM SIMD.   Finally, it should be noted that the fully interconnected model as described is weaker than a shared-memory computer for the same reason as the R-block shared memory: No more than one processor can gain access simultaneously to the memory block associated with another processor. Allowing the latter would yield a cost of $N^2 \times f(M/N)$, which is about the same as for the SM SIMD (not counting the quadratic cost of the two-way lines): This clearly would defeat our original purpose of getting a more feasible machine!

Simple Networks for SIMD Computers.   It is fortunate that in most applications a small subset of all pairwise connections is usually sufficient to obtain a good performance. The most popular of these networks are briefly outlined in what follows. Keep in mind that since two processors can communicate in a constant number of steps on a SM SIMD computer, any algorithm for an interconnection-network SIMD computer can be simulated on the former model in no more steps than required to execute it by the latter.

(i) Linear Array.   The simplest way to interconnect N processors is in the form of a one-dimensional array, as shown in Fig. 1.6 for $N = 6$. Here, processor P_i is linked to its two neighbors P_{i-1} and P_{i+1} through a two-way communication line. Each of the end processors, namely, P_1 and P_N, has only one neighbor.

(ii) Two-Dimensional Array.   A two-dimensional network is obtained by arranging the N processors into an $m \times m$ array, where $m = N^{1/2}$, as shown in Fig. 1.7 for $m = 4$. The processor in row j and column k is denoted by $P(j, k)$, where $0 \leqslant j \leqslant m - 1$ and $0 \leqslant k \leqslant m - 1$. A two-way communication line links $P(j, k)$ to its neighbors $P(j + 1, k)$, $P(j - 1, k)$, $P(j, k + 1)$, and $P(j, k - 1)$. Processors on the

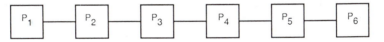

Figure 1.6   Linear array connection.

COLUMN
NUMBER   0   1   2   3

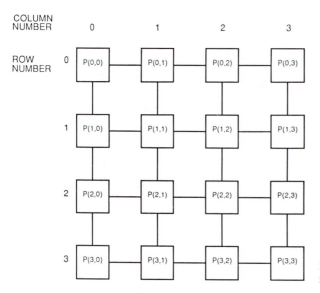

ROW
NUMBER

Figure 1.7 Two-dimensional array (or mesh) connection.

boundary rows and columns have fewer than four neighbors and hence fewer connections. This network is also known as the *mesh*.

Both the one- and two-dimensional arrays possess an interesting property: All the lines in the network have the same length. The importance of this feature, not enjoyed by other interconnections studied in this book, will become apparent when we analyze the time required by a network to solve a problem (see section 1.3.4.2).

(iii) Tree Connection.   In this network, the processors form a *complete binary tree*. Such a tree has d levels, numbered 0 to $d - 1$, and $N = 2^d - 1$ nodes each of which is a processor, as shown in Fig. 1.8 for $d = 4$. Each processor at level i is connected by a two-way line to its parent at level $i + 1$ and to its two children at level $i - 1$. The *root* processor (at level $d - 1$) has no parent and the *leaves* (all of which are at level 0) have no children. In this book, the terms *tree connection* (or *tree-connected computer*) are used to refer to such a tree of processors.

(iv) Perfect Shuffle Connection.   Let N processors P_0, $P_1, \ldots, P_{N-1}$ be available where N is a power of 2. In the *perfect shuffle* interconnection a one-way line links P_i to P_j, where

$$j = \begin{cases} 2i & \text{for } 0 \leqslant i \leqslant N/2 - 1, \\ 2i + 1 - N & \text{for } N/2 \leqslant i \leqslant N - 1, \end{cases}$$

as shown in Fig. 1.9 for $N = 8$. Equivalently, the binary representation of j is obtained by cyclically shifting that of i one position to the left.

In addition to these *shuffle* links, two-way lines connecting every even-numbered processor to its successor are sometimes added to the network. These connections, called the *exchange* links, are shown as broken lines in Fig. 1.9. In this case, the network is known as the *shuffle-exchange* connection.

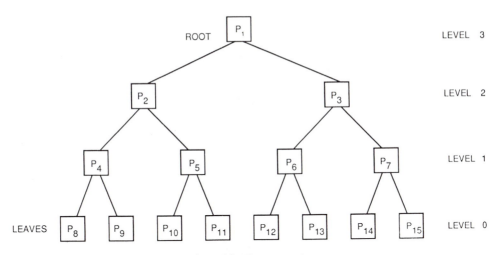

Figure 1.8   Tree connection.

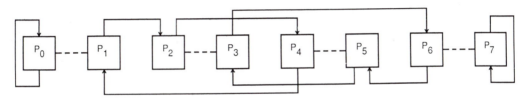

Figure 1.9   Perfect shuffle connection.

(v) Cube Connection.   Assume that $N = 2^q$ for some $q \geq 1$ and let N processors be available $P_0, P_1, \ldots, P_{N-1}$. A *q-dimensional cube* (or *hypercube*) is obtained by connecting each processor to q neighbors. The q neighbors P_j of P_i are defined as follows: The binary representation of j is obtained from that of i by complementing a single bit. This is illustrated in Fig. 1.10 for $q = 3$. The indices of $P_0, P_1, \ldots, P_7$ are given in binary notation. Note that each processor has three neighbors.

There are several other interconnection networks besides the ones just described. The decision regarding which of these to use largely depends on the application and in particular on such factors as the kinds of computations to be performed, the desired speed of execution, and the number of processors available. We conclude this section by illustrating a parallel algorithm for an SIMD computer that uses an interconnection network.

Example 1.5

Assume that the sum of n numbers $x_1, x_2, \ldots, x_n$ needs to be computed. There are $n - 1$ additions involved in this computation, and a sequential algorithm running on a conventional (i.e., SISD) computer will require n steps to complete it, as mentioned in

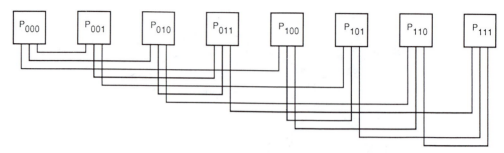

Figure 1.10   Cube connection.

example 1.1. Using a tree-connected SIMD computer with log n levels and $n/2$ leaves, the job can be done in log n steps as shown in Fig. 1.11 for $n = 8$.

The original input is received at the leaves, two numbers per leaf. Each leaf adds its inputs and sends the result to its parent. The process is now repeated at each subsequent level: Each processor receives two inputs from its children, computes their sum, and sends it to its parent. The final result is eventually produced by the root. Since at each level all the processors operate in parallel, the sum is computed in log n steps. This compares very favorably with the sequential computation.

The improvement in speed is even more dramatic when m sets, each of n numbers, are available and the sum of each set is to be computed. A conventional machine requires mn steps in this case. A naive application of the parallel algorithm produces the m sums in

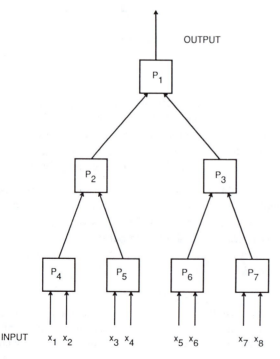

Figure 1.11   Adding eight numbers on a processor tree.

$m(\log n)$ steps. Through a process known as *pipelining*, however, we can do significantly better. Notice that once a set has been processed by the leaves, they are free to receive the next one. The same observation applies to all processors at higher levels. Hence each of the $m - 1$ sets that follow the initial one can be input to the leaves one step after their predecessor. Once the first sum exits from the root, a new sum is produced in the next step. The entire process therefore takes $\log n + m - 1$ steps.   □

It should be clear from our discussion so far that SIMD computers are considerably more versatile than those conforming to the MISD model. Numerous problems covering a wide variety of applications can be solved by parallel algorithms on SIMD computers. Also, as shown by examples 1.4 and 1.5, algorithms for these computers are relatively easy to design, analyze, and implement. In one respect, however, this class of problems is restricted to those that can be subdivided into a set of identical subproblems all of which are then solved simultaneously by the same set of instructions. Obviously, there are many computations that do not fit this pattern. In some problems it may not be possible or desirable to execute all instructions synchronously. Typically, such problems are subdivided into subproblems that are not necessarily identical and cannot or should not be solved by the same set of instructions. To solve these problems, we turn to the class of MIMD computers.

1.2.4 MIMD Computers

This class of computers is the most general and most powerful in our paradigm of parallel computation that classifies parallel computers according to whether the instruction and/or the data streams are duplicated. Here we have N processors, N streams of instructions, and N streams of data, as shown in Fig. 1.12. The processors here are of the type used in MISD computers in the sense that each possesses its own control unit in addition to its local memory and arithmetic and logic unit. This makes these processors more powerful than the ones used for SIMD computers.

Each processor operates under the control of an instruction stream issued by its control unit. Thus the processors are potentially all executing different programs on different data while solving different subproblems of a single problem. This means that the processors typically operate asynchronously. As with SIMD computers, communication between processors is performed through a shared memory or an interconnection network. MIMD computers sharing a common memory are often referred to as *multiprocessors* (or *tightly coupled machines*) while those with an interconnection network are known as *multicomputers* (or *loosely coupled machines*).

Since the processors on a multiprocessor computer share a common memory, the discussion in section 1.2.3.1 regarding the various modes of concurrent memory access applies here as well. Indeed, two or more processors executing an asynchronous algorithm may, by accident or by design, wish to gain access to the same memory location. We can therefore talk of EREW, CREW, ERCW, and CRCW SM MIMD computers and algorithms, and various methods should be established for resolving memory access conflicts in models that disallow them.

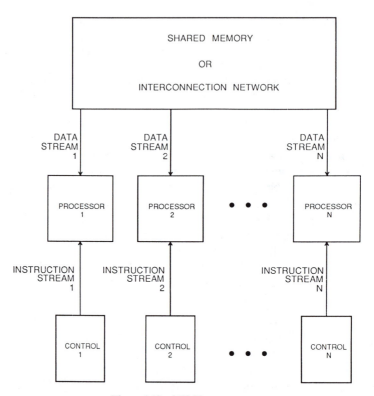

Figure 1.12 MIMD computer.

Multicomputers are sometimes referred to as *distributed systems*. The distinction is usually based on the physical distance separating the processors and is therefore often subjective. A rule of thumb is the following: If all the processors are in close proximity of one another (they are all in the same room, say), then they are a multicomputer; otherwise (they are in different cities, say) they are a distributed system. The nomenclature is relevant only when it comes to evaluating parallel algorithms. Because processors in a distributed system are so far apart, the number of data exchanges among them is significantly more important than the number of computational steps performed by any of them.

The following example examines an application where the great flexibility of MIMD computers is exploited.

Example 1.6

Computer programs that play games of strategy, such as *chess*, do so by generating and searching so-called *game trees*. The root of the tree is the current game configuration or *position* from which the program is to make a move. Children of the root represent all the positions reached through one move by the program. Nodes at the next level represent all positions reached through the opponent's reply. This continues up to some predefined number of levels. Each leaf position is now assigned a value representing its "goodness" from the program's point of view. The program then determines the path leading to the best position it can reach assuming that the opponent plays a perfect game. Finally, the original move on this path (i.e., an edge leaving the root) is selected for the program.

As there are typically several moves per position, game trees tend to be very large. In order to cut down on the search time, these trees are generated as they are searched. The idea is to explore the tree using the *depth-first search* method. From the given root position, paths are created and examined one by one. First, a complete path is built from the root to a leaf. The next path is obtained by backing up from the current leaf to a position all of whose descendants have not yet been explored and building a new path. During the generation of such a path it may happen that a position is reached that, based on information collected so far, definitely leads to leaves that are no better than the ones already examined. In this case the program interrupts its search along that path and all descendants of that position are ignored. A *cutoff* is said to have occurred. Search can now resume along a new path.

So far we have described the search procedure as it would be executed sequentially. One way to implement it on an MIMD computer would be to distribute the subtrees of the root among the processors and let as many subtrees as possible be explored in parallel. During the search the processors may exchange various pieces of information. For example, one processor may obtain from another the best move found so far: This may lead to further cutoffs. Another datum that may be communicated is whether a processor has finished searching its subtree(s). If there is a subtree that is still under consideration, then an idle processor may be assigned the job of searching part of that subtree.

This approach clearly does not lend itself to implementation on an SIMD computer as the sequence of operations involved in the search is not predictable in advance. At any given point, the instruction being executed varies from one processor to another: While one processor may be generating a new position, a second may be evaluating a leaf, a third may be executing a cutoff, a fourth may be backing up to start a new path, a fifth may be communicating its best move, a sixth may be signaling the end of its search, and so on.   □

1.2.4.1 Programming MIMD Computers.   As mentioned earlier, the MIMD model of parallel computation is the most general and powerful possible. Computers in this class are used to solve in parallel those problems that lack the regular structure required by the SIMD model. This generality does not come for free: Asynchronous algorithms are difficult to design, evaluate, and implement. In order to appreciate the complexity involved in programming MIMD computers, it is important to distinguish between the notion of a *process* and that of a *processor*. An asynchronous algorithm is a collection of processes some or all of which are executed simultaneously on a number of available processors. Initially, all processors are free. The parallel algorithm starts its execution on an arbitrarily chosen processor. Shortly thereafter it creates a number of computational tasks, or processes, to be performed. A process thus corresponds to a section of the algorithm: There may be several processes associated with the same algorithm section, each with a different parameter.

Once a process is created, it must be executed on a processor. If a free processor is available, the process is assigned to the processor that performs the computations specified by the process. Otherwise (if no free processor is available), the process is queued and waits for a processor to be free.

When a processor completes execution of a process, it becomes free. If a process is waiting to be executed, then it can be assigned to the processor just freed. Otherwise (if no process is waiting), the processor is queued and waits for a process to be created.

The order in which processes are executed by processors can obey any policy that assigns priorities to processes. For example, processes can be executed in a first-in-first-out or in a last-in-first-out order. Also, the availability of a processor is sometimes not sufficient for the processor to be assigned a waiting process. An additional condition may have to be satisfied before the process starts. Similarly, if a processor has already been assigned a process and an unsatisfied condition is encountered during execution, then the processor is freed. When the condition for resumption of that process is later satisfied, a processor (not necessarily the original one) is assigned to it. These are but a few of the scheduling problems that characterize the programming of multiprocessors. Finding efficient solutions to these problems is of paramount importance if MIMD computers are to be considered useful. Note that none of these scheduling problems arise on the less flexible but easier to program SIMD computers.

1.2.4.2 Special-Purpose Architectures.

In theory, any parallel algorithm can be executed efficiently on the MIMD model. The latter can therefore be used to build parallel computers with a wide variety of applications. Such computers are said to have a *general-purpose architecture*. In practice, by contrast, it is quite sensible in many applications to assemble several processors in a configuration specifically designed for the problem at hand. The result is a parallel computer well suited for solving that problem very quickly but that cannot in general be used for any other purpose. Such a computer is said to have a *special-purpose architecture*. With a particular problem in mind, there are several ways to design a special-purpose parallel computer. For example, a collection of specialized or very simple processors may be used in one of the standard networks such as the mesh. Alternatively, one may interconnect a number of standard processors in a custom geometry. These two approaches may also be combined.

Example 1.7

Black-and-white pictures are stored in computers in the form of two-dimensional arrays. Each array entry represents a *picture element*, or *pixel*. A 0 entry represents a white pixel, a 1 entry a black pixel. The larger the array, the more pixels we have, and hence the higher the *resolution*, that is, the precision with which the picture is represented. Once a picture is stored in that way, it can be processed, for example, to remove any noise that may be present, increase the sharpness, fill in missing details, and determine contours of objects.

Assume that it is desired to execute a very simple noise removal algorithm that gets rid of "salt" and "pepper" in pictures, that is, sparse white dots on a black background and sparse black dots on a white background, respectively. Such an algorithm can be implemented very efficiently on a set of very simple processors in a two-dimensional configuration where each processor is linked to its eight closest neighbors (i.e., the mesh with diagonal connections in addition to horizontal and vertical ones). Each processor corresponds to a pixel and stores its value. All the processors can now execute the following step in parallel: if a pixel is 0(1) and all its neighbors are 1(0), it changes its value to 1(0). □

One final observation is in order in concluding this section. Having studied a variety of approaches to building parallel computers, it is natural to ask: How is one to choose a parallel computer from among the available models? We already saw how one model can use its computational abilities to simulate an algorithm designed for another model. In fact, we shall show in the next section that one processor is capable of executing any parallel algorithm. This indicates that all the models of parallel computers are equivalent in terms of the problems that they *can* solve. What distinguishes one from another is the ease and speed with which it solves a particular problem. Therefore, the range of applications for which the computer will be used and the urgency with which answers to problems are needed are important factors in deciding what parallel computer to use. However, as with many things in life, the choice of a parallel computer is mostly dictated by economic considerations.

1.3 ANALYZING ALGORITHMS

This book is concerned with two aspects of parallel algorithms: their design and their analysis. A number of *algorithm design* techniques were illustrated in section 1.2 in connection with our description of the different models of parallel computation. The examples studied therein also dealt with the question of *algorithm analysis*. This refers to the process of determining how good an algorithm is, that is, how fast, how expensive to run, and how efficient it is in its use of the available resources. In this section we define more formally the various notions used in this book when analyzing parallel algorithms.

Once a new algorithm for some problem has been designed, it is usually evaluated using the following criteria: running time, number of processors used, and cost. Besides these standard metrics, a number of other technology-related measures are sometimes used when it is known that the algorithm is destined to run on a computer based on that particular technology.

1.3.1 Running Time

Since speeding up computations appears to be the main reason behind our interest in building parallel computers, the most important measure in evaluating a parallel algorithm is therefore its *running time*. This is defined as the time taken by the algorithm to solve a problem on a parallel computer, that is, the time elapsed from the moment the algorithm starts to the moment it terminates. If the various processors do not all begin and end their computation simultaneously, then the running time is equal to the time elapsed between the moment the first processor to begin computing starts and the moment the last processor to end computing terminates.

1.3.1.1 Counting Steps. Before actually implementing an algorithm (whether sequential or parallel) on a computer, it is customary to conduct a theoretical analysis of the time it will require to solve the computational problem at hand. This is usually done by counting the number of basic operations, or *steps*, executed by the algorithm in the worst case. This yields an expression describing the number of such steps as a function of the input size. The definition of what constitutes a step varies of course from one theoretical model of computation to another. Intuitively, however, comparing, adding, or swapping two numbers are commonly accepted basic operations in most models. Indeed, each of these operations requires a constant number of time units, or *cycles*, on a typical (SISD) computer. The running time of a parallel algorithm is usually obtained by counting two kinds of steps: *computational* steps and *routing* steps. A computational step is an arithmetic or logic operation performed on a datum within a processor. In a routing step, on the other hand, a datum travels from one processor to another via the shared memory or through the communication network. For a problem of size n, the parallel worst-case running time of an algorithm, a function of n, will be denoted by $t(n)$. Strictly speaking, the running time is also a function of the number of processors. Since the latter can always be expressed as a function of n, we shall write t as a function of the size of the input to avoid complicating our notation.

Example 1.8

In example 1.4 we studied a parallel algorithm that searches a file with n entries on an N-processor EREW SM SIMD computer. The algorithm requires $\log N$ parallel steps to broadcast the value to be searched for and n/N comparison steps within each processor. Assuming that each step (broadcast or comparison) requires one time unit, we say that the algorithms runs in $\log N + n/N$ time, that is, $t(n) = \log N + n/N$. □

In general, computational steps and routing steps do not necessarily require the same number of time units. A routing step usually depends on the distance between the processors and typically takes a little longer to execute than a computational step.

1.3.1.2 Lower and Upper Bounds. Given a computational problem for which a new sequential algorithm has just been designed, it is common practice among algorithm designers to ask the following two questions:

(i) Is it the fastest possible algorithm for the problem?

(ii) If not, how does it compare with other existing algorithms for the same problem?

The answer to the first question is usually obtained by comparing the number of steps executed by the algorithm to a known *lower bound* on the number of steps required to solve the problem in the worst case.

Example 1.9

Say that we want to compute the product of two $n \times n$ matrices. Since the resulting matrix has n^2 entries, at least this many steps are needed by any matrix multiplication algorithm simply to produce the output.   □

Lower bounds, such as the one in example 1.9, are usually known as *obvious* or *trivial* lower bounds, as they are obtained by counting the number of steps needed during input and/or output. A more sophisticated lower bound is derived in the next example.

Example 1.10

The problem of *sorting* is defined as follows: A set of n numbers in random order is given; arrange the numbers in nondecreasing order. There are $n!$ possible permutations of the input and $\log n!$ (i.e., on the order of $n \log n$) bits are needed to distinguish among them. Therefore, in the worst case, any algorithm for sorting requires on the order of $n \log n$ steps *at least* to recognize a particular output.   □

If the number of steps an algorithm executes in the worst case is equal to (or of the same order as) the lower bound, then the algorithm is the fastest possible and is said to be *optimal*. Otherwise, a faster algorithm may have to be invented, or it may be possible to improve the lower bound. In any case, if the new algorithm is faster than all *known* algorithms for the problem, then we say that it has established a new *upper bound* on the number of steps required to solve that problem in the worst case. Question (ii) is therefore always settled by comparing the running time of the new algorithm with the existing upper bound for the problem (established by the fastest previously known algorithm).

Example 1.11

To date, no algorithm is known for multiplying two $n \times n$ matrices in n^2 steps. The standard textbook algorithm requires on the order of n^3 operations. However, the upper bound on this problem is established at the time of this writing by an algorithm requiring on the order of n^x operations at most, where $x < 2.5$.

By contrast, several sorting algorithms exist that require on the order of at most $n \log n$ operations and are hence optimal.   □

In the preceding discussion, we used the phrase "on the order of" to express lower and upper bounds. We now introduce some notation for that purpose. Let $f(n)$ and $g(n)$ be functions from the positive integers to the positive reals:

  (i) The function $g(n)$ is said to be *of order at least $f(n)$*, denoted $\Omega(f(n))$, if there are positive constants c and n_0 such that $g(n) \geqslant cf(n)$ for all $n \geqslant n_0$.
  (ii) The function $g(n)$ is said to be *of order at most $f(n)$*, denoted $O(f(n))$, if there are positive constants c and n_0 such that $g(n) \leqslant cf(n)$ for all $n \geqslant n_0$.

This notation allows us to concentrate on the dominating term in an expression describing a lower or upper bound and to ignore any multiplicative constants.

Example 1.12

> For matrix multiplication, the lower bound is $\Omega(n^2)$ and the upper bound $O(n^{2.5})$. For sorting, the lower bound is $\Omega(n \log n)$ and the upper bound $O(n \log n)$.   □

Our treatment of lower and upper bounds in this section has so far concentrated on sequential algorithms. Clearly, the same general ideas also apply to parallel algorithms while taking two additional factors into consideration:

(i) the model of parallel computation used and

(ii) the number of processors involved.

Example 1.13

> An $n \times n$ mesh-connected SIMD computer (see Fig. 1.7) is used to compute the sum of n^2 numbers. Initially, there is one number per processor. Processor $P(n-1, n-1)$ is to produce the output. Since the number initially in $P(0, 0)$ has to be part of the sum, it must somehow find its way to $P(n-1, n-1)$. This requires at least $2(n-1)$ routing steps. Thus the lower bound on computing the sum is $\Omega(n)$ steps.   □

These ideas are further elaborated on in the following section.

1.3.1.3 Speedup.   In evaluating a parallel algorithm for a given problem, it is quite natural to do it in terms of the best available sequential algorithm for that problem. Thus a good indication of the quality of a parallel algorithm is the *speedup* it produces. This is defined as

Speedup =

$$\frac{\text{worst-case running time of fastest known sequential algorithm for problem}}{\text{worst-case running time of parallel algorithm}}.$$

Clearly, the larger the speedup, the better the parallel algorithm.

Example 1.14

> In example 1.4, a file of n entries is searched by an algorithm running on a CREW SM SIMD computer with N processors in $O(n/N)$ time. Since the running time of the best possible sequential algorithm is $O(n)$, the speedup is equal to $O(N)$.   □

For most problems, the speedup achieved in this example is usually the largest that can be obtained with N processors. To see this, assume that the fastest sequential algorithm for a problem requires time T_1, that a parallel algorithm for the same problem requires time T_2, and that $T_1/T_2 > N$. We now observe that any parallel algorithm can be simulated on a sequential computer. The simulation is carried out as follows: The (only) processor on the sequential computer executes the parallel steps serially by pretending that it is P_1, then that it is P_2, and so on. The time taken by the simulation is the sum of the times taken to imitate all N processors, which is at most N times T_2. But $NT_2 < T_1$, implying that the simulation we have just performed solves the problem faster than the sequential algorithm believed to be the fastest for that problem. This can mean one of two things:

(i) The sequential algorithm with running time T_1 is not really the fastest possible and we have just found a faster one with running time NT_2, thus improving the state of the art of sequential computing, or

(ii) there is an error in our analysis!

Suppose we know that a sequential algorithm for a given problem is indeed the fastest possible. Ideally, of course, one hopes to achieve the maximum speedup of N when solving such a problem using N processors operating in parallel. In practice, such a speedup cannot be achieved for every problem since

(i) it is not always possible to decompose a problem into N tasks, each requiring $(1/N)$th of the time taken by one processor to solve the original problem, and

(ii) in most cases the structure of the parallel computer used to solve a problem usually imposes restrictions that render the desired running time unattainable.

Example 1.15

The problem of adding n numbers discussed in example 1.5 is solved in $O(\log n)$ time on a tree-connected parallel computer using $n - 1$ processors. Here the speedup is $O(n/\log n)$ since the best possible sequential algorithm requires $O(n)$ additions. This speedup is far from the ideal $n - 1$ and is due to the fact that the n numbers were input at the leaves and the sum output at the root. Any algorithm for such a model necessarily requires $\Omega(\log n)$ time, that is, the time required for a single datum to propagate from input to output through all levels of the tree. □

1.3.2 Number of Processors

The second most important criterion in evaluating a parallel algorithm is the *number of processors* it requires to solve a problem. It costs money to purchase, maintain, and run computers. When several processors are present, the problem of maintenance, in particular, is compounded, and the price paid to guarantee a high degree of reliability rises sharply. Therefore, the larger the number of processors an algorithm uses to solve a problem, the more expensive the solution becomes to obtain. For a problem of size n, the number of processors required by an algorithm, a function of n, will be denoted by $p(n)$. Sometimes the number of processors is a constant independent of n.

Example 1.16

In example 1.5, the size of the tree depends on n, the number of terms to be added, and $p(n) = n - 1$.

On the other hand, in example 1.4, N, the number of processors on the shared-memory computer, is in no way related to n, the size of the file to be searched (except for the fact that $N \leqslant n$). Nevertheless, given a value of n, it is possible to express N in terms of n as follows: $N = n^x$ where $0 < x \leqslant 1$. Thus $p(n) = n^x$. □

1.3.3 Cost

The *cost* of a parallel algorithm is defined as the product of the previous two measures; hence

Cost = parallel running time × number of processors used.

In other words, cost equals the number of steps executed collectively by all processors in solving a problem in the worst case. This definition assumes that all processors execute the same number of steps. If this is not the case, then cost is an upper bound on the total number of steps executed. For a problem of size n, the cost of a parallel algorithm, a function of n, will be denoted by $c(n)$. Thus $c(n) = p(n) \times t(n)$.

Assume that a lower bound is known on the number of sequential operations required in the worst case to solve a problem. If the cost of a parallel algorithm for that problem matches this lower bound to within a constant multiplicative factor, then the algorithm is said to be *cost optimal*. This is because any parallel algorithm can be simulated on a sequential computer, as described in section 1.3.1. If the total numbers of steps executed during the simulation is equal to the lower bound, then this means that, when it comes to *cost*, this parallel algorithm cannot be improved upon as it executes the minimum number of steps possible. It may be possible, of course, to *reduce the running time* of a cost-optimal parallel algorithm by *using more processors*. Similarly, we may be able to *use fewer processors*, while retaining cost optimality, if we are willing to settle for a *higher running time*.

A parallel algorithm is *not cost optimal* if a sequential algorithm exists whose running time is smaller than the parallel algorithm's cost.

Example 1.17

In example 1.4, the algorithm for searching a file with n entries on an N-processor CREW SM SIMD computer has a cost of

$$N \times O(n/N) = O(n).$$

This cost is optimal since no randomly ordered file of size n can be searched for a particular value in fewer than n steps in the worst case: One step is needed to compare each entry with the given value.

In example 1.5, the cost of adding n numbers on an $(n-1)$-processor tree is $(n-1) \times O(\log n)$. This cost is not optimal since we know how to add n numbers optimally using $O(n)$ sequential additions. □

We note in passing that the preceding discussion leads to a method for obtaining model-independent lower bounds on parallel algorithms. Let $\Omega(T(n))$ be a lower bound on the number of sequential steps required to solve a problem of size n. Then $\Omega(T(n)/N)$ is a lower bound on the running time of any parallel algorithm that uses N processors to solve that problem.

Example 1.18

Since $\Omega(n \log n)$ steps is a lower bound on any sequential sorting algorithm, the equivalent lower bound on any parallel algorithm using n processors is $\Omega(\log n)$. □

When no optimal sequential algorithm is known for solving a problem, the *efficiency* of a parallel algorithm for that problem is used to evaluate its cost. This is defined as follows:

Efficiency =

$$\frac{\text{worst-case running time of fastest known sequential algorithm for problem}}{\text{cost of parallel algorithm}}.$$

Usually, efficiency ≤ 1; otherwise a faster sequential algorithm can be obtained from the parallel one!

Example 1.19

Let the worst-case running time of the fastest sequential algorithm to multiply two $n \times n$ matrices be $O(n^{2.5})$ time units. The efficiency of a parallel algorithm that uses n^2 processors to solve the problem in $O(n)$ time is $O(n^{2.5})/O(n^3)$. $\square$

Finally, let the cost of a parallel algorithm for a given problem match the running time of the fastest existing sequential algorithm for the same problem. Furthermore, assume that it is not known whether the sequential algorithm is optimal. In this case, the status of the parallel algorithm with respect to cost optimality is unknown. Thus in example 1.19, if the parallel algorithm had a cost of $O(n^{2.5})$, then its cost optimality would be an open question.

1.3.4 Other Measures

A digital computer can be viewed as a large collection of interconnected logical gates. These gates are built using transistors, resistors, and capacitors. In today's computers, gates come in packages called *chips*. These are tiny pieces of semiconductor material used to fabricate logical gates and the wires connecting them. The number of gates on a chip determines the level of *integration* being used to build the circuit. One particular technology that appears to be linked to future successes in parallel computing is Very Large Scale Integration (VLSI). Here, nearly a million logical gates can be located on a single 1-cm^2 chip. The chip is thus able to house a number of processors, and several such chips may be assembled to build a powerful parallel computer. When evaluating parallel algorithms for VLSI, the following criteria are often used: processor *area*, wire *length*, and *period* of the circuit.

1.3.4.1 Area.   If several processors are going to share the "real estate" on a chip, the area needed by the processors and wires connecting them as well as the interconnection geometry determine how many processors the chip will hold. Alternatively, if the number of processors per chip is fixed in advance, then the size of the chip itself is dictated by the total area the processors require. If two algorithms take the same amount of time to solve a problem, then the one occupying less area when implemented as a VLSI circuit is usually preferred. Note that when using the area as a measure of the goodness of a parallel algorithm, we are in fact using the criterion in section 1.3.2, namely, the number of processors needed by the algorithm. This is because the area occupied by each processor is normally a constant quantity.

1.3.4.2 Length.   This refers to the length of the wires connecting the processors in a given architecture. If the wires have constant length, then it usually means that the architecture is

   (i) *regular*, that is, has a pattern that repeats everywhere, and
   (ii) *modular*, that is, can be built of one (or just a few) repeated modules.

With these properties, extension of the design becomes easy, and the size of a parallel computer can be increased by simply adding more modules. The linear and two-dimensional arrays of section 1.2.3.2 enjoy this property. Also, fixed wire length means that the time taken by a signal to propagate from one processor to another is always constant. If, on the other hand, wire length varies from one section of the network to another, then propagation time becomes a function of that length. The tree, perfect shuffle, and cube interconnections in section 1.2.3.2 are examples of such networks. Again this measure is not unrelated to the criterion in section 1.3.1, namely, running time, since the duration of a routing step (and hence the algorithm's performance) depends on wire length.

1.3.4.3 Period.   Assume that several sets of inputs are available and queued for processing by a circuit in a pipeline fashion. Let $A_1, A_2, \ldots, A_n$ be a sequence of such inputs such that the time to process A_i is the same for all $1 \leqslant i \leqslant n$. The period of the circuit is the time elapsed between the moments when processing of A_i and A_{i+1} begin, which should be the same for all $1 \leqslant i \leqslant n$.

Example 1.20

   In example 1.5 several sums were to be computed on a tree-connected SIMD computer. We saw that once the leaves had processed one set of numbers to be added and sent it to their parents for further processing, they were ready to receive the next set. The period of this circuit is therefore 1: One time unit (the time for one addition) separates two inputs.   □

Evidently, a small period is a desirable property of a parallel algorithm. In general, the period is significantly smaller than the time required to completely process one input set. In example 1.20, the period is not only significantly smaller than the $O(\log n)$ time units required to compute the sum of n numbers, but also happens to be constant.

We conclude this section with a remark concerning the time taken by a parallel algorithm to receive its input and, once finished computing, to return its output. Our assumption throughout this book is that all the processors of a parallel computer are capable of reading the available input and producing the available output in parallel. Therefore, such simultaneous input or output operations will be regarded as requiring constant time.

1.4 EXPRESSING ALGORITHMS

So far we have used an informal language to describe parallel algorithms. In our subsequent treatment we would like to make this language a bit more formal while keeping our statements of algorithms as intuitive as possible. As a compromise, a high-level description will be used that combines plain English with widely known programming constructs.

A parallel algorithm will normally consist of two kinds of operations: sequential and parallel. In describing the former, we use statements similar to those of a typical structured programming language (such as Pascal, say). Examples of such statements include: **if ... then ... else, while ... do, for ... do,** assignment statements, input and output statements, and so on. The meanings of these statements are assumed to be known. A left-pointing arrow denotes the assignment operator; thus $a \leftarrow b$, means that the value of b is assigned to a. The logical operations **and, or, xor** (exclusive-or), and **not** are used in their familiar connotation. Thus, if a and b are two expressions, each taking one of the values **true** or **false**, then

(i) (a **and** b) is **true** if *both* a and b are **true**; otherwise (a **and** b) is **false**;

(ii) (a **or** b) is **true** if *at least one* of a and b is **true**; otherwise (a **or** b) is **false**;

(iii) (a **xor** b) is **true** if *exactly one* of a and b is **true**; otherwise (a **xor** b) is **false**; and

(iv) (**not** a) is **true** if a is **false**; otherwise (**not** a) is **false**.

Parallel operations, on the other hand, are expressed by two kinds of statements:

(i) When several steps are to be done at the same time, we write

> **do** steps i **to** j **in parallel**
>
> step i
> step $i+1$
> $\vdots$
> step j.   □

(ii) When several processors are to perform the same operation simultaneously, we write

> **for** $i = j$ **to** k **do in parallel**
> {The operations to be performed by P_i are stated here}
> **end for**   □

where i takes every integer value from j to k, or

> **for** $i = r, s, \ldots, t$ **do in parallel**
> {The operations to be performed by P_i are stated here}
> **end for**   □

where the integer values taken by i are enumerated, or

> **for all i in S do in parallel**
> {The operations to be performed by P_i are stated here}
> **end for**   □

where S is a given set of integers.

Comments in algorithms are surrounded with curly brackets { }, as shown in the preceding. Curly brackets are also used to denote a sequence of elements as, for example, in $A = \{a_0, a_1, \ldots, a_{n-1}\}$ or in $E = \{s_i \in S : s_i = m\}$. Both uses are fairly standard and easy to recognize from the context.

1.5 ORGANIZATION OF THE BOOK

The remainder of this book is organized in thirteen chapters. Each chapter is devoted to the study of parallel algorithms for a fundamental computational problem or problem area. The related operations of selection, merging, sorting, and searching are covered in chapters 2–5, respectively. Several computations of either a combinatorial or numerical nature are then examined, namely, generating permutations and combinations (chapter 6), matrix operations (chapter 7), numerical problems (chapter 8), and computing Fourier transforms (chapter 9). Four application areas are treated in chapters 10 (graph theory), 11 (computational geometry), 12 (traversing combinatorial spaces), and 13 (decision and optimization). Finally, chapter 14 addresses a number of basic problems for which the definition of a time unit (given in section 1.3.1.1) is interpreted as the time required to perform an operation on a pair of bits. Each chapter concludes with a set of problems, bibliographical remarks, and a list of references.

1.6 PROBLEMS

1.1 Show how an MISD computer can be used to handle multiple queries on a given object in a database.

1.2 Three applications of MISD computers are given in examples 1.2 and 1.3 and in problem 1.1. Can you think of other computations for which the MISD model is suitable?

1.3 There is no mention in section 1.2.2 of the possible communication among processors. Indeed, in most applications for which the MISD model is practical, virtually no communication is needed. In some problems, however, it may be necessary for the processors to exchange intermediate results. In addition, there should always be a mechanism to allow a processor to signal the end of its computation, which may lead the others to terminate their own. As with the SIMD and MIMD models, the processors can communicate through the common memory they already share and that generates the data stream. Alternatively, and for practical reasons, there could be a network connecting the processors (in addition to the memory). In the latter case, the memory's job is to issue the data stream while all communications are done through the network. Describe a problem that can be conveniently solved on an MISD computer where interprocessor communication is possible.

1.4 In section 1.2.3.1, while discussing simulating multiple accesses on an EREW SM SIMD computer, we mentioned that procedure *broadcast* was not suitable in the following situation: Several multiple-read operations are attempted by several subsets of the set of processors each subset trying to gain access to a different memory location. Strictly speaking, *broadcast* may be used, but the resulting algorithm may be inefficient. Show how this can be done and analyze the worst-case running time of the simulation.

1.5 Given a set of numbers $\{s_1, s_2, \ldots, s_N\}$, all sums of the form $s_1 + s_2$, $s_1 + s_2 + s_3, \ldots,$ $s_1 + s_2 + \cdots + s_N$ are to be computed. Design an algorithm for solving this problem using N processors on each of the four submodels of the SM SIMD model.

1.6 Show that a fully connected network of N processors is equivalent to an EREW SM SIMD computer with N processors and exactly N locations of shared memory.

1.7 Let an EREW SM SIMD computer have N processors and M locations of shared memory. Give a procedure for simulating this computer on a fully interconnected network of N processors each with up to M/N locations in its local memory. How many steps on the second computer are required to simulate one step on the first?

1.8 For each of the interconnection networks in section 1.2.3.2, describe a problem that can be solved efficiently on that network. Give an algorithm for each problem, derive its running time and cost, and determine whether it is cost optimal.

1.9 It is required to determine the largest of a set of n numbers. Describe an algorithm for solving this problem on each of the interconnection networks in section 1.2.3.2. Express the running time of each solution as a function of n.

1.10 Show how a fully connected network of N processors can be simulated on a cube-connected network with the same number of processors such that each step of a computation on the first network requires at most $O(\log^2 N)$ steps on the second.

1.11 Prove that an algorithm requiring $t(n)$ time to solve a problem of size n on a cube-connected computer with N processors can be simulated on a shuffle-exchange network with the same number of processors in $O(\log N) \times t(n)$ time.

1.12 The *plus–minus* 2^i (PM2I) interconnection network for an N-processor SIMD computer is defined as follows: P_j is connected to P_r and P_s, where $r = j + 2^i \bmod N$ and $s = j - 2^i \bmod N$, for $0 \leqslant i < \log N$.

  (i) Let A be an algorithm that requires T steps to run on a cube-connected computer. Prove that a PM2I-connected computer with the same number of processors can execute A in at most $2T$ steps.

  (ii) Let A be an algorithm that requires T steps to run on a PM2I-connected computer with N processors. Prove that a cube-connected computer also with N processors can execute A in at most $T \log N$ steps.

1.13 *Branch-and-bound* is the name of a well-known algorithm for solving combinatorial optimization problems. Let P be a problem for which we want to find a *least-cost* solution from among N *feasible* solutions. The number N is assumed to be so large as to preclude exhaustive enumeration. In branch-and-bound we think of the N feasible solutions as the leaves of a giant tree. Each node on a path from root to leaf represents a partial solution obtained by extending the partial solution represented by its parent. Starting with the empty solution at the root, the algorithm generates all of the root's descendants.

Expansion then continues from the node with least cost and the process is repeated. When the cost of a partial solution exceeds a certain bound, that node is no longer a candidate for expansion. Search continues until a leaf is reached and there are no more nodes to be expanded. This leaf represents a least-cost solution. Show how this algorithm can be made to run in parallel on an MIMD computer.

1.14 It is sometimes computationally infeasible (even with a parallel computer) to obtain exact answers to some combinatorial optimization problems. Instead, a *near-optimal* solution is computed using an approximation method. One such method is known as *local neighborhood search*. Let f be a combinatorial function that is to be minimized, say. We begin by computing the value of f at a randomly chosen point. The neighbors of that point are then examined and the value of f computed for each new point. Each time a point reduces the value of the function, we move to that point. This continues until no further improvement can be obtained. The point reached is labeled a local minimum. The entire process is repeated several times, each time from a new random point. Finally, a global minimum is computed from all local minima thus obtained. This is the approximate answer. Discuss various ways for obtaining a parallel version of this method that runs on an MIMD computer.

1.15 Example 1.6 and problems 1.13 and 1.14 describe three applications of MIMD computers. Describe other problems that can be solved naturally on an MIMD computer and for which neither the MISD nor SIMD models are appropriate. Propose an algorithm to solve each problem.

1.16 Three general classes of parallel computers were discussed in this chapter, namely, the MISD, SIMD, and MIMD models. Can you think of other models of parallel computation? For every model you propose explain why it does, or does not, belong to one of the preceding classes.

1.17 A satellite picture is represented as an $n \times n$ array of pixels each taking an integer value between 0 and 9, thus providing various *gray levels*. It is required to smooth the picture, that is, the value of pixel (i, j) is to be replaced by the average of its value and those of its eight neighbors $(i - 1, j)$, $(i - 1, j - 1)$, $(i, j - 1)$, $(i + 1, j - 1)$, $(i + 1, j)$, $(i + 1, j + 1)$, $(i, j + 1)$, and $(i - 1, j + 1)$, with appropriate rounding. Describe a special-purpose parallel architecture for this problem. Assume that N, the number of processors available, is less than n^2, the number of pixels. Give two different implementations of the smoothing process and analyze their running times.

1.18 Let A and B be two $n \times n$ matrices with elements a_{ij} and b_{ij}, respectively, for $i, j = 1, 2, \ldots, n$. It is required to compute $C = A \times B$ where the elements c_{ij} of the product matrix C are obtained from

$$c_{ij} = \sum_{k=1}^{n} a_{ik} \times b_{kj} \qquad \text{for } i, j = 1, 2, \ldots, n.$$

(a) Design a parallel algorithm for computing C on the following model of computation. The model consists of n^2 processors arranged in an $n \times n$ array (n rows and n columns). The processors are interconnected as follows:

1. The processors of each column are connected to form a ring, that is, every processor is connected to its top and bottom neighbors, and the topmost and bottommost processors of the column are also connected.

2. The processors of each row are connected to form a binary tree, that is, if the processors in the row are numbered $1, 2, \ldots, n$, then processor i is connected to processors $2i$ and $2i + 1$ if they exist.

The local memory of each processor consists of four locations at most.

(b) Analyze your algorithm.

1.19 Design a special-purpose architecture for solving a system of linear equations.

1.20 Example 1.7 and problems 1.17–1.19 describe applications of special-purpose parallel architectures. Can you think of other problems that can be efficiently solved on such architectures?

1.7 BIBLIOGRAPHICAL REMARKS

Several recent books have been devoted entirely or in part to the subject of parallel architectures. These include [Baer 1], [Cosnard], [Enslow], [Feilmeier], [Fernbach], [Hillis 1], [Hockney], [Hwang 1], [Hwang 2], [Karin], [Kuck 1], [Kuck 2], [Legendi], [Leighton], [Leiserson], [Lorin], [Mead], [Preston], [Reed], [Reijns], [Siegel], [Stone], [Uhr], [Ullman], and [Wu]. Some of the parallel computers that were built in research laboratories or have appeared on the market are described in [Baer 2], [Frenkel 1], [Frenkel 2], [Hillis 2], [Hord], [Jones 1], [Jones 2], [Lipovski], [Potter], and [Wah]. Reviews of parallel languages are provided in [Gelernter], [Howe], and [Karp]. Issues pertaining to parallel operating systems are addressed in [Evans] and [Oleinick]. The design and analysis of parallel algorithms are covered in [Akl 3], [Cook 1], [Cook 2], [Graham], [Jamieson], [Kronsjö], [Kuhn], [Kung], [Quinn], [Rodrigue], [Schendel], [Snyder], and [Traub].

Various approaches to simulating the shared-memory model by weaker models are given in [Alt], [Karlin], [Mehlhorn], [Parberry], [Stockmeyer], [Ullman], [Upfal 1], [Upfal 2], and [Vishkin]. Interconnection networks are reviewed in [Bhuyan] and [Wu].

The procedure described in example 1.6 for searching game trees on an MIMD computer is a simplified version of a parallel algorithm first proposed in [Akl 1]. Similar algorithms can be found in [Akl 2] and [Marsland].

Good references for sequential algorithms are [Horowitz] and [Reingold]. Fast sequential matrix multiplication algorithms, such as the one mentioned in example 1.11, are reviewed in [Strassen]. The branch-and-bound and local neighborhood search methods referred to in problems 1.13 and 1.14, respectively, are detailed in [Papadimitriou].

1.8 REFERENCES

[AKL 1]
Akl, S. G., Barnard, D. T., and Doran, R. J., Design, analysis and implementation of a parallel tree search algorithm, *IEEE Transactions on Pattern Analysis and Machine Intelligence*, Vol. PAMI-4, No. 2, March 1982, pp. 192–203.

[AKL 2]
Akl, S. G., and Doran, R. J., A comparison of parallel implementations of the Alpha–Beta and Scout tree search algorithms using the game of checkers, in Bramer, M. A., Ed., *Computer Game Playing*, Wiley, Chichester, England, 1983, pp. 290–303.

[AKL 3]
   Akl, S. G., *Parallel Sorting Algorithms*, Academic, Orlando, Fl., 1985.

[ALT]
   Alt, H., Hagerup, T., Mehlhorn, K., and Preparata, F. P., Deterministic simulation of idealized parallel computers on more realistic ones, *SIAM Journal on Computing*, Vol. 16, No. 5, October 1987, pp. 808–835.

[BAER 1]
   Baer, J.-L., *Computer Systems Architecture*, Computer Science Press, Potomac, Md., 1980.

[BAER 2]
   Baer, J.-L., Computer architecture, *Computer*, Vol. 17, No. 10, October 1984, pp. 77–87.

[BHUYAN]
   Bhuyan, L. N., Ed., Special Issue on Interconnection Networks for Parallel and Distributed Processing, *Computer*, Vol. 20, No. 6, June 1987.

[COOK 1]
   Cook, S. A., Towards a complexity theory of synchronous parallel computation, Technical Report No. 141/80, Department of Computer Science, University of Toronto, Toronto, 1980.

[COOK 2]
   Cook, S. A., A taxonomy of problems with fast parallel algorithms, *Information and Control*, Vol. 64, 1985, pp. 2–22.

[COSNARD]
   Cosnard, M., Quinton, P., Robert, Y., and Tchuente, M., Eds., *Parallel Algorithms and Architectures*, North-Holland, Amsterdam, 1986.

[ENSLOW]
   Enslow, P. H., Jr., *Multiprocessors and Parallel Processing*, Wiley-Interscience, New York, 1974.

[EVANS]
   Evans, D. J., *Parallel Processing Systems: An Advanced Course*, Cambridge University Press, Cambridge, England, 1982.

[FEILMEIER]
   Feilmeier, M., Joubert, G., and Schendel, U., Eds., *Parallel Computing 85*, North-Holland, Amsterdam, 1986.

[FERNBACH]
   Fernbach, S., Ed., *Supercomputers*, North-Holland, Amsterdam, 1986.

[FRENKEL 1]
   Frenkel, K. A., Evaluating two massively parallel machines, *Communications of the ACM*, Vol. 29, No. 8, August 1986, pp. 752–758.

[FRENKEL 2]
   Frenkel, K. A., Ed., Special Issue on Parallelism, *Communications of the ACM*, Vol. 29, No. 12, December 1986.

[GELERNTER]
   Gelernter, D., Ed., Special Issue on Domesticating Parallelism, *Computer*, Vol. 19, No. 8, August 1986.

[GRAHAM]
   Graham, R. L., Bounds on multiprocessing anomalies and related packing algorithms, Proceedings of the AFIPS 1972 Sprint Joint Computer Conference, Atlantic City, New Jersey, May 1972, pp. 205–217, AFIPS Press, Montvale, N.J., 1972.

[HILLIS 1]
  Hillis, W. D., *The Connection Machine*, MIT Press, Cambridge, Mass., 1985.

[HILLIS 2]
  Hillis, W. D., The connection machine, *Scientific American*, Vol. 256, No. 6, June 1987, pp. 108–115.

[HOCKNEY]
  Hockney, R. W., and Jesshope, C. R., *Parallel Computers*, Adam Hilger, Bristol, England, 1981.

[HORD]
  Hord, M. R., *The Illiac IV: The First Supercomputer*, Computer Science Press, Rockville, Md., 1982.

[HOROWITZ]
  Horowitz, E., and Sahni, S., *Fundamentals of Computer Algorithms*, Computer Science Press, Rockville, Md., 1978.

[HOWE]
  Howe, C. D., and Moxon, B., How to program parallel processors, *Spectrum*, Vol. 24, No. 9, September 1987, pp. 36–41.

[HWANG 1]
  Hwang, K., Ed., *Supercomputers: Design and Applications*, IEEE Computer Society Press, Los Angeles, 1984.

[HWANG 2]
  Hwang, K., and Briggs, F. A., *Computer Architecture and Parallel Processing*, McGraw-Hill, New York, 1984.

[JAMIESON]
  Jamieson, L. H., Gannon, D. B., and Douglass, R. J., Eds., *The Characteristics of Parallel Algorithms*, MIT Press, Cambridge, Mass., 1987.

[JONES 1]
  Jones, A. K., and Gehringer, E. F., Eds., The Cm* multiprocessor project: A research review, Technical Report No. CMU-CS-80-131, Department of Computer Science, Carnegie-Mellon University, Pittsburgh, July 1980.

[JONES 2]
  Jones, A. K., and Schwarz, P., Experience using multiprocessor systems—a status report, *Computing Surveys*, Vol. 12, No. 2, June 1980, pp. 121–165.

[KARIN]
  Karin, S., and Smith, N. P., *The Supercomputer Era*, Harcourt, Brace, Jovanevich, New York, 1987.

[KARLIN]
  Karlin, A. R., and Upfal, E., Parallel hashing—an efficient implementation of shared memory, Proceedings of the 18th Annual ACM Symposium on Theory of Computing, Berkeley, California, May 1986, pp. 160–168, Association for Computing Machinery, New York, N.Y., 1986.

[KARP]
  Karp, A. H., Programming for parallelism, *Computer*, Vol. 20, No. 5, May 1987, pp. 43–57.

[KRONSJÖ]
  Kronsjö, L., *Computational Complexity of Sequential and Parallel Algorithms*, Wiley, Chichester, England, 1985.

[KUCK 1]
Kuck, D. J., Lawrie, D. H., and Sameh, A. H., Eds., *High Speed Computer and Algorithm Organization*, Academic, New York, 1977.

[KUCK 2]
Kuck, D. J., *The Structure of Computers and Computations*, Vol. 1, Wiley, New York, 1978.

[KUHN]
Kuhn, R. H., and Padua, D. A., Eds., *Parallel Processing*, IEEE Computer Society Press, Los Angeles, 1981.

[KUNG]
Kung, H. T., The structure of parallel algorithms, in Yovits, M. C., Ed., *Advances in Computers*, Academic, New York, 1980, pp. 65–112.

[LEGENDI]
Legendi, T., Parkinson, D., Vollmar, R., and Wolf, G., Eds., *Parallel Processing by Cellular Automata and Arrays*, North-Holland, Amsterdam, 1987.

[LEIGHTON]
Leighton, F. T., *Complexity Issues in VLSI*, MIT Press, Cambridge, Mass., 1983.

[LEISERSON]
Leiserson, C. E., *Area-Efficient VLSI Computation*, MIT Press, Cambridge, Mass., 1983.

[LIPOVSKI]
Lipovski, G. J., and Malek, M., *Parallel Computing: Theory and Practice*, Wiley, New York, 1987.

[LORIN]
Lorin, H., *Parallelism in Hardware and Software: Real and Apparent Concurrency*, Prentice-Hall, Englewood Cliffs, N.J., 1972.

[MARSLAND]
Marsland, T. A., and Campbell, M., Parallel search of strongly ordered game trees, *Computing Surveys*, Vol. 14, No. 4, December 1982, pp. 533–551.

[MEAD]
Mead, C. A., and Conway, L. A., *Introduction to VLSI Systems*, Addison-Wesley, Reading, Mass., 1980.

[MEHLHORN]
Mehlhorn, K., and Vishkin, U., Randomized and deterministic simulations of PRAMs by parallel machines with restricted granularity of parallel memories, *Acta Informatica*, Vol. 21, 1984, pp. 339–374.

[OLEINICK]
Oleinick, P. N., *Parallel Algorithms on a Multiprocessor*, UMI Research Press, Ann Arbor, Mich., 1982.

[PAPADIMITRIOU]
Papadimitriou, C. H., and Steiglitz, K., *Combinatorial Optimization: Algorithms and Complexity*, Prentice-Hall, Englewood Cliffs, N.J., 1982.

[PARBERRY]
Parberry, I., Some practical simulations of impractical parallel computers, *Parallel Computing*, Vol. 4, 1987, pp. 93–101.

[POTTER]
Potter, J. L., Ed., *The Massively Parallel Processor*, MIT Press, Cambridge, Mass., 1985.

[PRESTON]

Preston, K., and Uhr, L., Eds., *Multicomputers and Image Processing: Algorithms and Programs*, Academic, New York, 1982.

[QUINN]

Quinn, M. J., *Designing Efficient Algorithms for Parallel Computers*, McGraw-Hill, New York, 1987.

[REED]

Reed, D. A., and Fujimoto, R. M., *Multicomputer Networks: Message-Based Parallel Processing*, MIT Press, Cambridge, Mass., 1987.

[REIJNS]

Reijns, G. L., and Barton, M. H., Eds., *Highly Parallel Computers*, North-Holland, Amsterdam, 1987.

[REINGOLD]

Reingold, E. M., Nievergelt, J., and Deo, N., *Combinatorial Algorithms*, Prentice-Hall, Englewood Cliffs, N.J., 1977.

[RODRIGUE]

Rodrigue, G., Ed., *Parallel Computations*, Academic, New York, 1982.

[SCHENDEL]

Schendel, U., *Introduction to Numerical Methods for Parallel Computers*, Wiley-Interscience, New York, 1984.

[SIEGEL]

Siegel, H. J., *Interconnection Networks for Large-Scale Parallel Processing*, Lexington Books, Lexington, Mass., 1985.

[SNYDER]

Snyder, L., Jamieson, L. H., Gannon, D. B., and Siegel, H. J., *Algorithmically Specialized Parallel Computers*, Academic, Orlando, Fl., 1985.

[STOCKMEYER]

Stockmeyer, L. J., and Vishkin, U., Simulation of parallel random access machines by circuits, *SIAM Journal on Computing*, Vol. 13, No. 2, May 1984, pp. 409–422.

[STONE]

Stone, H. S., Ed., *Introduction to Computer Architecture*, Science Research Associates, Chicago, 1980.

[STRASSEN]

Strassen, V., The asymptotic spectrum of tensors and the exponent of matrix multiplication, Proceedings of the 27th Annual IEEE Symposium on Foundations of Computer Science, Toronto, October 1986, IEEE Computer Society, Washington, D.C., 1986.

[TRAUB]

Traub, J. F., Ed., *Complexity of Sequential and Parallel Numerical Algorithms*, Academic, New York, 1973.

[UHR]

Uhr, L., *Algorithm-Structured Computer Arrays and Networks*, Academic, New York, 1984.

[ULLMAN]

Ullman, J. D., *Computational Aspects of VLSI*, Computer Science Press, Rockville, Md., 1984.

[UPFAL 1]

Upfal, E., A probabilistic relation between desirable and feasible models of parallel computation, Proceedings of the 16th Annual ACM Symposium on Theory of Computing, Washington, D.C., May 1984, pp. 258–265, Association for Computing Machinery, New York, N.Y., 1984.

[UPFAL 2]

Upfal, E., and Wigderson, A., How to share memory in a distributed system, Proceedings of the 25th Annual IEEE Symposium on Foundations of Computer Science, Singer Island, Florida, October 1984, pp. 171–180, IEEE Computer Society, Washington, D.C., 1984.

[VISHKIN]

Vishkin, U., Implementation of simultaneous memory address access in models that forbid it, *Journal of Algorithms*, Vol. 4, 1983, pp. 45–50.

[Wah]

Wah, B. W., Ed., Special Issue on New Computers for Artificial Intelligence Processing, *Computer*, Vol. 20, No. 1, January 1987.

[WU]

Wu, C.-L., and Feng, T.-Y., Eds., *Interconnection Networks for Parallel and Distributed Processing*, IEEE Computer Science Press, Los Angeles, 1984.

2

Selection

2.1 INTRODUCTION

Our study of parallel algorithm design and analysis begins by addressing the following problem: Given a sequence S of n elements and an integer k, where $1 \leqslant k \leqslant n$, it is required to determine the kth smallest element in S. This is known as the *selection problem*. It arises in many applications in computer science and statistics. Our purpose in this chapter is to present a parallel algorithm for solving this problem on the shared-memory SIMD model. The algorithm will be designed to meet a number of goals, and our analysis will then confirm that these goals have indeed been met.

We start in section 2.2 by defining the selection problem formally and deriving a lower bound on the number of steps required for solving it on a sequential computer. This translates into a lower bound on the cost of any parallel algorithm for selection. In section 2.3 an optimal sequential algorithm is presented. Our design goals are stated in section 2.4 in the form of properties generally desirable in any parallel algorithm. Two procedures that will be often used in this book are described in section 2.5. Section 2.6 contains the parallel selection algorithm and its analysis.

2.2 THE PROBLEM AND A LOWER BOUND

The problems studied in this and the next two chapters are intimately related and belong to a family of problems known as *comparison problems*. These problems are usually solved by comparing pairs of elements of an input sequence. In order to set the stage for our presentation we need the following definitions.

2.2.1 Linear Order

The elements of a set A are said to satisfy a *linear order* $<$ if and only if

(i) for any two elements a and b of A, $a < b$, $a = b$, or $b < a$, and
(ii) for any three elements a, b, and c of A, if $a < b$ and $b < c$, then $a < c$.

The symbol $<$ is to be read "precedes." An example of a set satisfying a linear order is the set of all integers. Another example is the set of letters of the Latin alphabet. We shall say that these sets are *linearly ordered*. Note that when the elements of A are numbers, it is customary to use the symbol $\leqslant$ to denote "less than or equal to."

2.2.2 Rank

For a sequence $S = \{s_1, s_2, \ldots, s_n\}$ whose elements are drawn from a linearly ordered set, the *rank* of an element s_i of S is defined as the number of elements in S preceding s_i plus 1. Thus, in $S = \{8, -3, 2, -5, 6, 0\}$ the rank of 0 is 3. Note that if $s_i = s_j$ then s_i precedes s_j if and only if $i < j$.

2.2.3 Selection

A sequence $S = \{s_1, s_2, \ldots, s_n\}$ whose elements are drawn from a linearly ordered set and an integer k, where $1 \leqslant k \leqslant n$, are given. It is required to determine the element with rank equal to k. Again, in $S = \{8, -3, 2, -5, 6, 0\}$ the element with rank 4 is 2. We shall denote the element with rank k by $s_{(k)}$.

In the ensuing discussion, it is assumed without loss of generality that S is a sequence of integers, as in the preceding example. Selection will therefore call for finding the kth *smallest* element. We also introduce the following useful notation. For a real number r, $\lfloor r \rfloor$ denotes the largest integer smaller than or equal to r (the "floor" of r), while $\lceil r \rceil$ denotes the smallest integer larger than or equal to r (the "ceiling" of r). Thus $\lfloor 3.9 \rfloor = 3$, $\lceil 3.1 \rceil = 4$, and $\lfloor 3.0 \rfloor = \lceil 3.0 \rceil = 3$.

2.2.4 Complexity

Three particular values of k in the definition of the selection problem immediately come to one's mind: $k = 1$, $k = n$, and $k = \lceil n/2 \rceil$. In the first two cases we would be looking for the smallest and largest elements of S, respectively. In the third case, $s_{(k)}$ would be the *median* of S, that is, the element for which half of the elements of S are smaller than (or equal to) it and the other half larger (or equal). It seems intuitive, at least in the sequential mode of thinking and computing, that the first two cases are easier to solve than when $k = \lceil n/2 \rceil$ or any other value. Indeed, for $k = 1$ or $k = n$, all one has to do is examine the sequence element by element, keeping track of the smallest (or largest) element seen so far until the result is obtained. No such obvious solution appears to work for $1 < k < n$.

Evidently, if S were presented in *sorted* order, that is, $S = \{s_{(1)}, s_{(2)}, \ldots, s_{(n)}\}$, then selection would be trivial: In one step we could obtain $s_{(k)}$. Of course, we do not assume that this is the case. Nor do we want to sort S first and then pick the kth element: This appears to be (and indeed is) a computationally far more demanding task than we need (particularly for large values of n) since sorting would solve the selection problem for *all* values of k, not just one.

Regardless of the value of k, one fact is certain: In order to determine the kth smallest element, we must examine each element of S at least once. This establishes a lower bound of $\Omega(n)$ on the number of (sequential) steps required to solve the problem. From chapter 1, we know that this immediately implies an $\Omega(n)$ lower bound on the *cost* of any parallel algorithm for selection.

2.3 A SEQUENTIAL ALGORITHM

In this section we study a sequential algorithm for the selection problem. There are two reasons for our interest in a sequential algorithm. First, our parallel algorithm is based on the sequential one and is a parallel implementation of it on an EREW SM SIMD computer. Second, the parallel algorithm assumes the existence of the sequential one and uses it as a procedure.

The algorithm presented in what follows in the form of procedure SEQUENTIAL SELECT is recursive in nature. It uses the *divide-and-conquer* approach to algorithm design. The sequence S and the integer k are the procedure's initial input. At each stage of the recursion, a number of elements of S are discarded from further consideration as candidates for being the kth smallest element. This continues until the kth element is finally determined. We denote by $|S|$ the size of a sequence S; thus initially, $|S| = n$. Also, let Q be a small integer constant to be determined later when analyzing the running time of the algorithm.

procedure SEQUENTIAL SELECT (S, k)

Step 1: **if** $|S| < Q$ **then** sort S and return the kth element directly

else subdivide S into $|S|/Q$ subsequences of Q elements each (with up to $Q-1$ leftover elements)
end if.

Step 2: Sort each subsequence and determine its median.

Step 3: Call SEQUENTIAL SELECT recursively to find m, the median of the $|S|/Q$ medians found in step 2.

Step 4: Create three subsequences S_1, S_2, and S_3 of elements of S smaller than, equal to, and larger than m, respectively.

Step 5: **if** $|S_1| \geqslant k$ **then** {the kth element of S must be in S_1}
call SEQUENTIAL SELECT recursively to find the kth element of S_1
else if $|S_1| + |S_2| \geqslant k$ **then** return m
else call SEQUENTIAL SELECT recursively to find the $(k - |S_1| - |S_2|)$th element of S_3
end if
end if. □

Note that the preceding statement of procedure SEQUENTIAL SELECT does not specify how the kth smallest element of S is actually returned. One way to do this would be to have an additional parameter, say, x, in the procedure's heading (besides

S and k) and return the kth smallest element in x. Another way would be to simply return the kth smallest as the first element of the sequence S.

Analysis.   A step-by-step analysis of $t(n)$, the running time of SEQUENTIAL SELECT, is now provided.

Step 1: Since Q is a constant, sorting S when $|S| < Q$ takes constant time. Otherwise, subdividing S requires $c_1 n$ time for some constant c_1.

Step 2: Since each of the $|S|/Q$ subsequences consists of Q elements, it can be sorted in constant time. Thus, $c_2 n$ time is also needed for this step for some constant c_2.

Step 3: There are $|S|/Q$ medians; hence the recursion takes $t(n/Q)$ time.

Step 4: One pass through S creates S_1, S_2, and S_3 given m; therefore this step is completed in $c_3 n$ time for some constant c_3.

Step 5: Since m is the median of $|S|/Q$ elements, there are $|S|/2Q$ elements larger than or equal to it, as shown in Fig. 2.1. Each of the $|S|/Q$ elements was itself the median of a set of Q elements, which means that it has $Q/2$ elements larger than or equal to it. It follows that $(|S|/2Q) \times (Q/2) = |S|/4$ elements of S are guaranteed to be larger than or equal to m. Consequently, $|S_1| \leqslant 3|S|/4$. By a similar reasoning, $|S_3| \leqslant 3|S|/4$. A recursive call in this step to SEQUENTIAL SELECT therefore requires $t(3n/4)$. From the preceding analysis we have

$$t(n) = c_4 n + t(n/Q) + t(3n/4), \quad \text{where } c_4 = c_1 + c_2 + c_3.$$

The time has now come to specify Q. If we choose Q so that

$$n/Q + 3n/4 < n,$$

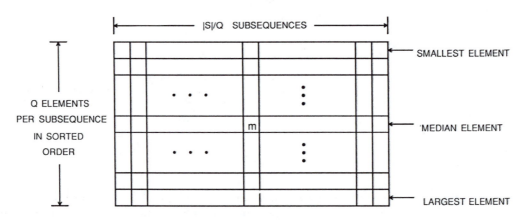

Figure 2.1   Main idea behind procedure SEQUENTIAL SELECT.

then the two recursive calls in the procedure are performed on ever-decreasing sequences. Any value of $Q \geqslant 5$ will do. Take $Q = 5$; thus

$$t(n) = c_4 n + t(n/5) + t(3n/4).$$

This recurrence can be solved by assuming that

$$t(n) \leqslant c_5 n \quad \text{for some constant } c_5.$$

Substituting, we get

$$t(n) \leqslant c_4 n + c_5(n/5) + c_5(3n/4)$$

$$= c_4 n + c_5(19n/20).$$

Finally, taking $c_5 = 20c_4$ yields

$$t(n) \leqslant c_5(n/20) + c_5(19n/20)$$

$$= c_5 n,$$

thus confirming our assumption. In other words, $t(n) = O(n)$, which is optimal in view of the lower bound derived in section 2.2.4.

2.4 DESIRABLE PROPERTIES FOR PARALLEL ALGORITHMS

Before we embark in our study of a parallel algorithm for the selection problem, it may be worthwhile to set ourselves some design goals. A number of criteria were described in section 1.3 for evaluating parallel algorithms. In light of these criteria, five important properties that we desire a parallel algorithm to possess are now defined.

2.4.1 Number of Processors

The first two properties concern the number of processors to be used by the algorithm. Let n be the size of the problem to be solved:

(i) *p(n) must be smaller than n:*   No matter how inexpensive computers become, it is unrealistic when designing a parallel algorithm to assume that we have at our disposal more (or even as many) processors as there are items of data. This is particularly true when n is very large. It is therefore important that $p(n)$ be expressible as a sublinear function of n, that is, $p(n) = n^x$, $0 < x < 1$.

(ii) *p(n) must be adaptive:*   In computing in general, and in parallel computing in particular, "appetite comes with eating." The availability of additional computing power always means that larger and more complex problems will be attacked than was possible before. Users of parallel computers will want to push their machines to their limits and beyond. Even if one could afford to have as many processors as data for a particular problem size, it may not be desirable to design an algorithm based on that assumption: A larger problem would render the algorithm totally useless.

Algorithms using a number of processors that is a sublinear function of n [and hence satisfying property (i)], such as $\log n$ or $n^{1/2}$, would not be acceptable either due to their inflexibility. What we need are algorithms that possess the "intelligence" to adapt to the actual number of processors available on the computer being used.

2.4.2 Running Time

The next two properties concern the worst-case running time of the parallel algorithm:

(i) *t(n) must be small:*   Our primary motive for building parallel computers is to speed up the computation process. It is therefore important that the parallel algorithms we design be fast. To be useful, a parallel algorithm should be significantly faster than the best sequential algorithm for the problem at hand.

(ii) *t(n) must be adaptive:*   Ideally, one hopes to have an algorithm whose running time decreases as more processors are used. In practice, it is usually the case that a limit is eventually reached beyond which no speedup is possible regardless of the number of processors used. Nevertheless, it is desirable that $t(n)$ vary inversely with $p(n)$ within the bounds set for $p(n)$.

2.4.3 Cost

Ultimately, we wish to have parallel algorithms for which $c(n) = p(n) \times t(n)$ always matches a known lower bound on the number of sequential operations required in the worst case to solve the problem. In other words, a parallel algorithm should be *cost optimal.*

In subsequent chapters we shall see that meeting the preceding objectives is usually difficult and sometimes impossible. In particular, when a set of processors are linked by an interconnection network, the geometry of the network often imposes limits on what can be accomplished by a parallel algorithm. It is a different story when the algorithm is to run on a shared-memory parallel computer. Here, it is not at all unreasonable to insist on these properties given how powerful and flexible the model is.

In section 2.6 we describe a parallel algorithm for selecting the kth smallest element of a sequence $S = \{s_1, s_2, \ldots, s_n\}$. The algorithm runs on an EREW SM SIMD computer with N processors, where $N < n$. The algorithm enjoys all the desirable properties formulated in this section:

(i) It uses $p(n) = n^{1-x}$ processors, where $0 < x < 1$. The value of x is obtained from $N = n^{1-x}$. Thus $p(n)$ is sublinear and adaptive.

(ii) It runs in $t(n) = O(n^x)$ time, where x depends on the number of processors available on the parallel computer. The value of x is obtained in (i). Thus $t(n)$ is smaller than the running time of the optimal sequential algorithm described in section 2.3. It is also adaptive: The larger is $p(n)$, the smaller is $t(n)$, and vice versa.

(iii) It has a cost of $c(n) = n^{1-x} \times O(n^x) = O(n)$, which is optimal in view of the lower bound derived in section 2.2.4.

In closing this section we note that all real quantities of the kind just described (e.g., n^{1-x} and n^x) should in practice be rounded to a convenient integer, according to our assumption in chapter 1. When dealing with numbers of processors and running times, though, it is important that this rounding be done pessimistically. Thus, the real n^{1-x} representing the number of processors used by an algorithm should be interpreted as $\lfloor n^{1-x} \rfloor$: This is to ensure that the resulting integer does not exceed the actual number of processors. Conversely, the real n^x representing the worst-case running time of an algorithm should be interpreted as $\lceil n^x \rceil$: This guarantees that the resulting integer is not smaller than the true worst-case running time.

2.5 TWO USEFUL PROCEDURES

In the EREW SM SIMD model no two processors can gain access to the same memory location simultaneously. However, two situations may arise in a typical parallel algorithm:

(i) All processors need to read a datum held in a particular location of the common memory.

(ii) Each processor has to compute a function of data held by other processors and therefore needs to receive these data.

Clearly, a way must be found to efficiently simulate these two operations that cannot be performed in one step on the EREW model. In this section, we present two procedures for performing these simulations. The two procedures are used by the algorithm in this chapter as well as by other parallel algorithms to be studied subsequently. In what follows we assume that N processors $P_1, P_2, \ldots, P_N$ are available on an EREW SM SIMD computer.

2.5.1 Broadcasting a Datum

Let D be a location in memory holding a datum that all N processors need at a given moment during the execution of an algorithm. As mentioned in section 1.2.3.1, this is a special case of the more general multiple-read situation and can be simulated on an EREW computer by the broadcasting process described in example 1.4. We now give this process formally as procedure BROADCAST. The procedure assumes the presence of an array A of length N in memory. The array is initially empty and is used by the procedure as a working space to distribute the contents of D to the processors. Its ith position is denoted by $A(i)$.

procedure BROADCAST (D, N, A)

Step 1: Processor P_1
      (i) reads the value in D,
      (ii) stores it in its own memory, and
      (iii) writes it in $A(1)$.

Step 2: **for** $i = 0$ **to** $(\log N - 1)$ **do**
      for $j = 2^i + 1$ **to** 2^{i+1} **do in parallel**
        Processor P_j
          (i) reads the value in $A(j - 2^i)$,
          (ii) stores it in its own memory, and
          (iii) writes it in $A(j)$.
      end for
    end for. □

The working of BROADCAST is illustrated in Fig. 2.2 for $N = 8$ and $D = 5$. When the procedure terminates, all processors have stored the value of D in their local memories for later use. Since the number of processors having read D doubles in each iteration, the procedure terminates in $O(\log N)$ time. The memory requirement of BROADCAST is an array of length N. Strictly speaking, an array of half that length will do since in the last iteration of the procedure all the processors have received the value in D and need not write it back in A [see Fig. 2.2(d)]. BROADCAST can be easily modified to prevent this final write operation and hence use an array A of length $N/2$.

Besides being generally useful in broadcasting data to processors during the execution of an algorithm, procedure BROADCAST becomes particularly important when starting an adaptive algorithm such as the one to be described in section 2.6. Initially, each of the N processors knows its own index i, $1 \leq i \leq N$, and the available number of processors N. When a problem is to be solved, the problem size n must be communicated to all processors. This can be done using procedure BROADCAST before executing the algorithm. Each processor now computes x from $N = n^{1-x}$, and the algorithm is performed. Therefore, we shall assume henceforth that the parameter x is known to all processors when an adaptive algorithm starts its computation.

2.5.2 Computing All Sums

Assume that each processor P_i holds in its local memory a number a_i, $1 \leq i \leq N$. It is often useful to compute, for each P_i, the sum $a_1 + a_2 + \cdots + a_i$. In example 1.5 an algorithm was demonstrated for computing the sum of N numbers in $O(\log N)$ time on a tree-connected computer with $O(N)$ processors. Clearly this algorithm can be implemented on a shared-memory machine to compute the sum in the same amount of time using the same number of processors. The question here is: Can the power

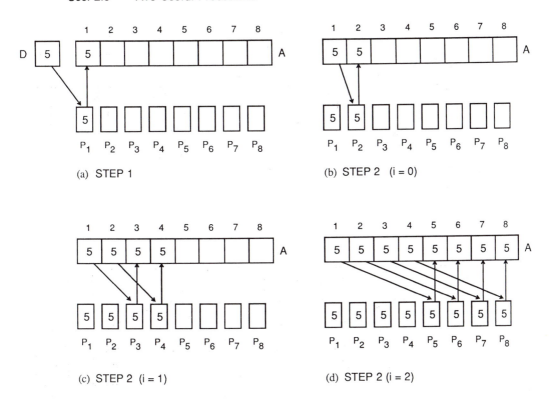

Figure 2.2 Distributing a datum to eight processors using procedure BROADCAST.

of the shared-memory model be exploited to compute *all* sums of the form $a_1 + a_2 + \cdots + a_i$, $1 \le i \le N$, known as the *prefix sums*, using N processors in $O(\log N)$ time? As it turns out, this is indeed possible. The idea is to keep as many processors busy as long as possible and exploit the associativity of the addition operation. Procedure ALLSUMS given formally in the following accomplishes exactly that:

procedure ALLSUMS $(a_1, a_2, \dots, a_N)$

   for $j = 0$ **to** $\log N - 1$ **do**
     for $i = 2^j + 1$ **to** N **do in parallel**
       Processor P_i
         (i) obtains a_{i-2^j} from P_{i-2^j} through shared memory and
         (ii) replaces a_i with $a_{i-2^j} + a_i$.
   end for
   end for. □

The working of ALLSUMS is illustrated in Fig. 2.3 for $N = 8$ with A_{ij} referring to the sum $a_i + a_{i+1} + \cdots + a_j$. When the procedure terminates, a_i has been replaced by

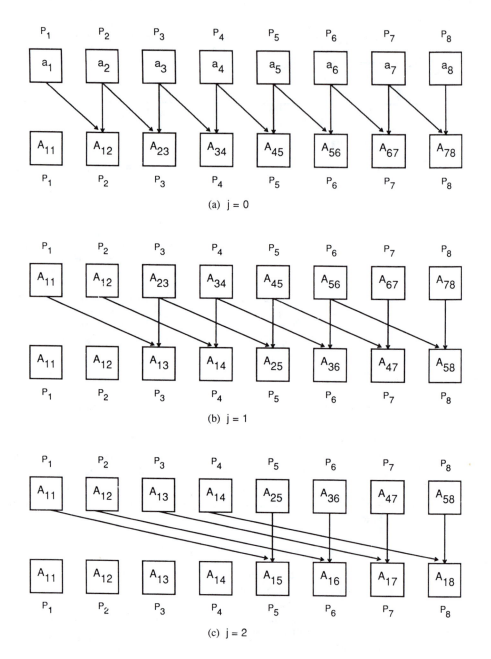

Figure 2.3 Computing the prefix sums of eight numbers using procedure ALLSUMS.

$a_1 + a_2 + \cdots + a_i$ in the local memory of P_i, for $1 \leq i \leq N$. The procedure requires $O(\log N)$ time since the number of processors that have finished their computation doubles at each stage.

It is important to note that procedure ALLSUMS can be modified to solve any problem where the addition operation is replaced by any other associative binary operation. Examples of such operations on numbers are multiplication, finding the larger or smaller of two numbers, and so on. Other operations that apply to a pair of logical quantities (or a pair of bits) are **and, or,** and **xor.** Various aspects of the problem of computing the prefix sums in parallel are discussed in detail in chapters 13 and 14.

2.6 AN ALGORITHM FOR PARALLEL SELECTION

We are now ready to study an algorithm for parallel selection on an EREW SM SIMD computer. The algorithm presented as procedure PARALLEL SELECT makes the following assumptions (some of these were stated earlier):

1. A sequence of integers $S = \{s_1, s_2, \ldots, s_n\}$ and an integer k, $1 \leq k \leq n$, are given, and it is required to determine the kth smallest element of S. This is the initial input to PARALLEL SELECT.

2. The parallel computer consists of N processors $P_1, P_2, \ldots, P_N$.

3. Each processor has received n and computed x from $N = n^{1-x}$, where $0 < x < 1$.

4. Each of the n^{1-x} processors is capable of storing a sequence of n^x elements in its local memory.

5. Each processor can execute procedures SEQUENTIAL SELECT, BROADCAST, and ALLSUMS.

6. M is an array in shared memory of length N whose ith position is $M(i)$.

procedure PARALLEL SELECT (S, k)

Step 1:   **if** $|S| \leq 4$ **then** P_1 uses at most five comparisons to return the kth element
         else
               (i) S is subdivided into $|S|^{1-x}$ subsequences S_i of length $|S|^x$ each, where $1 \leq i \leq |S|^{1-x}$, and
               (ii) subsequence S_i is assigned to processor P_i.
         end if.

Step 2:   **for** $i = 1$ **to** $|S|^{1-x}$ **do in parallel**
               (2.1) $\{P_i$ obtains the median m_i, i.e., the $\lceil |S_i|/2 \rceil$th element, of its associated subsequence$\}$
                     SEQUENTIAL SELECT $(S_i, \lceil |S_i|/2 \rceil)$
               (2.2) P_i stores m_i in $M(i)$
         end for.

Step 3:   {The procedure is called recursively to obtain the median m of M}

$$\text{PARALLEL SELECT } (M, \lceil |M|/2 \rceil).$$

Step 4:   The sequence S is subdivided into three subsequences:

$L = \{s_i \in S: s_i < m\}$,
$E = \{s_i \in S: s_i = m\}$, and
$G = \{s_i \in S: s_i > m\}$.

Step 5:   **if** $|L| \geqslant k$ **then** PARALLEL SELECT (L, k)
          else if $|L| + |E| \geqslant k$ **then** return m
              else PARALLEL SELECT $(G, k - |L| - |E|)$
              end if
          end if. □

Note that the precise mechanism used by procedure PARALLEL SELECT to return the kth smallest element of S is unspecified in the preceding statement. However, any of the ways suggested in section 2.3 in connection with procedure SEQUENTIAL SELECT can be used here.

Analysis.   We have deliberately given a high-level description of PARALLEL SELECT to avoid obscuring the main ideas of the algorithm. In order to obtain an accurate analysis of the procedure's running time, however, various implementation details must be specified. As usual, we denote by $t(n)$ the time required by PARALLEL SELECT for an input of size n. A function describing $t(n)$ is now obtained by analyzing each step of the procedure.

Step 1: To perform this step, each processor needs the beginning address A of sequence S in the shared memory, its size $|S|$, and the value of k. These quantities can be broadcast to all processors using procedure BROADCAST: This requires $O(\log n^{1-x})$ time. If $|S| \leqslant 4$, then P_1 returns the kth element in constant time. Otherwise, P_i computes the address of the first and last elements in S_i from $A + (i - 1)n^x$ and $A + in^x - 1$, respectively; this can be done in constant time. Thus, step 1 takes $c_1 \log n$ time units for some constant c_1.

Step 2: SEQUENTIAL SELECT finds the median of a sequence of length n^x in $c_2 n^x$ time units for some constant c_2.

Step 3: Since PARALLEL SELECT is called with a sequence of length n^{1-x}, this step requires $t(n^{1-x})$ time.

Step 4: The sequence S can be subdivided into L, E, and G as follows:

(i) First m is broadcast to all the processors in $O(\log n^{1-x})$ time using procedure BROADCAST.

(ii) Each processor P_i now splits S_i into three subsequences L_i, E_i, and G_i of elements smaller than, equal to, and larger than m, respectively. This can be done in time linear in the size of S_i, that is, $O(n^x)$ time.

(iii) The subsequences L_i, E_i, and G_i are now merged to form L, E, and G. We show how this can be done for the L_i; similar procedures with the same running time can be derived for merging the E_i and G_i, respectively. Let $a_i = |L_i|$. For each i, $1 \leqslant i \leqslant n^{1-x}$, the sum

$$z_i = \sum_{j=1}^{i} a_j$$

is computed. All these sums can be obtained by n^{1-x} processors in $O(\log n^{1-x})$ time using procedure ALLSUMS. Now let $z_0 = 0$. All processors simultaneously merge their L_i subsequences to form L: Processor P_i copies L_i into L starting at position $z_{i-1} + 1$. This can be done in $O(n^x)$ time.

Hence the time required by this step is $c_3 n^x$ for some constant c_3.

Step 5: The size of L needed in this step has already been obtained in step 4 through the computation of $z_{n^{1-x}}$. The same remark applies to the sizes of E and G. Now we must determine how much time is taken by each of the two recursive steps. Since m is the median of M, $n^{1-x}/2$ elements of S are guaranteed to be larger than it. Furthermore, every element of M is smaller than at least $n^x/2$ elements of S. Thus $|L| \leqslant 3n/4$. Similarly, $|G| \leqslant 3n/4$. Consequently, step 5 requires at most $t(3n/4)$ time.

The preceding analysis yields the following recurrence for $t(n)$:

$$t(n) = c_1 \log n + c_2 n^x + t(n^{1-x}) + c_3 n^x + t(3n/4),$$

whose solution is $t(n) = O(n^x)$ for $n > 4$. Since $p(n) = n^{1-x}$, we have

$$c(n) = p(n) \times t(n) = n^{1-x} \times O(n^x) = O(n).$$

This cost is optimal in view of the $\Omega(n)$ lower bound derived in section 2.2. Note, however, that n^x is asymptotically larger than $\log n$ for any x. (Indeed we have used this fact in our analysis of PARALLEL SELECT.) Since $N = n^{1-x}$ and $n/n^x < n/\log n$, it follows that PARALLEL SELECT is cost optimal provided $N < n/\log n$.

Example 2.1

This example illustrates the working of PARALLEL SELECT. Let $S = \{3, 14, 16, 20, 8, 31, 22, 12, 33, 1, 4, 9, 10, 5, 13, 7, 24, 2, 14, 26, 18, 34, 36, 25, 14, 27, 32, 35, 33\}$, that is, $n = 29$ and let $k = 21$, that is, we need to determine the twenty-first element of S. Assume further that the EREW SM SIMD computer available consists of five processors, ($N = 5$). Hence $|S|^{1-x} = 5$, implying that $1 - x = 0.47796$. The input sequence is initially in the shared memory as shown in Fig. 2.4(a). After step 1, each processor has been assigned a subsequence of S: The first four processors receive six elements each, and the fifth receives five, as in Fig. 2.4(b). Now each processor finds the median of its subsequence in step 2 and places it in a shared-memory array M; this is illustrated in Fig. 2.4(c). When PARALLEL SELECT is called recursively in step 3, it returns the median $m = 14$ of M. The three subsequences of S, namely, L, E, and G of elements smaller than, equal to, and larger than 14, respectively, are formed in step 4, as shown in Fig. 2.4(d). Since $|L| = 11$ and $|E| = 3$, $|L| + |E| < k$ and PARALLEL SELECT is called recursively in step 5 with $S = G$ and $k = 21 - (11 + 3) = 7$. Since $|G| = 15$, we use $15^{1-x} = 3.6485$, that is, three, processors during this recursive step.

Again in step 1, each processor is assigned five elements, as shown in Fig. 2.4(e). The sequence M of medians obtained in step 2 is shown in Fig. 2.4(f). The median $m = 26$

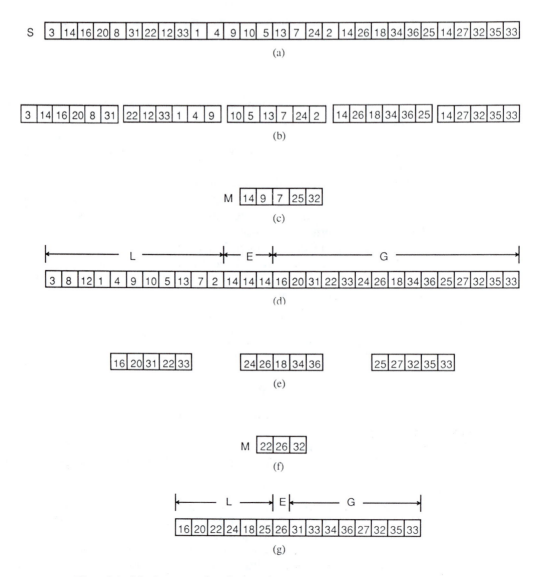

Figure 2.4 Selecting twenty-first element of a sequence using procedure PARALLEL SELECT.

of M is determined in step 3. The three subsequences L, E, and G created in step 4 are illustrated in Fig. 2.4(g). Since $|L| = 6$ and $|E| = 1$, the only element of E, namely, 26, is returned as the twenty-first element of the input. ☐

We conclude this section with the following observation. In designing PARALLEL SELECT, we adopted the approach of taking a sequential algorithm for a problem and turning it into a parallel algorithm. We were quite successful in obtaining an algorithm for the EREW SM SIMD model that is fast, adaptive, and cost optimal while using a number of processors that is sublinear in the size of the input. There are problems however, for which this approach does not work that well. In these cases a parallel algorithm (not based on any sequential algorithm) must be derived by exploiting the inherent parallelism in the problem. We shall study such algorithms in subsequent chapters. Taken to the extreme, this latter approach can sometimes offer surprises: A parallel algorithm provides an insight that leads to an improvement over the best existing sequential algorithm.

2.7 PROBLEMS

2.1 In an interconnection-network SIMD computer, one of the N processors holds a datum that it wishes to make known to all other processors. Show how this can be done on each of the networks studied in chapter 1. Which of these networks accomplish this task in the same order of time as required by procedure BROADCAST?

2.2 Consider an SIMD computer where the N processors are linked together by a perfect shuffle interconnection network. Now assume that the line connecting two processors can serve as a two-way link; in other words, if P_i can send data to P_j (using a perfect shuffle link), then P_j can also send data back to P_i (the latter link being referred to as a *perfect unshuffle* connection). In addition, assume that for $i < N - 1$, each P_i is linked by a direct one-way link to P_{i+1}; call these the *nearest-neighbor* links. Each processor P_i holds an integer a_i. It is desired that a_i in P_i be replaced with $a_0 + a_1 + \cdots + a_i$ for all i. Can this task be accomplished using the unshuffle and nearest-neighbor links in the same order of time as required by procedure ALLSUMS?

2.3 A parallel selection algorithm that uses $O(n/\log^s n)$ processors and runs in $O(\log^s n)$ time for some $0 \leqslant s \leqslant 1$ would be faster than PARALLEL SELECT since $\log^s n$ is asymptotically smaller than n^x for any x and s. Can you find such an algorithm?

2.4 If PARALLEL SELECT were to be implemented on a CREW SM SIMD computer, would it run any faster?

2.5 Design and analyze a parallel algorithm for solving the selection problem on a CRCW SM SIMD computer.

2.6 A tree-connected computer with n leaves stores one integer of a sequence S per leaf. For a given k, $1 \leqslant k \leqslant n$, design an algorithm that runs on this computer and selects the kth smallest element of S.

2.7 Repeat problem 2.6 for a linear array of n processors with one element of S per processor.

2.8 Repeat problem 2.6 for an $n^{1/2} \times n^{1/2}$ mesh of processors with one element of S per processor.

2.9 Consider the following variant of the linear array interconnection network for SIMD computers. In addition to the usual links connecting the processors, a further communication path known as a *bus* is available, as shown in Fig. 2.5. At any given time during the execution of an algorithm, precisely one of the processors is allowed to broadcast one of the input data to the other processors using the bus. All processors receive the datum simultaneously. The time required by the broadcast operation is assumed to be constant. Repeat problem 2.6 for this modified linear array.

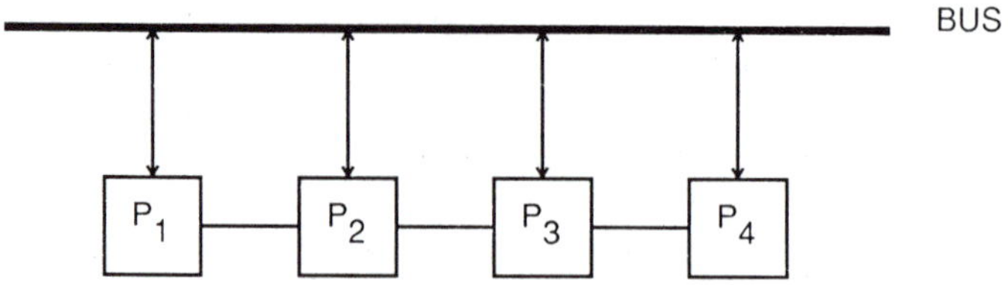

Figure 2.5   Linear array with a bus.

2.10 Modify the mesh interconnection network for SIMD machines to include a bus and repeat problem 2.6 for the modified model.

2.11 Design an algorithm for solving the selection problem for the case $k = 1$ (i.e., finding the smallest element of a sequence) on each of the following two models: (i) a mesh-connected SIMD computer and (ii) the machine in problem 2.10.

2.12 A problem related to selection is that of determining the k smallest elements of a sequence S (in any order). On a sequential computer this can be done as follows: First determine the kth smallest element (using SEQUENTIAL SELECT); then one pass through S suffices to determine the $k - 1$ elements smaller than k. The running time of this algorithm is linear in the size of S. Design a parallel algorithm to solve this problem on your chosen submodel of each of the following models and analyze its running time and cost: (i) shared-memory SIMD, (ii) interconnection-network SIMD, and (iii) specialized architecture.

2.13 Modify procedure BROADCAST to obtain a formal statement of procedure STORE described in section 1.2.3.1. Provide a different version of your procedure for each of the write conflict resolution policies mentioned in chapter 1.

2.14 In steps 1 and 2 of procedure SEQUENTIAL SELECT, a simple sequential algorithm is required for sorting short sequences. Describe one such algorithm.

2.8 BIBLIOGRAPHICAL REMARKS

As mentioned in section 2.1, the problem of selection has a number of applications in computer science and statistics. In this book, for example, we invoke a procedure for selecting the kth smallest out of n elements in our development of algorithms for parallel merging (chapter 3), sorting (chapter 4), and convex hull computation (chapter 11). An application to image analysis is cited in [Chandran]. In statistics, selection is referred to as the computation of *order statistics*. In particular, computing the median element of a set of data is a standard procedure in statistical analysis. The idea upon which procedure SEQUENTIAL SELECT is based was first proposed in [Blum]. Sequential algorithms for sorting short sequences, as required by that procedure, can be found in [Knuth].

Procedures BROADCAST and ALLSUMS are adapted from [Akl 2]. Another way of computing the prefix sums of n numbers is through a specialized network of processors. One such network is suggested by Fig. 2.3. It consists of $\log n$ rows of n processors each. The processors are connected by the lines illustrating the flow of data in Fig. 2.3. The top row of processors receives the n numbers as input, and all the prefix sums are produced by the bottom row as output. This network has a cost of $n \log^2 n$. Networks with lower cost and their applications are described in [Fich], [Kogge 1], [Kogge 2], [Ladner], [Reif], and [Stone]. A parallel algorithm to compute the prefix sums on an EREW SM SIMD computer for the case where the input numbers are presented in a linked list is proposed in [Kruskal].

Procedure PARALLEL SELECT was first presented in [Akl 1]. Other parallel algorithms for selecting the kth smallest out of n elements on the EREW SM SIMD computer are described in [Cole 2] and [Vishkin]. The algorithm in [Cole 2] uses $n/(\log n \log^* n)$ processors and runs in time $O(\log n \log^* n)$, where $\log^* n$ is the least i such that the ith iterate of the logarithm function (i.e., $\log^{(i)} n$) is less than or equal to 2. Note that this algorithm is cost optimal and faster than PARALLEL SELECT but is not adaptive. The algorithm in [Vishkin] runs in $O(n/N)$ time using $N \leqslant n/(\log n \log \log n)$ processors. This algorithm is both adaptive and cost optimal; however, when compared with PARALLEL SELECT, its running time is seen to be larger and its range of optimality smaller. Finally, a parallel selection algorithm is obtained in [Akl 3] that runs in $O(\log \log n)$ time using $O(n/\log \log n)$ processors. Examples of parallel algorithms that aid in the design of sequential algorithms are provided in [Megiddo].

A model of parallel computation is described in [Valiant], where only the time taken to perform comparisons among pairs of input elements is counted. Thus, the time taken in routing data from one processor to another, the time taken to specify what comparisons are to be performed, and any other computations besides comparisons are all ignored. This is appropriately known as the *comparison model*. A lower bound of $\Omega(\log \log n)$ on the time required by n processors to select using this model is derived in [Valiant]. This bound is achieved by an algorithm described in [Ajtai]. It runs in $O(\log \log n)$ time and is essentially a refinement of an earlier $O((\log \log n)^2)$ algorithm appearing in [Cole 1].

A number of algorithms exist for selection on a tree-connected SIMD computer. An algorithm in [Tanimoto] finds the kth smallest element on a tree machine with n leaves in $O(k + \log n)$ time. Note that when $k = n/2$, this algorithm requires $O(n)$ time, which is no better than sequential selection. This is improved in [Stout 1], where an algorithm is described whose running time is strictly less than n^a for any $a > 0$. It is shown in [Aggarwal] how a further speedup can be achieved for the case where the elements of S are taken from a field of size $O(n^{1+y})$ for some constant $y > 0$: Selection can now be performed in $O(\log^2 n)$ time. In chapter 14 we shall study an algorithm for selection on the tree that was first proposed in [Cooper]. This algorithm takes the time to operate on two bits (rather than two entire numbers) as its unit of time.

The selection problem has also been tackled on variants of basic models. An algorithm is proposed in [Stout 2] that runs on a mesh-connected computer with a broadcast ability. The model in [Chandran] is a cube-connected computer where each communication between two processors counts as one routing step regardless of how many elements are exchanged.

Variations on the problem of selection itself have also been studied. Algorithms for finding the largest element of a sequence (a special case of selection) appear in [Bokhari], [Shiloach], and [Valiant]. A special-purpose architecture for selecting the k smallest out of n elements is described in [Wah].

Finally, all the results discussed so far were obtained by *worst-case* analyses. Sometimes it is useful to derive the time required by a parallel algorithm *on the average*. Here, the elements of the input are assumed to obey a given probability distribution, and the *expected* running time is obtained. Algorithms specifically designed to achieve a good running time on the average are said to be *probabilistic*. Examples of such probabilistic algorithms are provided in [Greenberg] for the tree-connected SIMD model and in [Reischuck] for the comparison model.

2.9 REFERENCES

[AGGARWAL]

Aggarwal, A., A comparative study of X-tree, pyramid and related machines, Proceedings of the 25th Annual IEEE Symposium on Foundations of Computer Science, Singer Island, Florida, October 1984, pp. 89–99, IEEE Computer Society, Washington, D.C., 1984.

[AJTAI]

Ajtai, M., Komlós, J., Steiger, W. L., and Szemerédi, E., Deterministic selection in $O(\log \log N)$ parallel time, Proceedings of the 18th Annual ACM Symposium on Theory of Computing, Berkeley, California, May 1986, pp. 188–195, Association for Computing Machinery, New York, N.Y., 1986.

[AKL 1]

Akl, S. G., An optimal algorithm for parallel selection, *Information Processing Letters*, Vol. 19, No. 1, July 1984, pp. 47–50.

[AKL 2]

Akl, S. G., *Parallel Sorting Algorithms*, Academic, Orlando, Fl., 1985.

[AKL 3]

Akl, S. G., Parallel selection in $O(\log \log n)$ time using $O(n/\log \log n)$ processors, Technical Report No. 88-221, Department of Computing and Information Science, Queen's University, Kingston, Ontario, March 1988.

[BLUM]

Blum, M., Floyd, R. W., Pratt, V., Rivest, R. L., and Tarjan, R. E., Time bounds for selection, *Journal of Computer and System Sciences*, Vol. 7, No. 4, 1972, pp. 448–461.

[BOKHARI]

Bokhari, S. H., Finding maximum on an array processor with global bus, *IEEE Transactions on Computers*, Vol. C-33, No. 2, February 1984, pp. 133–139.

[CHANDRAN]

Chandran, S., and Rosenfeld, A., Order statistics on a hypercube, Center for Automation Research, University of Maryland, College Park, Md., 1986.

[COLE 1]

Cole, R., and Yap, C. K., A parallel median algorithm, *Information Processing Letters*, Vol. 20, No. 3, April 1985, pp. 137–139.

[COLE 2]

Cole, R., and Vishkin, U., Deterministic coin tossing and accelerating cascades: Micro and macro techniques for designing parallel algorithms, Proceedings of the 18th Annual ACM Symposium on Theory of Computing, Berkeley, California, May 1986, pp. 206–219, Association for Computing Machinery, New York, N.Y., 1986.

[COOPER]

Cooper, J., and Akl, S. G., Efficient selection on a binary tree, *Information Processing Letters*, Vol. 23, No. 3, October 1986, pp. 123–126.

[FICH]

Fich, F. E., New bounds for parallel prefix circuits, Proceedings of the 15th Annual ACM Symposium on Theory of Computing, Boston, Massachusetts, May 1983, pp. 100–109, Association for Computing Machinery, New York, N.Y., 1983.

[GREENBERG]

Greenberg, A. G., and Manber, U., A probabilistic pipeline algorithm for k-selection on the tree machine, *IEEE Transactions on Computers*, Vol. C-36, No. 3, March 1987, pp. 359–362.

[KNUTH]

Knuth, D. E., *The Art of Computer Programming*, Vol. 3, *Sorting and Searching*, Addison-Wesley, Reading, Mass., 1973.

[KOGGE 1]

Kogge, P. M., Parallel solution of recurrence problems, *IBM Journal of Research and Development*, March 1974, pp. 138–148.

[KOGGE 2]

Kogge, P. M., and Stone, H. S., A parallel algorithm for the efficient solution of a general class of recurrence equations, *IEEE Transactions on Computers*, Vol. C-22, No. 8, August 1973, pp. 786–792.

[KRUSKAL]

Kruskal, C. P., Rudolph, L., and Snir, M., The power of parallel prefix, *IEEE Transactions on Computers*, Vol. C-34, No. 10, October 1985, pp. 965–968.

[LADNER]

Ladner, R. E., and Fischer, M. J., Parallel prefix computation, *Journal of the ACM*, Vol. 27, No. 4, October 1980, pp. 831–838.

[MEGIDDO]

Megiddo, N., Applying parallel computation algorithms in the design of serial algorithms, *Journal of the ACM*, Vol. 30, No. 4, October 1983, pp. 852–865.

[REIF]

Reif, J. H., Probabilistic parallel prefix computation, Proceedings of the 1984 International Conference on Parallel Processing, Bellaire, Michigan, August 1984, pp. 291–298, IEEE Computer Society, Washington, D.C., 1984.

[REISCHUK]

Reischuk, R., A fast probabilistic parallel sorting algorithm, Proceedings of the 22nd Annual IEEE Symposium on Foundations of Computer Science, Nashville, Tennessee, October 1981, pp. 212–219, IEEE Computer Society, Washington, D.C., 1981.

[SHILOACH]

Shiloach, Y., and Vishkin, U., Finding the maximum, merging, and sorting in a parallel computation model, *Journal of Algorithms*, Vol. 2, 1981, pp. 88–102.

[STONE]

Stone, H. S., Ed., *Introduction to Computer Architecture*, Science Research Associates, Chicago, 1980.

[STOUT 1]

Stout, Q. F., Sorting, merging, selecting, and filtering on tree and pyramid machines, Proceedings of the 1983 International Conference on Parallel Processing, Bellaire, Michigan, August 1983, pp. 214–221, IEEE Computer Society, Washington, D.C., 1983.

[STOUT 2]

Stout, Q. F., Mesh-connected computers with broadcasting, *IEEE Transactions on Computers*, Vol. C-32, No. 9, September 1983, pp. 826–830.

[TANIMOTO]

Tanimoto, S. L., Sorting, histogramming, and other statistical operations on a pyramid machine, Technical Report 82-08-02, Department of Computer Science, University of Washington, Seattle, 1982.

[VALIANT]

Valiant, L. G., Parallelism in comparison problems, *SIAM Journal on Computing*, Vol. 4, No. 3, September 1975, pp. 348–355.

[VISHKIN]

Vishkin, U., An optimal parallel algorithm for selection, Department of Computer Science, Courant Institute of Mathematical Sciences, New York, 1983.

[WAH]

Wah, B. W., and Chen, K.-L., A partitioning approach to the design of selection networks, *IEEE Transactions on Computers*, Vol. C-33, No. 3, March 1984, pp. 261–268.

3

Merging

3.1 INTRODUCTION

We mentioned in chapter 2 that selection belongs to a class of problems known as comparison problems. The second such problem to be studied in this book is that of *merging*. It is defined as follows: Let $A = \{a_1, a_2, \ldots, a_r\}$ and $B = \{b_1, b_2, \ldots, b_s\}$ be two sequences of numbers sorted in nondecreasing order; it is required to *merge* A and B, that is, to form a third sequence $C = \{c_1, c_2, \ldots, c_{r+s}\}$, also sorted in nondecreasing order, such that each c_i in C belongs to either A or B and each a_i and each b_i appears exactly once in C. In computer science, merging arises in a variety of contexts including database applications in particular and file management in general. Many of these applications, of course, involve the merging of nonnumeric data. Furthermore, it is often necessary once the merging is complete to delete duplicate entries from the resulting sequence. A typical example is the merging of two mailing lists each sorted alphabetically. These variants offer no new insights and can be handled quite easily once the basic problem stated above has been solved.

Merging is very well understood in the sequential model of computation and a simple algorithm exists for its solution. In the worst case, when $r = s = n$, say, the algorithm runs in $O(n)$ time. This is optimal since every element of A and B must be examined at least once, thus making $\Omega(n)$ steps necessary in order to merge. Our purpose in this chapter is to show how the problem can be solved on a variety of parallel computational models. In view of the lower bound just stated, it should be noted that $\Omega(n/N)$ time is needed by any parallel merging algorithm that uses N processors.

We begin in section 3.2 by describing a special-purpose parallel architecture for merging. A parallel algorithm for the CREW SM SIMD model is presented in section 3.3 that is adaptive and cost optimal. Since the algorithm invokes a sequential procedure for merging, that procedure is also described in section 3.3. It is shown in section 3.4 how the concurrent-read operations can be removed from the parallel algorithm of section 3.3 by simulating it on an EREW computer. Finally, an adaptive and optimal algorithm for the EREW SM SIMD model is presented in section 3.5 whose running time is smaller than that of the simulation in section 3.4. The algorithm is based on a sequential procedure for finding the median of two sorted sequences, also described in section 3.5.

3.2 A NETWORK FOR MERGING

In chapter 1 we saw that special-purpose parallel architectures can be obtained in any one of the following ways:

(i) using specialized processors together with a conventional interconnection network,

(ii) using a custom-designed interconnection network to link standard processors, or

(iii) using a combination of (i) and (ii).

In this section we shall take the third of these approaches. Merging will be accomplished by a collection of very simple processors communicating through a special-purpose network. This special-purpose parallel architecture is known as an *(r, s)-merging network*. All the processors to be used are identical and are called *comparators*. As illustrated by Fig. 3.1, a comparator receives two inputs and produces two outputs. The only operation a comparator is capable of performing is to compare the values of its two inputs and then place the smaller and larger of the two on its top and bottom output lines, respectively.

Using these comparators, we proceed to build a network that takes as input the two sorted sequences $A = \{a_1, a_2, \ldots, a_r\}$ and $B = \{b_1, b_2, \ldots, b_s\}$ and produces as output a single sorted sequence $C = \{c_1, c_2, \ldots, c_{r+s}\}$. The following presentation is greatly simplified by making two assumptions:

1. the two input sequences are of the same size, that is, $r = s = n \geqslant 1$, and

2. n is a power of 2.

We begin by considering merging networks for the first three values of n. When $n = 1$, a single comparator clearly suffices: It produces as output its two inputs in

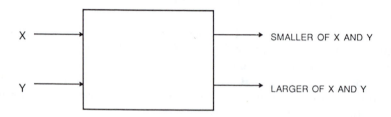

X   →   → SMALLER OF X AND Y

Y   →   → LARGER OF X AND Y

Figure 3.1 Comparator.

sorted order. When $n = 2$, the two sequences $A = \{a_1, a_2\}$ and $B = \{b_1, b_2\}$ are correctly merged by the network in Fig. 3.2. This is easily verified. Processor P_1 compares the smallest element of A to the smallest element of B. Its top output must be the smallest element in C, that is, c_1. Similarly, the bottom output of P_2 must be c_4. One additional comparison is performed by P_3 to produce the two middle elements of C. When $n = 4$, we can use two copies of the network in Fig. 3.2 followed by three comparators, as shown in Fig. 3.3 for $A = \{3, 5, 7, 9\}$ and $B = \{2, 4, 6, 8\}$.

In general, an (n, n)-merging network is obtained by the following recursive construction. First, the odd-numbered elements of A and B, that is, $\{a_1, a_3, a_5, \ldots, a_{n-1}\}$ and $\{b_1, b_3, b_5, \ldots, b_{n-1}\}$, are merged using an $(n/2, n/2)$-merging network to produce a sequence $\{d_1, d_2, d_3, \ldots, d_n\}$. Simultaneously, the even-numbered elements of the two sequences, $\{a_2, a_4, a_6, \ldots, a_n\}$ and $\{b_2, b_4, b_6, \ldots, b_n\}$, are also merged using an $(n/2, n/2)$-merging network to produce a sequence $\{e_1, e_2, e_3, \ldots, e_n\}$. The final sequence $\{c_1, c_2, \ldots, c_{2n}\}$ is now obtained from

$$c_1 = d_1, \quad c_{2n} = e_n, \quad c_{2i} = \min(d_{i+1}, e_i), \quad \text{and} \quad c_{2i+1} = \max(d_{i+1}, e_i)$$

$$\text{for } i = 1, 2, \ldots, n - 1.$$

The final comparisons are accomplished by a rank of $n - 1$ comparators as illustrated in Fig. 3.4. Note that each of the $(n/2, n/2)$-merging networks is constructed by applying the same rule recursively, that is, by using two $(n/4, n/4)$-merging networks followed by a rank of $(n/2) - 1$ comparators.

The merging network in Fig. 3.4 is based on a method known as *odd–even merging*. That this method works in general is shown as follows. First note that $d_1 = \min(a_1, b_1)$ and $e_n = \max(a_n, b_n)$, which means that c_1 and c_{2n} are computed properly. Now observe that in the sequence $\{d_1, d_2, \ldots, d_n\}$, i elements are smaller than or equal to d_{i+1}. Each of these is an odd-numbered element of either A or B. Therefore, $2i$ elements of A and B are smaller than or equal to d_{i+1}. In other words,

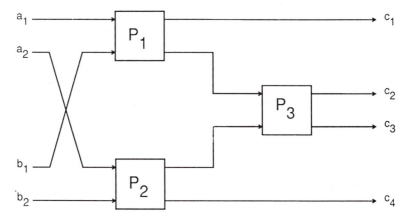

Figure 3.2 Merging two sequences of two elements each.

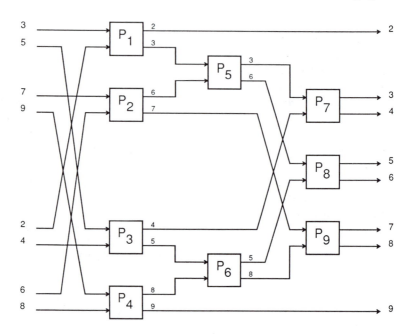

Figure 3.3   Merging two sequences of four elements each.

$d_{i+1} \geqslant c_{2i}$. Similarly, $e_i \geqslant c_{2i}$. On the other hand, in the sequence $\{c_1, c_2, \ldots, c_{2n}\}$, $2i$ elements from A and B are smaller than or equal to c_{2i+1}. This means that c_{2i+1} is larger than or equal to $(i + 1)$ odd-numbered elements belonging to either A or B. In other words, $c_{2i+1} \geqslant d_{i+1}$. Similarly, $c_{2i+1} \geqslant e_i$. Since $c_{2i} \leqslant c_{2i+1}$, the preceding inequalities imply that $c_{2i} = \min(d_{i+1}, e_i)$, and $c_{2i+1} = \max(d_{i+1}, e_i)$, thus establishing the correctness of odd–even merging.

Analysis.   Our analysis of odd–even merging will concentrate on the time, number of processors, and total number of operations required to merge.

(i) Running Time.   We begin by assuming that a comparator can read its input, perform a comparison, and produce its output all in one time unit. Now, let $t(2n)$ denote the time required by an (n, n)-merging network to merge two sequences of length n each. The recursive nature of such a network yields the following recurrence for $t(2n)$:

$$t(2) = 1 \qquad \text{for } n = 1 \quad \text{(see Fig. 3.1),}$$

$$t(2n) = t(n) + 1 \quad \text{for } n > 1 \quad \text{(see Fig. 3.4),}$$

whose solution is easily seen to be $t(2n) = 1 + \log n$. This is significantly faster than the best, namely, $O(n)$, running time achievable on a sequential computer.

(ii) Number of Processors.   Here we are interested in counting the number of comparators required to odd–even merge. Let $p(2n)$ denote the number of compara-

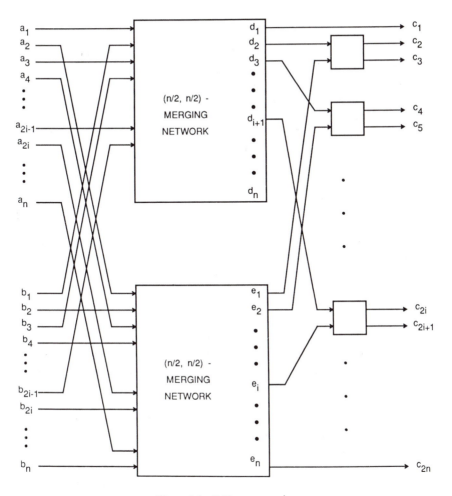

Figure 3.4 Odd–even merging.

tors in an (n, n)-merging network. Again, we have a recurrence:

$$p(2) = 1 \qquad\qquad \text{for } n = 1 \quad \text{(see Fig. 3.1)},$$
$$p(2n) = 2p(n) + (n - 1) \quad \text{for } n > 1 \quad \text{(see Fig. 3.4)},$$

whose solution $p(2n) = 1 + n \log n$ is also straightforward.

  (iii) Cost. Since $t(2n) = 1 + \log n$ and $p(2n) = 1 + n \log n$, the total number of comparisons performed by an (n, n)-merging network, that is, the network's cost, is

$$c(2n) = p(2n) \times t(2n)$$

$$= O(n \log^2 n).$$

Our network is therefore not cost optimal as it performs more operations than the $O(n)$ sufficient to merge sequentially.

Discussion.   In this section we presented an example of a special-purpose architecture for merging. These *merging networks*, as we called them, have the following interesting property: The sequence of comparisons they perform is fixed in advance. Regardless of the input, the network will always perform the same number of comparisons in a predetermined order. This is why such networks are sometimes said to be *oblivious* of their input.

Our analysis showed that the (n, n)-merging network studied is extremely fast, especially when compared with the best possible sequential merging algorithm. For example, it can merge two sequences of length 2^{20} elements each in twenty-one steps; the same result would require more than two million steps on a sequential computer. Unfortunately, such speed is achieved by using an unreasonable number of processors. Again, for $n = 2^{20}$, our (n, n)-merging network would consist of over twenty million comparators! In addition, the architecture of the network is highly irregular, and the wires linking the comparators have lengths that vary with n. This suggests that, although theoretically appealing, merging networks would be impractical for large values of n.

3.3 MERGING ON THE CREW MODEL

Our study of odd–even merging identified a problem associated with merging networks in general, namely, their inflexibility. A fixed number of comparators are assembled in a fixed configuration to merge sequences of fixed size. Although this may prove adequate for some applications, it is desirable in general to have a parallel algorithm that adapts to the number of available processors on the parallel computer at hand. This section describes one such algorithm. In addition to being adaptive, the algorithm is also cost optimal: Its running time multiplied by the number of processors used equals, to within a constant multiplicative factor, the lower bound on the number of operations required to merge. The algorithm runs on the CREW SM SIMD model. It assumes the existence, and makes use of, a sequential procedure for merging two sorted sequences. We therefore begin by presenting this procedure.

3.3.1 Sequential Merging

Two sequences of numbers $A = \{a_1, a_2, \ldots, a_r\}$ and $B = \{b_1, b_2, \ldots, b_s\}$ sorted in nondecreasing order are given. It is required to merge A and B to form a third sequence C, also sorted in nondecreasing order. The merging process is to be performed by a single processor. This can be done by the following algorithm. Two pointers are used, one for each sequence. Initially, the pointers are positioned at elements a_1 and b_1, respectively. The smaller of a_1 and b_1 is assigned to c_1, and the pointer to the sequence from which c_1 came is advanced one position. Again, the two elements pointed to are compared: The smaller becomes c_2 and the pointer to it is advanced. This continues until one of the two input sequences is exhausted; the elements left over in the other sequence are now copied in C. The algorithm is given in what follows as procedure SEQUENTIAL MERGE. Its description is greatly simplified by assuming the existence of two fictional elements a_{r+1} and b_{s+1}, both of which are equal to infinity.

procedure SEQUENTIAL MERGE (A, B, C)

Step 1: (1.1) $i \leftarrow 1$
        (1.2) $j \leftarrow 1$.

Step 2: **for** $k = 1$ **to** $r + s$ **do**
        if $a_i < b_j$ **then** (i) $c_k \leftarrow a_i$
                            (ii) $i \leftarrow i + 1$
                else (i) $c_k \leftarrow b_j$
                        (ii) $j \leftarrow j + 1$

        end if
    end for. □

The procedure takes sequences A and B as input and returns sequence C as output. Since each comparison leads to one element of C being defined, there are exactly $r + s$ such comparisons, and in the worst case, when $r = s = n$, say, the algorithm runs in $O(n)$ time. In view of the $\Omega(n)$ lower bound on merging derived in section 3.1, procedure SEQUENTIAL MERGE is optimal.

3.3.2 Parallel Merging

A CREW SM SIMD computer consists of N processors $P_1, P_2, \ldots, P_N$. It is required to design a parallel algorithm for this computer that takes the two sequences A and B as input and produces the sequence C as output, as defined earlier. Without loss of generality, we assume that $r \leqslant s$.

It is desired that the parallel algorithm satisfy the properties stated in section 2.4, namely, that

(i) the number of processors used by the algorithm be sublinear and adaptive,

(ii) the running time of the algorithm be adaptive and significantly smaller than the best sequential algorithm, and

(iii) the cost be optimal.

We now describe an algorithm that satisfies these properties. It uses N processors where $N \leqslant r$ and in the worst case when $r = s = n$ runs in $O((n/N) + \log n)$ time. The algorithm is therefore cost optimal for $N \leqslant n/\log n$. In addition to the basic arithmetic and logic functions usually available, each of the N processors is assumed capable of performing the following two sequential procedures:

1. Procedure SEQUENTIAL MERGE described in section 3.3.1.

2. Procedure BINARY SEARCH described in what follows. The procedure takes as input a sequence $S = \{s_1, s_2, \ldots, s_n\}$ of numbers sorted in nondecreasing order and a number x. If x belongs to S, the procedure returns the index k of an element s_k in S such that $x = s_k$. Otherwise, the procedure returns a zero. Binary search is based on the divide-and-conquer principle. At each stage, a comparison is performed between x and an element of S. Either the two are equal and the procedure terminates or half of the elements of the sequence under consideration are discarded. The process continues until the number of elements left is 0 or 1, and after at most one additional comparison the procedure terminates.

procedure BINARY SEARCH (S, x, k)

Step 1:   (1.1) $i \leftarrow 1$
           (1.2) $h \leftarrow n$
           (1.3) $k \leftarrow 0$.

Step 2:   **while** $i \leqslant h$ **do**
           (2.1) $m \leftarrow \lfloor (i+h)/2 \rfloor$
           (2.2) **if** $x = s_m$ **then** (i) $k \leftarrow m$
                                          (ii) $i \leftarrow h+1$
                        else if $x < s_m$ **then** $h \leftarrow m-1$
                                              else $i \leftarrow m+1$
                        end if
                 end if
           end while.   □

Since the number of elements under consideration is reduced by one-half at each step, the procedure requires $O(\log n)$ time in the worst case.

We are now ready to describe our first parallel merging algorithm for a shared-memory computer. The algorithm is presented as procedure CREW MERGE.

procedure CREW MERGE (A, B, C)

Step 1:   {Select $N-1$ elements of A that subdivide that sequence into N subsequences of approximately the same size. Call the subsequence formed by these $N-1$ elements A'. A subsequence B' of $N-1$ elements of B is chosen similarly. This step is executed as follows:}
           for $i = 1$ **to** $N-1$ **do in parallel**
                Processor P_i determines a_i' and b_i' from
                (1.1) $a_i' \leftarrow a_{i\lceil r/N \rceil}$
                (1.2) $b_i' \leftarrow b_{i\lceil s/N \rceil}$

           end for.

Step 2:   {Merge A' and B' into a sequence of triples $V = \{v_1, v_2, \ldots, v_{2N-2}\}$, where each triple consists of an element of A' or B' followed by its position in A' or B' followed by the name of its sequence of origin, that is, A or B. This is done as follows:}
           (2.1) **for** $i = 1$ **to** $N-1$ **do in parallel**
                (i) Processor P_i uses BINARY SEARCH on B' to find the smallest j such that $a_i' < b_j'$

(ii) **if** j exists **then** $v_{i+j-1} \leftarrow (a_i', i, A)$
      else $v_{i+N-1} \leftarrow (a_i', i, A)$
   end if
end for

(2.2) **for** $i = 1$ **to** $N-1$ **do in parallel**
   (i) Processor P_i uses BINARY SEARCH on A' to find the smallest j such that $b_i' < a_j'$
   (ii) **if** j exists **then** $v_{i+j-1} \leftarrow (b_i', i, B)$
         else $v_{i+N-1} \leftarrow (b_i', i, B)$
      end if
   end for.

Step 3:   {Each processor merges and inserts into C the elements of two subsequences, one from A and one from B. The indices of the two elements (one in A and one in B) at which each processor is to begin merging are first computed and stored in an array Q of ordered pairs. This step is executed as follows:}

(3.1) $Q(1) \leftarrow (1, 1)$
(3.2) **for** $i = 2$ **to** N **do in parallel**
      if $v_{2i-2} = (a_k', k, A)$ **then** processor P_i
         (i) uses BINARY SEARCH on B to find the smallest j such that $b_j > a_k'$
         (ii) $Q(i) \leftarrow (k\lceil r/N \rceil, j)$
      else processor P_i

         (i) uses BINARY SEARCH on A to find the smallest j such that $a_j > b_k'$
         (ii) $Q(i) \leftarrow (j, k\lceil s/N \rceil)$
      end if
   end for
(3.3) **for** $i = 1$ **to** N **do in parallel**
      Processor P_i uses SEQUENTIAL MERGE and $Q(i) = (x, y)$ to merge two subsequences one beginning at a_x and the other at b_y and places the result of the merge in array C beginning at position $x + y - 1$. The merge continues until
         (i) an element larger than or equal to the first component of v_{2i} is encountered in each of A and B (when $i \leqslant N-1$)
         (ii) no elements are left in either A or B (when $i = N$)
      end for. $\square$

Before analyzing the running time of the algorithm, we make the following two observations:

(i) In general instances, an element a_i of A is compared to an element b_j of B to determine which is smaller; if it turns out that $a_i = b_j$, then the algorithm decides arbitrarily that a_i is smaller.

(ii) Concurrent-read operations are performed whenever procedure BINARY SEARCH is invoked, namely, in steps 2.1, 2.2, and 3.2. Indeed, in each of these instances several processors are executing a binary search over the same sequence.

Analysis. A step-by-step analysis of CREW MERGE follows:

Step 1: With all processors operating in parallel, each processor computes two subscripts. Therefore this step requires constant time.

Step 2: This step consists of two applications of procedure BINARY SEARCH to a sequence of length $N - 1$, each followed by an assignment statement. This takes $O(\log N)$ time.

Step 3: Step 3.1 consists of a constant-time assignment, and step 3.2 requires at most $O(\log s)$ time. To analyze step 3.3, we first observe that V contains $2N - 2$ elements that divide C into $2N - 1$ subsequences with maximum size equal to $(\lceil r/N \rceil + \lceil s/N \rceil)$. This maximum size occurs if, for example, one element a_i' of A' equals an element b_j' of B'; then the $\lceil r/N \rceil$ elements smaller than or equal to a_i' (and larger than or equal to a_{i-1}') are also smaller than or equal to b_j', and similarly, the $\lceil s/N \rceil$ elements smaller than or equal to b_j' (and larger than or equal to b_{j-1}') are also smaller than or equal to a_i'. In step 3 each processor creates two such subsequences of C whose total size is therefore no larger than $2(\lceil r/N \rceil + \lceil s/N \rceil)$, except P_N, which creates only one subsequence of C. It follows that procedure SEQUENTIAL MERGE takes at most $O((r + s)/N)$ time.

In the worst case, $r = s = n$, and since $n \geqslant N$, the algorithm's running time is dominated by the time required by step 3. Thus

$$t(2n) = O((n/N) + \log n).$$

Since $p(2n) = N$, $c(2n) = p(2n) \times t(2n) = O(n + N \log n)$, and the algorithm is cost optimal when $N \leqslant n/\log n$.

Example 3.1

Assume that a CREW SM SIMD computer with $N = 4$ processors is available and it is required to merge $A = \{2, 3, 4, 6, 11, 12, 13, 15, 16, 20, 22, 24\}$ and $B = \{1, 5, 7, 8, 9, 10, 14, 17, 18, 19, 21, 23\}$, that is, $r = s = 12$.

The two subsequences $A' = \{4, 12, 16\}$ and $B' = \{7, 10, 18\}$ are found in step 1 and then merged in step 2 to obtain

$$V = \{(4, 1, A), (7, 1, B), (10, 2, B), (12, 2, A), (16, 3, A), (18, 3, B)\}.$$

In steps 3.1 and 3.2, $Q(1) = (1, 1)$, $Q(2) = (5, 3)$, $Q(3) = (6, 7)$, and $Q(4) = (10, 9)$ are determined. In step 3.3 processor P_1 begins at elements $a_1 = 2$ and $b_1 = 1$ and merges all elements of A and B smaller than 7, thus creating the subsequence $\{1, 2, 3, 4, 5, 6\}$ of C. Similarly, processor P_2 begins at $a_5 = 11$ and $b_3 = 7$ and merges all elements smaller than 12, thus creating $\{7, 8, 9, 10, 11\}$. Processor P_3 begins at $a_6 = 12$ and $b_7 = 14$ and creates $\{12, 13, 14, 15, 16, 17\}$. Finally P_4 begins at $a_{10} = 20$ and $b_9 = 18$ and creates $\{18, 19, 20, 21, 22, 23, 24\}$. The resulting sequence C is therefore $\{1, 2, 3, \underline{4}, 5, 6, \underline{7}, 8, 9, \underline{10}, 11, \underline{12}, 13, 14, 15, \underline{16}, 17, \underline{18}, 19, 20, 21, 22, 23, 24\}$. The elements of A' and B' are shown underlined in C. $\square$

3.4 MERGING ON THE EREW MODEL

As we saw in the previous section, concurrent-read operations are performed at several places of procedure CREW MERGE. We now show how this procedure can be adapted to run on an N-processor EREW SM SIMD computer that, by definition, disallows any attempt by more than one processor to read from a memory location. The idea of the adaptation is quite simple: All we have to do is find a way to simulate multiple-read operations. Once such a simulation is found, it can be used by the parallel merge algorithm (and in general by any algorithm with multiple-read operations) to perform every read operation from the EREW memory. Of course, we require the simulation to be efficient. Simply queuing all the requests to read from a given memory location and serving them one after the other is surely inadequate: It can increase the running time by a factor of N in the worst case. On the other hand, using procedure BROADCAST of chapter 2 is inappropriate: A multiple-read operation from a memory location may not necessarily involve all processors. Typically, several arbitrary subsets of the set of processors attempt to gain access to different locations, one location per subset. In chapter 1 we described a method for performing the simulation in this general case. This is now presented more formally as procedure MULTIPLE BROADCAST in what follows.

Assume that an algorithm designed to run on a CREW SM SIMD computer requires a total of M locations of shared memory. In order to simulate this algorithm on the EREW model with N processors, where $N = 2^q$ for $q \geqslant 1$, we increase the size of the memory from M to $M(2N - 1)$. Thus, each of the M locations is thought of as the root of a binary tree with N leaves. Such a tree has $q + 1$ levels and a total of $2N - 1$ nodes, as shown in Fig. 3.5 for $N = 16$. The nodes of the tree represent consecutive locations in memory. Thus if location D is the root, then its left and right children are $D + 1$ and $D + 2$, respectively. In general, the left and right children of $D + x$ are $D + 2x + 1$ and $D + 2x + 2$, respectively.

Assume that processor P_i wishes at some point to read from some location $d(i)$ in memory. It places its request at location $d(i) + (N - 1) + (i - 1)$, a leaf of the tree rooted at $d(i)$. This is done by initializing two variables local to P_i:

1. level(i), which stores the current level of the tree reached by P_i's request, is initialized to 0, and
2. loc(i), which stores the current node of the tree reached by P_i's request, is initialized to $(N - 1) + (i - 1)$. Note that P_i need only store the position in the tree relative to $d(i)$ that its request has reached and not the actual memory location $d(i) + (N - 1) + (i - 1)$.

The simulation consists of two stages: the *ascent* stage and the *descent* stage. During the ascent stage, the processors proceed as follows: At each level a processor P_i occupying a left child is first given priority to advance its request one level up the tree.

LEVEL

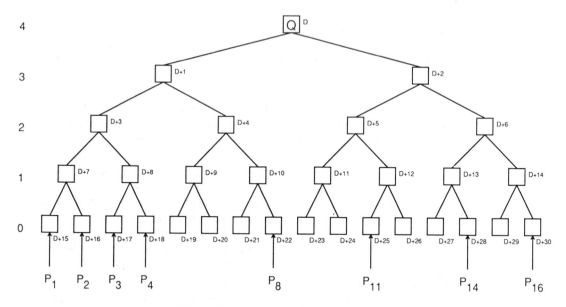

Figure 3.5 Memory organization for multiple broadcasting.

It does so by marking the parent location with a special marker, say, [*i*]. It then updates its level and location. In this case, a request at the right child is immobilized for the remainder of the procedure. Otherwise (i.e., if there was no processor occupying the left child) a processor occupying the right child can now "claim" the parent location. This continues until at most two processors reach level (log *N*) − 1. They each in turn read the value stored in the root, and the descent stage commences. The value just read goes down the tree of memory locations until every request to read by a processor has been honored. Procedure MULTIPLE BROADCAST follows.

procedure MULTIPLE BROADCAST (*d*(1), *d*(2), ..., *d*(*N*))

Step 1: **for** *i* = 1 **to** *N* **do in parallel**
  {*P_i* initializes level(*i*) and loc(*i*)}
  (1.1) level(*i*)←0
  (1.2) loc(*i*) ← *N* + *i* − 2
  (1.3) store [*i*] in location *d*(*i*) + loc(*i*)
  end for.

Step 2: **for** *v* = 0 **to** (log *N*) − 2 **do**
  (2.1) **for** *i* = 1 **to** *N* **do in parallel**
    {*P_i* at a left child advances up its tree}
    (2.1.1) *x* ← ⌊(loc(*i*) − 1)/2⌋
    (2.1.2) **if** loc(*i*) is odd and level(*i*) = *v*

    then (i) $loc(i) \leftarrow x$
          (ii) store $[i]$ in location $d(i) + loc(i)$
          (iii) $level(i) \leftarrow level(i) + 1$
    end if
  end for
  (2.2) **for** $i = 1$ **to** N **do in parallel**
      {P_i at a right child advances up its tree if possible}
      if $d(i) + x$ does not already contain a marker $[j]$ for some $1 \leqslant j \leqslant N$
      then (i) $loc(i) \leftarrow x$
            (ii) store $[i]$ in location $d(i) + loc(i)$
            (iii) $level(i) \leftarrow level(i) + 1$
      end if
  end for
  end for.

Step 3: **for** $v = (\log N) - 1$ **down to** 0 **do**
      (3.1) **for** $i = 1$ **to** N **do in parallel**
          {P_i at a left child reads from its parent and then moves down the tree}
          (3.1.1) $x \leftarrow \lfloor(loc(i) - 1)/2\rfloor$
          (3.1.2) $y \leftarrow (2 \times loc(i)) + 1$
          (3.1.3) **if** $loc(i)$ is odd and $level(i) = v$
                then (i) read the contents of $d(i) + x$
                     (ii) write the contents of $d(i) + x$ in location
                          $d(i) + loc(i)$
                     (iii) $level(i) \leftarrow level(i) - 1$
                     (iv) **if** location $d(i) + y$ contains $[i]$
                          then $loc(i) \leftarrow y$
                          else $loc(i) \leftarrow y + 1$
                          end if
                end if
      end for
      (3.2) **for** $i = 1$ **to** N **do in parallel**
          {P_i at a right child reads from its parent and then moves down the tree}
          if $loc(i)$ is even and $level(i) = v$
          then (i) read the contents of $d(i) + x$
             (ii) write the contents of $d(i) + x$ in location $d(i) + loc(i)$
             (iii) $level(i) \leftarrow level(i) - 1$
             (iv) **if** location $d(i) + y$ contains $[i]$
                  then $loc(i) \leftarrow y$
                  else $loc(i) \leftarrow y + 1$
                  end if
          end if
      end for
  end for. □

Step 1 of the procedure consists of three constant-time operations. Each of the ascent and descent stages in steps 2 and 3, respectively, requires $O(\log N)$ time. The overall running time of procedure MULTIPLE BROADCAST is therefore $O(\log N)$.

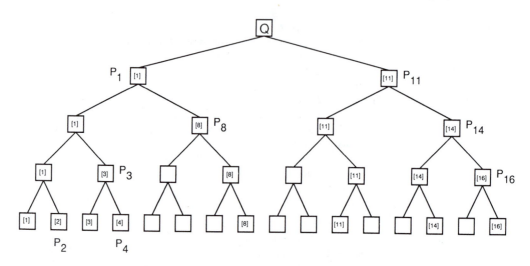

Figure 3.6 Memory contents after step 2 of procedure MULTIPLE BROADCAST.

Example 3.2

Let $N = 16$ and assume that at a given moment during the execution of a CREW parallel algorithm processors P_1, P_2, P_3, P_4, P_8, P_{11}, P_{14}, and P_{16} need to read a quantity Q from a location D in memory. When simulating this multiple-read operation on an EREW computer using MULTIPLE BROADCAST, the processors place their requests at the appropriate leaves of a tree of locations rooted at D during step 1, as shown in Fig. 3.5. Figure 3.6 shows the positions of the various processors and the contents of memory locations at the end of step 2. The contents of the memory locations at the end of step 3 are shown in Fig. 3.7. □

Note that:

1. The markers $[i]$ are chosen so that they can be easily distinguished from data values such as Q.
2. If during a multiple-read step of the CREW algorithm being simulated, a processor P_i does not wish to read from memory, then $d(i)$ may be chosen arbitrarily among the M memory locations used by the algorithm.
3. When the procedure terminates, the value of level(i) is negative and that of loc(i) is out of bounds. These values are meaningless. This is of no consequence, however, since level(i) and loc(i) are always initialized in step 1.

We are now ready to analyze the running time $t(2n)$ of an adaptation of procedure CREW MERGE for the EREW model. Since every read operation (simple or multiple) is simulated using procedure MULTIPLE BROADCAST in $O(\log N)$ time, the adapted procedure is at most $O(\log N)$ times slower than procedure CREW

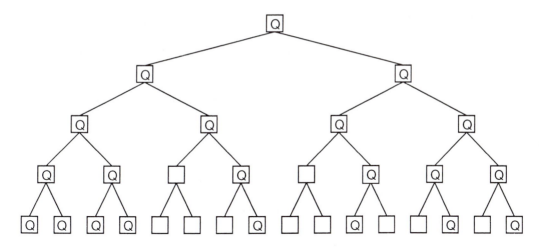

Figure 3.7   Memory contents at end of procedure MULTIPLE BROADCAST.

MERGE, that is,

$$t(2n) = O(\log N) \times O(n/N + \log n)$$

$$= O((n/N)\log n + \log^2 n).$$

The algorithm has a cost of

$$c(2n) = O(n \log n + N \log^2 n)$$

which is not optimal. Furthermore, since procedure CREW MERGE uses $O(n)$ locations of shared memory, the storage requirements of its adaptation for the EREW model are $O(Nn)$. In the following section an algorithm for merging on the EREW model is described that is cost optimal and uses only $O(n)$ shared-memory locations.

3.5 A BETTER ALGORITHM FOR THE EREW MODEL

We saw in the previous section how a direct simulation of the CREW merging algorithm on the EREW model is not cost optimal. This is due to the logarithmic factor always introduced by procedure MULTIPLE BROADCAST. Clearly, in order to match the performance of procedure CREW MERGE, another approach is needed. In this section we describe an adaptive and cost-optimal parallel algorithm for merging on the EREW SM SIMD model of computation. The algorithm merges two sorted sequences $A = \{a_1, a_2, \ldots, a_r\}$ and $B = \{b_1, b_2, \ldots, b_s\}$ into a single sequence $C = \{c_1, c_2, \ldots, c_{r+s}\}$. It uses N processors $P_1, P_2, \ldots, P_N$, where $1 \leqslant N \leqslant r + s$ and, in the worst case when $r = s = n$, runs in $O((n/N) + \log N \log n)$ time. A building block of the algorithm is a sequential procedure for finding the *median* of two sorted sequences. This procedure is presented in section 3.5.1. The merging algorithm itself is the subject of section 3.5.2.

3.5.1 Finding the Median of Two Sorted Sequences

In this section we study a variant of the selection problem visited in chapter 2. Given two sorted sequences $A = \{a_1, a_2, \ldots, a_r\}$ and $B = \{b_1, b_2, \ldots, b_s\}$, where $r, s \geqslant 1$, let $A.B$ denote the sequence of length $m = r + s$ resulting from merging A and B. It is required to find the median, that is, the $\lceil m/2 \rceil$th element, of $A.B$. Without actually forming $A.B$, the algorithm we are about to describe returns a pair (a_x, b_y) that satisfies the following properties:

1. Either a_x or b_y is the median of $A.B$, that is, either a_x or b_y is larger than precisely $\lceil m/2 \rceil - 1$ elements and smaller than precisely $\lfloor m/2 \rfloor$ elements.

2. If a_x is the median, then b_y is either
    (i) the largest element in B smaller than or equal to a_x or
    (ii) the smallest element in B larger than or equal to a_x.
   Alternatively, if b_y is the median, then a_x is either
    (i) the largest element in A smaller than or equal to b_y or
    (ii) the smallest element in A larger than or equal to b_y.

3. If more than one pair satisfies 1 and 2, then the algorithm returns the pair for which $x + y$ is smallest.

We shall refer to (a_x, b_y) as the *median pair* of $A.B$. Thus x and y are the *indices of the median pair*. Note that a_x is the median of $A.B$ if either

(i) $a_x > b_y$ and $x + y - 1 = \lceil m/2 \rceil - 1$ or
(ii) $a_x < b_y$ and $m - (x + y - 1) = \lfloor m/2 \rfloor$.

Otherwise b_y is the median of $A.B$.

Example 3.3

Let $A = \{2, 5, 7, 10\}$ and $B = \{1, 4, 8, 9\}$ and observe that the median of $A.B$ is 5 and belongs to A. There are two median pairs satisfying properties 1 and 2:

(i) $(a_2, b_2) = (5, 4)$, where 4 is the largest element in B smaller than or equal to 5;
(ii) $(a_2, b_3) = (5, 8)$, where 8 is the smallest element in B larger than or equal to 5.
   The median pair is therefore $(5, 4)$. □

The algorithm, described in what follows as procedure TWO-SEQUENCE MEDIAN, proceeds in stages. At the end of each stage, some elements are removed from consideration from both A and B. We denote by n_A and n_B the number of elements of A and B, respectively, still under consideration at the beginning of a stage and by w the smaller of $\lfloor n_A/2 \rfloor$ and $\lfloor n_B/2 \rfloor$. Each stage is as follows: The medians a and b of the elements still under consideration in A and in B, respectively, are compared. If $a \geqslant b$, then the largest (smallest) w elements of $A(B)$ are removed from consideration. Otherwise, that is, if $a < b$, then the smallest (largest) w elements of $A(B)$ are removed from consideration. This process is repeated until there is only one element left still under consideration in one or both of the two sequences. The median pair is then determined from a small set of candidate pairs. The procedure keeps track of the elements still under consideration by using two pointers to each sequence: low_A and $high_A$ in A and low_B and $high_B$ in B.

procedure TWO-SEQUENCE MEDIAN (A, B, x, y)

Step 1: (1.1) $low_A \leftarrow 1$
        (1.2) $low_B \leftarrow 1$
        (1.3) $high_A \leftarrow r$
        (1.4) $high_B \leftarrow s$
        (1.5) $n_A \leftarrow r$
        (1.6) $n_B \leftarrow s$.

Step 2: **while** $n_A > 1$ **and** $n_B > 1$ **do**
        (2.1) $u \leftarrow low_A + \lceil (high_A - low_A - 1)/2 \rceil$
        (2.2) $v \leftarrow low_B + \lceil (high_B - low_B - 1)/2 \rceil$
        (2.3) $w \leftarrow \min(\lfloor n_A/2 \rfloor, \lfloor n_B/2 \rfloor)$
        (2.4) $n_A \leftarrow n_A - w$
        (2.5) $n_B \leftarrow n_B - w$
        (2.6) **if** $a_u \geq b_v$
            then (i) $high_A \leftarrow high_A - w$
                  (ii) $low_B \leftarrow low_B + w$
            else (i) $low_A \leftarrow low_A + w$
                  (ii) $high_B \leftarrow high_B - w$
        end if
        end while.

Step 3: Return as x and y the indices of the pair from $\{a_{u-1}, a_u, a_{u+1}\} \times \{b_{v-1}, b_v, b_{v+1}\}$ satisfying properties 1–3 of a median pair. □

Note that procedure TWO-SEQUENCE MEDIAN returns the indices of the median pair (a_x, b_y) rather than the pair itself.

Example 3.4

Let $A = \{10, 11, 12, 13, 14, 15, 16, 17, 18\}$ and $B = \{3, 4, 5, 6, 7, 8, 19, 20, 21, 22\}$. The following variables are initialized during step 1 of procedure TWO-SEQUENCE MEDIAN: $low_A = low_B = 1$, $high_A = n_A = 9$, and $high_B = n_B = 10$.

In the first iteration of step 2, $u = v = 5$, $w = \min(4, 5) = 4$, $n_A = 5$, and $n_B = 6$. Since $a_5 > b_5$, $high_A = low_B = 5$. In the second iteration, $u = 3$, $v = 7$, $w = \min(2, 3) = 2$, $n_A = 3$, and $n_B = 4$. Since $a_3 < b_7$, $low_A = 3$ and $high_B = 8$. In the third iteration, $u = 4$, $v = 6$, $w = \min(1, 2) = 1$, $n_A = 2$, and $n_B = 3$. Since $a_4 > b_6$, $high_A = 4$ and $low_B = 6$. In the fourth and final iteration of step 2, $u = 3$, $v = 7$, $w = \min(1, 1) = 1$, $n_A = 1$, and $n_B = 2$. Since $a_3 < b_7$, $low_A = 4$ and $high_B = 7$.

In step 3, two of the nine pairs in $\{11, 12, 13\} \times \{8, 19, 20\}$ satisfy the first two properties of a median pair. These pairs are $(a_4, b_6) = (13, 8)$ and $(a_4, b_7) = (13, 19)$. The procedure thus returns $(4, 6)$ as the indices of the median pair. □

Analysis. Steps 1 and 3 require constant time. Each iteration of step 2 reduces the smaller of the two sequences by half. For constants c_1 and c_2 procedure TWO-SEQUENCE MEDIAN thus requires $c_1 + c_2\log(\min\{r, s\})$ time, which is $O(\log n)$ in the worst case.

3.5.2 Fast Merging on the EREW Model

We now make use of procedure TWO-SEQUENCE MEDIAN to construct a parallel merging algorithm for the EREW model. The algorithm, presented in what follows as procedure EREW MERGE, has the following properties:

1. It requires a number of processors that is sublinear in the size of the input and adapts to the actual number of processors available on the EREW computer.
2. Its running time is small and varies inversely with the number of processors used.
3. Its cost is optimal.

Given two sorted sequences $A = \{a_1, a_2, \ldots, a_r\}$ and $B = \{b_1, b_2, \ldots, b_s\}$, the algorithm assumes the existence of N processors $P_1, P_2, \ldots, P_N$, where N is a power of 2 and $1 \leqslant N \leqslant r + s$. It merges A and B into a sorted sequence $C = \{c_1, c_2, \ldots, c_{r+s}\}$ in two stages as follows:

Stage 1: Each of the two sequences A and B is partitioned into N (possibly empty) subsequences $A_1, A_2, \ldots, A_N$ and $B_1, B_2, \ldots, B_N$ such that

(i) $|A_i| + |B_i| = (r + s)/N$ for $1 \leqslant i \leqslant N$ and
(ii) all elements in $A_i.B_i$ are smaller than or equal to all elements in $A_{i+1}.B_{i+1}$ for $1 \leqslant i \leqslant N$.

Stage 2: All pairs A_i and B_i, $1 \leqslant i \leqslant N$, are merged simultaneously and placed in C.

The first stage can be implemented efficiently with the help of procedure TWO-SEQUENCE MEDIAN. Stage 2 is carried out using procedure SEQUENTIAL MERGE. In the following procedure $A[i,j]$ is used to denote the subsequence $\{a_i, a_{i+1}, \ldots, a_j\}$ of A if $i \leqslant j$; otherwise $A[i,j]$ is empty. We define $B[i,j]$ similarly.

procedure EREW MERGE (A, B, C)

Step 1: (1.1) Processor P_1 obtains the quadruple $(1, r, 1, s)$
         (1.2) **for** $j = 1$ **to** $\log N$ **do**
                 for $i = 1$ **to** 2^{j-1} **do in parallel**
                 Processor P_i having received the quadruple (e, f, g, h)
                 (1.2.1) {Finds the median pair of two sequences}
                         TWO-SEQUENCE MEDIAN $(A[e, f], B[g, h], x, y)$

(1.2.2) {Computes four pointers p_1, p_2, q_1, and q_2 as follows:}
if a_x is the median
then (i) $p_1 \leftarrow x$
$\qquad$ (ii) $q_1 \leftarrow x + 1$
$\qquad$ (iii) **if** $b_y \leqslant a_x$ **then** (a) $p_2 \leftarrow y$
$\qquad\qquad\qquad\qquad\qquad$ (b) $q_2 \leftarrow y + 1$
$\qquad\qquad\qquad\qquad$ **else** (a) $p_2 \leftarrow y - 1$
$\qquad\qquad\qquad\qquad\qquad$ (b) $q_2 \leftarrow y$
$\qquad\qquad$ **end if**
else (i) $p_2 \leftarrow y$
$\qquad$ (ii) $q_2 \leftarrow y + 1$
$\qquad$ (iii) **if** $a_x \leqslant b_y$ **then** (a) $p_1 \leftarrow x$
$\qquad\qquad\qquad\qquad\qquad$ (b) $q_1 \leftarrow x + 1$
$\qquad\qquad\qquad\qquad$ **else** (a) $p_1 \leftarrow x - 1$
$\qquad\qquad\qquad\qquad\qquad$ (b) $q_1 \leftarrow x$
$\qquad\qquad$ **end if**
end if
(1.2.3) Communicates the quadruple (e, p_1, g, p_2) to P_{2i-1}
(1.2.4) Communicates the quadruple (q_1, f, q_2, h) to P_{2i}
end for
end for.

Step 2: **for** $i = 1$ **to** N **do in parallel**
$\qquad$ Processor P_i having received the quadruple (a, b, c, d)
$\qquad$ (2.1) $w \leftarrow 1 + ((i - 1)(r + s))/N$
$\qquad$ (2.2) $z \leftarrow \min\{i(r + s)/N, (r + s)\}$
$\qquad$ (2.3) SEQUENTIAL MERGE $(A[a, b], B[c, d], C[w, z])$
end for. $\square$

It should be clear that at any time during the execution of the procedure the subsequences on which processors are working are all disjoint. Hence, no concurrent-read operation is ever needed.

Example 3.5

Let $A = \{10, 11, 12, 13, 14, 15, 16, 17, 18\}$, $B = \{3, 4, 5, 6, 7, 8, 19, 20, 21, 22\}$, and $N = 4$.

In step 1.1 processor P_1 receives $(1, 9, 1, 10)$. During the first iteration of step 1.2 processor P_1 determines the indices of the median pair of A and B, namely, $(4, 6)$. It keeps $(1, 4, 1, 6)$ and communicates $(5, 9, 7, 10)$ to P_2. During the second iteration, P_1 computes the indices of the median pair of $A[1, 4] = \{10, 11, 12, 13\}$ and $B[1, 6] = \{3, 4, 5, 6, 7, 8\}$, namely, 1 and 5. Simultaneously, P_2 does the same with $A[5, 9] = \{14, 15, 16, 17, 18\}$ and $B[7, 10] = \{19, 20, 21, 22\}$ and obtains 9 and 7. Processor P_1 keeps $(1, 0, 1, 5)$ and communicates $(1, 4, 6, 6)$ to P_2. Similarly, P_2 communicates $(5, 9, 7, 6)$ to P_3 and $(10, 9, 7, 10)$ to P_4.

In step 2, processors P_1 to P_4 simultaneously create $C[1, 19]$ as follows. Having last received $(1, 0, 1, 5)$, P_1 computes $w = 1$ and $z = 5$ and copies $B[1, 5] = \{3, 4, 5, 6, 7\}$ into $C[1, 5]$. Similarly, P_2, having last received $(1, 4, 6, 6)$, computes $w = 6$ and $z = 10$ and merges $A[1, 4]$ and $B[6, 6]$ to obtain $C[6, 10] = \{8, 10, 11, 12, 13\}$. Processor P_3, having last received $(5, 9, 7, 6)$, computes $w = 11$ and $z = 15$ and copies

$A[5, 9] = \{14, 15, 16, 17, 18\}$ into $C[11, 15]$. Finally P_4, having last received $(10, 9, 7, 10)$, computes $w = 16$ and $z = 19$ and copies $B[7, 10] = \{19, 20, 21, 22\}$ into $C[16, 19]$. □

Analysis. In order to analyze the time requirements of procedure EREW MERGE, note that in step 1.1 processor P_1 reads from memory in constant time. During the jth iteration of step 1.2, each processor involved has to find the indices of the median pair of $(r + s)/2^{j-1}$ elements. This is done using procedure TWO-SEQUENCE MEDIAN in $O(\log[(r + s)/2^{j-1}])$ time, which is $O(\log(r + s))$. The two other operations in step 1.2 take constant time as they involve communications among processors through the shared memory. Since there are $\log N$ iterations of step 1.2, step 1 is completed in $O(\log N \times \log(r + s))$ time.

In step 2 each processor merges at most $(r + s)/N$ elements. This is done using procedure SEQUENTIAL MERGE in $O((r + s)/N)$ time. Together, steps 1 and 2 take $O((r + s)/N + \log N \times \log(r + s))$ time. In the worst case, when $r = s = n$, the time required by procedure EREW MERGE can be expressed as

$$t(2n) = O(n/N + \log^2 n),$$

yielding a cost of $c(2n) = O(n + N \log^2 n)$. In view of the $\Omega(n)$ lower bound on the number of operations required to merge, this cost is optimal when $N \leqslant n/\log^2 n$.

3.6 PROBLEMS

3.1 The odd–even merging network described in section 3.2 is just one example from a wide class of merging networks. Show that, in general, any (r, s)-merging network built of comparators must require $\Omega(\log(r + s))$ time in order to completely merge two sorted sequences of length r and s, respectively.

3.2 Show that, in general, any (r, s)-merging network must require $\Omega(s \log r)$ comparators when $r \leqslant s$.

3.3 Use the results in problems 3.1 and 3.2 to draw conclusions about the running time and number of comparators needed by the (n, n) odd–even merging network of section 3.2.

3.4 The odd–even merging network described in section 3.2 requires the two input sequences to be of equal length n. Modify that network so it becomes an (r, s)-merging network, where r is not necessarily equal to s.

3.5 The sequence of comparisons in the odd–even merging network can be viewed as a parallel algorithm. Describe an implementation of that algorithm on an SIMD computer where the processors are connected to form a linear array. The two input sequences to be merged initially occupy processors P_1 to P_r and P_{r+1} to P_s, respectively. When the algorithm terminates, P_i should contain the ith smallest element of the output sequence.

3.6 Repeat problem 3.5 for an $m \times m$ mesh-connected SIMD computer. Here the two sequences to be merged are initially horizontally adjacent, that is, one sequence occupies the upper part of the mesh and the second the lower part, as shown in Fig. 3.8(a). The output should be returned, as in Fig. 3.8(b), that is, in *row-major order*: The ith element resides in row j and column k, where $i = jm + k + 1$. Note that for simplicity, only the processors and their contents are shown in the figure, whereas the communications links have been omitted.

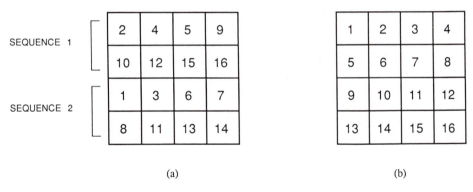

(a)   (b)

Figure 3.8   Merging two horizontal sequences on mesh-connected SIMD computer.

3.7   Repeat problem 3.6 for the case where the two input sequences are initially vertically adjacent, that is, one sequence occupies the left part of the mesh and the second the right part, as shown in Fig. 3.9. The result of the merge should appear as in Fig. 3.8(b).

3.8   A sequence $\{a_1, a_2, \ldots, a_{2n}\}$ is said to be *bitonic* if either
(i) there is an integer $1 \leqslant j \leqslant 2n$ such that

$$a_1 \leqslant a_2 \leqslant \cdots \leqslant a_j \geqslant a_{j+1} \geqslant \cdots \geqslant a_{2n}$$

or

(ii) the sequence does not initially satisfy condition (i) but can be shifted cyclically until condition (i) is satisfied.
For example, $\{2, 5, 8, 7, 6, 4, 3, 1\}$ is a bitonic sequence as it satisfies condition (i). Similarly, the sequence $\{2, 1, 3, 5, 6, 7, 8, 4\}$, which does not satisfy condition (i), is also bitonic as it can be shifted cyclically to obtain $\{1, 3, 5, 6, 7, 8, 4, 2\}$. Let $\{a_1, a_2, \ldots, a_{2n}\}$ be a bitonic sequence and let $d_i = \min\{a_i, a_{n+i}\}$ and $e_i = \max\{a_i, a_{n+i}\}$ for $1 \leqslant i \leqslant n$. Show that
(a) $\{d_1, d_2, \ldots, d_n\}$ and $\{e_1, e_2, \ldots, e_n\}$ are each bitonic and
(b) $\max\{d_1, d_2, \ldots, d_n\} \leqslant \min\{e_1, e_2, \ldots, e_n\}$.

3.9   Two sequences $A = \{a_1, a_2, \ldots, a_n\}$ and $B = \{a_{n+1}, a_{n+2}, \ldots, a_{2n}\}$ are given that when concatenated form a bitonic sequence $\{a_1, a_2, \ldots, a_{2n}\}$. Use the two properties of bitonic sequences derived in problem 3.8 to design an (n, n)-merging network for merging A and B.

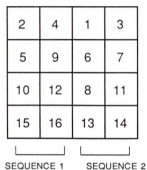

SEQUENCE 1   SEQUENCE 2

Figure 3.9   Merging two vertical sequences on mesh-connected SIMD computer.

Analyze the running time and number of comparators required. How does your network compare with odd–even merging in those respects?

3.10 Is it necessary for the *bitonic* merging network in problem 3.9 that the two input sequences be of equal length?

3.11 The sequence of comparisons in the bitonic merging network can be viewed as a parallel algorithm. Repeat problem 3.5 for this algorithm.

3.12 Repeat problem 3.6 for the bitonic merging algorithm.

3.13 Repeat problem 3.7 for the bitonic merging algorithm.

3.14 Design an algorithm for merging on a tree-connected SIMD computer. The two input sequences to be merged, of length r and s, respectively, are initially distributed among the leaves of the tree. Consider the two following situations:
   (i) The tree has at least $r + s$ leaves; initially leaves $1, \ldots, r$ store the first sequence and leaves $r + 1, \ldots, r + s$ store the second sequence, one element per leaf.
   (ii) The tree has fewer than $r + s$ leaves; initially, each leaf stores a subsequence of the input.
Analyze the running time and cost of your algorithm.

3.15 The running time analysis in problem 3.14 probably indicates that merging on the tree is no faster than procedure SEQUENTIAL MERGE. Show how merging on the tree can be more appealing than sequential merging when several pairs of sequences are queued for merging.

3.16 Consider the following variant of a tree-connected SIMD computer. In addition to the edges of the tree, two-way links connect processors at the same level (into a linear array), as shown in Fig. 3.10 for a four-leaf tree computer. Assume that such a parallel computer, known as a *pyramid*, has n processors at the base storing two sorted sequences of total length n, one element per processor. Show that $\Omega(n/\log n)$ is a lower bound on the time required for merging on the pyramid.

3.17 Develop a parallel algorithm for merging two sequences of total length n on a pyramid with n base processors. Analyze the running time of your algorithm.

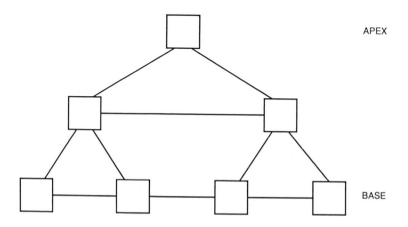

Figure 3.10   Processor pyramid.

3.18 Procedure CREW MERGE assumes that N, the number of processors available to merge two sequences of length r and s, respectively, is smaller than or equal to r when $r \leqslant s$. Modify the procedure so it can handle the case when $r < N \leqslant s$.

3.19 Modify procedure CREW MERGE to use $N \geqslant s \geqslant r$ processors. Analyze the running time and cost of the modified procedure.

3.20 Show that procedure CREW MERGE can be simulated on an EREW computer in $O((n/N) + \log^2 n)$ time if a way can be found to distinguish between simple read operations (each processor needs to gain access to a different memory location) and multiple-read operations.

3.21 Establish the correctness of procedure TWO-SEQUENCE MEDIAN.

3.22 Modify procedure TWO-SEQUENCE MEDIAN so that given two sequences A and B of length r and s, respectively, and an integer $1 \leqslant k \leqslant r + s$, it returns the kth smallest element of $A.B$. Show that the running time of the new procedure is the same as that of procedure TWO-SEQUENCE MEDIAN.

3.23 Establish the correctness of procedure EREW MERGE.

3.24 Procedure EREW MERGE assumes that N, the number of processors available, is a power of 2. Can you modify the procedure for the case where N is not a power of 2?

3.25 Can the range of cost optimality of procedure EREW MERGE, namely, $N \leqslant n/\log^2 n$, be expanded to, say, $N \leqslant n/\log n$?

3.26 Can procedure EREW MERGE be modified (or a totally new algorithm for the EREW model be developed) to match the $O((n/N) + \log n)$ running time of procedure CREW MERGE?

3.27 Using the results in problems 1.6 and 1.10, show that an algorithm for an N-processor EREW SM SIMD computer requiring $O(N)$ locations of shared memory and time T can be simulated on a cube-connected network with the same number of processors in time $T \times O(\log^2 N)$.

3.28 Analyze the memory requirements of procedure EREW MERGE. Then, assuming that $N = r + s$, use the result in problem 3.27 to determine whether the procedure can be simulated on a cube with N processors in $O(\log^4 N)$ time.

3.29 Assume that $r + s$ processors are available for merging two sequences A and B of length r and s, respectively, into a sequence C. Now consider the following simpler variant of procedure CREW MERGE.

> **for** $i = 1$ **to** $r + s$ **do in parallel**
> P_i finds the ith smallest element of $A.B$ (using the procedure in problem 3.22) and places it in the ith position of C
> **end for**.

Analyze the running time and cost of this procedure.

3.30 Adapt the procedure in problem 3.29 for the case where N processors are available, where $N < r + s$. Compare the running time and cost of the resulting procedure to those of procedure CREW MERGE.

3.31 Develop a parallel merging algorithm for the CRCW model.

3.32 Show how each of the parallel merging algorithms studied in this chapter can lead to a parallel sorting algorithm.

3.33 Modify procedure MULTIPLE BROADCAST to obtain a formal statement of procedure MULTIPLE STORE described in section 1.2.3.1. Provide a different version of your procedure for each of the write conflict resolution policies mentioned in chapter 1.

3.7 BIBLIOGRAPHICAL REMARKS

Merging networks are discussed in [Akl 1], [Batcher], [Hong], [Knuth], [Perl], [Tseng], and [Yao]. The odd–even and bitonic merging networks were first proposed in [Batcher]. These two networks are shown to be asymptotically the best possible merging networks with respect to their running time (in [Hong]) and number of comparators needed (in [Yao]). Various implementations of the odd–even and bitonic merging algorithms on one- and two-dimensional arrays of processors are described in [Kumar], [Nassimi], and [Thompson].

Procedure CREW MERGE is based on ideas presented in [Shiloach]. A second parallel merging procedure for the CREW model when $N \geqslant s \geqslant r$ is described in [Shiloach] whose running time is $O((\log r)/\log(N/s))$. Ideas similar to those in [Shiloach] are presented in [Barlow]. These results are improved in [Borodin] and [Kruskal]. It is shown in [Borodin] how $r + s$ processors can merge two sequences of length r and s, respectively, where $r \leqslant s$ in $O(\log \log r)$ time. An adaptive algorithm is described in [Kruskal] that uses $N \leqslant r + s$ processors and runs in time $O((r + s)/N + \log[(r + s)/N] + \log \log N)$. When $r = s = n$ and $N = n/\log \log n$, this last algorithm runs in $O(\log \log n)$ time and is therefore cost optimal.

The concept of multiple broadcasting is attributed to [Eckstein]. Let A be an algorithm designed to run in time t and space s on an N-processor CREW SM SIMD computer. As shown in section 3.4, procedure MULTIPLE BROADCAST allows A to be simulated on an N-processor EREW SM SIMD computer in time $O(t \times \log N)$ and space $O(s \times p)$. In [Vishkin] and [Wah] variants of this procedure are given that perform the simulation using only $O(s + p)$ space. Procedures TWO-SEQUENCE MEDIAN and EREW MERGE first appeared in [Akl 2]. Algorithms for merging on a tree and a pyramid are given in [Akl 1] and [Stout], respectively.

Three parallel merging algorithms are described in [Valiant] to run on the *comparison model* of computation where only comparisons among input elements are counted in analyzing the running time of an algorithm. The first merges two lists of length r and s, respectively, where $r \leqslant s$, using $(rs)^{1/2}$ processors in $O(\log \log r)$ time. The second uses $c(rs)^{1/2}$ processors, where $c \geqslant 2$, and runs in $O(\log \log r - \log \log c)$ time. The third uses N processors, where $N \leqslant r$, and runs in $O((r + s)/N + \log[(rs \log N)/N])$. A fourth algorithm for the comparison model is described in [Gavril] that uses $N \leqslant r$ processors and runs in $O(\log r + r/N + (r/N)\log s/r)$ time. An $\Omega(\log \log n)$ lower bound on the time required to merge two sequences of length n each on the comparison model is derived in [Borodin]. Essentially the same lower bound is obtained in [Häggkvist]. It is interesting to note that this lower bound is matched by the CREW algorithm in [Kruskal] mentioned earlier where all operations (not just comparisons) are counted.

3.8 REFERENCES

[AKL 1]
  Akl, S. G., *Parallel Sorting Algorithms*, Academic, Orlando, Fl., 1985.
[AKL 2]
  Akl, S. G., and Santoro, N., Optimal parallel merging and sorting without memory conflicts, *IEEE Transactions on Computers*, Vol. C-36, No. 11, November 1987, pp. 1367–1369.

[BARLOW]

Barlow, R. H., Evans, D. J., and Shanehchi, J., A parallel merging algorithm, *Information Processing Letters*, Vol. 13, No. 3, December 1981, pp. 103–106.

[BATCHER]

Batcher, K. E., Sorting networks and their applications, Proceedings of the AFIPS 1968 Spring Joint Computer Conference, Atlantic City, New Jersey, April 30–May 2, 1968, pp. 307–314, AFIPS Press, Montvale, N.J., 1968.

[BORODIN]

Borodin, A., and Hopcroft, J. E., Routing, merging and sorting on parallel models of computation, *Journal of Computer and System Sciences*, Vol. 30, 1985, pp. 130–145.

[ECKSTEIN]

Eckstein, D. M., Simultaneous memory accesses, Technical Report #79-6, Department of Computer Science, Iowa State University, Ames, Iowa, August 1979.

[GAVRIL]

Gavril, F., Merging with parallel processors, *Communications of the ACM*, Vol. 18, No. 10, October 1975, pp. 588–591.

[HÄGGKVIST]

Häggkvist, R., and Hell, P., Sorting and merging in rounds, *SIAM Journal on Algebraic and Discrete Methods*, Vol. 3, No. 4, December 1982, pp. 465–473.

[HONG]

Hong, Z., and Sedgewick, R., Notes on merging networks, Proceedings of the 14th Annual ACM Symposium on Theory of Computing, San Francisco, California, May 1982, pp. 296–302, Association for Computing Machinery, New York, N.Y., 1982.

[KNUTH]

Knuth, D. E., *The Art of Computer Programming*, Vol. 3, *Sorting and Searching*, Addison-Wesley, Reading, Mass., 1973.

[KRUSKAL]

Kruskal, C. P., Searching, merging, and sorting in parallel computation, *IEEE Transactions on Computers*, Vol. C-32, No. 10, October 1983, pp. 942–946.

[KUMAR]

Kumar, M., and Hirschberg, D. S., An efficient implementation of Batcher's odd-even merge algorithm and its application in parallel sorting schemes, *IEEE Transactions on Computers*, Vol. C-32, No. 3, March 1983, pp. 254–264.

[NASSIMI]

Nassimi, D., and Sahni, S., Bitonic sort on a mesh-connected parallel computer, *IEEE Transactions on Computers*, Vol. C-28, No. 1, January 1979, pp. 2–7.

[PERL]

Perl, Y., The bitonic and odd-even networks are more than merging, Technical Report DCS-TR-123, Department of Computer Science, Rutgers University, New Brunswick, N.J., February 1983.

[SHILOACH]

Shiloach, Y., and Vishkin, U., Finding the maximum, merging, and sorting in a parallel computation model, *Journal of Algorithms*, Vol. 2, 1981, pp. 88–102.

[STOUT]

Stout, Q. F., Sorting, merging, selecting and filtering on tree and pyramid machines, Proceedings of the 1983 International Conference on Parallel Processing, Bellaire, Michigan, August 1983, pp. 214–221, IEEE Computer Society, Washington, D.C., 1983.

[THOMPSON]

Thompson, C. D., and Kung, H. T., Sorting on a mesh-connected parallel computer, *Communications of the ACM*, Vol. 20, No. 4, April 1977, pp. 263–271.

[TSENG]

Tseng, S. S., and Lee, R. C. T., A new parallel sorting algorithm based upon min-mid-max operations, *BIT*, Vol. 24, 1984, pp. 187–195.

[VALIANT]

Valiant, L. G., Parallelism in comparison problems, *SIAM Journal of Computing*, Vol. 4, No. 3, September 1975, pp. 348–355.

[VISHKIN]

Vishkin, U., Implementation of simultaneous memory address access in models that forbid it, *Journal of Algorithms*, Vol. 4, 1983, pp. 45–50.

[WAH]

Wah, W., and Akl, S. G., Simulating multiple memory accesses in logarithmic time and linear space, Technical Report No. 87-196, Department of Computing and Information Science, Queen's University, Kingston, Ontario, July 1987.

[YAO]

Yao, A. C.-C., and Yao, F. F., Lower bounds on merging networks, *Journal of the ACM*, Vol. 23, No. 3, July 1976, pp. 566–571.

4

Sorting

4.1 INTRODUCTION

In the previous two chapters we described parallel algorithms for two comparison problems: selection and merging. We now turn our attention to a third such problem: *sorting*. Among all computational tasks studied by computer scientists over the past forty years, sorting appears to have received the most attention. Entire books have been devoted to the subject. And although the problem and its many solutions seem to be quite well understood, hardly a month goes by without a new article appearing in a technical journal that describes yet another facet of sorting. There are two reasons for this interest. The problem is important to practitioners, as sorting data is at the heart of many computations. It also has a rich theory: The design and analysis of algorithms is an important area of computer science today thanks mainly to the early work on sorting.

The problem is defined as follows. We are given a sequence $S = \{s_1, s_2, \ldots, s_n\}$ of n items on which a linear order $<$ is defined. The elements of S are initially in random order. The purpose of sorting is to arrange the elements of S into a new sequence $S' = \{s'_1, s'_2, \ldots, s'_n\}$ such that $s'_i < s'_{i+1}$ for $i = 1, 2, \ldots, n - 1$. We saw in chapter 1 (example 1.10) that any algorithm for sorting must require $\Omega(n \log n)$ operations in the worst case. As we did in the previous two chapters, we shall assume henceforth, without loss of generality, that the elements of S are numbers (of arbitrary size) to be arranged in nondecreasing order.

Numerous algorithms exist for sorting on a sequential computational model. One such algorithm is given in what follows as the recursive procedure QUICKSORT. The notation $a \leftrightarrow b$ means that the variables a and b exchange their values.

procedure QUICKSORT (S)

if $|S| = 2$ **and** $s_2 < s_1$
then $s_1 \leftrightarrow s_2$
else if $|S| > 2$ **then**
     (1) {Determine m, the median element of S}
         SEQUENTIAL SELECT (S, $\lceil |S|/2 \rceil$)

(2) {Split S into two subsequences S_1 and S_2}
    (2.1) $S_1 \leftarrow \{s_i : s_i \leqslant m\}$ and $|S_1| = \lceil |S|/2 \rceil$
    (2.2) $S_2 \leftarrow \{s_i : s_i \geqslant m\}$ and $|S_2| = \lfloor |S|/2 \rfloor$
(3) QUICKSORT(S_1)
(4) QUICKSORT(S_2)
   end if
  end if. □

At each level of the recursion, procedure QUICKSORT finds the median of a sequence S and then splits S into two subsequences S_1 and S_2 of elements smaller than or equal to and larger than or equal to the median, respectively. The algorithm is now applied recursively to each of S_1 and S_2. This continues until S consists of either one or two elements, in which case recursion is no longer needed. We also insist that $|S_1| = \lceil |S|/2 \rceil$ and $|S_2| = \lfloor |S|/2 \rfloor$ to ensure that the recursive calls to procedure QUICKSORT are on sequences smaller than S so that the procedure is guaranteed to terminate when all elements of S are equal. This is done by placing all elements of S smaller than m in S_1; if $|S_1| < \lceil |S|/2 \rceil$, then elements equal to m are added to S_1 until $|S_1| = \lceil |S|/2 \rceil$. From chapter 2 we know that procedure SEQUENTIAL SELECT runs in time linear in the size of the input. Similarly, creating S_1 and S_2 requires one pass through S, which is also linear.

For some constant c, we can express the running time of procedure QUICKSORT as

$$t(n) = cn + 2t(n/2)$$

$$= O(n \log n),$$

which is optimal.

Example 4.1

Let $S = \{6, 5, 9, 2, 4, 3, 5, 1, 7, 5, 8\}$. The first call to procedure QUICKSORT produces 5 as the median element of S, and hence $S_1 = \{2, 4, 3, 1, 5, 5\}$ and $S_2 = \{6, 9, 7, 8, 5\}$. Note that $S_1 = \lceil \frac{11}{2} \rceil = 6$ and $S_2 = \lfloor \frac{11}{2} \rfloor = 5$. A recursive call to QUICKSORT with S_1 as input produces the two subsequences $\{2, 1, 3\}$ and $\{4, 5, 5\}$. The second call with S_2 as input produces $\{6, 5, 7\}$ and $\{9, 8\}$. Further recursive calls complete the sorting of these sequences. □

Because of the importance of sorting, it was natural for researchers to also develop several algorithms for sorting on parallel computers. In this chapter we study a number of such algorithms for various computational models. Note that, in view of the $\Omega(n \log n)$ operations required in the worst case to sort sequentially, no parallel sorting algorithm can have a cost inferior to $O(n \log n)$. When its cost is $O(n \log n)$, a parallel sorting algorithm is of course cost optimal. Similarly, a lower bound on the time required to sort using N processors operating in parallel is $\Omega((n \log n)/N)$ for $N \leqslant n \log n$.

We begin in section 4.2 by describing a special-purpose parallel architecture for sorting. The architecture is a *sorting network* based on the odd–even merging algorithm studied in chapter 3. In section 4.3 a parallel sorting algorithm is presented for an SIMD computer where the processors are connected to form a linear array. Sections 4.4–4.6 are devoted to the shared-memory SIMD model.

4.2 A NETWORK FOR SORTING

Recall how an (r, s)-merging network was constructed in section 3.2 for merging two sorted sequences. It is rather straightforward to use a collection of merging networks to build a sorting network for the sequence $S = \{s_1, s_2, \ldots, s_n\}$, where n is a power of 2. The idea is the following. In a first stage, a rank of $n/2$ comparators is used to create $n/2$ sorted sequences each of length 2. In a second stage, pairs of these are now merged into sorted sequences of length 4 using a rank of $(2, 2)$-merging networks. Again, in a third stage, pairs of sequences of length 4 are merged using $(4, 4)$-merging networks into sequences of length 8. The process continues until two sequences of length $n/2$ each are merged by an $(n/2, n/2)$-merging network to produce a single sorted sequence of length n. The resulting architecture is known as an *odd–even sorting network* and is illustrated in Fig. 4.1 for $S = \{8, 4, 7, 2, 1, 5, 6, 3\}$. Note that, as in the case of merging, the odd–even sorting network is oblivious of its input.

Analysis.   As we did for the merging network, we shall analyze the running time, number of comparators, and cost of the odd–even sorting network. Since the size of the merged sequences doubles after every stage, there are $\log n$ stages in all.

(i) Running Time.   Denote by $s(2^i)$ the time required in the ith stage to merge two sorted sequences of 2^{i-1} elements each. From section 3.2 we have the recurrence

$$s(2) = 1 \qquad \text{for } i = 1,$$
$$s(2^i) = s(2^{i-1}) + 1 \quad \text{for } i > 1,$$

whose solution is $s(2^i) = i$. Therefore, the time required by an odd–even sorting network to sort a sequence of length n is

$$t(n) = \sum_{i=1}^{\log n} s(2^i) = O(\log^2 n).$$

Note that this is significantly faster than the (optimal) sequential running time of $O(n \log n)$ achieved by procedure QUICKSORT.

(ii) Number of Processors.   Denote by $q(2^i)$ the number of comparators required in the ith stage to merge two sorted sequences of 2^{i-1} elements each. From section 3.2 we have the recurrence

$$q(2) = 1 \qquad \text{for } i = 1,$$
$$q(2^i) = 2q(2^{i-1}) + 2^{i-1} - 1 \quad \text{for } i > 1,$$

whose solution is $q(2^i) = (i - 1)2^{i-1} + 1$. Therefore, the number of comparators

88

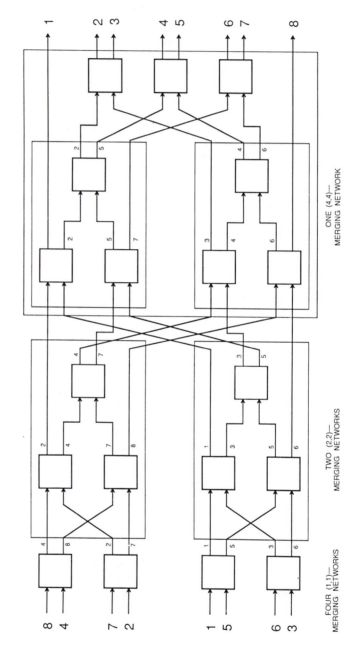

Figure 4.1 Odd–even sorting networks for sequence of eight elements.

needed by an odd–even sorting network to sort a sequence of length n is

$$p(n) = \sum_{i=1}^{\log n} 2^{(\log n) - i} q(2^i)$$

$$= O(n \log^2 n).$$

(iii) Cost.   Since $t(n) = O(\log^2 n)$ and $p(n) = O(n \log^2 n)$, the total number of comparisons performed by an odd–even sorting network, that is, the network's cost, is

$$c(n) = p(n) \times t(n)$$

$$= O(n \log^4 n).$$

Our sorting network is therefore not cost optimal as it performs more operations than the $O(n \log n)$ sufficient to sort sequentially.

Since the odd—even sorting network is based on the odd–even merging one, the remarks made in section 3.2 apply here as well. In particular:

- **(i)** The network is extremely fast. It can sort a sequence of length 2^{20} within, on the order of, $(20)^2$ time units. This is to be contrasted with the time required by procedure QUICKSORT, which would be in excess of 20 million time units.
- **(ii)** The number of comparators is too high. Again for $n = 2^{20}$, the network would need on the order of 400 million comparators.
- **(iii)** The architecture is highly irregular and the wires linking the comparators have lengths that vary with n.

We therefore reach the same conclusion as for the merging network of section 3.2: The odd–even sorting network is impractical for large input sequences.

4.3 SORTING ON A LINEAR ARRAY

In this section we describe a parallel sorting algorithm for an SIMD computer where the processors are connected to form a linear array as depicted in Fig. 1.6. The algorithm uses n processors $P_1, P_2, \ldots, P_n$ to sort the sequences $S = \{s_1, s_2, \ldots, s_n\}$. At any time during the execution of the algorithm, processor P_i holds one element of the input sequence; we denote this element by x_i for all $1 \leqslant i \leqslant n$. Initially $x_i = s_i$. It is required that, upon termination, x_i be the ith element of the sorted sequence. The algorithm consists of two steps that are performed repeatedly. In the first step, all odd-numbered processors P_i obtain x_{i+1} from P_{i+1}. If $x_i > x_{i+1}$, then P_i and P_{i+1} exchange the elements they held at the beginning of this step. In the second step, all even-numbered processors perform the same operations as did the odd-numbered ones in the first step. After $\lceil n/2 \rceil$ repetitions of these two steps in this order, no further exchanges of elements can take place. Hence the algorithm terminates with $x_i < x_{i+1}$

for all $1 \leqslant i \leqslant n - 1$. The algorithm is given in what follows as procedure ODD-EVEN TRANSPOSITION.

procedure ODD-EVEN TRANSPOSITION (S)
    for $j = 1$ **to** $\lceil n/2 \rceil$ **do**
       (1) **for** $i = 1, 3, \ldots, 2\lfloor n/2 \rfloor - 1$ **do in parallel**
           if $x_i > x_{i+1}$
           then $x_i \leftrightarrow x_{i+1}$
           end if
        end for
       (2) **for** $i = 2, 4, \ldots, 2\lfloor (n-1)/2 \rfloor$ **do in parallel**
           if $x_i > x_{i+1}$
           then $x_i \leftrightarrow x_{i+1}$
           end if
        end for
    end for. □

Example 4.2

Let $S = \{6, 5, 9, 2, 4, 3, 5, 1, 7, 5, 8\}$. The contents of the linear array for this input during the execution of procedure ODD-EVEN TRANSPOSITION are illustrated in Fig. 4.2. Note that although a sorted sequence is produced after four iterations of steps 1 and 2, two more (redundant) iterations are performed, that is, a total of $\lceil \frac{11}{2} \rceil$ as required by the procedure's statement. □

Analysis. Each of steps 1 and 2 consists of one comparison and two routing operations and hence requires constant time. These two steps are executed $\lceil n/2 \rceil$ times. The running time of procedure ODD-EVEN TRANSPOSITION is therefore $t(n) = O(n)$. Since $p(n) = n$, the procedure's cost is given by $c(n) = p(n) \times t(n) = O(n^2)$, which is not optimal.

From this analysis, procedure ODD-EVEN TRANSPOSITION does not appear to be too attractive. Indeed,

(i) with respect to procedure QUICKSORT, it achieves a speedup of $O(\log n)$ only,

(ii) it uses a number of processors equal to the size of the input, which is unreasonable, and

(iii) it is not cost optimal.

The only redeeming feature of procedure ODD-EVEN TRANSPOSITION seems to be its extreme simplicity. We are therefore tempted to salvage its basic idea in order to obtain a new algorithm with optimal cost. There are two obvious ways for doing this: either (1) reduce the running time or (2) reduce the number of processors used. The first approach is hopeless: The running time of procedure ODD-EVEN TRANSPOSITION is the smallest possible achievable on a linear array with n processors. To see this, assume that the largest element in S is initially in P_1 and must therefore move $n - 1$ steps across the linear array before settling in its final position in P_n. This requires $O(n)$ time.

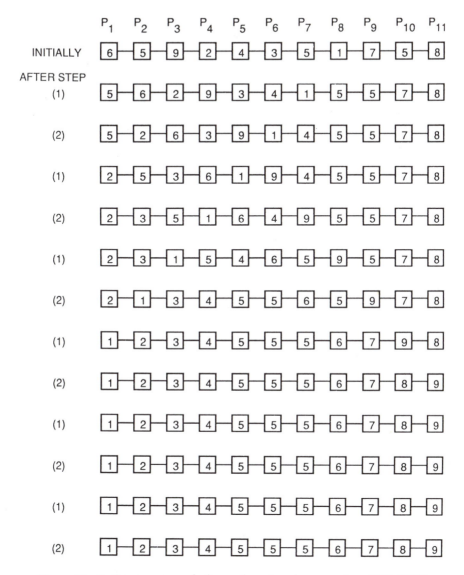

Figure 4.2 Sorting sequence of eleven elements using procedure ODD-EVEN TRANSPOSITION.

Now consider the second approach. If N processors, where $N < n$, are available, then they can simulate the algorithm in $n \times t(n)/N$ time. The cost remains $n \times t(n)$, which as we know is not optimal. A more subtle simulation, however, allows us to achieve cost optimality. Assume that each of the N processors in the linear array holds a subsequence of S of length n/N. (It may be necessary to add some dummy elements to S if n is not a multiple of N.) In the new algorithm, the comparison-exchange operations of procedure ODD-EVEN TRANSPOSITION are now replaced with merge-split operations on subsequences. Let S_i denote the subsequence held by processor P_i. Initially, the S_i are random subsequences of S. In step 1, each P_i sorts S_i using procedure QUICKSORT. In step 2.1 each odd-numbered processor P_i merges the two subsequences S_i and S_{i+1} into a sorted sequence $S_i' = \{s_1', s_2', \ldots, s_{2n/N}'\}$. It retains the first half of S_i' and assigns to its neighbor P_{i+1} the second half. Step 2.2 is identical to 2.1 except that it is performed by all even-numbered processors. Steps 2.1 and 2.2 are repeated alternately. After $\lceil N/2 \rceil$ iterations no further exchange of elements can take place between two processors. The algorithm is given in what follows as procedure MERGE SPLIT. When it terminates, the sequence $S = S_1$, $S_2, \ldots, S_N$ is sorted.

procedure MERGE SPLIT (S)

Step 1: **for** $i = 1$ **to** N **do in parallel**
        QUICKSORT (S_i)
        end for.

Step 2: **for** $j = 1$ **to** $\lceil N/2 \rceil$ **do**
       (2.1) **for** $i = 1, 3, \ldots, 2\lfloor N/2 \rfloor - 1$ **do in parallel**
            (i) SEQUENTIAL MERGE (S_i, S_{i+1}, S_i')
            (ii) $S_i \leftarrow \{s_1', s_2', \ldots, s_{n/N}'\}$
            (iii) $S_{i+1} \leftarrow \{s_{(n/N)+1}', s_{(n/N)+2}', \ldots, s_{2n/N}'\}$
         end for
       (2.2) **for** $i = 2, 4, \ldots, 2\lfloor (N-1)/2 \rfloor$ **do in parallel**
            (i) SEQUENTIAL MERGE (S_i, S_{i+1}, S_i')
            (ii) $S_i \leftarrow \{s_1', s_2', \ldots, s_{n/N}'\}$
            (iii) $S_{i+1} \leftarrow \{s_{(n/N)+1}', s_{(n/N)+2}', \ldots, s_{2n/N}'\}$
         end for
     end for. ☐

Example 4.3

Let $S = \{8, 2, 5, 10, 1, 7, 3, 12, 6, 11, 4, 9\}$ and $N = 4$. The contents of the various processors during the execution of procedure MERGE SPLIT for this input is illustrated in Fig. 4.3. ☐

Analysis. Step 1 requires $O((n/N)\log(n/N))$ steps. Transferring S_{i+1} to P_i, merging by SEQUENTIAL MERGE, and returning S_{i+1} to P_{i+1} all require $O(n/N)$ time. The total running time of procedure MERGE SPLIT is therefore

$$t(n) = O((n/N)\log(n/N)) + \lceil N/2 \rceil \times O(n/N)$$

$$= O((n \log n)/N) + O(n),$$

and its cost is

$$c(n) = O(n \log n) + O(nN),$$

which is optimal when $N \leqslant \log n$.

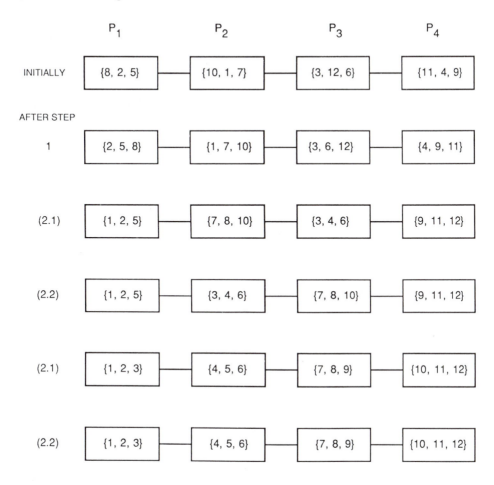

Figure 4.3 Sorting sequence of twelve elements using procedure MERGE SPLIT.

4.4 SORTING ON THE CRCW MODEL

It is time to turn our attention to the shared-memory SIMD model. In the present and the next two sections we describe parallel algorithms for sorting on the various incarnations of this model. We begin with the most powerful submodel, the CRCW SM SIMD computer. We then proceed to the weaker CREW model (section 4.5), and finally we study algorithms for the weakest shared-memory computer, namely, the EREW model (section 4.6).

Whenever an algorithm is to be designed for the CRCW model of computation, one must specify how write conflicts, that is, multiple attempts to write into the same memory location, can be resolved. For the purposes of the sorting algorithm to be described, we shall assume that write conflicts are created whenever several processors attempt to write potentially different integers into the same address. The conflict is resolved by storing the *sum* of these integers in that address.

Assume that n^2 processors are available on such a CRCW computer to sort the sequence $S = \{s_1, s_2, \ldots, s_n\}$. The sorting algorithm to be used is based on the idea of *sorting by enumeration*: The position of each element s_i of S in the sorted sequence is determined by computing c_i, the number of elements smaller than it. If two elements s_i and s_j are equal, then s_i is taken to be the larger of the two if $i > j$; otherwise s_j is the larger. Once all the c_i have been computed, s_i is placed in position $1 + c_i$ of the sorted sequence. To help visualize the algorithm, we assume that the processors are arranged into n rows of n elements each and are numbered as shown in Fig. 4.4. The shared memory contains two arrays: The input sequence is stored in array S, while the counts c_i are stored in array C. The sorted sequence is returned in array S. The ith row of processors is "in charge" of element s_i: Processors $P(i, 1), P(i, 2), \ldots, P(i, n)$ compute c_i and store s_i in position $1 + c_i$ of S. The algorithm is given as procedure CRCW SORT:

procedure CRCW SORT (S)

Step 1:   **for** $i = 1$ **to** n **do in parallel**
       for $j = 1$ **to** n **do in parallel**
          if $(s_i > s_j)$ **or** $(s_i = s_j$ **and** $i > j)$
          then $P(i, j)$ writes 1 in c_i
          else $P(i, j)$ writes 0 in c_i
          end if
       end for
      end for.

Step 2:   **for** $i = 1$ **to** n **do in parallel**
       $P(i, 1)$ stores s_i in position $1 + c_i$ of S
      end for. $\square$

Example 4.4

Let $S = \{5, 2, 4, 5\}$. The two elements of S that each of the 16 processors compares and the contents of arrays S and C after each step of procedure CRCW SORT are shown in Fig. 4.5. $\square$

Analysis.   Each of steps 1 and 2 consists of an operation requiring constant time. Therefore $t(n) = O(1)$. Since $p(n) = n^2$, the cost of procedure CRCW SORT is

$$c(n) = O(n^2),$$

which is not optimal.

We have managed to sort in constant time on an extremely powerful model that

1. allows concurrent-read operations; that is, each input element s_i is read simultaneously by all processors in row i and all processors in column i;
2. allows concurrent-write operations; that is,
   (i) all processors in a given row are allowed to write simultaneously into the same memory location and

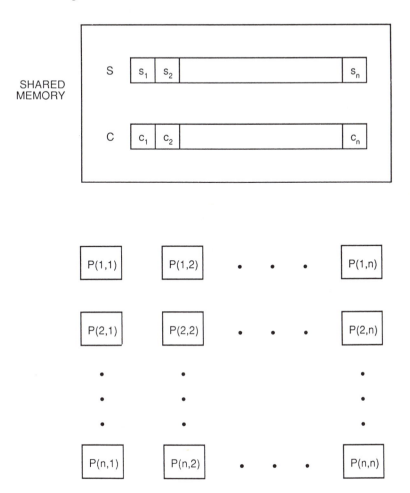

Figure 4.4 Processor and memory organization for sorting on CRCW SM SIMD model.

(ii) the write conflict resolution process is itself very powerful—all numbers to
be stored in a memory location are added and stored in constant time;
and

3. uses a very large number of processors; that is, the number of processors grows
quadratically with the size of the input.

For these reasons, particularly the last one, the algorithm is most likely to be of no
great practical value. Nevertheless, procedure CRCW SORT is interesting in its own
right: It demonstrates how sorting can be accomplished in constant time on a model
that is not only acceptable theoretically, but has also been proposed for a number of
contemplated and existing parallel computers.

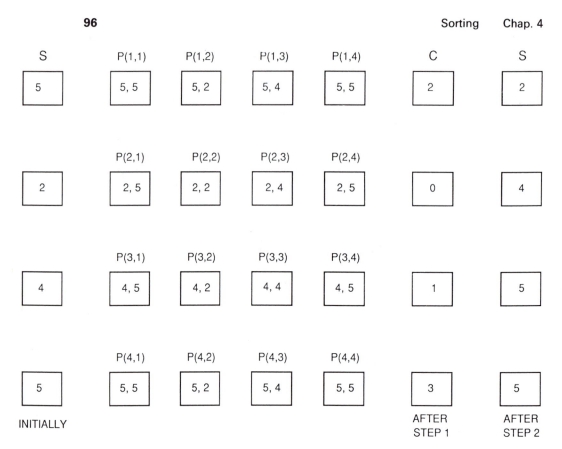

Figure 4.5 Sorting sequence of four elements using procedure CRCW SORT.

4.5 SORTING ON THE CREW MODEL

In this section we attempt to deal with two of the objections raised with regards to procedure CRCW SORT: its excessive use of processors and its tolerance of write conflicts. Our purpose is to design an algorithm that is free of write conflicts and uses a reasonable number of processors. In addition, we shall require the algorithm to also satisfy our usual desired properties for shared-memory SIMD algorithms. Thus the algorithm should have

  (i) a sublinear and adaptive number of processors,
  (ii) a running time that is small and adaptive, and
 (iii) a cost that is optimal.

In sequential computation, a very efficient approach to sorting is based on the idea of merging successively longer sequences of sorted elements. This approach is even more attractive in parallel computation, and we have already invoked it twice in this chapter in sections 4.2 and 4.3. Once again we shall use a merging algorithm in order to sort. Procedure CREW MERGE developed in chapter 3 will serve as a basis for the CREW sorting algorithm of this section. The idea is quite simple. Assume that a CREW SM SIMD computer with N processors $P_1, P_2, \ldots, P_N$ is to be used to sort the sequence $S = \{s_1, s_2, \ldots, s_n\}$, where $N \leqslant n$. We begin by distributing the elements of S evenly among the N processors. Each processor sorts its allocated subsequence sequentially using procedure QUICKSORT. The N sorted subsequences are now merged pairwise, simultaneously, using procedure CREW MERGE for each pair. The resulting subsequences are again merged pairwise and the process continues until one sorted sequence of length n is obtained.

The algorithm is given in what follows as procedure CREW SORT. In it we denote the initial subsequence of S allocated to processor P_i by S_i. Subsequently, S_j^k is used to denote a subsequence obtained by merging two subsequences and P_j^k the set of processors that performed the merge.

procedure CREW SORT (S)

Step 1: **for** $i = 1$ **to** N **do in parallel**
        Processor P_i
        (1.1) reads a distinct subsequence S_i of S of size n/N
        (1.2) QUICKSORT (S_i)
        (1.3) $S_i^1 \leftarrow S_i$
        (1.4) $P_i^1 \leftarrow \{P_i\}$
    end for.

Step 2: (2.1) $u \leftarrow 1$
    (2.2) $v \leftarrow N$
    (2.3) **while** $v > 1$ **do**
        (2.3.1) **for** $m = 1$ **to** $\lfloor v/2 \rfloor$ **do in parallel**
            (i) $P_m^{u+1} \leftarrow P_{2m-1}^u \cup P_{2m}^u$
            (ii) The processors in the set P_m^{u+1} perform
                CREW MERGE ($S_{2m-1}^u, S_{2m}^u, S_m^{u+1}$)
        end for
        (2.3.2) **if** v is odd **then** (i) $P_{\lceil v/2 \rceil}^{u+1} \leftarrow P_v^u$
                           (ii) $S_{\lceil v/2 \rceil}^{u+1} \leftarrow S_v^u$
        end if
        (2.3.3) $u \leftarrow u + 1$
        (2.3.4) $v \leftarrow \lceil v/2 \rceil$
    end while. □

Analysis. The dominating operation in step 1 is the call to QUICKSORT, which requires $O((n/N)\log(n/N))$ time. During each iteration of step 2.3, $\lfloor v/2 \rfloor$ pairs of subsequences with $n/\lfloor v/2 \rfloor$ elements per pair are to be merged simultaneously using $N/\lfloor v/2 \rfloor$ processors per pair. Procedure CREW MERGE thus requires $O([(n/\lfloor v/2 \rfloor)/(N/\lfloor v/2 \rfloor)] + \log(n/\lfloor v/2 \rfloor))$, that is, $O((n/N) + \log n)$ time. Since step 2.3 is iterated $\lfloor \log N \rfloor$ times, the total running time of procedure CREW SORT is

$$t(n) = O((n/N)\log(n/N)) + O((n/N)\log N + \log n \log N)$$
$$= O((n/N)\log n + \log^2 n).$$

Since $p(n) = N$, the procedure's cost is given by

$$c(n) = O(n \log n + N \log^2 n),$$

which is optimal for $N \leqslant n/\log n$.

Example 4.5

Let $S = \{2, 8, 5, 10, 15, 1, 12, 6, 14, 3, 11, 7, 9, 4, 13, 16\}$ and $N = 4$. During step 1, processors P_1, P_2, P_3, and P_4 receive the subsequences $S_1 = \{2, 8, 5, 10\}$, $S_2 = \{15, 1, 12, 6\}$, $S_3 = \{14, 3, 11, 7\}$, and $S_4 = \{9, 4, 13, 16\}$, respectively, which they sort locally. At the end of step 1, $S_1^1 = \{2, 5, 8, 10\}$, $S_2^1 = \{1, 6, 12, 15\}$, $S_3^1 = \{3, 7, 11, 14\}$, $S_4^1 = \{4, 9, 13, 16\}$, $P_1^1 = \{P_1\}$, $P_2^1 = \{P_2\}$, $P_3^1 = \{P_3\}$, and $P_4^1 = \{P_4\}$.

During the first iteration of step 2.3, the processors in $P_1^2 = P_1^1 \cup P_2^1 = \{P_1, P_2\}$ cooperate to merge the elements of S_1^1 and S_2^1 to produce $S_1^2 = \{1, 2, 5, 6, 8, 10, 12, 15\}$. Simultaneously, the processors in $P_2^2 = P_3^1 \cup P_4^1 = \{P_3, P_4\}$ merge S_3^1 and S_4^1 into $S_2^2 = \{3, 4, 7, 9, 11, 13, 14, 16\}$.

During the second iteration of step 2.3, the processors in $P_1^3 = P_1^2 \cup P_2^2 = \{P_1, P_2, P_3, P_4\}$ cooperate to merge S_1^2 and S_2^2 into $S_1^3 = \{1, 2, \ldots, 16\}$ and the procedure terminates. $\square$

4.6 SORTING ON THE EREW MODEL

Two of the criticisms expressed with regards to procedure CRCW SORT were addressed by procedure CREW SORT, which adapts to the number of existing processors and disallows multiple-write operations into the same memory location. Still, procedure CREW SORT tolerates multiple-read operations. Our purpose in this section is to deal with this third difficulty. Three parallel algorithms for sorting on the EREW model are described, each representing an improvement over its predecessor. We assume throughout this section that N processors $P_1, P_2, \ldots, P_N$ are available on an EREW SM SIMD computer to sort the sequence $S = \{s_1, s_2, \ldots, s_n\}$, where $N < n$.

4.6.1 Simulating Procedure CREW SORT

The simplest way to remove read conflicts from procedure CREW SORT is to use procedure MULTIPLE BROADCAST. Each attempt to read from memory now takes $O(\log N)$ time. Simulating procedure CREW SORT on the EREW model therefore requires

$$t(n) = O((n/N)\log n + \log n \log N) \times O(\log N)$$

$$= O([(n/N) + \log N]\log n \log N)$$

time and has a cost of

$$c(n) = O((n + N \log N)\log n \log N),$$

which is not cost optimal.

4.6.2 Sorting by Conflict-Free Merging

A more subtle way to avoid concurrent-read operations from the same memory location in procedure CREW SORT is to remove the need for them. This can be accomplished by replacing the call to produce CREW MERGE in step 2.3.1 with a call to procedure EREW MERGE. This step therefore requires $O((n/N) + \log n \log N)$. Since there are $O(\log N)$ iterations of this step, the overall running time of the modified procedure, including step 1, is

$$t(n) = O((n/N)\log(n/N)) + O((n/N)\log N + \log n \log^2 N)$$

$$= O([(n/N) + \log^2 n]\log n),$$

yielding a cost of

$$c(n) = O((n + N \log^2 n)\log n).$$

Therefore the modified procedure is cost optimal when $N \leq n/\log^2 n$. This range of optimality is therefore narrower than the one enjoyed by procedure CREW SORT.

4.6.3 Sorting by Selection

Our analysis so far indicates that perhaps another approach should be used if the performance of procedure CREW SORT is to be matched on the EREW model. We now study one such approach. The idea is to adapt the sequential procedure QUICKSORT to run on a parallel computer. We begin by noting that, since $N < n$, we can write $N = n^{1-x}$, where $0 < x < 1$.

Now, let m_i be defined as the $\lceil i(n/2^{1/x}) \rceil$th smallest element of S, for $1 \leq i \leq 2^{1/x} - 1$. The m_i's can be used to divide S into $2^{1/x}$ subsequences of size $n/2^{1/x}$ each. These subsequences, denoted by $S_1, S_2, \ldots, S_j, S_{j+1}, S_{j+2}, \ldots, S_{2j}$, where $j = 2^{(1/x)-1}$, satisfy the following property: Every element of S_i is smaller than or equal to every element of S_{i+1} for $1 \leq i \leq 2j - 1$. This is illustrated in Fig. 4.6. The subdivision process can now be applied recursively to each of the subsequences S_i until the entire sequence S is sorted in nondecreasing order.

This algorithm can be performed in parallel by first invoking procedure PARALLEL SELECT to determine the elements m_i and then creating the sub-sequences S_i. The algorithm is applied in parallel to the subsequences $S_1, S_2, \ldots, S_j$ using N/j processors per subsequence. The same is then done with the subsequences $S_{j+1}, S_{j+2}, \ldots, S_{2j}$. Note that the number of processors used to sort each subsequence of size $n/2^{1/x}$, namely, $n^{1-x}/2^{(1/x)-1}$, is exactly the number required for a proper recursive application of the algorithm, that is, $(n/2^{1/x})^{1-x}$.

It is important, of course, that $2^{1/x}$ be an integer of finite size: This ensures that a bound can be placed on the running time and that all the m_i exist. Initially, the N available processors compute x from $N = n^{1-x}$. If x does not satisfy the conditions (i) $\lceil 1/x \rceil \leq 10$ (say) and (ii) $n \geq 2^{\lceil 1/x \rceil}$, then the smallest real number larger than x and

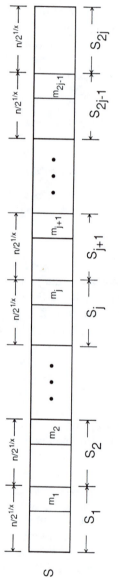

Figure 4.6 Dividing sequence for sorting by selection.

satisfying (i) and (ii) is taken as x. Let $k = 2^{\lceil 1/x \rceil}$. The algorithm is given as procedure EREW SORT:

procedure EREW SORT (S)

    if $|S| \leqslant k$
    then QUICKSORT (S)
    else (1) **for** $i = 1$ **to** $k - 1$ **do**
                PARALLEL SELECT $(S, \lceil i|S|/k \rceil)$ {Obtain m_i}
          end for
        (2) $S_1 \leftarrow \{s \in S : s \leqslant m_1\}$
        (3) **for** $i = 2$ **to** $k - 1$ **do**
                $S_i \leftarrow \{s \in S : m_{i-1} \leqslant s \leqslant m_i\}$
          end for
        (4) $S_k \leftarrow \{s \in S : s \geqslant m_{k-1}\}$
        (5) **for** $i = 1$ **to** $k/2$ **do in parallel**
                EREW SORT (S_i)
          end for
        (6) **for** $i = (k/2) + 1$ **to** k **do in parallel**
                EREW SORT (S_i)
          end for
    end if.   □

Note that in steps 2–4 the sequence S_i is created using the method outlined in chapter 2 in connection with procedure PARALLEL SELECT. Also in step 3, the elements of S smaller than m_i and larger than or equal to m_{i-1} are first placed in S_i. If $|S_i| < \lceil |S|/k \rceil$, then elements equal to m_i are added to S_i so that either $|S_i| = \lceil |S|/k \rceil$ or no element is left to add to S_i. This is reminiscent of what we did with QUICKSORT. Steps 2 and 4 are executed in a similar manner.

Example 4.6

Let $S = \{5, 9, 12, 16, 18, 2, 10, 13, 17, 4, 7, 18, 18, 11, 3, 17, 20, 19, 14, 8, 5, 17, 1, 11, 15, 10, 6\}$ (i.e., $n = 27$) and let five processors P_1, P_2, P_3, P_4, P_5 be available on an EREW SM SIMD computer (i.e., $N = 5$). Thus $5 = (27)^{1-x}$, $x \simeq 0.5$, and $k = 2^{\lceil 1/x \rceil} = 4$. The working of procedure EREW SORT for this input is illustrated in Fig. 4.7. During step 1, $m_1 = 6$, $m_2 = 11$, and $m_3 = 17$ are computed. The four subsequences S_1, S_2, S_3, and S_4 are created in steps 2–4 as shown in Fig. 4.7(b). In step 5 the procedure is applied recursively and simultaneously to S_1 and S_2. Note that $|S_1| = |S_2| = 7$, and therefore 7^{1-x} is rounded down to 2 (as suggested in chapter 2). In other words two processors are used to sort each of the subsequences S_1 and S_2 (the fifth processor remaining idle). For S_1, processors P_1 and P_2 compute $m_1 = 2$, $m_2 = 4$, and $m_3 = 5$, and the four subsequences $\{1, 2\}$, $\{3, 4\}$, $\{5, 5\}$, and $\{6\}$ are created each of which is already in sorted order. For S_2, processors P_3 and P_4 compute $m_1 = 8, m_2 = 10$, and $m_3 = 11$, and the four subsequences $\{7, 8\}$, $\{9, 10\}$, $\{10, 11\}$, and $\{11\}$ are created each of which is already in sorted order. The sequence S at the end of step 5 is illustrated in Fig. 4.7(c). In step 6 the procedure is applied recursively and simultaneously to S_3 and S_4. Again since $|S_3| = 7$ and $|S_4| = 6$, 7^{1-x} and 6^{1-x} are rounded down to 2 and two processors are used to sort each of the two subsequences S_3

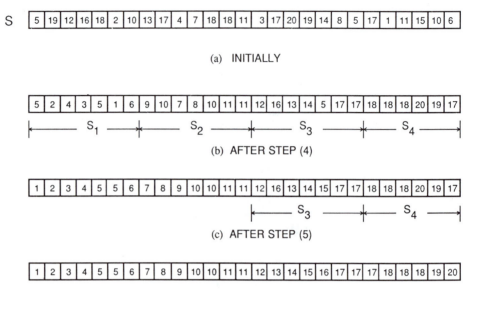

Figure 4.7 Sorting sequence of twenty-seven elements using procedure EREW SORT.

and S_4. For S_3, $m_1 = 13$, $m_2 = 15$, and $m_3 = 17$ are computed, and the four subsequences $\{12, 13\}$, $\{14, 15\}$, $\{16, 17\}$, and $\{17\}$ are created each of which is already sorted. For S_4, $m_1 = 18$, $m_2 = 18$, and $m_3 = 20$ are computed, and the four subsequences $\{17, 18\}$, $\{18, 18\}$, $\{19, 20\}$, and an empty subsequence are created. The sequence S after step 5 is shown in Fig. 4.7(d). □

Analysis. The call to QUICKSORT takes constant time. From the analysis of procedure PARALLEL SELECT in chapter 2 we know that steps 1–4 require cn^x time units for some constant c. The running time of procedure EREW SORT is therefore

$$t(n) = cn^x + 2t(n/k)$$

$$= O(n^x \log n).$$

Since $p(n) = n^{1-x}$, the procedure's cost is given by

$$c(n) = p(n) \times t(n) = O(n \log n),$$

which is optimal. Note, however, that since $n^{1-x} < n/\log n$, cost optimality is restricted to the range $N < n/\log n$.

Procedure EREW SORT therefore matches CREW SORT in performance:

(i) It uses a number of processors N that is sublinear in the size of the input n and adapts to it,

(ii) it has a running time that is small and varies inversely with N, and

(iii) its cost is optimal for $N < n/\log n$.

Procedure EREW SORT has the added advantage, of course, of running on a weaker model of computation that does not allow multiple-read operations from the same memory location.

It is also interesting to observe that procedure EREW SORT is a "mirror image" of procedure CREW SORT in the following way. Both algorithms can be modeled in theory by a binary tree. In procedure CREW SORT, subsequences are input at the leaves, one subsequence per leaf, and sorted locally; they are then merged pairwise by parent nodes until the output is produced at the root. By contrast, in procedure EREW SORT, the sequence to be sorted is input at the root and then split into two independent subsequences $\{S_1, S_2, \ldots, S_j\}$ and $\{S_{j+1}, S_{j+2}, \ldots, S_{2j}\}$; splitting then continues at each node until each leaf receives a subsequence that, once locally sorted, is produced as output.

4.7 PROBLEMS

4.1 Use the (n, n)-merging network defined in problem 3.9 to obtain a network for sorting arbitrary (i.e., not necessarily bitonic) input sequences. Analyze the running time and number of processors used by this network and compare these with the corresponding quantities for the network in section 4.2.

4.2 Consider the following parallel architecture consisting of n^2 processors placed in a square array with n rows and n columns. The processors in each row are interconnected to form a binary tree. The processors in each column are interconnected similarly. The tree interconnections are the only links among the processors. Show that this architecture, known as the *mesh of trees*, can sort a sequence of n elements in $O(\log n)$ time.

4.3 The odd–even sorting network of section 4.2 uses $O(n \log^2 n)$ processors to sort a sequence of length n in $O(\log^2 n)$ time. For some applications, this may be too slow. On the other hand, the architecture in problem 4.2 sorts in $O(\log n)$ time using n^2 processors. Again, when n is large, this number of processors is prohibitive. Can you design a network that combines the features of these two algorithms, that is, one that uses $O(n \log^2 n)$ processors and sorts in $O(\log n)$ time?

4.4 It may be argued that the number of processors used in problem 4.3, namely, $O(n \log^2 n)$, is still too large. Is it possible to reduce this to $O(n \log n)$ and still achieve an $O(\log n)$ running time?

4.5 Inspect the network obtained in problem 4.1. You will likely notice that it consists of m columns of $n/2$ processors each, where m is a function of n obtained from your analysis. It is required to exploit this regular structure to obtain a sorting network consisting of a single column of $n/2$ processors that sorts a sequence of length n in $O(m)$ time. The idea is to keep the processors busy all the time as follows. The input sequence is fed to the processors and an output is obtained equal to that obtained from the first column of the bitonic sorting network. This output is permuted appropriately and fed back to the processors to obtain the output of the second column. This continues for m iterations, until the sequence is fully sorted. Such a scheme is illustrated in Fig. 4.8 for $n = 8$.

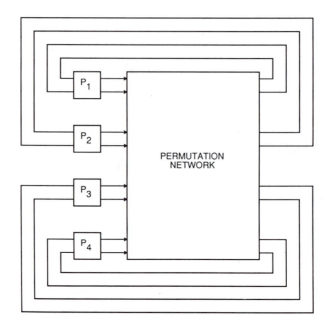

Figure 4.8 Sorting using permutation network.

4.6 The sorting network in problem 4.5 has a cost of $O(nm)$. Is this optimal? The answer, of course, depends on m. If the cost is not optimal, apply the same idea used in procedure MERGE SPLIT to obtain an optimal algorithm.

4.7 Can you design a sorting network that uses $O(n)$ processors to sort a sequence of length n in $O(\log n)$ time?

4.8 Establish the correctness of procedure ODD-EVEN TRANSPOSITION.

4.9 As example 4.2 illustrates, a sequence may be completely sorted several iterations before procedure ODD-EVEN TRANSPOSITION actually terminates. In fact, if the sequence is initially sorted, the $O(n)$ iterations performed by the procedure would be redundant. Is it possible, within the limitations of the linear array model, to modify the procedure so that an early termination is obtained if at any point the sequence becomes sorted?

4.10 Procedure ODD-EVEN TRANSPOSITION assumes that all elements of the input sequence are available and reside initially in the array of processors. It is conceivable that in some applications, the inputs arrive sequentially and are received one at a time by the leftmost processor P_1. Similarly, the output is produced one element at a time from P_1. Modify procedure ODD-EVEN TRANSPOSITION so that it runs under these conditions and completes the sort in exactly the same number of steps as before (i.e., without an extra time penalty for input and output).

4.11 When several sequences are queued for sorting, the procedure in problem 4.9 has a period of $2n$. Show that this period can be reduced to n by allowing both P_1 and P_n to handle input and output. In this way, m sequences of n elements each are sorted in $(m + 1)n$ steps instead of $2mn$.

4.12 In section 4.3 we showed how procedure ODD-EVEN TRANSPOSITION can be modified so that its cost becomes optimal. Show that it is possible to obtain a cost-optimal sorting algorithm on the linear array for the case of sequential input. One approach to consider is the following. For a sequence of length n, the linear array consists of $1 + \log n$ processors. The leftmost processor receives the input, the rightmost produces the output. Each processor is connected to its neighbors by two lines, as shown in Fig. 4.9 for $n = 8$. This array can be made to sort in $O(n)$ time by implementing an adapted version of the sequential procedure Mergesort. This procedure consists of $\log n$ stages. In stage i sorted subsequences of length 2^i are created, $i = 1, 2, \ldots, \log n$. In the parallel adaptation, the steps are run overlapped on the linear array.

4.13 In procedure MERGE SPLIT each processor needs at least $4n/N$ storage locations to merge two sequences of length n/N each. Modify the procedure to require only $1 + n/N$ locations per processor.

4.14 A variant of the linear array that uses a bus was introduced in problem 2.9. Design an algorithm for sorting on this model, where P_1 receives the input sequence of size n and P_n produces the output.

4.15 The n elements of a sequence are input to an $n^{1/2} \times n^{1/2}$ mesh-connected SIMD computer, one element per processor. It is required to sort this sequence in row-major order. Derive a lower bound on the running time required to solve this problem.

4.16 Use the results of problems 3.6 and 3.7 to obtain an algorithm for odd–even sorting on an $m \times m$ mesh-connected SIMD computer. Analyze your algorithm.

4.17 Is the algorithm obtained in problem 4.16 cost optimal? If not, apply the same idea used in procedure MERGE SPLIT to obtain a cost-optimal algorithm.

4.18 Use the results of problems 3.12 and 3.13 to obtain an algorithm for bitonic sorting on an $m \times m$ mesh-connected SIMD computer. Analyze your algorithm.

4.19 Repeat problem 4.17 for the algorithm in problem 4.18.

4.20 The algorithm in problem 4.16 returns a sequence sorted in row-major order. Another indexing that may sometimes be desirable is known as *snakelike row-major order*: The ith element resides in row j and column k, where

$$i = \begin{cases} jm + k + 1 & \text{for } j \text{ even,} \\ jm + m - k & \text{for } j \text{ odd.} \end{cases}$$

This is illustrated in Fig. 4.10 for $n = 16$. Show that after a sequence has been sorted into row-major order, its elements may be rearranged into snakelike row-major order in $2(n^{1/2} - 1)$ routing steps.

4.21 Another indexing for sequences sorted on two-dimensional arrays is the *shuffled row-major order*. Let element i, $1 \leqslant i \leqslant n$, reside in row j and column k in a row-major ordering. If i' is the integer obtained by applying a perfect shuffle to the bits in the binary representation of $i - 1$, then element $i' + 1$ occupies position (j, k) in a shuffled row-major indexing. This is

Figure 4.9   Cost-optimal sorting on linear array for case of sequential input.

1	2	3	4
8	7	6	5
9	10	11	12
16	15	14	13

Figure 4.10 Snakelike row-major order.

illustrated in Fig. 4.11 for $n = 16$. Show that if n elements have already been sorted according to row-major order and if each processor can store $n^{1/2}$ elements, then the n elements can be sorted into shuffled row-major order using an additional $4(n^{1/2} - 1)$ routing steps.

4.22 A variant of the mesh interconnection network that uses a bus was introduced in problem 2.10. Repeat problem 4.15 for this model.

4.23 Design a parallel algorithm for sorting on the model of problem 2.10.

4.24 Design an algorithm for sorting on a tree-connected SIMD computer. The input sequence is initially distributed among the leaves of the tree. Analyze the running time, number of processors used, and cost of your algorithm.

4.25 Repeat problem 4.24 for the case where the sequence to be sorted is presented to the root.

4.26 Derive a lower bound for sorting a sequence of length n on the pyramid machine defined in problem 3.16.

4.27 Design an algorithm for sorting on the pyramid machine.

4.28 Show that any parallel algorithm that uses a cube-connected SIMD computer with N processors to sort a sequence of length n, where $N \geqslant n$, requires $\Omega(\log N)$ time.

4.29 Implement the idea of sorting by enumeration on a cube-connected SIMD computer and analyze the running time of your implementation.

4.30 Show that any parallel algorithm that uses the perfect shuffle interconnection network with N processors to sort a sequence of length n, where $N = 2^m \geqslant n$, requires $\Omega(\log N)$ time.

4.31 Consider a CRCW SM SIMD computer where write conflicts are resolved as follows: The write operation is allowed if and only if all processors writing simultaneously in the same memory location are attempting to store the same value. Describe an algorithm for this

1	2	5	6
3	4	7	8
9	10	13	14
11	12	15	16

Figure 4.11 Shuffled row-major order.

model that can determine the minimum of n numbers $\{x_1, x_2, \ldots, x_n\}$ in constant time using n^2 processors. If more than one of the numbers qualify, the one with the smallest subscript should be returned.

4.32 Show how procedure CRCW SORT can be modified to run on an EREW model and analyze its running time.

4.33 Show that procedure CREW SORT can be simulated on an EREW computer in $O([(n/N) + \log^2 n]\log n)$ time if a way can be found to distinguish between simple read operations and multiple-read operations, as in problem 3.20.

4.34 In procedure EREW SORT, why are steps 5 and 6 not executed simultaneously?

4.35 Derive an algorithm for sorting by enumeration on the EREW model. The algorithm should use $n^{1 + 1/k}$ processors, where k is an arbitrary integer, and run in $O(k \log n)$ time.

4.36 Let the elements of the sequence S to be sorted belong to the set $\{0, 1, \ldots, m - 1\}$. A sorting algorithm known as *sorting by bucketing* first distributes the elements among a number of *buckets* that are then sorted individually. Show that sorting can be completed in $O(\log n)$ time on the EREW model using n processors and $O(mn)$ memory locations.

4.37 The amount of memory required for bucketing in problem 4.36 can be reduced when the elements to be sorted are binary strings in the interval $[0, 2^b - 1]$ for some b. The algorithm consists of b iterations. During iteration $i, i = 0, 1, \ldots, b - 1$, each element to be sorted is placed in one of two buckets depending on whether its ith bit is 0 or 1; the sequence is then reconstructed using procedure ALLSUMS so that all elements with a 0 ith bit precede all the elements with a 1 ith bit. Show that in this case sorting can be completed in $O(b \log n)$ time using $O(n)$ processors and $O(n)$ memory locations.

4.38 Assume that an interconnection network SIMD computer with n processors can sort a sequence of length n in $O(f(n))$ time. Show that this network can simulate an algorithm requiring time T on an EREW SM SIMD computer with n memory locations and n processors in $O(Tf(n))$ time.

4.39 Design an asynchronous algorithm for sorting a sequence of length n by enumeration on a multiprocessor computer with N processors.

4.40 Adapt procedure QUICKSORT to run on the model of problem 4.39.

4.8 BIBLIOGRAPHICAL REMARKS

An extensive treatment of parallel sorting is provided in [Akl 2]. Taxonomies of parallel sorting algorithms can be found in [Bitton] and [Lakshmivarahan]. The odd–even sorting network was first presented in [Batcher]. Other sorting networks are proposed in [Lee], [Miranker], [Tseng], [Winslow], and [Wong]. The theoretically fastest possible network for sorting using $O(n)$ processors is described in [Leighton] based on ideas appearing in [Ajtai]: It sorts a sequence of length n in $O(\log n)$ time and is therefore cost optimal. However, the asymptotic expression for the running time of this network hides an enormous constant, which makes it infeasible in practice.

Procedure ODD-EVEN TRANSPOSITION is attributed to [Demuth]. The idea on which procedure MERGE SPLIT is based comes from [Baudet]. Other algorithms for sorting on a linear array are described in [Akl 1], [Todd], and [Yasuura]. Parallel sorting algorithms for a variety of interconnection-network SIMD computers have been proposed. These include algorithms for the perfect shuffle ([Stone]), the mesh ([Kumar], [Nassimi 1], and [Thompson]), the tree ([Bentley], [Horowitz 2], and [Orenstein]), the pyramid ([Stout]), and the cube ([Nassimi 2]).

It is particularly interesting to point out the difference between the tree- and mesh-connected computers in their ability to sort a sequence $S = \{s_1, s_2, \ldots, s_n\}$. Assume that a tree with n leaf processors $P_1, P_2, \ldots, P_n$ is available. Initially, P_i contains s_i. It is required to sort S such that P_i contains the ith element of the sorted sequence. Clearly, any parallel algorithm for solving this problem requires $\Omega(n)$ time in the worst case since all the values in the right subtree of the root may have to be exchanged (through the root) with those in the left subtree. It is shown in [Akl 2] how an $O(\log n)$-processor tree-connected computer can sort S in $O(n)$ time for an optimal cost of $O(n \log n)$. Now consider an $n^{1/2} \times n^{1/2}$ mesh with processors $P_1, P_2, \ldots, P_n$ arranged in row-major order. Initially P_i contains s_i. Again, it is required to sort S such that P_i contains the ith element of the sorted sequence. Suppose that the maximum and minimum elements of S are initially in P_1 and P_n, respectively. Since these two elements must be exchanged for the outcome of the sorting to be correct, $\Omega(n^{1/2})$ steps are required to sort on the mesh. An algorithm is described in [Akl 2] for sorting S on an n-processor mesh-connected computer in $O(n^{1/2})$ time. It is also shown in [Akl 2] how an N-processor mesh can sort S with a running time of

$$t(n) = O((n/N)\log(n/N) + (n/N)O(N^{1/2}) + (2n/N)O(\log^2 N^{1/2})),$$

for an optimal cost of $O(n \log n)$ when $N < \log^2 n$.

Procedure CRCW SORT is based on ideas appearing in [Kučera]. A proposal is made in [Gottlieb] for a computer architecture implementing the concurrent-read, concurrent-write features of the model in section 4.4. Procedure CREW SORT is adapted from [Shiloach]. Other parallel sorting algorithms for the CREW model were proposed in [Hirschberg], [Kruskal], and [Preparata]. The procedure in section 4.6.2 and procedure EREW SORT are from [Akl 3] and [Akl 1], respectively. Other issues of interest when studying parallel sorting are external sorting, covered in [Akl 4], [Bonnucelli], and [Even], and parallel probabilistic sorting algorithms, examples of which appear in [Horowitz 2], [Reif], and [Reischuk]. The importance of parallel sorting in simulating powerful models of parallel computation on weaker ones is outlined in [Parberry]. A description of the sequential sorting procedure Mergesort mentioned in problem 4.12 can be found in [Horowitz 1].

4.9 REFERENCES

[AJTAI]
Ajtai, M., Komlós, J., and Szemerédi, E., An $O(n \log n)$ sorting network, Proceedings of the 15th Annual ACM Symposium on Theory of Computing, Boston, Massachusetts, April 1983, pp. 1–9, Association for Computing Machinery, New York, N.Y., 1983.

[AKL 1]
Akl, S. G., Optimal parallel algorithms for computing convex hulls and for sorting, *Computing*, Vol. 33, No. 1, 1984, pp. 1–11.

[AKL 2]
Akl, S. G., *Parallel Sorting Algorithms*, Academic, Orlando, Fl., 1985.

[AKL 3]
Akl, S. G., and Santoro, N., Optimal parallel merging and sorting without memory conflicts, *IEEE Transactions on Computers*, Vol. C-36, No. 11, November 1987, pp. 1367–1369.

[AKL 4]
Akl, S. G., and Schmeck, H., Systolic sorting in a sequential input/output environment, *Parallel Computing*, Vol. 3, No. 1, March 1986, pp. 11–23.

[BATCHER]
Batcher, K. E., Sorting networks and their applications, Proceedings of the AFIPS 1968 Spring Joint Computer Conference, Atlantic City, New Jersey, April 30–May 2, 1968, pp. 307–314, AFIPS Press, Montvale, N.J., 1968.

[BAUDET]
Baudet, G. M., and Stevenson, D., Optimal sorting algorithms for parallel computers, *IEEE Transactions on Computers*, Vol. C-27, No. 1, January 1978, pp. 84–87.

[BENTLEY]
Bentley, J. L., and Brown, D. J., A general class of recurrence tradeoffs, Proceedings of the 21st Annual IEEE Symposium on Foundations of Computer Science, Syracuse, New York, October 1980, pp. 217–228, IEEE Computer Society, Washington, D.C., 1980.

[BITTON]
Bitton, D., DeWitt, D. J., Hsiao, D. K., and Menon, J., A taxonomy of parallel sorting, *Computing Surveys*, Vol. 13, No. 3, September 1984, pp. 287–318.

[BONNUCELLI]
Bonnucelli, M. A., Lodi, E., and Pagli, L., External sorting in VLSI, *IEEE Transactions on Computers*, Vol. C-33, No. 10, October 1984, pp. 931–934.

[DEMUTH]
Demuth, H. B., Electronic data sorting, Ph.D. thesis, Stanford University, Stanford, California, October 1956.

[EVEN]
Even, S., Parallelism in tape sorting, *Communications of the ACM*, Vol. 17, No. 4, April 1974, pp. 202–204.

[GOTTLIEB]
Gottlieb, A., Grishman, R., Kruskal, C. P., McAuliffe, K. P., Rudolph, L., and Snir, M., The NYU Ultracomputer: Designing an MIMD shared memory parallel computer, *IEEE Transactions on Computers*, Vol. C-32, No. 2, 1983, pp. 175–189.

[HIRSCHBERG]
Hirschberg, D. S., Fast parallel sorting algorithms, *Communications of the ACM*, Vol. 21, No. 8, August 1978, pp. 657–661.

[HOROWITZ 1]
Horowitz, E., and Sahni, S., *Fundamentals of Computer Algorithms*, Computer Science Press, Rockville, Md., 1978.

[HOROWITZ 2]
Horowitz, E., and Zorat, A., Divide-and-conquer for parallel processing, *IEEE Transactions on Computers*, Vol. C-32, No. 6, June 1983, pp. 582–585.

[KRUSKAL]
Kruskal, C. P., Searching, merging and sorting in parallel computations, *IEEE Transactions on Computers*, Vol. C-32, No. 10, October 1983, pp. 942–946.

[KUČERA]
Kučera, L., Parallel computation and conflicts in memory access, *Information Processing Letters*, Vol. 14, April 1982, pp. 93–96.

[KUMAR]
Kumar, M., and Hirschberg, D. S., An efficient implementation of Batcher's odd-even merge algorithm and its application in parallel sorting schemes, *IEEE Transactions on Computers*, Vol. C-32, No. 3, March 1983, pp. 254–264.

[LAKSHMIVARAHAN]

Lakshmivarahan, S., Dhall, S. K., and Miller, L. L., Parallel sorting algorithms, in Yovits, M. C., Ed., *Advances in Computers*, Academic, New York, 1984, pp. 295–354.

[LEE]

Lee, D. T., Chang, H., and Wong, C. K., An on-chip compare/steer bubble sorter, *IEEE Transactions on Computers*, Vol. C-30, No. 6, June 1981, pp. 396–405.

[LEIGHTON]

Leighton, F. T., Tight bounds on the complexity of parallel sorting, *IEEE Transactions on Computers*, Vol. C-34, No. 4, April 1985, pp. 344–354.

[MIRANKER]

Miranker, G., Tang, L., and Wong, C. K., A "zero-time" VLSI sorter, *IBM Journal of Research and Development*, Vol. 27, No. 2, March 1983, pp. 140–148.

[NASSIMI 1]

Nassimi, D., and Sahni, S., Bitonic sort on a mesh-connected parallel computer, *IEEE Transactions on Computers*, Vol. C-28, No. 1, January 1979, pp. 2–7.

[NASSIMI 2]

Nassimi, D., and Sahni, S., Parallel permutation and sorting algorithms and a new generalized connection network, *Journal of the ACM*, Vol. 29, No. 3, July 1982, pp. 642–667.

[ORENSTEIN]

Orenstein, J. A., Merrett, T. H., and Devroye, L., Linear sorting with $O(\log n)$ processors, *BIT*, Vol. 23, 1983, pp. 170–180.

[PARBERRY]

Parberry, I., Some practical simulations of impractical parallel computers, *Parallel Computing*, Vol. 4, 1987, pp. 93–101.

[PREPARATA]

Preparata, F. P., New parallel sorting schemes, *IEEE Transactions on Computers*, Vol. C-27, No. 7, July 1978, pp. 669–673.

[REIF]

Reif, J. H., and Valiant, L. G., A logarithmic time sort for linear size networks, *Journal of the ACM*, Vol. 34, No. 1, January 1987, pp. 60–76.

[REISCHUK]

Reischuk, R., A fast probabilistic parallel sorting algorithm, Proceedings of the 22nd Annual IEEE Symposium on Foundations of Computer Science, Nashville, Tennessee, October 1981, pp. 212–219, IEEE Computer Society, Washington, D.C., 1981.

[SHILOACH]

Shiloach, Y., and Vishkin, V., Finding the maximum, merging and sorting in a parallel computation model, *Journal of Algorithms*, Vol. 2, 1981, pp. 88–102.

[STONE]

Stone, H. S., Parallel processing with the perfect shuffle, *IEEE Transactions on Computers*, Vol. C-20, No. 2, February 1971, pp. 153–161.

[STOUT]

Stout, Q. F., Sorting, merging, selecting and filtering on tree and pyramid machines, Proceedings of the 1983 International Conference on Parallel Processing, Bellaire, Michigan, August 1983, pp. 214–221, IEEE Computer Society, Washington, D.C., 1983.

[THOMPSON]
Thompson, C. D., and Kung, H. T., Sorting on a mesh-connected parallel computer, *Communications of the ACM*, Vol. 20, No. 4, April 1977, pp. 263–271.

[TODD]
Todd, S., Algorithms and hardware for a merge sort using multiple processors, *IBM Journal of Research and Development*, Vol. 22, No. 5, September 1978, pp. 509–517.

[TSENG]
Tseng, S. S., and Lee, R. C. T., A new parallel sorting algorithm based upon min-mid-max operations, *BIT*, Vol. 24, 1984, pp. 187–195.

[WINSLOW]
Winslow, L. E., and Chow, Y.-C., The analysis and design of some new sorting machines, *IEEE Transactions on Computers*, Vol. C-32, No. 7, July 1983, pp. 677–683.

[WONG]
Wong, F. S., and Ito, M. R., Parallel sorting on a re-circulating systolic sorter, *The Computer Journal*, Vol. 27, No. 3, 1984, pp. 260–269.

[YASUURA]
Yasuura, H., Tagaki, N., and Yajima, S., The parallel enumeration sorting scheme for VLSI, *IEEE Transactions on Computers*, Vol. C-31, No. 12, December 1982, pp. 1192–1201.

5

Searching

5.1 INTRODUCTION

Searching is one of the most fundamental operations in the field of computing. It is used in any application where we need to find out whether an element belongs to a list or, more generally, retrieve from a file information associated with that element. In its most basic form the *searching problem* is stated as follows: Given a sequence $S = \{s_1, s_2, \ldots, s_n\}$ of integers and an integer x, it is required to determine whether $x = s_k$ for some s_k in S.

In sequential computing, the problem is solved by scanning the sequence S and comparing x with its successive elements until either an integer equal to x is found or the sequence is exhausted without success. This is given in what follows as procedure SEQUENTIAL SEARCH. As soon as an s_k in S is found such that $x = s_k$, the procedure returns k; otherwise 0 is returned.

procedure SEQUENTIAL SEARCH (S, x, k)

Step 1: (1.1) $i \leftarrow 1$
(1.2) $k \leftarrow 0$.
Step 2: **while** $(i \leqslant n$ **and** $k = 0)$ **do**
if $s_i = x$ **then** $k \leftarrow i$ **end if**
$i \leftarrow i + 1$
end while. $\square$

In the worst case, the procedure takes $O(n)$ time. This is clearly optimal since every element of S must be examined (when x is not in S) before declaring failure. Alternatively, if S is sorted in nondecreasing order, then procedure BINARY SEARCH of section 3.3.2 can return the index of an element of S equal to x (or 0 if no such element exists) in $O(\log n)$ time. Again, this is optimal since this many bits are needed to distinguish among the n elements of S.

In this chapter we discuss parallel searching algorithms. We begin by considering the case where S is sorted in nondecreasing order and show how searching can be performed on the SM SIMD model. As it turns out, our EREW searching algorithm is no faster than procedure BINARY SEARCH. On the other hand, the CREW algorithm matches a lower bound on the number of parallel steps required to search a sorted sequence, assuming that all the elements of S are distinct. When this assumption is removed, a CRCW algorithm is needed to achieve the best possible speedup. We then turn to the more general case where the elements of S are in random order. Here, although the SM SIMD algorithms are faster than procedure SEQUENTIAL SEARCH, the same speedup can be achieved on a weaker model, namely, a tree-connected SIMD computer. Finally, we present a parallel search algorithm for a mesh-connected SIMD computer that, under some assumptions about signal propagation time along wires, is superior to the tree algorithm.

5.2 SEARCHING A SORTED SEQUENCE

We assume throughout this section that the sequence $S = \{s_1, s_2, \ldots, s_n\}$ is sorted in nondecreasing order, that is, $s_1 \leqslant s_2 \leqslant \cdots \leqslant s_n$. Typically, a file with n records is available, which is sorted on the s field of each record. This file is to be searched using s as the *key*; that is, given an integer x, a record is sought whose s field equals x. If such a record is found, then the information stored in the other fields may now be retrieved. The format of a record is illustrated in Fig. 5.1. Note that if the values of the s fields are not unique and *all* records whose s fields equal a given x are needed, then the search algorithm is continued until the file is exhausted. For simplicity we begin by assuming that the s_i are distinct; this assumption is later removed.

5.2.1 EREW Searching

Assume that an N-processor EREW SM SIMD computer is available to search S for a given element x, where $1 < N \leqslant n$. To begin, the value of x must be made known to all processors. This can be done using procedure BROADCAST in $O(\log N)$ time. The sequence S is then subdivided into N subsequences of length n/N each, and processor P_i is assigned $\{s_{(i-1)(n/N)+1}, s_{(i-1)(n/N)+2}, \ldots, s_{i(n/N)}\}$. All processors now perform procedure BINARY SEARCH on their assigned subsequences. This requires $O(\log(n/N))$ in the worst case. Since the elements of S are all distinct, at most one processor finds an s_k equal to x and returns k. The total time required by this EREW searching algorithm is therefore $O(\log N) + O(\log(n/N))$, which is $O(\log n)$. Since this is precisely the time required by procedure BINARY SEARCH (running on a single processor!), no speedup is achieved by this approach.

Figure 5.1 Format of record in file to be searched.

5.2.2 CREW Searching

Again, assume that an N-processor CREW SM SIMD computer is available to search S for a given element x, where $1 < N \leqslant n$. The same algorithm described for the EREW computer can be used here except that in this case all processors can read x simultaneously in constant time and then proceed to perform procedure BINARY SEARCH on their assigned subsequences. This requires $O(\log(n/N))$ time in the worst case, which is faster than procedure BINARY SEARCH applied sequentially to the entire sequence.

It is possible, however, to do even better. The idea is to use a parallel version of the binary search approach. Recall that during each iteration of procedure BINARY SEARCH the middle element s_m of the sequence searched is probed and tested for equality with the input x. If $s_m > x$, then all the elements larger than s_m are discarded; otherwise all the elements smaller than s_m are discarded. Thus, the next iteration is applied to a sequence half as long as previously. The procedure terminates when the probed element equals x or when all elements have been discarded. In the parallel version, there are N processors and hence an $(N + 1)$-ary search can be used. At each stage, the sequence is split into $N + 1$ subsequences of equal length and the N processors simultaneously probe the elements at the boundary between successive subsequences. This is illustrated in Fig. 5.2. Every processor compares the element s of S it probes with x:

1. If $s > x$, then if an element equal to x is in the sequence at all, it must precede s; consequently, s and all the elements that follow it (i.e., to its right in Fig. 5.2) are removed from consideration.

2. The opposite takes place if $s < x$.

Thus each processor splits the sequence into two parts: those elements to be discarded as they definitely do not contain an element equal to x and those that might and are hence kept. This narrows down the search to the intersection of all the parts to be kept, that is, the subsequence between two elements probed in this stage. This subsequence, shown hachured in Fig. 5.2, is searched in the next stage by the same process. This continues until either an element equal to x is found or all the elements of S are discarded. Since every stage is applied to a sequence whose length is $1/(N + 1)$ the length of the sequence searched during the previous stage less 1, $O(\log_{N+1}(n + 1))$ stages are needed. We now develop the algorithm formally and then show that this is precisely the number of steps it requires in the worst case.

Let g be the smallest integer such that $n \leqslant (N + 1)^g - 1$, that is, $g = \lceil \log(n + 1)/\log(N + 1) \rceil$. It is possible to prove by induction that g stages are sufficient to search a sequence of length n for an element equal to an input x. Indeed, the statement is true for $g = 0$. Assume it is true for $(N + 1)^{g-1} - 1$. Now, to search a sequence of length $(N + 1)^g - 1$, processor P_i, $i = 1, 2, \ldots, N$, compares x to s_j where $j = i(N + 1)^{g-1}$, as shown in Fig. 5.3. Following this comparison, only a subsequence of length $(N + 1)^{g-1} - 1$ needs to be searched, thus proving our claim. This subsequence, shown hachured in Fig. 5.3, can be determined as follows. Each processor P_i uses a variable c_i that takes the value *left* or *right* according to whether the part of the sequence P_i decides to keep is to the left or right of the element it compared to x during this stage. Initially, the value of each c_i is irrelevant and can be assigned arbitrarily. Two constants $c_0 = $ right and $c_{N+1} = $ left are also used. Following the comparison between x and an element s_{j_i} of S, P_i assigns a value to c_i (unless $s_{j_i} = x$, in which case the value of c_i is again irrelevant). If $c_i \neq c_{i-1}$ for some i, $1 \leq i \leq N$, then the sequence to be searched next runs from s_q to s_r, where $q = (i-1)(N+1)^{g-1} + 1$ and $r = i(N+1)^{g-1} - 1$. Precisely one processor updates q and r in the shared memory, and all remaining processors can simultaneously read the updated values in constant time. The algorithm is given in what follows as procedure CREW SEARCH. The procedure takes S and x as input: If $x = s_k$ for some k, then k is returned; otherwise a 0 is returned.

procedure CREW SEARCH (S, x, k)

Step 1:   {Initialize indices of sequence to be searched}
          (1.1) $q \leftarrow 1$
          (1.2) $r \leftarrow n$.

Step 2:   {Initialize results and maximum number of stages}
          (2.1) $k \leftarrow 0$
          (2.2) $g \leftarrow \lceil \log(n+1)/\log(N+1) \rceil$.

Step 3:   **while** $(q \leq r$ **and** $k = 0)$ **do**
          (3.1) $j_0 \leftarrow q - 1$
          (3.2) **for** $i = 1$ **to** N **do in parallel**
                (i) $j_i \leftarrow (q-1) + i(N+1)^{g-1}$
                    {P_i compares x to s_j and determines the part of the sequence to be kept}
                (ii) **if** $j_i \leq r$
                     then if $s_{j_i} = x$
                          then $k \leftarrow j_i$
                          else if $s_{j_i} > x$
                               then $c_i \leftarrow$ left
                               else $c_i \leftarrow$ right
                               end if
                          end if
                     else (a) $j_i \leftarrow r + 1$
                          (b) $c_i \leftarrow$ left
                     end if
                     {The indices of the subsequence to be searched in the next iteration are computed}
                (iii) **if** $c_i \neq c_{i-1}$ **then** (a) $q \leftarrow j_{i-1} + 1$
                                              (b) $r \leftarrow j_i - 1$
                      end if
                (iv) **if** $(i = N$ **and** $c_i \neq c_{i+1})$ **then** $q \leftarrow j_i + 1$
                     end if
                end for
          (3.3) $g \leftarrow g - 1$.
          end while. $\square$

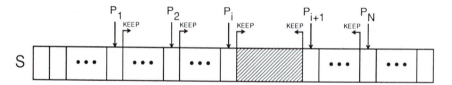

Figure 5.2   Searching sorted sequence with N processors.

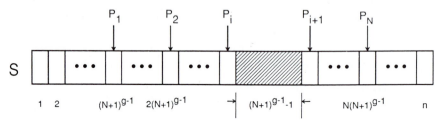

Figure 5.3   Derivation of number of stages required to search sequence.

Analysis

Steps 1, 2, 3.1, and 3.3 are performed by one processor, say, P_1, in constant time. Step 3.2 also takes constant time. As proved earlier, there are at most g iterations of step 3. It follows that procedure CREW SEARCH runs in $O(\log(n+1)/\log(N+1))$ time, that is, $t(n) = O(\log_{N+1}(n+1))$. Hence $c(n) = O(N\log_{N+1}(n+1))$, which is not optimal.

Example 5.1

Let $S = \{1, 4, 6, 9, 10, 11, 13, 14, 15, 18, 20, 23, 32, 45, 51\}$ be the sequence to be searched using a CREW SM SIMD computer with N processors. We illustrate two successful and one unsuccessful searches.

1. Assume that $N = 3$ and that it is required to find the index k of the element in S equal to 45 (i.e., $x = 45$). Initially, $q = 1$, $r = 15$, $k = 0$, and $g = 2$. During the first iteration of step 3, P_1 computes $j_1 = 4$ and compares s_4 to x. Since $9 < 45$, $c_1 = $ right. Simultaneously, P_2 and P_3 compare s_8 and s_{12}, respectively, to x: Since $14 < 45$ and $23 < 45$, $c_2 = $ right and $c_3 = $ right. Now $c_3 \neq c_4$; therefore $q = 13$ and r remains unchanged. The new sequence to be searched runs from s_{13} to s_{15}, as shown in Fig. 5.4(a), and $g = 1$. In the second iteration, illustrated in Fig. 5.4(b), P_1 computes $j_1 = 12 + 1$ and compares s_{13} to x: Since $32 < 45$, $c_1 = $ right. Simultaneously, P_2 compares s_{14} to x, and since they are equal, it sets k to 14 (c_2 remains unchanged). Also, P_3 compares s_{15} to x: Since $51 > 45$, $c_3 = $ left. Now $c_3 \neq c_2$: Thus $q = 12 + 2 + 1 = 15$ and $r = 12 + 3 - 1 = 14$. The procedure terminates with $k = 14$.

2. Say now that $x = 9$, with N still equal to 3. In the first iteration, P_1 compares s_4 to x: Since they are equal, k is set to 4. All simultaneous and subsequent computations in this iteration are redundant since the following iteration is not performed and the procedure terminates early with $k = 4$.

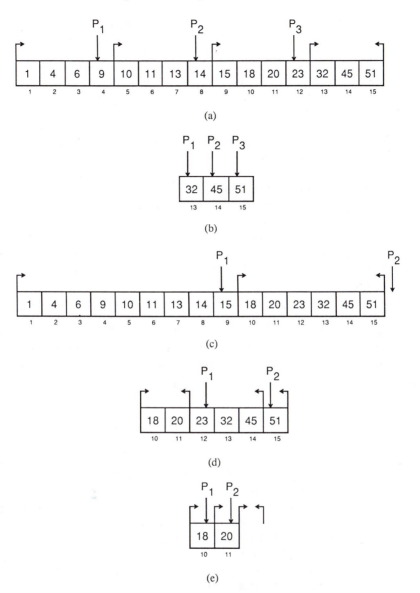

Figure 5.4 Searching sequence of fifteen elements using procedure CREW SEARCH.

3. Finally, let $N = 2$ and $x = 21$. Initially, $g = 3$. In the first iteration P_1 computes $j_1 = 9$ and compares s_9 to x: Since $15 < 21$, $c_1 =$ right. Simultaneously, P_2 computes $j_2 = 18$: Since $18 > 15$, j_2 points to an element outside the sequence. Thus P_2 sets $j_2 = 16$ and $c_2 =$ left. Now $c_2 \neq c_1$: Therefore $q = 10$ and $r = 15$, that is, the sequence to be searched in the next iteration runs from s_{10} to s_{15}, and $g = 2$. This is illustrated in Fig. 5.4(c). In the second iteration, P_1 computes $j_1 = 9 + 3$ and

compares s_{12} to x: since $23 > 21$, $c_1 =$ left. Simultaneously, P_2 computes $j_2 = 15$: Since $51 > 21$, $c_2 =$ left. Now $c_1 \neq c_0$, and therefore $r = 11$ and q remains unchanged, as shown in Fig. 5.4(d). In the final iteration, $g = 1$ and P_1 computes $j_1 = 9 + 1$ and compares s_{10} to x: Since $18 < 21$, $c_1 =$ right. Simultaneously, P_2 computes $j_2 = 9 + 2$ and compares s_{11} to x: Since $20 < 21$, $c_2 =$ right. Now $c_2 \neq c_3$, and therefore $q = 12$. Since $q > r$, the procedure terminates unsuccessfully with $k = 0$. $\square$

We conclude our discussion of parallel searching algorithms for the CREW model with the following two observations:

1. Under the assumption that the elements of S are sorted and distinct, procedure CREW SEARCH, although not cost optimal, achieves the best possible running time for searching. This can be shown by noting that any algorithm using N processors can compare an input element x to at most N elements of S simultaneously. After these comparisons and the subsequent deletion of elements from S definitely not equal to x, a subsequence must be left whose length is at least

$$\lceil (n - N)/(N + 1) \rceil \geqslant (n - N)/(N + 1) = [(n + 1)/(N + 1)] - 1.$$

   After g repetitions of the same process, we are left with a sequence of length $[(n + 1)/(N + 1)^g] - 1$. It follows that the number of iterations required by any such parallel algorithm is no smaller than the minimum g such that

$$[(n + 1)/(N + 1)^g] - 1 \leqslant 0,$$

   which is

$$\lceil \log(n + 1)/\log(N + 1) \rceil.$$

2. Two parallel algorithms were presented in this section for searching a sequence of length n on a CREW SM SIMD computer with N processors. The first required $O(\log(n/N))$ time and the second $O(\log(n + 1)/\log(N + 1))$. In both cases, if $N = n$, then the algorithm runs in constant time. The fact that the elements of S are distinct still remains a condition for achieving this constant running time, as we shall see in the next section. However, we no longer need S to be sorted. The algorithm is simply as follows: In one step each P_i, $i = 1, 2, \ldots, n$, can read x and compare it to s_i; if x is equal to one element of S, say, s_k, then P_k returns k; otherwise k remains 0.

5.2.3 CRCW Searching

In the previous two sections, we assumed that all the elements of the sequence S to be searched are distinct. From our discussion so far, the reason for this assumption may have become apparent: If each s_i is not unique, then possibly more than one processor will succeed in finding a member of S equal to x. Consequently, possibly several processors will attempt to return a value in the variable k, thus causing a write conflict, an occurrence disallowed in both the EREW and CREW models. Of course, we can remove the uniqueness assumption and still use the EREW and CREW searching algorithms described earlier. The idea is to invoke procedure STORE (see problem 2.13) whose job is to resolve write conflicts: Thus, in $O(\log N)$ time we can get the smallest numbered of the successful processors to return the index k it has computed, where $s_k = x$. The asymptotic running time of the EREW search algorithm in section 5.2.1 is not affected by this additional overhead. However, procedure CREW SEARCH now runs in

$$t(n) = O(\log(n + 1)/\log(N + 1)) + O(\log N).$$

In order to appreciate the effect of this additional $O(\log N)$ term, note that when $N = n$, $t(n) = O(\log n)$. In other words, procedure CREW SEARCH with n processors is no faster than procedure BINARY SEARCH, which runs on one processor!

Clearly, in order to maintain the efficiency of procedure CREW SEARCH while giving up the uniqueness assumption, we must run the algorithm on a CRCW SM SIMD computer with an appropriate write conflict resolution rule. Whatever the rule and no matter how many processors are successful in finding a member of S equal to x, only one index k will be returned, and that in constant time.

5.3 SEARCHING A RANDOM SEQUENCE

We now turn to the more general case of the search problem. Here the elements of the sequence $S = \{s_1, s_2, \ldots, s_n\}$ are not assumed to be in any particular order and are not necessarily distinct. As before, we have a file with n records that is to be searched using the s field of each record as the key. Given an integer x, a record is sought whose s field equals x; if such a record is found, then the information stored in the other fields may now be retrieved. This operation is referred to as *querying* the file. Besides querying, search is useful in file *maintenance*, such as inserting a new record and updating or deleting an existing record. Maintenance, as we shall see, is particularly easy when the s fields are in random order.

We begin by studying parallel search algorithms for shared-memory SIMD computers. We then show how the power of this model is not really needed for the search problem. As it turns out, performance similar to that of SM SIMD algorithms can be obtained using a tree-connected SIMD computer. Finally, we demonstrate that a mesh-connected computer is superior to the tree for searching if signal propagation time along wires is taken into account when calculating the running time of algorithms for both models.

5.3.1 Searching on SM SIMD Computers

The general algorithm for searching a sequence in random order on a SM SIMD computer is straightforward and similar in structure to the algorithm in section 5.2.1.

We have an N-processor computer to search $S = \{s_1, s_2, \ldots, s_n\}$ for a given element x, where $1 < N \leqslant n$. The algorithm is given as procedure SM SEARCH:

procedure SM SEARCH (S, x, k)

    Step 1:   **for** $i = 1$ **to** N **do in parallel**
               Read x
        end for.

    Step 2:   **for** $i = 1$ **to** N **do in parallel**
            (2.1) $S_i \leftarrow \{s_{(i-1)(n/N)+1}, s_{(i-1)(n/N)+2}, \ldots, s_{i(n/N)}\}$
            (2.2) SEQUENTIAL SEARCH (S_i, x, k_i)
        end for.

    Step 3:   **for** $i = 1$ **to** N **do in parallel**
              if $k_i > 0$ **then** $k \leftarrow k_i$ **end if**
        end for. ☐

Analysis

We now analyze procedure SM SEARCH for each of the four incarnations of the shared-memory model of SIMD computers.

    5.3.1.1 EREW.   Step 1 is implemented using procedure BROADCAST and requires $O(\log N)$ time. In step 2, procedure SEQUENTIAL SEARCH takes $O(n/N)$ time in the worst case. Finally, procedure STORE (with an appropriate conflict resolution rule) is used in step 3 and runs in $O(\log N)$ time. The overall asymptotic running time is therefore

$$t(n) = O(\log N) + O(n/N),$$

and the cost is

$$c(n) = O(N \log N) + O(n),$$

which is not optimal.

    5.3.1.2 ERCW.   Steps 1 and 2 are as in the EREW case, while step 3 now takes constant time. The overall asymptotic running time remains unchanged.

    5.3.1.3 CREW.   Step 1 now takes constant time, while steps 2 and 3 are as in the EREW case. The overall asymptotic running time remains unchanged.

    5.3.1.4 CRCW.   Both steps 1 and 3 take constant time, while step 2 is as in the EREW case. The overall running time is now $O(n/N)$, and the cost is

$$c(n) = N \times O(n/N) = O(n),$$

which is optimal.

In order to put the preceding results in perspective, let us consider a situation where the following two conditions hold:

1. There are as many processors as there are elements in S, that is, $N = n$.
2. There are q queries to be answered, that is, q values of x are queued waiting for processing.

In the case of the EREW, ERCW, and CREW models, the time to process one query is now $O(\log n)$. For q queries, this time is simply multiplied by a factor of q. This is of course an improvement over the time required by procedure SEQUENTIAL SEARCH, which would be on the order of qn. For the CRCW computer, procedure SM SEARCH now takes constant time. Thus q queries require a constant multiple of q time units to be answered.

Surprisingly, a performance slightly inferior to that of the CRCW algorithm but still superior to that of the EREW algorithm can be obtained using a much weaker model, namely, the tree-connected SIMD computer. Here a binary tree with $O(n)$ processors processes the queries in a pipeline fashion: Thus the q queries require a constant multiple of $\log n + (q - 1)$ time units to be answered. For large values of q (i.e., $q > \log n$), this behavior is equivalent to that of the CRCW algorithm. We now turn to the description of this tree algorithm.

5.3.2 Searching on a Tree

A tree-connected SIMD computer with n leaves is available for searching a file of n records. Such a tree is shown in Fig. 5.5 for $n = 16$. Each leaf of the tree stores one record of the file to be searched. The root is in charge of receiving input from the outside world and passing a copy of it to each of its two children. It is also responsible for producing output received from its two children to the outside world. As for the intermediate nodes, each of these is capable of:

1. receiving one input from its parent, making two copies of it, and sending one copy to each of its two children; and
2. receiving two inputs from its children, combining them, and passing the result to its parent.

The next two sections illustrate how the file stored in the leaves can be queried and maintained.

5.3.2.1 Querying.   Given an integer x, it is required to search the file of records on the s field for x, that is, determine whether there is a value in $S = \{s_1, s_2, \ldots, s_n\}$ equal to x. Such a query only requires a yes or no answer. This is the most basic form of querying and is even simpler than the one that we have been concerned with so far in this chapter. The tree-connected computer handles this query

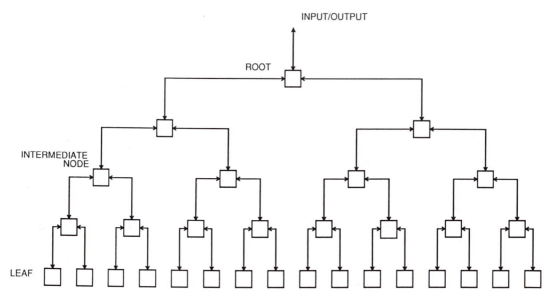

Figure 5.5 Tree-connected computer for searching.

in three stages:

> *Stage 1:* The root reads x and passes it to its two children. In turn, these send x to their children. The process continues until a copy of x reaches each leaf.
>
> *Stage 2:* Simultaneously, all leaves compare the s field of the record they store to x: If they are equal, the leaf produces a 1 as output: otherwise a 0 is produced.
>
> *Stage 3:* The outputs of the leaves are combined by going upward in the tree: Each intermediate node computes the logical **or** of its two inputs (i.e., 0 **or** 0 = 0, 0 **or** 1 = 1, 1 **or** 0 = 1, and 1 **or** 1 = 1) and passes the result to its parent. The process continues until the root receives two bits, computes their logical **or**, and produces either a 1 (for yes) or a 0 (for no).

It takes $O(\log n)$ time to go down the tree, constant time to perform the comparison at the leaves, and again $O(\log n)$ time to go back up the tree. Therefore, such a query is answered in $O(\log n)$ time.

Example 5.2

> Let $S = \{25, 14, 36, 18, 15, 17, 19, 17\}$ and $x = 17$. The three stages above are illustrated in Fig. 5.6. □

Assume now that q such queries are queued waiting to be processed. They can be pipelined down the tree since the root and intermediate nodes are free to handle the next query as soon as they have passed the current one along to their children. The same remark applies to the leaves: As soon as the result of one comparison has been

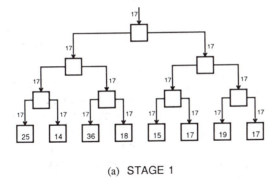

(a) STAGE 1

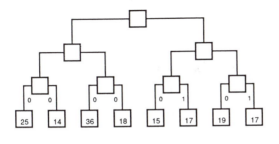

(b) STAGE 2

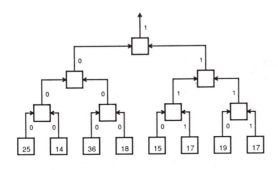

(c) STAGE 3

Figure 5.6 Searching sequence of eight elements using tree.

produced, each leaf is ready to receive a new value of x. The results are also pipelined upward: The root and intermediate nodes can compute the logical **or** of the next pair of bits as soon as the current pair has been cleared. Typically, the root and intermediate nodes will receive data flowing downward (queries) and upward (results) simultaneously: We assume that both can be handled in a single time unit; otherwise, and in order to keep both flows of data moving, a processor can switch its attention from one direction to the other alternately. It takes $O(\log n)$ time for the answer to the first query to be produced at the root. The answer to the second query is obtained in the following time unit. The answer to the last query emerges $q - 1$ time units after the first answer. Thus the q answers are obtained in a total of $O(\log n) + O(q)$ time.

We now examine some variations over the basic form of a query discussed so far.

1. *Position* If a query is successful and element s_k is equal to x, it may be desired to know the index k. Assume that the leaves are numbered $1, \ldots, n$ and that leaf i contains s_i. Following the comparison with x, leaf i produces the pair $(1, i)$ if $s_i = x$; otherwise it produces $(0, i)$. All intermediate nodes and the root now operate as follows. If two pairs $(1, i)$ and $(0, j)$ are received, then the pair $(1, i)$ is sent upward. Otherwise, if both pairs have a 1 as a first element or if both pairs have a 0 as a first element, then the pair arriving from the left son is sent upward. In this way, the root produces either

(i) $(1, k)$ where k is the smallest index of an element in S equal to x or
(ii) $(0, k)$ indicating that no match for x was found and, therefore, that the value of k is meaningless.

With this modification, the root in example 5.2 would produce $(1, 6)$.

This variant of the basic query can itself be extended in three ways:

(a) When a record is found whose s field equals x, it may be desirable to obtain the entire record as an answer to the query (or perhaps some of its fields). The preceding approach can be generalized by having the leaf that finds a match return a triple of the form $(1, i,$ required information$)$. The intermediate nodes and root behave as before.

(b) Sometimes, the positions of *all* elements equal to x in S may be needed. In this case, when an intermediate node, or the root, receives two pairs $(1, i)$ and $(1, j)$, *two* pairs are sent upward consecutively. In this way the indices of all members of S equal to x will eventually emerge from the root.

(c) The third extension is a combination of (a) and (b): All records whose s fields match x are to be retrieved. This is handled by combining the preceding two solutions

It should be noted, however, that for each of the preceding extensions care must be taken with regards to timing if several queries are being pipelined. This is because the result being sent upward by each node is no longer a single bit but rather many bits of information from potentially several records (in the worst case the answer consists of the n entire records). Since the answer to a query is now of unpredictable length, it is no longer guaranteed that a query will be answered in $O(\log n)$ time, that the period is constant, or that q queries will be processed in $O(\log n) + O(q)$ time.

2. *Count* Another variant of the basic query asks for the *number* of records whose s field equals x. This is handled exactly as the basic query, except that now the intermediate nodes and the root compute the sum of their inputs (instead of the logical **or**). With this modification, the root in example 5.2 would produce a 2.

3. *Closest Element* Sometimes it may be useful to find the element of S whose value is *closest* to x. As with the basic query, x is first sent to the leaves. Leaf i now computes the absolute value of $s_i - x$, call it a_i, and produces (i, a_i) as output.

Each intermediate node and the root now receive two pairs (i, a_i) and (j, a_j): The pair with the smaller a component is sent upward. With this modification and $x = 38$ as input, the root in example 5.2 would produce $(3, 2)$ as output. Note that the case of two pairs with identical a components is handled either by choosing one of the two arbitrarily or by sending both upward consecutively.

4. *Rank* The *rank* of an element x in S is defined as the number of elements of S smaller than x plus 1. We begin by sending x to the leaves and then having each leaf i produce a 1 if $s_i < x$, and a 0 otherwise. Now the rank of x in S is computed by making all intermediate nodes *add* their inputs and send the result upward. The root adds 1 to the sum of its two inputs before producing the rank. With this modification, the root's output in example 5.2 would be 3.

It should be emphasized that each of the preceding variants, if carefully timed, should have the same running time as the basic query (except, of course, when the queries being processed do not have constant-length answers as pointed out earlier).

5.3.2.2 Maintenance.   We now address the problem of maintaining a file of records stored at the leaves of a tree, that is, inserting a new record and updating or deleting an existing record.

1. *Insertion* In a typical file, records are inserted and deleted continually. It is therefore reasonable to assume that at any given time a number of leaves are unoccupied. We can keep track of the location of these unoccupied leaves by storing in each intermediate node and at the root

(i) the number of unoccupied leaves in its left subtree and
(ii) the number of unoccupied leaves in its right subtree.

A new record received by the root is inserted into an unoccupied leaf as follows:

(i) The root passes the record to the one of its two subtrees with unoccupied leaves. If both have unoccupied leaves, the root makes an arbitrary decision; if neither does, the root signals an *overflow* situation.
(ii) When an intermediate node receives the new record, it routes it to its subtree with unoccupied leaves (again, making an arbitrary choice, if necessary).
(iii) The new record eventually reaches an unoccupied leaf where it is stored.

Note that whenever the root, or an intermediate node, sends the new record to a subtree, the number of unoccupied leaves associated with that subtreee is decreased by

1. It should be clear that insertion is greatly facilitated by the fact that the file is not to be maintained in any particular order.

2. *Update* Say that every record whose *s* field equals *x* must be updated with new information in (some of) its other fields. This is accomplished by sending *x* and the new information to all leaves. Each leaf *i* for which $s_i = x$ implements the change.

3. *Deletion* If every record whose *s* field equals *x* must be deleted, then we begin by sending *x* to all leaves. Each leaf *i* for which $s_i = x$ now declares itself as unoccupied by sending a 1 to its parent. This information is carried upward until it reaches the root. On its way, it increments by 1 the appropriate count in each node of the number of unoccupied leaves in the left or right subtree.

Each of the preceding maintenance operations takes $O(\log n)$ time. As before, *q* operations can be pipelined to require $O(\log n) + O(q)$ time in total.

We conclude this section with the following observations.

1. We have obtained a search algorithm for a tree-connected computer that is more efficient than that described for a much stronger model, namely, the EREW SM SIMD. Is there a paradox here? Not really. What our result indicates is that we managed to find an algorithm that does not require the full power of the shared-memory model and yet is more efficient than an existing EREW algorithm. Since any algorithm for an interconnection network SIMD computer can be simulated on the shared-memory model, the tree algorithm for searching can be turned into an EREW algorithm with the same performance.

2. It may be objected that our comparison of the tree and shared-memory algorithms is unfair since we are using $2n - 1$ processors on the tree and only *n* on the EREW computer. This objection can be easily taken care of by using a tree with $n/2$ leaves and therefore a total of $n - 1$ processors. Each leaf now stores two records and performs two comparisons for every given *x*.

3. If a tree with *N* leaves is available, where $1 < N \leqslant n$, then n/N records are stored per leaf. A query now requires

  (i) $O(\log N)$ time to send *x* to the leaves,
 (ii) $O(n/N)$ time to search the records within each leaf for one with an *s* field equal to *x*, and
(iii) $O(\log N)$ time to send the answer back to the root,

that is, a total of $O(\log N) + O(n/N)$. This is identical to the time required by the algorithms that run on the more powerful EREW, ERCW, or CREW SM SIMD computers. Pipelining, however, is not as attractive as before: Searching within each leaf no longer requires constant time and *q* queries are not guaranteed to be answered in $O(\log n) + O(q)$ time.

4. Throughout the preceding discussion we have assumed that the *wire delay*, that is, the time it takes a datum to propagate along a wire, from one level of the tree to the next is a constant. Thus for a tree with n leaves, each query or maintenance operation under this assumption requires a running time of $O(\log n)$ to be processed. In addition, the time between two consecutive inputs or two consecutive outputs is constant: In other words, searching on the tree has a constant *period* (provided, of course, that the queries have constant-length answers). However, a direct hardware implementation of the tree-connected computer would obviously have connections between levels whose length grows exponentially with the level number. As Fig. 5.5 illustrates, the wire connecting a node at level i to its parent at level $i + 1$ has length proportional to 2^i. The maximum *wire length* for a tree with n leaves is $O(n)$ and occurs at level $\log n - 1$. Clearly, this approach is undesirable from a practical point of view, as it results in a very poor utilization of the *area* in which the processors and wires are placed. Furthermore, it would yield a running time of $O(n)$ per query if the propagation time is taken to be proportional to the wire length. In order to prevent this, we can embed the tree in a mesh, as shown in Fig. 5.7. Figure 5.7 illustrates an *n*-

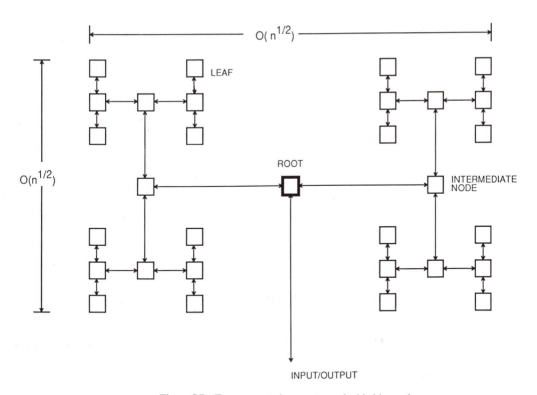

Figure 5.7   Tree-connected computer embedded in mesh.

node tree, with $n = 31$, where

(i) the maximum wire *length* is $O(n^{1/2})$,

(ii) the *area* used is $O(n)$, and

(iii) the *running time* per query or maintenance operation is $O(n^{1/2})$ and the *period* is $O(n^{1/2})$, assuming that the propagation time of a signal across a wire grows linearly with the length of the wire.

This is a definite improvement over the previous design, but not sufficiently so to make the tree the preferred architecture for search problems. In the next section we describe a parallel algorithm for searching on a mesh-connected SIMD computer whose behavior is superior to that of the tree algorithm under the linear propagation time assumption.

5.3.3 Searching on a Mesh

In this section we show how a two-dimensional array of processors can be used to solve the various searching problems described earlier. Consider the n-processor mesh-connected SIMD computer illustrated in Fig. 5.8 for $n = 16$, where each processor stores one record of the file to be searched. This architecture has the following characteristics:

1. The wire *length* is constant, that is, independent of the size of the array;

2. the *area* used is $O(n)$; and

3. the *running time* per query or maintenance operation is $O(n^{1/2})$ and the *period* is constant regardless of any assumption about wire delay.

Clearly, this behavior is a significant improvement over that of the tree architecture under the assumption that the propagation time of a signal along a wire is linearly proportional to the length of that wire. (Of course, if the wire delay is assumed to be a constant, then the tree is superior for the searching problem since $\log n < n^{1/2}$ for sufficiently large n.)

5.3.3.1 Querying. In order to justify the statement in 3 regarding the running time and period of query and maintenance operations on the mesh, we describe an algorithm for that architecture that solves the basic query problem; namely, given an integer x, it is required to search the file of records on the s field for x. We then show that the algorithm produces a yes or no answer to such a query in $O(n^{1/2})$ time and that q queries can be processed in $O(q) + O(n^{1/2})$ time. Let us denote by $s_{i,j}$ the s field of the record held by processor $P(i, j)$. The algorithm consists of two stages: unfolding and folding.

Unfolding. Processor $P(1, 1)$ reads x. If $x = s_{1,1}$, it produces an output $b_{1,1}$ equal to 1; otherwise $b_{1,1} = 0$. It then communicates $(b_{1,1}, x)$ to $P(1, 2)$. If $x = s_{1,2}$ or $b_{1,1} = 1$, then $b_{1,2} = 1$; otherwise $b_{1,2} = 0$. Now simultaneously, the two row

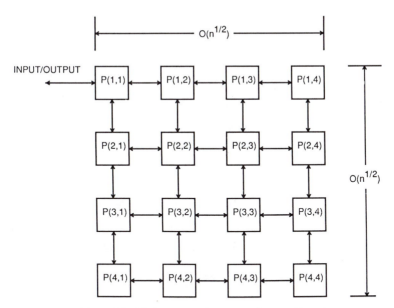

Figure 5.8 Mesh-connected computer for searching.

neighbors $P(1, 1)$ and $P(1, 2)$ send $(b_{1,1}, x)$ and $(b_{1,2}, x)$ to $P(2, 1)$ and $P(2, 2)$, respectively. Once $b_{2,1}$ and $b_{2,2}$ have been computed, the two column neighbors $P(1, 2)$ and $P(2, 2)$ communicate $(b_{1,2}, x)$ and $(b_{2,2}, x)$ to $P(1, 3)$ and $P(2, 3)$, respectively. This *unfolding* process, which alternates row and column propagation, continues until x reaches $P(n^{1/2}, n^{1/2})$.

Folding.   At the end of the unfolding stage every processor has had a chance to "see" x and compare it to the s field of the record it holds. In this second stage, the reverse action takes place. The output bits are propagated from row to row and from column to column in an alternating fashion, right to left and bottom to top, until the answer emerges from $P(1, 1)$. The algorithm is given as procedure MESH SEARCH:

procedure MESH SEARCH (S, x, answer)

    Step 1:   \{$P(1, 1)$ reads the input\}
                if $x = s_{1,1}$ **then** $b_{1,1} \leftarrow 1$
                                else $b_{1,1} \leftarrow 0$
        end if.

    Step 2:   \{Unfolding\}
                for $i = 1$ **to** $n^{1/2} - 1$ **do**
                    (2.1) **for** $j = 1$ **to** i **do in parallel**
                            (i) $P(j, i)$ transmits $(b_{j,i}, x)$ to $P(j, i + 1)$
                            (ii) **if** $(x = s_{j,i+1}$ **or** $b_{j,i} = 1)$ **then** $b_{j,i+1} \leftarrow 1$
                                                    else $b_{j,i+1} \leftarrow 0$
                        end if
                    end for

(2.2) **for** $j = 1$ **to** $i + 1$ **do in parallel**
    (i) $P(i, j)$ transmits $(b_{i,j}, x)$ to $P(i + 1, j)$
    (ii) **if** $(x = s_{i+1,j}$ **or** $b_{i,j} = 1)$ **then** $b_{i+1,j} \leftarrow 1$
                  else $b_{i+1,j} \leftarrow 0$
    end if
   end for
end for.

Step 3: {Folding}
   for $i = n^{1/2}$ **downto 2 do**
   (3.1) **for** $j = 1$ **to** i **do in parallel**
      $P(j, i)$ transmits $b_{j,i}$ to $P(j, i - 1)$
   end for
   (3.2) **for** $j = 1$ **to** $i - 1$ **do in parallel**
      $b_{j,i-1} \leftarrow b_{j,i}$
   end for
   (3.3) **if** $(b_{i,i-1} = 1$ **or** $b_{i,i} = 1)$ **then** $b_{i,i-1} \leftarrow 1$
                    else $b_{i,i-1} \leftarrow 0$
   end if
   (3.4) **for** $j = 1$ **to** $i - 1$ **do in parallel**
      $P(i, j)$ transmits $b_{i,j}$ to $P(i - 1, j)$
   end for
   (3.5) **for** $j = 1$ **to** $i - 2$ **do in parallel**
      $b_{i-1,j} \leftarrow b_{i,j}$
   end for
   (3.6) **if** $(b_{i-1,i-1} = 1$ **or** $b_{i,i-1} = 1)$ **then** $b_{i-1,i-1} \leftarrow 1$
                    else $b_{i-1,i-1} \leftarrow 0$
   end if
  end for.

Step 4: {$P(1,1)$ produces the output}
   if $b_{1,1} = 1$ **then** answer $\leftarrow$ yes
             else answer $\leftarrow$ no
   end if. $\square$

Analysis

As each of steps 1 and 4 takes constant time and steps 2 and 3 consist of $n^{1/2} - 1$ constant-time iterations, the time to process a query is $O(n^{1/2})$. Notice that after the first iteration of step 2, processor $P(1, 1)$ is free to receive a new query. The same remark applies to other processors in subsequent iterations. Thus queries can be processed in pipeline fashion. Inputs are submitted to $P(1, 1)$ at a constant rate. Since the answer to a basic query is of fixed length, outputs are also produced by $P(1, 1)$ at a constant rate following the answer to the first query. Hence the *period* is constant.

Example 5.3

Let a set of 16 records stored in a 4×4 mesh-connected SIMD computer be as shown in Fig. 5.9. Each square in Fig. 5.9(a) represents a processor and the number inside it is the s

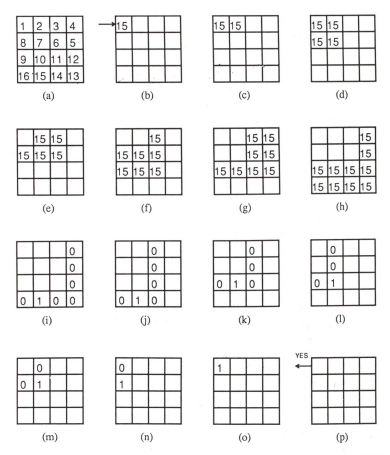

Figure 5.9 Searching sequence of sixteen elements using procedure MESH SEARCH.

field of the associated record. Wires connecting the processors are omitted for simplicity. It is required to determine whether there exists a record with s field equal to 15 (i.e., $x = 15$). Figures 5.9(b)–5.9(h) illustrate the propagation of 15 in the array. Figure 5.9(i) shows the relevant b values at the end of step 2. Figures 5.9(j)–5.9(o) illustrate the folding process. Finally Fig. 5.9(p) shows the result as produced in step 4. Note that in Fig. 5.9(e) processor $P(1, 1)$ is shown empty indicating that it has done its job propagating 15 and is now ready to receive a new query.   □

Some final comments are in order regarding procedure MESH SEARCH.

1. No justification was given for transmitting $b_{i,j}$ along with x during the unfolding stage. Indeed, if only one query is to be answered, no processor needs to communicate its b value to a neighbor: All processors can compute and retain their outputs; these can then be combined during the folding stage. However, if

several queries are to be processed in pipeline fashion, then each processor must first transmit its current b value before computing the next one. In this way the $b_{i,j}$ are continually moving, and no processor needs to store its b value.

2. When several queries are being processed in pipeline fashion, the folding stage of one query inevitably encounters the unfolding stage of another. As we did for the tree, we assume that a processor simultaneously receiving data from opposite directions can process them in a single time unit or that every processor alternately switches its attention from one direction to the other.

3. It should be clear that all variations over the basic query problem described in section 5.3.2.1 can be easily handled by minor modifications to procedure MESH SEARCH.

5.3.3.2 Maintenance. All three maintenance operations can be easily implemented on the mesh.

1. *Insertion* Each processor in the top row of the mesh keeps track of the number of unoccupied processors in its column. When a new record is to be inserted, it is propagated along the top row until a column is found with an unoccupied processor. The record is then propagated down the column and inserted in the first unoccupied processor it encounters. The number of unoccupied processors in that column is reduced by 1.

2. *Updating* All records to be updated are first located using procedure MESH SEARCH and then the change is implemented.

3. *Deletion* When a record is to be deleted, it is first located, an indicator is placed in the processor holding it signifying it is unoccupied, and the count at the processor in the top row of the column is incremented by 1.

5.4 PROBLEMS

5.1 Show that $\Omega(\log n)$ is a lower bound on the number of steps required to search a sorted sequence of n elements on an EREW SM SIMD computer with n processors.

5.2 Consider the following variant of the EREW SM SIMD model. In one step, a processor can perform an arbitrary number of computations locally or transfer an arbitrary number of data (to or from the shared memory). Regardless of the amount of processing (computations or data transfers) done, one step is assumed to take a constant number of time units. Note, however, that a processor is allowed to gain access to a unique memory location during each step (as customary for the EREW model). Let n processors be available on this model to search a sorted sequence $S = \{s_1, s_2, \ldots, s_n\}$ of length n for a given value x. Suppose that any subsequence of S can be encoded to fit in one memory location. Show that under these conditions the search can be performed in $O(\log^{1/2} n)$ time. [*Hint:* Imagine that the data structure used to store the sequence in shared memory is a binary tree, as shown in Fig. 5.10(a) for $n = 31$. This tree can be encoded as shown in Fig. 5.10(b).]

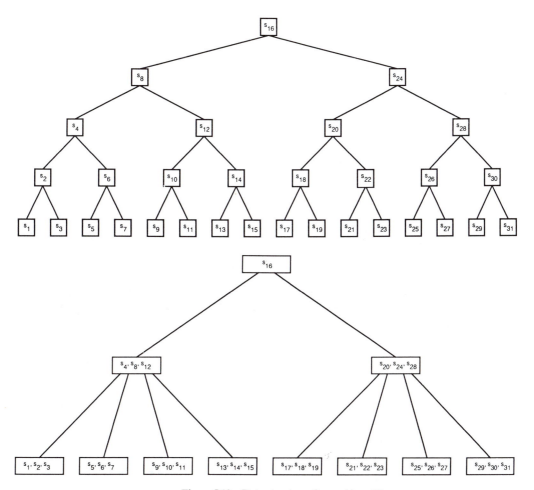

Figure 5.10 Data structures for problem 5.2.

5.3 Prove that $\Omega(\log^{1/2} n)$ is a lower bound on the number of steps required to search a sorted sequence of n elements using n processors on the EREW SM SIMD computer of problem 5.2.

5.4 Let us reconsider problem 5.2 but without the assumption that arbitrary subsequences of S can be encoded to fit in one memory location and communicated in one step. Instead, we shall store the sequence in a tree with d levels such that a node at level i contains $d - i$ elements of S and has $d - i + 1$ children, as shown in Fig. 5.11 for $n = 23$. Each node of this tree is assigned to a processor that has sufficient local memory to store the elements of S contained in that node. However, a processor can read only one element of S at every step. The key x to be searched for is initially available to the processor in charge of the root. An additional array in memory, with as many locations as there are processors, allows processor P_i to communicate x to P_j by depositing it in the location associated with P_j. Show that $O(n)$ processors can search a sequence of length n in $O(\log n / \log \log n)$.

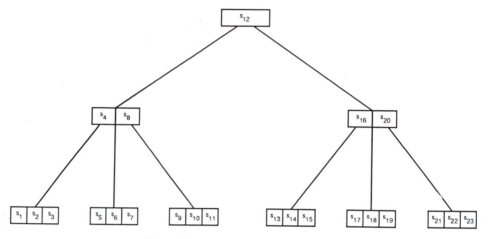

Figure 5.11   Data structure for problem 5.4.

5.5   Let $M(N, r, s)$ be the number of comparisons required by an N-processor CREW SM SIMD computer to merge two sorted sequences of length r and s, respectively. Prove that $M(N, 1, s) = \lceil \log(s + 1)/\log(N + 1) \rceil$.

5.6   Let $1 \leqslant r \leqslant N$ and $r \leqslant s$. Prove that

$$M(N, r, s) \leqslant \lceil \log(s + 1)/\log(\lfloor N/r \rfloor + 1) \rceil.$$

5.7   Let $1 \leqslant N \leqslant r \leqslant s$. Prove that

$$M(n, r, s) \leqslant \lceil r/N \rceil \lceil \log(s + 1) \rceil.$$

5.8   Consider an interconnection-network SIMD computer with n processors where each processor has a fixed-size local memory and is connected to each of the other $n - 1$ processors by a two-way link. At any given step a processor can perform any amount of computations locally but can communicate at most one input to at most one other processor. A sequence S is stored in this computer one element per processor. It is required to search S for an element x initially known to one of the processors. Show that $\Omega(\log n)$ steps are required to perform the search.

5.9   Assume that the size of the local memory of the processors in the network of problem 5.8 is no longer fixed. Show that if each processor can send or receive one element of S or x at a time, then searching S for some x can be done in $O(\log n/\log \log n)$ time.

5.10 Reconsider the model in problem 5.8 but without any restriction on the kind of information that can be communicated in one step from one processor to another. Show that in this case the search can be performed in $O(\log^{1/2} n)$ time.

5.11 Let the model of computation described in problem 2.9, that is, a linear array of N processors with a bus, be available. Each processor has a copy of a sorted sequence S of n distinct elements. Describe an algorithm for searching S for a given value x on this model and compare its running time to that of procedure CREW SEARCH.

5.12 An algorithm is described in example 1.4 for searching a file with n entries on a CRCW SM SIMD computer. The n entries are not necessarily distinct or sorted in any order. The algorithm uses a location F in shared memory to determine whether early termination is possible. Give a formal description of this algorithm.

5.13 Give a formal description of the tree algorithm for searching described in section 5.3.2.1.

5.14 Given a sequence S and a value x, describe tree algorithms for solving the following extensions to the basic query:

(a) Find the *predecessor* of x in S, that is, the largest element of S smaller than x.

(b) Find the *successor* of x in S, that is, the smallest element of S larger than x.

5.15 A file of n records is stored in the leaves of a tree machine one record per leaf. Each record consists of several fields. Given $((i, x_i), (j, x_j), \ldots, (m, x_m))$, it is required to find the records with the ith field equal to x_i, the jth field equal to x_j, and so on. Describe an algorithm for solving this version of the search problem.

5.16 Consider a tree-connected SIMD computer where each node contains a record (not just the leaves). Describe algorithms for querying and maintaining such a file of records.

5.17 Repeat problem 5.14 for a mesh-connected SIMD computer.

5.18 Consider the following modification to procedure MESH SEARCH. As usual, $P(1, 1)$ receives the input. During the unfolding stage processor $P(i, j)$ can send data simultaneously to $P(i + 1, j)$ and $P(i, j + 1)$. When the input reaches $P(n^{1/2}, n^{1/2})$, this processor can compute the final answer and produce it as output (i.e., there is no folding stage). Describe the modified procedure formally and analyze its running time.

5.19 Repeat problem 5.11 for the case where the number of processors is n and each processor stores one element of a sequence S of n distinct elements.

5.20 A binary sequence of length n consisting of a string of 0's followed by a string of 1's is given. It is required to find the length of the string of 0's using an EREW SM SIMD computer with N processors, $1 < N \leqslant n$. Show that this can be done in $O(\log(n/N))$ time.

5.21 In a storage and retrieval technique known as *hashing*, the location of a data element in memory is determined by its value. Thus, for every element x, the address of x is $f(x)$, where f is an appropriately chosen function. This approach is used when the data space (set of potential values to be stored) is larger than the storage space (memory locations) but not all data need be stored at once. Inevitably, *collisions* occur, that is, $f(x) = f(y)$ for $x \neq y$, and several strategies exist for resolving them. Describe a parallel algorithm for the hashing function, collision resolution strategy, and model of computation of your choice.

5.22 The algorithms in this chapter addressed the *discrete* search problem, that is, searching for a value in a given sequence. Similar algorithms can be derived for the *continuous* case, that is, searching for points at which a continuous function takes a given value. Describe parallel algorithms for locating (within a given tolerance) the point at which a certain function (i) assumes its largest value and (ii) is equal to zero.

5.23 It was shown in section 5.2.2 that procedure CREW SEARCH achieves the best possible running time for searching. In view of the lower bound in problem 5.1, show that no procedure faster than MULTIPLE BROADCAST of section 3.4 exists for simulating a CREW algorithm on an EREW computer.

5.5 BIBLIOGRAPHICAL REMARKS

The problem of searching a sorted sequence in parallel has attracted a good deal of attention since searching is an often-performed and time-consuming operation in most database, information retrieval, and office automation applications. Algorithms similar to procedure

CREW SEARCH for searching on the EREW and CREW models, as well as variations of these models, are described in [Coraor], [Kruskal], [Munro], and [Snir]. In [Baer] a parallel computer is described that consists of N processors connected via a switch to M memory blocks. During each computational step several processors can gain access to several memory blocks simultaneously, but no more than one processor can gain access to a given memory block (recall Fig. 1.4). A sorted sequence is distributed among the memory blocks. Various implementations of the binary search algorithm for this model are proposed in [Baer]. A brief discussion of how to speed up information retrieval operations through parallel processing is provided in [Salton 1].

Several algorithms for searching on a tree-connected computer are described in [Atallah], [Bentley], [Bonuccelli], [Chung], [Leiserson 1], [Leiserson 2], [Ottman], [Somani], and [Song]. Some of these algorithms allow for records to be stored in all nodes of the tree, while others allow additional connections among the nodes (such as, e.g., connecting the leaves as a linear array). The organization of a commercially available tree-connected computer for database applications is outlined in [Seaborn]. Also, various ways to implement tree-connected computers in VLSI are provided in [Bhatt] and [Schmeck 1]. An algorithm analogous to procedure MESH SEARCH can be found in [Schmeck 2]. The idea that the propagation time of a signal along a wire should be taken as a function of the length of the wire in parallel computational models is suggested in [Chazelle] and [Thompson].

Other parallel algorithms for searching on a variety of architectures are proposed in the literature. It is shown in [Kung 2], for example, how database operations such as intersection, duplicate removal, union, join, and division can be performed on one- and two-dimensional arrays of processors. Other parallel search algorithms are described in [Boral], [Carey], [Chang], [DeWitt 1], [DeWitt 2], [Ellis 1], [Ellis 2], [Fisher], [Hillyer], [Kim], [Lehman], [Potter], [Ramamoorthy], [Salton 2], [Schuster], [Stanfill], [Stone], [Su], [Tanaka], and [Wong]. In [Rudolph] and [Weller] the model of computation is a so-called *parallel pipelined* computer, which consists of N components of M processors each. Each component can initiate a comparison every $1/M$ units of time; thus up to NM comparisons may be in progress at one time. The algorithms in [Rudolph] and [Weller] implement a number of variations of binary search. Several questions related to querying and maintaining files on an MIMD computer are addressed in [Kung 1], [Kwong 1], and [Kwong 2]. Parallel hashing algorithms are presented in [Mühlbacher]. Finally, parallel search in the continuous case is the subject of [Gal] and [Karp].

5.6 REFERENCES

[ATALLAH]
Atallah, M. J., and Kosaraju, S. R., A generalized dictionary machine for VLSI, *IEEE Transactions on Computers*, Vol. C-34, No. 2, February 1985, pp. 151–155.

[BAER]
Baer, J.-L., Du, H. C., and Ladner, R. E., Binary Search in a multiprocessing environment, *IEEE Transactions on Computers*, Vol. C-32, No. 7, July 1983, pp. 667–676.

[BENTLEY]
Bentley, J. L., and Kung, H. T., Two papers on a tree-structured parallel computer, Technical Report No. CMU-CS-79-142, Department of Computer Science, Carnegie-Mellon University, Pittsburgh, August 1979.

[BHATT]
Bhatt, S. N., and Leiserson, C. E., How to assemble tree machines, Proceedings of the 14th Annual ACM Symposium on Theory of Computing, San Francisco, California, May 1982, pp. 77–84, Association for Computing Machinery, New York, N.Y., 1982.

[BONUCCELLI]
Bonuccelli, M. A., Lodi, E., Lucio, F., Maestrini, P., and Pagli, L., A VLSI tree machine for relational data bases, Proceedings of the 10th Annual ACM International Symposium on Computer Architecture, Stockholm, Sweden, June 1983, pp. 67–73, Association for Computing Machinery, New York, N.Y., 1983.

[BORAL]
Boral, H., and DeWitt, D. J., Database machines: An idea whose time has passed? A critique of the future of database machines, in Leilich, H. O., and Missikoff, M., Eds., *Database Machines*, Springer-Verlag, Berlin, 1983.

[CAREY]
Carey, M. J., and Thompson, C. D., An efficient implementation of search trees on $\lceil \log N + 1 \rceil$ processors, *IEEE Transactions on Computers*, Vol. C-33, No. 11, November 1984, pp. 1038–1041.

[CHANG]
Chang, S.-K., Parallel balancing of binary search trees, *IEEE Transactions on Computers*, Vol. C-23, No. 4, April 1974, pp. 441–445.

[CHAZELLE]
Chazelle, B., and Monier, L., A model of computation for VLSI with related complexity results, *Journal of the ACM*, Vol. 32, No. 3, July 1985, pp. 573–588.

[CHUNG]
Chung, K. M., Lucio, F., and Wong, C. K., Magnetic bubble memory structures for efficient sorting and searching, in Lavington, S. H., Ed., *Information Processing 80*, North-Holland, Amsterdam, 1980.

[CORAOR]
Coraor, L. D., A multiprocessor organization for large data list searches, Ph.D. thesis, Department of Electrical Engineering, University of Iowa, Iowa City, July 1978.

[DEWITT 1]
DeWitt, D. J., DIRECT—a multiprocessor organization for supporting relational database management systems, *IEEE Transactions on Computers*, Vol. C-28, No. 6, June 1979, pp. 395–406.

[DEWITT 2]
DeWitt, D. J., and Hawthorn, P. B., A performance evaluation of database machine architectures, Proceedings of the 7th International Conference on Very Large Data Bases, Cannes, France, September 1981, pp. 199–213, VLDB Endowment, Cannes, France, 1981.

[ELLIS 1]
Ellis, C., Concurrent search and insertion in 2-3 trees, *Acta Informatica*, Vol. 14, 1980, pp. 63–86.

[ELLIS 2]
Ellis, C., Concurrent search and insertion in AVL trees, *IEEE Transactions on Computers*, Vol. C-29, No. 9, September 1980, pp. 811–817.

[FISHER]
Fisher, A. L., Dictionary machines with a small number of processors, Proceedings of the

11th Annual ACM International Symposium on Computer Architecture, Ann Arbor, Michigan, June 1984, pp. 151–156, Association for Computing Machinery, New York, N.Y., 1984.

[GAL]

Gal, S., and Miranker, W. L., Optimal sequential and parallel search for finding a root, *Journal of Combinatorial Theory (A)*, Vol. 23, 1977, pp. 1–14.

[HILLYER]

Hillyer, B. K., Shaw, D. E., and Nigam, A., NOV-VON's performance on certain database benchmarks, *IEEE Transactions on Software Engineering*, Vol. SE-12, No. 4, April 1986, pp. 577–583.

[KARP]

Karp, R. M., and Miranker, W. L., Parallel minimax search for a maximum, *Journal of Combinatorial Theory*, Vol. 4, 1968, pp. 19–35.

[KIM]

Kim, W., Gajski, D., and Kuck, D. J., A parallel-pipelined query processor, *ACM Transactions on Database Systems*, Vol. 9, No. 2, June 1984, pp. 214–242.

[KRUSKAL]

Kruskal, C. P., Searching, merging, and sorting in parallel computation, *IEEE Transactions on Computers*, Vol. C-32, No. 10, October 1983, pp. 942–946.

[KUNG 1]

Kung, H. T., and Lehman, P. L., Concurrent manipulation of binary search trees, *ACM Transactions on Database Systems*, Vol. 5, No. 3, September 1980, pp. 354–382.

[KUNG 2]

Kung, H. T., and Lehman, P. L., Systolic (VLSI) arrays for relational database operations, Technical Report No. CMU-CS-80-114, Department of Computer Science, Carnegie-Mellon University, Pittsburgh, 1980.

[KWONG 1]

Kwong, Y. S., and Wood, D., Concurrency in B-trees, S-trees and T-trees, Technical Report No. 79-CS-17, Unit for Computer Science, McMaster University, Hamilton, Ontario, 1979.

[KWONG 2]

Kwong, Y. S., and Wood, D., On B-trees: Routing schemes and concurrency, Technical Report No. 80-CS-5, Unit for Computer Science, McMaster University, Hamilton, Ontario, 1980.

[LEHMAN]

Lehman, P. L., and Yao, S. B., Efficient locking for concurrent operations on B-trees, *ACM Transactions on Database Systems*, Vol. 6, No. 4, December 1981, pp. 650–670.

[LEISERSON 1]

Leiserson, C. E., Systolic priority queues, Technical Report No. CMU-CS-79-115, Department of Computer Science, Carnegie-Mellon University, Pittsburgh, 1979.

[LEISERSON 2]

Leiserson, C. E., *Area-Efficient VLSI Computation*, MIT Press, Cambridge, Mass., 1983.

[MÜHLBACHER]

Mühlbacher, J. R., Full table scatter storage parallel searching, *Computing*, Vol. 26, 1986, pp. 9–18.

[MUNRO]

Munro, J. I., and Robertson, E. L., Parallel algorithms and serial data structures, *Proceedings of the 17th Annual Allerton Conference on Communications, Control and Computing,* Monticello, Illinois, October 1979, pp. 21–26, University of Illinois, Urbana-Champaign, Illinois, 1979.

[OTTMAN]

Ottman, T. A., Rosenberg, A. L., and Stockmeyer, L. J., A dictionary machine (for VLSI), *IEEE Transactions on Computers,* Vol. C-31, No. 9, September 1982, pp. 892–897.

[POTTER]

Potter, J. L., Programming the MPP, in Potter, J. L., Ed., *The Massively Parallel Processor,* MIT Press, Cambridge, Mass., 1985, pp. 218–229.

[RAMAMOORTHY]

Ramamoorthy, C. V., Turner, J. L., and Wah, B. W., A design of a fast cellular associative memory for ordered retrieval, *IEEE Transactions on Computers,* Vol. C-27, No. 9, September 1978, pp. 800–815.

[RUDOLPH]

Rudolph, D., and Schlosser, K.-H., Optimal searching algorithms for parallel pipelined computers, in Feilmeier, M., Joubert, J., and Schendel, U., Eds., *Parallel Computing 83,* North-Holland, Amsterdam, 1984.

[SALTON 1]

Salton, G., Automatic information retrieval, *Computer,* Vol. 13, No. 9, September 1980, pp. 41–56.

[SALTON 2]

Salton, G., and Buckley, C., Parallel text search methods, *Communications of the ACM,* Vol. 31, No. 2, February 1988, pp. 202–215.

[SCHMECK 1]

Schmeck, H., On the maximum edge length in VLSI layouts of complete binary trees, *Information Processing Letters,* Vol. 23, No. 1, July 1986, pp. 19–23.

[SCHMECK 2]

Schmeck, H., and Schröder, H., Dictionary machines for different models of VLSI, *IEEE Transactions on Computers,* Vol. C-34, No. 2, February 1985, pp. 151–155.

[SCHUSTER]

Schuster, S. A., Ngyuen, H. B., and Ozkarahan, E. A., RAP.2: An associative processor for databases and its applications, *IEEE Transactions on Computers,* Vol. C-28, No. 6, June 1979, pp. 446–458.

[SEABORN]

Seaborn, T., The genesis of a database computer, *Computer,* Vol. 17, No. 11, November 1984, pp. 42–56.

[SNIR]

Snir, M., On parallel searching, *SIAM Journal on Computing,* Vol. 14, No. 3, August 1985, pp. 688–708.

[SOMANI]

Somani, A. K., and Agarwal, V. K., An efficient VLSI dictionary machine, *Proceedings of the 11th Annual ACM International Symposium on Computer Architecture,* Ann Arbor, Michigan, June 1984, pp. 142–150, Association for Computing Machinery, New York, N.Y., 1984.

[SONG]

Song, S. W., A highly concurrent tree machine for database applications, Proceedings of the 1980 International Conference on Parallel Processing, Harbor Springs, Michigan, August 1980, pp. 259–268, IEEE Computer Society, Washington, D.C., 1980.

[STANFILL]

Stanfill, C., and Kahle, B., Parallel free text search on the connection machine system, *Communications of the ACM*, Vol. 29, No. 12, December 1986, pp. 1229–1239.

[STONE]

Stone, H. S., Parallel querying of large databases: A case study, *Computer*, Vol. 20, No. 10, October 1987, pp. 11–21.

[SU]

Su, S. Y. W., Associative programming in CASSM and its applications, Proceedings of the 3rd International Conference on Very Large Data Bases, Tokyo, Japan, October 1977, pp. 213–228, VLDB Endowment, Tokyo, Japan, 1977.

[TANAKA]

Tanaka, Y., Nozaka, Y., and Masuyama, A., Pipeline searching and sorting modules as components of a data flow database computer, in Lavington, S. H., Ed., *Information Processing 80*, North-Holland, Amsterdam, 1980.

[THOMPSON]

Thompson, C. D., The VLSI complexity of sorting, *IEEE Transactions on Computers*, Vol. C-32, No. 12, December 1983, pp. 1171–1184.

[WELLER]

Weller, D. L., and Davidson, E. S., Optimal searching algorithms for parallel-pipelined computers, in Goos, G., and Hartmanis, J., Ed., *Parallel Processing*, Springer-Verlag, Berlin, 1975, pp. 291–305.

[WONG]

Wong, C. K., and Chang, S.-K., Parallel generation of binary search trees, *IEEE Transactions on Computers*, Vol. C-23, No. 3, March 1974, pp. 268–271.

6

Generating Permutations and Combinations

6.1 INTRODUCTION

The enumeration of combinatorial objects occupies an important place in computer science due to its many applications in science and engineering. In this chapter we describe a number of parallel algorithms for the two fundamental problems of generating permutations and combinations. We begin with some definitions.

Let S be a set consisting of n distinct items, say, the first n positive integers; thus $S = \{1, 2, \ldots, n\}$. An m-*permutation* of S is obtained by selecting m distinct integers out of the n and arranging them in some order. Thus for $n = 10$ and $m = 4$, a 4-permutation might be (5 7 9 2). Two m-permutations are *distinct* if they differ with respect to the items they contain or with respect to the order of the items. The number of distinct m-permutations of n items is denoted by ^nP_m, where

$$^nP_m = n!/(n - m)!.$$

Thus for $n = 4$, there are twenty-four distinct 3-permutations. Note that when $m = n$, $^nP_n = n!$.

Now let $x = (x_1 x_2 \ldots x_m)$ and $y = (y_1 y_2 \ldots y_m)$ be two m-permutations of S. We say that x *precedes* y *in lexicographic order* if there exists an i, $1 \leqslant i \leqslant m$, such that $x_j = y_j$ for all $j < i$ and $x_i < y_i$. The 3-permutations of $\{1, 2, 3, 4\}$ in lexicographic order are

$$
\begin{array}{cccc}
(1\ 2\ 3), & (1\ 2\ 4), & (1\ 3\ 2), & (1\ 3\ 4), \\
(1\ 4\ 2), & (1\ 4\ 3), & (2\ 1\ 3), & (2\ 1\ 4), \\
(2\ 3\ 1), & (2\ 3\ 4), & (2\ 4\ 1), & (2\ 4\ 3), \\
(3\ 1\ 2), & (3\ 1\ 4), & (3\ 2\ 1), & (3\ 2\ 4), \\
(3\ 4\ 1), & (3\ 4\ 2), & (4\ 1\ 2), & (4\ 1\ 3), \\
(4\ 2\ 1), & (4\ 2\ 3), & (4\ 3\ 1), & (4\ 3\ 2).
\end{array}
$$

Note that, since $S = \{1, 2, 3, 4\}$, lexicographic order coincides with increasing numerical order. Had the elements of S been letters of the alphabet, lexicographic order would have been equivalent to the order used to list words in a dictionary.

An *m-combination* of S is obtained by selecting m distinct integers out of the n and arranging them in increasing order. Thus for $n = 6$ and $m = 3$, one 3-combination is (2 4 5). Two *m-combinations* are *distinct* if they differ with respect to the items they contain. The number of distinct *m-combinations* of n items is denoted by ^nC_m [and sometimes $\binom{n}{m}$], where

$$^nC_m = n!/(n - m)!\,m!.$$

Thus for $n = 4$, there are four distinct 3-combinations. Since *m-combinations* are a special case of *m-permutations*, the definition of lexicographic order applies to them as well. The 3-combinations of $\{1, 2, 3, 4\}$ in lexicographic order are

$$(1\ 2\ 3), \qquad (1\ 2\ 4), \qquad (1\ 3\ 4), \qquad (2\ 3\ 4).$$

It should be clear that each of the two integers ^nP_m and ^nC_m can be computed sequentially in $O(m)$ time.

This chapter addresses the problems of generating all *m-permutations* and *m-combinations* of n items in lexicographic order. We begin by describing a number of sequential algorithms in section 6.2. Two of these algorithms are concerned with generating *m-permutations* and *m-combinations* in lexicographic order, respectively. The other algorithms in section 6.2 implement two numbering systems that associate a unique integer with each *m-permutation* and each *m-combination*, respectively. Three parallel *m-permutation* generation algorithms for the EREW SM SIMD model of computation are described in section 6.3. The first of these algorithms is a direct parallelization of the sequential algorithm in section 6.2. It uses m processors and runs in $O(^nP_m\log m)$ time. The second algorithm is based on the numbering system for *m-permutations* described in section 6.2 and is both adaptive and cost optimal. It uses N processors, where $1 < N \leqslant {}^nP_m/n$, and runs in $O(\lceil {}^nP_m/N\rceil m)$ time. The third algorithm applies to the case where $m = n$; it uses N processors, where $1 < N \leqslant n$, and runs in $O(\lceil n!/N\rceil n)$ time for an optimal cost of $O(n!\,n)$. Section 6.4 is devoted to two parallel *m-combination* generation algorithms for EREW SM SIMD computers. The first uses m processors and runs in $O(^nC_m\log m)$ time. This algorithm is neither adaptive nor cost optimal. The second algorithm enjoys both of these properties and is based on the numbering system for *m-combinations* described in section 6.2. It uses N processors, where $1 < N \leqslant {}^nC_m/n$, and runs in $O(\lceil {}^nC_m/N\rceil m)$ time.

6.2 SEQUENTIAL ALGORITHMS

In this section we describe a number of sequential algorithms. The first algorithm generates all *m-permutations* of n items in lexicographic order. We also show how all *m-permutations* of n items can be put into one-to-one correspondence with the integers $1, \ldots, {}^nP_m$. Two algorithms, one for mapping a given permutation to an integer and another that performs the inverse mapping, are described. We then move to combination-related algorithms. Three algorithms are described: The first generates all m-combinations of n items in lexicographic order; the second maps a given combination to a unique integer $1, \ldots, {}^nC_m$; and the third generates a unique combination corresponding to a given integer $1, \ldots, {}^nC_m$. All the algorithms presented in this section will then be used in our development of parallel permutation and combination generation algorithms. We continue to assume that $S = \{1, 2, \ldots, n\}$.

6.2.1 Generating Permutations Lexicographically

Our algorithm for generating all m-permutations of $\{1, 2, \ldots, n\}$ proceeds as follows. Beginning with the permutation $(1\,2\ldots m)$ all m-permutations are generated in lexicographic order, until the last permutation, namely, $(n\,n-1\ldots n-m+1)$, is generated. Given $(p_1\,p_2\ldots p_m)$ the next permutation is obtained by calling a procedure NEXT PERMUTATION. This procedure uses a bit array $u = u_1,\ u_2, \ldots, u_n$ as follows:

   (i) When the procedure begins execution all the entries of u are 1.
   (ii) For each element p_i in the given permutation $(p_1\,p_2\ldots p_m)$, if $p_i = j$, then u_j is set to 0.
   (iii) When the procedure terminates, all entries of u are 1.

In order to generate the next permutation, the procedure begins by determining whether the current permutation is *updatable*. A permutation $(p_1\,p_2\ldots p_m)$ is updatable if for at least one of its elements p_i there exists a j such that $p_i < j \leqslant n$ and $u_j = 1$. Thus the only permutation that is not updatable is $(n\,n-1\ldots n-m+1)$. Having determined that a permutation $(p_1\,p_2\ldots p_m)$ is updatable, the rightmost element p_i and the smallest index j for which the preceding condition holds are located: p_i is made equal to j and u_j to 0. All the elements $p_{i+1}, p_{i+2}, \ldots, p_m$ to the *right* of p_i are now updated. This is done as follows: $p_{i+k}, 1 \leqslant k \leqslant m - i$, is made equal to s if u_s is the kth position in u that is equal to 1. The algorithm is given as procedure SEQUENTIAL PERMUTATIONS followed by procedure NEXT PERMUTATION, which it calls:

procedure SEQUENTIAL PERMUTATIONS (n, m)

   Step 1:   (1.1) $(p_1 p_2 \ldots p_m) \leftarrow (1\ 2 \ldots m)$
   　　　　 (1.2) produce $(p_1\,p_2\ldots p_m)$ as output
   　　　　 (1.3) $u_1, u_2, \ldots, u_n \leftarrow (1, 1, \ldots, 1)$.

   Step 2:   **for** $i = 1$ **to** $({}^nP_m - 1)$ **do**
   　　　　　　 NEXT PERMUTATION $(n, m, p_1, p_2, \ldots, p_m)$
   　　　　 end for. $\square$

procedure NEXT PERMUTATION $(n, m, p_1, p_2, \ldots, p_m)$

if $(p_1 \, p_2 \ldots p_m) \neq (n \, n - 1 \ldots n - m + 1)$

then (1) **for** $i = 1$ **to** m **do**

$$u_{p_i} \leftarrow 0$$

end for

(2) $f \leftarrow n$

(3) {Find the largest unused integer}

while $u_f \neq 1$ **do**

$$f \leftarrow f - 1$$

end while

(4) $k \leftarrow m + 1$

(5) $i \leftarrow 0$

(6) {Find rightmost updatable element}

while $i = 0$ **do**

(6.1) $k \leftarrow k - 1$

(6.2) $u_{p_k} \leftarrow 1$

(6.3) **if** $p_k < f$

     then {update p_k}

         (i) find smallest j such that

$$p_k < j \leqslant n \text{ and } u_j = 1$$

         (ii) $i \leftarrow k$

         (iii) $p_i \leftarrow j$

         (iv) $u_{p_i} \leftarrow 0$

     else {largest unused integer is set equal to p_k}

$$f \leftarrow p_k$$

     end if

end while

(7) {Update elements to the right of p_i}

for $k = 1$ **to** $m - i$ **do**

if u_s is kth position in u that is 1

then $p_{i+k} \leftarrow s$

end if

end for

(8) {Reinitialize array u}

for $k = 1$ **to** i **do**

$$u_{p_k} \leftarrow 1$$

end for

(9) produce $(p_1 \, p_2 \ldots p_m)$ as output

end if. □

Analysis. Procedure SEQUENTIAL PERMUTATIONS consists of one execution of step 1 requiring $O(n)$ time and $^nP_m - 1$ executions of step 2. In step 2 each call to procedure NEXT PERMUTATION performs $O(m)$ steps. This can be seen as follows. Steps 1, 3, 8, and 9 take $O(m)$ time, while steps 2, 4, and 5 require constant time. Since only m positions of array u are 0 after step 1, both steps 6 and 7 take $O(m)$ steps. The overall running time of procedure SEQUENTIAL PERMUTATIONS is $O(^nP_m m)$. This behavior is optimal in view of the fact that $\Omega(^nP_m m)$ time is required to produce ^nP_m lines of output, each m elements long.

6.2.2 Numbering Permutations

We now show that a one-to-one correspondence exists between the integers $1, \ldots, {}^nP_m$ and the set of m-permutations of $\{1, 2, \ldots, m\}$ listed in lexicographic order. Specifically, we define a function *rankp* with the following properties:

(i) Let $(p_1 \, p_2 \ldots p_m)$ be one of the ${}^nP_m$ m-permutations of $\{1, 2, \ldots, n\}$; then $\text{rankp}(p_1, p_2, \ldots, p_m)$ is an integer in $\{1, 2, \ldots, {}^nP_m\}$.

(ii) Let $(p_1 \, p_2 \, \cdots \, p_m)$ and $(q_1 \, q_2 \, \cdots \, q_m)$ be two m-permutations of $\{1, 2, \ldots, n\}$; then $(p_1 \, p_2 \, \cdots \, p_m)$ precedes $(q_1 \, q_2 \, \cdots \, q_m)$ lexicographically if and only if $\text{rankp}(p_1, p_2, \ldots, p_m) < \text{rankp}(q_1, q_2, \ldots, q_m)$.

(iii) Let $d = \text{rankp}(p_1, p_2, \ldots, p_m)$; then $(p_1 \, p_2 \ldots p_m)$ can be obtained from $\text{rankp}^{-1}(d)$, that is, rankp is invertible, as can be deduced from (i) and (ii).

For the permutation $(p_1 \, p_2 \ldots p_m)$ define the sequence $\{r_1, r_2, \ldots, r_m\}$ as follows:

$$r_i = p_i - i + \sum_{j=1}^{i-1} [p_i < p_j] \quad \text{where } [p_i < p_j] = \begin{cases} 1 & \text{if } p_i < p_j, \\ 0 & \text{otherwise.} \end{cases}$$

The string $r_1 r_2 \ldots r_m$ can be seen as a mixed radix integer where

$$0 \leqslant r_m \leqslant n - m,$$
$$0 \leqslant r_{m-1} \leqslant n - m + 1,$$
$$\vdots$$
$$0 \leqslant r_2 \leqslant n - 2,$$
$$0 \leqslant r_1 \leqslant n - 1.$$

Expressing $r_1 r_2 \ldots r_m$ as a decimal number gives us the integer corresponding to $(p_1 \, p_2 \ldots p_m)$:

$$\text{rankp}(p_1, p_2, \ldots, p_m) = 1 + \sum_{i=1}^{m-1} r_i \prod_{j=0}^{m-i-1} (n - i - j).$$

Let $d = \text{rankp}(p_1, p_2, \ldots, p_m)$; the permutation $(p_1 \, p_2 \ldots p_m)$ can be obtained from d as follows. A sequence $\{r_1, r_2, \ldots, r_m\}$ is computed from

$$r_i = \left\lfloor \left(d - 1 - \sum_{j=1}^{i-1} r_j \prod_{k=0}^{m-j-1} (n - j - k) \right) \bigg/ \prod_{k=0}^{m-i-1} (n - i - k) \right\rfloor \quad \text{for } i = 1, 2, \ldots, m.$$

Then $(p_1 \, p_2 \ldots p_m)$ is defined recursively by

$$p_i = r_i + i - d_i \quad \text{for } i = 1, 2, \ldots, m,$$

where d_i is the smallest nonnegative integer such that

$$d_i = \sum_{j=1}^{i-1} [r_i + i - d_i < p_j].$$

Functions rankp and rankp^{-1} are given below as procedures **RANKP** and **RANKPINV**, respectively.

procedure RANKP $(n, m, p_1, p_2, \ldots, p_m, d)$

Step 1: **for** $i = 1$ **to** m **do**
    (1.1) $d \leftarrow -i$
    (1.2) **for** $j = 1$ **to** $i - 1$ **do**
        if $p_i < p_j$ **then** $d \leftarrow d + 1$ **end if**
    end for
    (1.3) $s_i \leftarrow p_i + d$
  end for.

Step 2: $d \leftarrow s_m.$

Step 3: $i \leftarrow 1.$

Step 4: **for** $j = m - 1$ **downto** 1 **do**
    (4.1) $i \leftarrow (n - j) \times i$
    (4.2) $d \leftarrow d + (s_j \times i)$
  end for.

Step 5: $d \leftarrow d + 1.$ $\square$

procedure RANKPINV $(n, m, d, p_1, p_2, \ldots, p_m)$

Step 1: $d \leftarrow d - 1.$

Step 2: **for** $i = 1$ **to** n **do**
    $s_i \leftarrow 0$
  end for.

Step 3: $a \leftarrow 1.$

Step 4: **for** $i = m - 1$ **downto** 1 **do**
    $a \leftarrow a \times (n - m + i)$
  end for.

Step 5: **for** $i = 1$ **to** m **do**
    (5.1) $b \leftarrow \lfloor d/a \rfloor$
    (5.2) $d \leftarrow d - (a \times b)$
    (5.3) **if** $n > i$ **then** $a \leftarrow a/(n - i)$ **end if**
    (5.4) $k \leftarrow 0$
    (5.5) $j \leftarrow 0$
    (5.6) {Find the $(b + 1)$st position in s equal to 0}
        while $k < b + 1$ **do**
            (i) $j \leftarrow j + 1$
            (ii) **if** $s_j = 0$ **then** $k \leftarrow k + 1$ **end if**
        end while
    (5.7) $p_i \leftarrow j$
    (5.8) $s_j \leftarrow 1$
  end for. $\square$

Analysis.   In procedure RANKP, steps 2, 3, and 5 take constant time while step 4 consists of a constant time loop executed m times. Step 1 consists of two nested $O(m)$ time loops plus two constant time steps. The procedure therefore requires $O(m^2)$ time. The running time of procedure RANKPINV is dominated by step 5, which requires $O(mn)$ time.

6.2.3 Generating Combinations Lexicographically

We now give a sequential algorithm for generating all m-combinations of $\{1, 2, \ldots, n\}$ in lexicographic order. The algorithm begins by generating the initial combination, namely $(1\,2\ldots m)$. Then, every one of the $^nC_m - 1$ subsequent m-combinations is derived from its predecessor $(c_1\,c_2\ldots c_m)$ as follows. First observe that the last combination to be generated is $((n-m+1)(n-m+2)\ldots n)$. A combination $(c_1\,c_2\ldots c_m)$ is therefore *updatable* if for some j, $1 \leqslant j \leqslant m$, $c_j < n - m + j$. If $(c_1\,c_2\ldots c_m)$ is updatable, then the largest j satisfying the above condition is determined. The next combination in lexicographic order can now be obtained by

1. incrementing c_j by one, and
2. setting $c_{j+1} \leftarrow c_j + 1$, $c_{j+2} \leftarrow c_{j+1} + 1, \ldots, c_m \leftarrow c_{m-1} + 1$.

The algorithm is given below as procedure SEQUENTIAL COMBINATIONS along with procedure NEXT COMBINATIONS which it calls.

procedure SEQUENTIAL COMBINATIONS (n, m)

Step 1:   (1.1) $(c_1\,c_2\ldots c_m) \leftarrow (1\,2\ldots m)$
           (1.2) produce $(c_1\,c_2\ldots c_m)$ as output.

Step 2:   **for** $i = 1$ **to** $^nC_m - 1$ **do**
                 NEXT COMBINATION $(n, m, c_1, c_2, \ldots, c_m)$
           end for.   □

procedure NEXT COMBINATION $(n, m, c_1, c_2, \ldots, c_m)$

Step 1: $j \leftarrow m$.

Step 2:   **while** $(j > 0)$ **do**
                 if $c_j < n - m + j$
                 then
                     (2.1) $c_j \leftarrow c_j + 1$
                     (2.2) **for** $i = j + 1$ **to** m **do**
                               $c_i \leftarrow c_{i-1} + 1$
                           end for
                     (2.3) produce $(c_1\,c_2\ldots c_m)$ as output
                 else $j \leftarrow j - 1$
                 end if
           end while.   □

Analysis. Procedure NEXT COMBINATION scans a given m-combination once from right to left and then (from an updatable position) left to right. This takes $O(m)$ steps in the worst case. Procedure SEQUENTIAL COMBINATIONS requires $O(m)$ time in step 1 to produce the initial permutation. Step 2 consists of $^nC_m - 1$ iterations each of which is a call to procedure NEXT COMBINATION and thus requires $O(m)$ time. The overall running time of procedure SEQUENTIAL COMBINATIONS is $O(^nC_m m)$. This behavior is optimal since $\Omega(^nC_m m)$ steps are required to produce ^nC_m lines of output, each m elements long.

6.2.4 Numbering Combinations

As we did with m-permutations, we now show that a one-to-one correspondence exists between the integers $1, \ldots, ^nC_m$ and the set of m-combinations of $\{1, 2, \ldots, n\}$ listed in lexicographic order. Let $(c_1 c_2 \ldots c_m)$ represent one such combination (where, by definition, $c_1 < c_2 < \cdots < c_m$). We define

$$\text{complement}(n, c_1, c_2, \ldots, c_m) = (d_1 d_2 \ldots d_m)$$

as the *complement* of $(c_1 c_2 \ldots c_m)$ with respect to $\{1, 2, \ldots, n\}$, where

$$d_i = (n + 1) - c_{m-i+1}.$$

The following function takes n and $(c_1 c_2 \ldots c_m)$ as input and returns $(d_1 d_2 \ldots d_m)$ as output in $O(m)$ time.

> **function** COMPLEMENT $(n, c_1, c_2, \ldots, c_m)$
>
> Step 1: **for** $i = 1$ **to** m **do**
> $$d_i \leftarrow (n + 1) - c_{m-i+1}$$
> **end for.**
>
> Step 2: COMPLEMENT $\leftarrow (d_1 d_2 \ldots d_m)$. □

Now let the *reverse* of $(c_1 c_2 \ldots c_m)$ be given by $(c_m c_{m-1} \ldots c_2 c_1)$. The mapping

$$\text{order}(c_1, c_2, \ldots, c_m) = \sum_{i=1}^{m} {}^{c_i - 1}C_i$$

has the following properties:

1. if $(c_1 c_2 \ldots c_m)$ and $(c'_1 c'_2 \ldots c'_m)$ are two m-combinations of $\{1, 2, \ldots, n\}$ and the reverse of $(c_1 c_2 \ldots c_m)$ precedes the reverse of $(c'_1 c'_2 \ldots c'_m)$ in lexicographic order, then

$$\text{order}(c_1, c_2, \ldots, c_m) < \text{order}(c'_1, c'_2, \ldots, c'_m);$$

2. order$(1, 2, \ldots, m) = 0$ and order$((n - m + 1), (n - m + 2), \ldots, n) = {}^nC_m - 1$ implying that the transformation *order* maps the ${}^nC_m$ different m-combinations onto $\{0, 1, \ldots, {}^nC_m - 1\}$ while preserving reverse lexicographic order.

The following function takes $(c_1\, c_2 \ldots c_m)$ as input and returns order $(c_1, c_2, \ldots, c_m)$ as output in $O(m^2)$ time:

function ORDER $(c_1, c_2, \ldots, c_m)$

Step 1:   sum $\leftarrow 0$.
Step 2:   **for** $i = 1$ **to** m **do**
$$\text{sum} \leftarrow \text{sum} + {}^{c_i - 1}C_i$$
end for.

Step 3:   ORDER $\leftarrow$ sum. $\square$

Using order and complement, we can define the following one-to-one mapping of the ${}^nC_m$ possible combinations onto $\{1, 2, \ldots, {}^nC_m\}$, which preserves lexicographic ordering:

$$\text{rankc}(n, c_1, c_2, \ldots, c_m) = {}^nC_m - \text{order}(\text{complement}(n, c_1, c_2, \ldots, c_m)).$$

Thus rankc$(n, 1, 2, \ldots, m) = 1$, rankc$(n, 1, 2, \ldots, m, m + 1) = 2$, $\ldots$, rankc$(n, (n - m + 1), (n - m + 2), \ldots, n) = {}^nC_m$. The following procedure is an implementation of the preceding mapping: It takes n and the combinations $(c_1\, c_2 \ldots c_m)$ as input and returns the ordinal position h of the latter in $O(m^2)$ time.

procedure RANKC $(n, c_1, c_2, \ldots, c_m, h)$

Step 1: $h \leftarrow {}^nC_m$.

Step 2: $(d_1\, d_2 \ldots d_m) \leftarrow$ COMPLEMENT$(n, c_1, c_2, \ldots, c_m)$.

Step 3: $h \leftarrow h - $ ORDER$(d_1, d_2, \ldots, d_m)$. $\square$

We now turn to the question of inverting the rankc mapping. Specifically, given an integer h, where $1 \leqslant h \leqslant {}^nC_m$, it is required to determine the combination $(c_1\, c_2 \ldots c_m)$ such that rankc$(n, c_1, c_2, \ldots, c_m) = h$. We begin by defining the inverse of order with respect to $\{1, 2, \ldots, n\}$ as follows. Let order$(c_1, c_2, \ldots, c_m) = g$. Then

$$\text{orderinverse}(n, m, g) = (c_1\, c_2 \ldots c_m)$$

where c_i is equal to the largest j such that

(i) $i \leqslant j \leqslant n$ and
(ii) $(g - \sum_{k = i + 1}^{m} {}^{c_k - 1}C_k) \geqslant {}^{j - 1}C_i$.

The following function is an implementation of the preceding mapping. It takes n, m, and g as input and returns a combination $(c_1\, c_2 \ldots c_m)$ as output in $O(mn)$ time.

function ORDERINV(n, m, g)

Step 1:   **for** $i = m$ **downto** 1 **do**
          (1.1) $j \leftarrow n$
          (1.2) $c_i \leftarrow 0$
          (1.3) $t \leftarrow {}^{n-1}C_i$
          (1.4) **while** $(c_i = 0)$ **do**
               (i) **if** $g \geqslant t$
                 then $c_i \leftarrow j$
                 end if
               (ii) $t \leftarrow (t \times (j - i))/j$
               (iii) $j \leftarrow j - 1$
          end while
          (1.5) $g \leftarrow g - {}^{c_i-1}C_i$
    end for.

Step 2:   ORDERINV $\leftarrow (c_1\, c_2 \dots c_m)$. $\square$

We are finally in a position to define the inverse of rankc. If rankc(n, c_1, $c_2, \dots, c_m$) = h, then

$$\text{rankc}^{-1}(n, m, h) = \text{complement}(n, \text{orderinverse}(n, m, {}^{n}C_m - h)).$$

The following procedure RANKCINV takes n, m, and h as input and returns the combination $(c_1\, c_2 \dots c_m)$ as output in $O(mn)$ time.

procedure RANKCINV(n, m, h, c_1, $c_2, \dots, c_m$)

Step 1: $(d_1\, d_2 \dots d_m) \leftarrow$ ORDERINV(n, m, ${}^{n}C_m - h$).

Step 2: $(c_1\, c_2 \dots c_m) \leftarrow$ COMPLEMENT(n, d_1, $d_2, \dots, d_m$). $\square$

6.3 GENERATING PERMUTATIONS IN PARALLEL

We set the stage in the previous section to address the problem of generating permutations in parallel. Our first algorithm is a parallel version of the algorithm in section 6.2.1.

6.3.1 Adapting a Sequential Algorithm

We begin by making a few observations regarding procedure NEXT PERMU-TATION.

1. Given an m-permutation $(p_1\, p_2 \dots p_m)$ the procedure first checks whether it is updatable.

2. If the permutation is updatable, then its rightmost element p_m is checked first to determine whether it can be incremented; if it can, then the procedure increments it and terminates.

3. Determining whether p_m can be incremented requires scanning no more than m positions of array u whose entries indicate which of the integers $\{1, 2, \ldots, n\}$ currently appear in $(p_1 \, p_2 \ldots p_m)$ and which do not. This scanning also yields the new value of p_m in case the latter can be incremented.

4. If the rightmost element cannot be incremented, then the procedure finds the first element to the left of p_m that is smaller than its right neighbor. This element, call it p_k, is incremented by the procedure and all elements to its right are updated.

5. Determining the new value of p_k requires scanning no more than m positions of u.

9. Updating all positions to the right of p_k requires scanning no more than the *first* m positions of u.

These observations indicate that the algorithm in section 6.2.1 lends itself quite naturally to parallel implementation. Assume that m processors are available on an EREW SM SIMD computer. We give our first parallel m-permutation generator as procedure PARALLEL PERMUTATIONS. The procedure takes n and m as input and produces all ^nP_m m-permutations of $\{1, 2, \ldots, n\}$. It assumes that processor P_i has access to position i of an output register where each successive permutation is produced. There are three arrays in shared memory:

1. $p = p_1, p_2, \ldots, p_m$, which stores the current permutation.

2. $u = u_1, u_2, \ldots, u_n$, where $u_i = 0$ if i is in the current permutation $(p_1 \, p_2 \ldots p_m)$; otherwise $u_i = 1$. Initially, $u_i = 1$ for $1 \leqslant i \leqslant n$.

3. $x = x_1, x_2, \ldots, x_m$ is used to store intermediate results.

Procedure PARALLEL PERMUTATIONS also invokes the following four procedures for EREW SM SIMD computers:

1. Procedure BROADCAST (a, m, x) studied in chapter 2, which uses an array $x_1, x_2, \ldots, x_m$ to distribute the value of a to m processors $P_1, P_2, \ldots, P_m$.

2. Procedure ALLSUMS $(x_1, x_2, \ldots, x_m)$ also studied in chapter 2, which uses m processors to compute the prefix sums of the array $x_1, x_2, \ldots, x_m$ and replace x_i with $x_1 + x_2 + \cdots + x_i$ for $1 \leqslant i \leqslant n$.

3. Procedure MINIMUM $(x_1, x_2, \ldots, x_m)$ given in what follows, which uses m processors to find the smallest element in the array $x_1, x_2, \ldots, x_m$ and return it in x_1:

```
procedure MINIMUM (x₁, x₂, ..., xₘ)

    for j = 0 to (log m − 1) do
        for i = 1 to m in steps of 2^(j+1) do in parallel
            (1) P_i obtains x_(i+2^j) through shared memory
            (2) if x_(i+2^j) < x_i then x_i ← x_(i+2^j) end if
        end for
    end for.  □
```

4. Procedure MAXIMUM $(x_1, x_2, \ldots, x_m)$, which uses m processors to find the largest element in the array $x_1, x_2, \ldots, x_m$ and return it in x_1. This procedure is identical to procedure MINIMUM, except that step 2 now reads

$$\text{if } x_{i+2^i} > x_i \text{ then } x_i \leftarrow x_{i+2^i} \text{ end if.}$$

5. Procedure PARALLEL SCAN (p_s, n), which is helpful in searching for the next available integer to increment a given element p_s of an m-permutation $(p_1 p_2 \ldots p_m)$ of $\{1, 2, \ldots, n\}$. Given p_s and n, array u in shared memory is used to determine which of the m integers $p_s + 1, p_s + 2, \ldots, p_s + m$ satisfy the two conditions of

(i) being smaller than or equal to n and

(ii) being not present in $(p_1 p_2 \ldots p_m)$

and are therefore available for incrementing p_s. Array x in shared memory is used to keep track of these integers.

procedure PARALLEL SCAN (p_s, n)

    for $i = 1$ **to** m **do in parallel**
      if $p_s + i \leqslant n$ **and** $u_{p_s+i} = 1$
      then $x_i \leftarrow p_s + i$
      else $x_i \leftarrow \infty$
      end if
    end for. ☐

From chapter 2 we know that procedures BROADCAST and ALLSUMS run in $O(\log m)$ time. Procedures MINIMUM and MAXIMUM clearly require $O(\log m)$ time as well. Procedure PARALLEL SCAN takes constant time. We are now ready to state procedure PARALLEL PERMUTATIONS:

procedure PARALLEL PERMUTATIONS (n, m)

  Step 1: (1.1) **for** $i = 1$ **to** m **do in parallel**
          (i) $p_i \leftarrow 1$
          (ii) produce p_i as output
         end for
      (1.2) {Initialize array u}
         for $i = 1$ **to** $\lceil n/m \rceil$ **do**
           for $j = 1$ **to** m **do in parallel**
              (i) $k \leftarrow (i-1)m + j$
              (ii) **if** $k \leqslant n$ **then** $u_k \leftarrow 1$ **end if**
           end for
         end for.

Step 2:   **for** $t = 1$ **to** $(^nP_m - 1)$ **do**
    (2.1) **for** $i = 1$ **to** m **do in parallel**
        $u_{p_i} \leftarrow 0$
    end for
    (2.2) {Check whether rightmost element of $(p_1 p_2 \ldots p_m)$ can be incremented; i.e., if there is a j, $p_m \leqslant j \leqslant n$, such that $j \neq p_k$ for $1 \leqslant k \leqslant m - 1$}
        (i) BROADCAST (p_m, m, x)
        (ii) PARALLEL SCAN (p_m, n)
    (2.3) {If several j satisfying the condition in (2.2) are found, the smallest is assigned to p_m}
        (i) {The smallest of the x_i is found and placed in x_1}
            MINIMUM $(x_1, x_2, \ldots, x_m)$
        (ii) **if** $x_1 \neq \infty$ **then** (a) $u_{\bar{p}_m} \leftarrow 1$
                                (b) $p_m \leftarrow x_1$
                                (c) $k \leftarrow m - 1$
                                (d) **Go to** step (2.7)
        end if
    (2.4) {Rightmost element cannot be incremented; find rightmost element p_k such that $p_k < p_{k+1}$}
        (i) **for** $i = 1$ **to** $m - 1$ **do in parallel**
            if $p_i < p_{i+1}$ **then** $x_i \leftarrow i$
                            else $x_i \leftarrow -1$
            end if
        end for
        (ii) {The largest of the x_i is found and placed in x_1}
            MAXIMUM $(x_1, x_2, \ldots, x_m)$
        (iii) $k \leftarrow x_1$
        (iv) BROADCAST (k, m, x)
        (v) BROADCAST (p_k, m, x)
    (2.5) {Increment p_k: the smallest available integer larger than p_k is assigned to p_k}
        (i) **for** $i = k$ **to** m **do in parallel**
            $u_{p_i} \leftarrow 1$
        end for
        (ii) PARALLEL SCAN (p_k, n)
        (iii) MINIMUM $(x_1, x_2, \ldots, x_m)$
        (iv) $p_k \leftarrow x_1$
        (v) $u_{p_k} \leftarrow 0$
    (2.6) {Find the smallest $m - k$ integers that are available and assign their values to $p_{k+1}, p_{k+2}, \ldots, p_m$, respectively. This reduces to finding the first $m - k$ positions of u that are equal to 1}
        (i) **for** $i = 1$ **to** m **do in parallel**
            $x_i \leftarrow u_i$
        end for
        (ii) ALLSUMS $(x_1, x_2, \ldots, x_m)$
        (iii) **for** $i = 1$ **to** m **do in parallel**
            if $x_i \leqslant (m - k)$ **and** $u_i = 1$
            then $p_{k + x_i} \leftarrow i$
            end if
        end for

(2.7) {Clean up array u and output current m-permutation}
    (i) **for** $i = 1$ **to** k **do in parallel**
        $u_{p_i} \leftarrow 1$
        end for
    (ii) **for** $i = 1$ **to** m **do in parallel**
        produce p_i as output
        end for
end for. □

Analysis. Step 1 takes $O(n/m)$ time. There are $^nP_m - 1$ iterations of step 2, each requiring $O(\log m)$ time, as can be easily verified. The overall running time of PARALLEL PERMUTATIONS is therefore $O(^nP_m \log m)$. Since m processors are used, the procedure's cost is $O(^nP_m m \log m)$.

Example 6.1

We illustrate the working of procedure PARALLEL PERMUTATIONS by showing how a permutation is updated. Let $S = \{1, 2, 3, 4, 5\}$ and let $(p_1 p_2 p_3 p_4) = (5 1 4 3)$ be a 4-permutation to be updated during an iteration of step 2. In step 2.1 array u is set up as shown in Fig. 6.1(a). In step 2.2, $p_4 = 3$ is broadcast to all four processors to check whether any of the integers $p_4 + 1, p_4 + 2, p_4 + 3$, and $p_4 + 4$ is available. The processors assign values to array x as shown in Fig. 6.1(b). This leads to the discovery in step 2.3 that p_4 cannot be incremented. In step 2.4 the processors assign values to array x to indicate the positions of those elements in the permutation that are smaller than their right neighbor, as shown in Fig. 6.1(c). The largest entry in x is determined to be 2; this means that p_2 is to be incremented and all the positions to its right are to be updated. Now 2 and p_2 are broadcast to the four processors. In step 2.5 array u is updated to indicate that the old values of p_2, p_3, and p_4 are now available, as shown in Fig. 6.1(d). The processors now check whether any of the integers $p_2 + 1, p_2 + 2, p_2 + 3$, and $p_2 + 4$ is available and indicate their findings by setting up array x as shown in Fig. 6.1(e). The smallest entry in x is found to be 2: p_2 is assigned the value 2 and u_2 is set to 0, as shown in Fig. 6.1(f). In step 2.6 the smallest two available integers are found by setting array x equal to the first four positions of array u. Now procedure ALLSUMS is applied to array x with the result shown in Fig. 6.1(g). Since $x_1 < 4 - 2$ and $u_1 = 1$, p_{2+1} is assigned the value 1. Similarly, since $x_3 = 4 - 2$ and $u_3 = 1$, p_{2+2} is assigned the value 3. Finally, in step 2.7 positions 2 and 5 of array u are set to 1 and the 4-permutation $(p_1 p_2 p_3 p_4) = (5 2 1 3)$ is produced as output. □

Discussion. We conclude this section with two remarks on procedure PARALLEL PERMUTATIONS.

1. The procedure has a cost of $O(^nP_m m \log m)$, which is not optimal in view of the $O(^nP_m m)$ operations sufficient to generate all m-permutations of n items by procedure SEQUENTIAL PERMUTATIONS.

2. The procedure is not adaptive as it requires the presence of m processors in order to function properly. As pointed out earlier, it is usually reasonable to assume that the number of processors on a shared memory parallel computer is not only fixed but also smaller than the size of the typical problem.

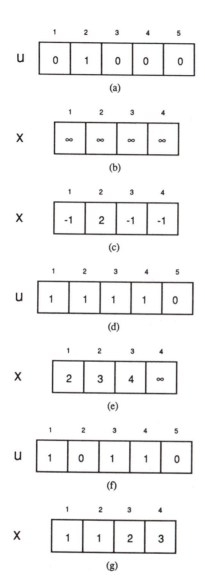

Figure 6.1 Updating permutation using procedure   PARALLEL   PERMUTATIONS.

The preceding remarks lead naturally to the following questions:

1. Can a parallel permutation algorithm be derived that uses N processors, where $1 < N \leqslant {}^{n}P_m$?
2. Would the algorithm be cost optimal?

These two questions are answered affirmatively in the following section.

6.3.2 An Adaptive Permutation Generator

In this section we describe an adaptive and cost-optimal parallel algorithm for generating all m-permutations of $\{1, 2, \ldots, n\}$. The algorithm is designed to run on an EREW SM SIMD computer with N processors $P_1, P_2, \ldots, P_N$, where $1 < N \leqslant {}^nP_m$. It makes use of procedure NEXT PERMUTATION and RANKPINV described in section 6.2. The idea of the algorithm is to let each processor generate a subset of the permutations lexicographically. Furthermore, all the permutations generated by P_i precede in lexicographic order those generated by P_{i+1}, $1 \leqslant i < N$. Thus P_i begins with the jth permutation, where $j = (i - 1)\lceil {}^nP_m/N\rceil + 1$, and then generates the next $\lceil {}^nP_m/N\rceil - 1$ permutations. The algorithm is given as procedure ADAPTIVE PERMUTATIONS:

procedure ADAPTIVE PERMUTATIONS (n, m)

    for $i = 1$ **to** N **do in parallel**
        (1) $j \leftarrow (i - 1)\lceil {}^nP_m/N\rceil + 1$
        (2) **if** $j \leqslant {}^nP_m$ **then**
            (2.1) RANKPINV $(n, m, j, p_1, p_2, \ldots, p_m)$
            (2.2) produce the jth permutation $(p_1 p_2 \ldots p_m)$ as output
            (2.3) **for** $i = 1$ **to** $\lceil {}^nP_m/N\rceil - 1$ **do**
                NEXT PERMUTATION $(n, m, p_1, p_2, \ldots, p_m)$
            end for
        end if
    end for. $\square$

    Analysis.   Step 1 requires $O(m)$ operations. Generating the jth permutation in step 2.1 takes $O(mn)$ operations and producing it as output in step 2.2 another $O(m)$. There are $\lceil {}^nP_m/N\rceil - 1$ iterations of step 2.3 each involving $O(m)$ operations. The overall running time of procedure ADAPTIVE PERMUTATIONS is therefore dominated by the larger of $O(mn)$ and $O(\lceil {}^nP_m/N\rceil m)$. Assuming that $n \leqslant \lceil {}^nP_m/N\rceil$, that is, $1 < N \leqslant {}^nP_m/n$, the procedure runs in $O(\lceil {}^nP_m/N\rceil m)$ time with an optimal cost of $O({}^nP_m m)$.

    Three points are worth noting regarding procedure ADAPTIVE PERMUTATIONS.

    The first two are:

1. Once the values of n and m are made known to all the processors, using procedure BROADCAST, say, the shared memory is no longer needed. Indeed the processors, once started, independently execute the same algorithm and never need to communicate among themselves.

2. Steps 2.1–2.3 may not be executed at all by some processors. This is illustrated by the following example.

Example 6.2

Let $n = 5$, $m = 3$, and $N = 13$. Thus $\lceil {^n}P_m/N \rceil = \lceil \frac{60}{13} \rceil = 5$. Processor P_1 computes $j = 1$, uses procedure RANKPINV to generate the first permutation in lexicographic order, namely, (1 2 3), and then calls procedure NEXT PERMUTATION four times to generate (1 2 4), (1 2 5), (1 3 2), and (1 3 4). Simultaneously, P_2 generates the sixth through the tenth permutations, namely, (1 3 5), (1 4 2), (1 4 3), (1 4 5), and (1 5 2). Similarly, P_3, P_4, ..., P_{12} each generates five 3-permutations. As for P_{13}, it computes $j = 12 \times 5 + 1 = 61$, finds it larger than ${^5}P_3$, and consequently does not execute steps 2.1–2.3.   □

The third point regarding procedure ADAPTIVE PERMUTATIONS is:

3. Although step 2.3 is iterated $\lceil {^n}P_m/N \rceil - 1$ times by the processors that execute it, fewer permutations than this number may be generated. This is illustrated by the following example.

Example 6.3

Again let $n = 5$ and $m = 3$ but this time assume that $N = 7$. Thus $\lceil {^5}P_3/7 \rceil = 9$. Each of processors $P_1, \ldots, P_6$ generates nine 3-permutations. Processor P_7, however, generates only six 3-permutations, namely, the fifty-fifth through the sixtieth. During each of the final three iterations of step 2.3 executed by P_7, procedure NEXT PERMUTATION detects that $(p_1 p_2 p_3) = (5 4 3)$, that is, the last permutation has been reached, and consequently does nothing.   □

6.3.3 Parallel Permutation Generator for Few Processors

Sometimes only few processors can be used to generate all m-permutations of n items. Assume, for example, that N processors are available, where $1 < N \leqslant n$. A surprisingly simple parallel algorithm can be developed for this situation. The algorithm runs on an EREW SM SIMD computer and is adaptive and cost optimal. Unlike procedure ADAPTIVE PERMUTATIONS, however, it does not make use of the numbering system of section 6.2.2. We illustrate the algorithm for the special case where $m = n$, that is, when all $n!$ permutations of n items are to be generated.

Let $S = \{1, 2, \ldots, n\}$, as before, and consider the permutation $(1\ 2 \ldots i - 1\ i\ i + 1 \ldots n)$ of S. For each i, $1 \leqslant i \leqslant n$, an $n - 1$ permutation is defined as follows:

$$(1\ 2 \ldots i - 1\ i\ i + 1 \ldots n) - i = (1\ 2 \ldots i - 1\ i + 1 \ldots n).$$

For ease of presentation, we begin by assuming that $N = n$, that is, that there are as many processors available as items to permute. The idea is to let processor P_i, for $1 \leqslant i \leqslant n$, begin with the permutation $(i\ 1\ 2 \ldots i - 1\ i + 1 \ldots n)$ and generate all subsequent permutations in lexicographic order, which have i in the first position. There are exactly $(n - 1)!$ such permutations.

In general, for N processors, where $1 < N \leqslant n$, each processor generates $\lceil n!/N \rceil$ permutations. In other words, each processor does the job of $\lceil n/N \rceil$ processors in the informal description of the previous paragraph. The algorithm is given as procedure FULL PERMUTATIONS:

procedure FULL PERMUTATIONS (n)

    for $j = 1$ **to** N **do in parallel**
        for $i = (j - 1) \lceil n/N \rceil + 1$ **to** $j \lceil n/N \rceil$ **do**
            if $i \leqslant n$ **then**
                (1) $(p_1 \, p_2 \ldots p_{n-1}) = (1 \, 2 \ldots i - 1 \, i \, i + 1 \ldots n) - i$
                (2) produce $(i \, p_1 \, p_2 \ldots p_{n-1})$ as output
                (3) **for** $k = 1$ **to** $((n - 1)! - 1)$ **do**
                      NEXT PERMUTATION $(n, n, i, p_1, p_2, \ldots, p_{n-1})$
                end for
            end if
        end for
    end for. $\square$

Analysis. Procedure NEXT PERMUTATION is called $\lceil n/N \rceil [(n-1)! - 1]$ times, each call requiring $O(n)$ steps to generate a permutation. Steps 1 and 2 are also executed $\lceil n/N \rceil$ times and require $O(n)$ time. The overall running time of procedure FULL PERMUTATIONS is therefore

$$t(n) = O(\lceil n!/N \rceil n).$$

Since $p(n) = N$, the procedure has an optimal cost of $c(n) = O(n! \, n)$.

6.4 GENERATING COMBINATIONS IN PARALLEL

We now turn to the problem of generating all ^nC_m m-combinations of $S = \{1, 2, \ldots, n\}$ in lexicographic order. On the surface, this may appear to be a special case of the problem addressed in the previous section; indeed each m-combination is an m-permutation. It is not clear, however, how an algorithm for generating m-permutations, such as procedure PARALLEL PERMUTATIONS, for example, can be made to *efficiently* generate combinations *only*. It appears therefore that a special approach will have to be developed for this problem. In this section we describe two algorithms for generating m-combinations in parallel. Both algorithms are designed to run on the EREW SM SIMD model of computation.

6.4.1 A Fast Combination Generator

We begin by restating the following properties of m-combinations of n items, listed in lexicographic order.

Property 1.   For $1 \leqslant m \leqslant n$, the first combination in lexicographic order is $(1\,2\ldots m)$, and the last one is $(n - m + 1\ n - m + 2 \ldots n)$.

Property 2.   Denote the last combination by $(x_1\,x_2\ldots x_m)$. If $(y_1\,y_2\ldots y_m)$ is one of the *other* possible combinations, then

(i) $y_1 < y_2 < \cdots < y_m$ and $y_i \leqslant x_i$ for $1 \leqslant i \leqslant m$.

(ii) If there is a subscript i, $2 \leqslant i \leqslant m$, such that all y's from y_i to y_m equal x_i to x_m, respectively, and $y_{i-1} < x_{i-1}$, then the next successive combination is given by $(y_1'\,y_2'\ldots y_m')$ where $y_j' = y_j$ for $1 \leqslant j \leqslant i - 2$, and $y_j' = y_{i-1} + j - i + 2$ for $i - 1 \leqslant j \leqslant m$. Otherwise, the next successive combination is given by $(y_1\,y_2\ldots y_{m-1}\ y_m + 1)$.

The preceding discussion leads naturally to our first parallel combination generator. The first combination generated is $(1\,2\ldots m)$. Now, if $(y_1\,y_2\ldots y_m)$ is the combination just generated, then the next successive combination is given by property 2(ii). The algorithm uses five arrays b, c, x, y, and z, each of length m, in shared memory. The ith position of each of these arrays is denoted by b_i, c_i, x_i, y_i, and z_i, respectively. The first of these arrays, array b, is used for broadcasting. Array c is simply an output buffer where every new combination generated is placed. The last three arrays are used to store intermediate results:

1. Array x holds the last combination, namely,

$$x_i = n - m + i \qquad \text{for } 1 \leqslant i \leqslant m.$$

2. Array y holds the current combination being generated.

3. Array z keeps track of those positions in y that have reached their limiting values; thus for $1 \leqslant i \leqslant m$

$$z_i = \begin{cases} \textbf{true} & \text{if } y_i = x_i, \\ \textbf{false} & \text{otherwise.} \end{cases}$$

The algorithm is given in what follows as procedure PARALLEL COMBINATIONS. It uses m processors P_1, $P_2, \ldots, P_m$ and invokes procedure BROADCAST.

procedure PARALLEL COMBINATIONS (n, m)

Step 1:   {Initialization}
        for $i = 1$ **to** m **do in parallel**
          (1.1) $x_i \leftarrow n - m + i$
          (1.2) $y_i \leftarrow i$
          (1.3) **if** $y_i = x_i$ **then** $z_i \leftarrow$ **true**
                           else $z_i \leftarrow$ **false**
          end if
          (1.4) $c_i \leftarrow i$
        end for.

Step 2: {The value of z_1 if broadcast}
BROADCAST (z_1, m, b).

Step 3: **while** $z_1 =$ **false do**
    (3.1) $k \leftarrow 0$
    (3.2) {Find rightmost element of current combination that has not reached its
    limiting value}
        for $i = 2$ **to** m **do in parallel**
          if $z_{i-1} =$ **false and** $z_i =$ **true**
          then (i) $y_{i-1} \leftarrow y_{i-1} + 1$
              (ii) $k \leftarrow i$
          end if
        end for
    (3.3) BROADCAST (k, m, b)
    (3.4) {If no element has reached its limiting value, increment y_m; otherwise update
    all elements from y_k to y_m}
        if $k = 0$ **then** $y_m \leftarrow y_m + 1$
        else (i) BROADCAST (y_{k-1}, m, b)
            (ii) **for** $i = k$ **to** m **do in parallel**
               $y_i \leftarrow y_{k-1} + (i - k + 1)$
            end for
        end if
    (3.5) **for** $i = 1$ **to** m **do in parallel**
          (i) $c_i \leftarrow y_i$
          (ii) **if** $y_i = x_i$ **then** $z_i =$ **true**
                  else $z_i =$ **false**
          end if
        end for
    (3.6) BROADCAST (z_1, m, b)
    end while. □

Note that step 3.1 is executed by one processor, say, P_1. Also, in step 3.2 at most one processor finds $z_{i-1} =$ **false** and $z_i =$ **true** and updates y_{i-1} and k. Finally in the **then** part of step 3.4 only one processor, say, P_m, increments y_m.

Analysis.   Steps 1, 3.1, 3.2, and 3.5 take constant time. In steps 2, 3.3, 3.4, and 3.6 procedure BROADCAST requires $O(\log m)$ time. Since step 3 is executed ($^nC_m - 1$) times, the overall running time of procedure PARALLEL COMBINATIONS is $O(^nC_m \log m)$, and its cost $O(^nC_m m \log m)$, which is not optimal.

Example 6.4

The behavior of PARALLEL COMBINATIONS is illustrated in Fig. 6.2 for the case where $n = 5$ and $m = 3$. The figure shows the contents of each of the arrays y, z, and c as well as the value of k after each step of the procedure where they are modified by an assignment. Note that t and f represent **true** and **false**, respectively. Also, $(x_1 \, x_2 \, x_3) = (3 \, 4 \, 5)$ throughout. □

AFTER STEP	y_1	y_2	y_3	z_1	z_2	z_3	c_1	c_2	c_3	k
1	1	2	3	f	f	f	1	2	3	
(3.1)										0
(3.4)	1	2	4							
(3.5)				f	f	f	1	2	4	
(3.1)										0
(3.4)	1	2	5							
(3.5)				f	f	t	1	2	5	
(3.1)										0
(3.2)	1	3	5							3
(3.4)	1	3	4							
(3.5)				f	f	f	1	3	4	
(3.1)										0
(3.4)	1	3	5							
(3.5)				f	f	t	1	3	5	
(3.1)										0
(3.2)	1	4	5							3
(3.4)	1	4	5							
(3.5)				f	t	t	1	4	5	
(3.1)										0
(3.2)	2	4	5							2
(3.4)	2	3	4							
(3.5)				f	f	f	2	3	4	
(3.1)										0
(3.4)	2	3	5							
(3.5)				f	f	t	2	3	5	
(3.1)										0
(3.2)	2	4	5							3
(3.4)	2	4	5							
(3.5)				f	t	t	2	4	5	
(3.1)										0
(3.2)	3	4	5							2
(3.4)	3	4	5							
(3.5)				t	t	t	3	4	5	

Figure 6.2 Generating combinations of three out of five items using procedure PARALLEL COMBINATIONS.

Discussion.   When stating desirable properties of algorithms in chapter 2, we said that

(i) a parallel algorithm should be adaptive, that is, capable of modifying its behavior according to the number of processors actually available on the parallel computer being used,

(ii) its running time should vary with the number of processors used, and

(iii) its cost should be optimal.

Procedure PARALLEL COMBINATIONS does not satisfy any of the preceding criteria:

(i) It requires the availability of m processors.

(ii) Although quite fast, its running time does not decrease with an increasing number of processors.

(iii) Its cost exceeds the $O(^nC_m m)$ operations sufficient to generate all m combinations of n items by procedure SEQUENTIAL COMBINATIONS.

The purpose of the next section is to exhibit an algorithm satisfying these three desirable properties.

6.4.2 An Adaptive Combination Generator

We conclude our treatment of combination generators by describing an adaptive and cost-optimal parallel algorithm for generating all m-combinations of $\{1, 2, \ldots, n\}$. The algorithm is designed to run on an EREW SM SIMD computer with N processors P_1, $P_2, \ldots, P_N$, where $1 < N \leq {}^nC_m$. It makes use of procedures NEXT COMBINATION and RANKCINV described in section 6.2. The idea of the algorithm is to let each processor generate a subset of the combinations lexicographically. Furthermore, all the combinations generated by P_i precede in lexicographic order those generated by P_{i+1}, $1 \leq i < N$. Thus P_i begins with the jth combination, where $j = (i - 1)\lceil {}^nC_m/N \rceil + 1$ and then generates the next $\lceil {}^nC_m/N \rceil - 1$ combinations. The algorithm, which is similar to the one in section 6.3.2, is given as procedure ADAPTIVE COMBINATIONS:

procedure ADAPTIVE COMBINATIONS (n, m)

    for $i = 1$ **to** N **do in parallel**
        (1) $j \leftarrow (i - 1) \lceil {}^nC_m/N \rceil + 1$
        (2) **if** $j \leq {}^nC_m$ **then**
            (2.1) RANKCINV $(n, m, j, c_1, c_2, \ldots, c_m)$
            (2.2) produce the jth combination $(c_1 c_2 \ldots c_m)$ as output
            (2.3) **for** $i = 1$ **to** $\lceil {}^nC_m/N \rceil - 1$ **do**
                NEXT COMBINATION $(n, m, c_1, c_2, \ldots, c_m)$
            end for
        end if
    end for. $\square$

Analysis.   Step 1 requires $O(m)$ operations. Generating the jth combination in step 2.1 takes $O(mn)$ operations and producing it as output in step 2.2 another $O(mn)$. Each of the $\lceil {}^nC_m/N \rceil - 1$ iterations of step 2.3 involves $O(m)$ operations. The overall running time of procedure ADAPTIVE COMBINATIONS is therefore dominated by the larger of $O(mn)$ and $O(\lceil {}^nC_m/N \rceil m)$. Assuming that $n \leqslant \lceil {}^nC_m/N \rceil$, that is, $1 < N \leqslant {}^nC_m/n$, the procedure runs in $O(\lceil {}^nC_m/N \rceil m)$ time with an optimal cost of $O({}^nC_m m)$.

The three comments made in section 6.3.3 regarding procedure ADAPTIVE PERMUTATIONS are also valid here:

1. The shared memory is only needed to broadcast n and m.

2. Steps 2.1–2.3 may not be executed at all by some processors.

3. Fewer than $\lceil {}^nC_m/N \rceil - 1$ combinations may be generated in step 2.3.

Example 6.5

Let $n = 7$, $m = 1$, and $N = 5$. Then $\lceil {}^7C_1/5 \rceil = 2$. Processor P_1 computes $j = 1$ and generates the first two combinations. Processors P_2 and P_3 compute $j = 3$ and $j = 5$, respectively, and each generates an additional two combinations. Processor P_4 computes $j = 7$ and succeeds in generating the one and last combination. Processor P_5 computes $j = 9$ and since $9 > {}^7C_1$, it does not execute step 2.   □

6.5 PROBLEMS

6.1   In procedure PARALLEL PERMUTATIONS, the processors make extensive use of the shared memory to communicate. Design a parallel algorithm for generating all m-permutations of n items in $O({}^nP_m \log m)$ time using m processors that never need to communicate (through shared memory or otherwise). Once the values of n and m have been made known to the processors, the latter operate independently and generate all ${}^nP_m$ permutations lexicographically.

6.2   Once the algorithm in problem 6.1 has been developed, it is not difficult to make it adaptive. Given N processors, $1 < N \leqslant {}^nP_m$, the modified algorithm would run in $O({}^nP_m m \log m/N)$ time, which would not be cost optimal. On the other hand, procedure ADAPTIVE PERMUTATIONS is both adaptive and cost optimal. Design an adaptive and cost-optimal parallel algorithm for generating permutations that uses neither the shared memory nor the numbering system of section 6.2.2.

6.3   Is it possible to design a parallel algorithm for generating all m-permutations of n items on the EREW SM SIMD model of computation in $O({}^nP_m)$ time using m processors? Would the permutations be in lexicographic order?

6.4   Procedure ADAPTIVE PERMUTATIONS is cost optimal only when the number of processors N lies in the range $1 < N \leqslant {}^nP_m/n$. Can the procedure be modified (or a new procedure designed) to extend this range of optimality? Is there a parallel algorithm that is cost optimal for all values of N from 2 to ${}^nP_m$?

6.5   Can you generalize procedure FULL PERMUTATIONS to generate all m-permutations, where m can take any value from 1 to n?

6.6   Consider the sorting networks described in chapter 4. These networks can be used as permutation generators as follows. Let $S = \{1, 2, 3, 4, 5\}$ and assume that we wish to generate the permutation $(5\,3\,2\,1\,4)$ from the *initial* permutation $(1\,2\,3\,4\,5)$. We begin by assigning each integer in the initial permutation an index (or subscript) indicating its position in the desired permutation. This gives $(1_4\,2_3\,3_2\,4_5\,5_1)$. The sequence of indices can now be *sorted* on a sorting network: When two indices are to be swapped, each carries its associated integer along. The result is $(5_1\,3_2\,2_3\,1_4\,4_5)$ as required. For a given n, can all $n!$ permutations be generated in this fashion? Would they be in lexicographic order? Analyze the running time, number of processors, and cost of your algorithm.

6.7   Repeat problem 6.6 for each of the interconnection networks described in chapter 1.

6.8   Is there any advantage to using the approach in problem 6.6 on the shared-memory SIMD model of computation? How would the resulting algorithm compare with those in section 6.3?

6.9   A *permutation network* is a circuit that is hard wired to effect a particular permutation of its input. It takes n inputs and produces n outputs. An example of a permutation network for $n = 4$ is shown in Fig. 6.3. For input $(1\,2\,3\,4)$ the network produces $(2\,4\,1\,3)$. Feeding $(2\,4\,1\,3)$ back into the network (using the dotted lines) yields $(4\,3\,2\,1)$. Repeating the process yields $(3\,1\,4\,2)$ and then $(1\,2\,3\,4)$, that is, the original permutation. This means that the network in Fig. 6.3 is capable of producing only four of the twenty-four permutations of four items. Can you design a network capable of generating all permutations?

6.10 The permutation network in Fig. 6.3 is an example of a *single-stage* network. A two-stage network is illustrated in Fig. 6.4 for $n = 4$. In general, *multistage* networks can be designed. How many permutations does the network of Fig. 6.4 (with feedback as shown in dotted lines) generate? Can you design a network capable of generating all 4! permutations? How many stages would it have?

6.11 Modify procedure PARALLEL COMBINATIONS to run using N processors, where $1 < N \leqslant m$. Show that the running time of the modified procedure is $O(^nC_m(m/N + \log N))$, which is cost optimal for $n \leqslant m/\log N$.

6.12 In procedure PARALLEL COMBINATIONS, the processors make extensive use of the shared memory to communicate. Design a parallel algorithm for generating all m-combinations of n items in $O(^nC_m \log m)$ time using m processors that never need to communicate (through the shared memory or otherwise). Once the value of n and m have been made known to the processors, the latter operate independently and generate all ^nC_m combinations lexicographically.

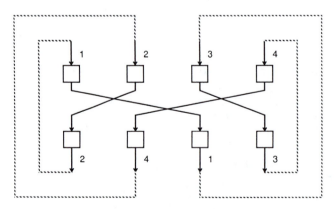

Figure 6.3   Permutation network.

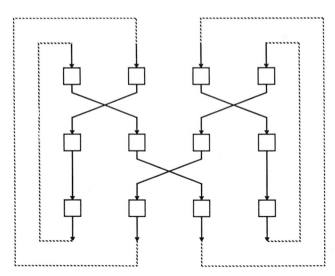

Figure   6.4 Two-stage   permutation
network.

6.13 Once the algorithm in problem 6.12 has been developed, it is not difficult to make it adaptive. Given N processors, $1 < N \leqslant {}^nC_m$, the modified algorithm would run in $O({}^nC_m m \log m/N)$ time, which would not be cost optimal. On the other hand, procedure ADAPTIVE COMBINATIONS is both adaptive and cost optimal. Design an adaptive and cost-optimal parallel algorithm for generating combinations that uses neither the shared memory nor the numbering system in section 6.2.4.

6.14 Is it possible to design a parallel algorithm for generating all m-combinations of n items on the EREW SM SIMD model of computation in $O({}^nC_m)$ time using m processors? Would the combinations be in lexicographic order?

6.15 Establish the validity of property 2 in section 6.4.1 by induction on the index i.

6.16 Procedure ADAPTIVE COMBINATIONS is cost optimal only when the number of processors N lies in the range $1 < N \leqslant {}^nC_m/n$. Can this procedure be modified (or a new procedure designed) to extend this range of optimality? Is there a parallel algorithm that is cost optimal for all values of N from 2 to ${}^nC_m$?

6.17 An n-permutation of $\{1, 2, \ldots, n\}$ is said to be a *derangement* if for each i, $1 \leqslant i \leqslant n$, integer i does not appear in position i in the permutation. Thus for $n = 5$, $(2\,5\,4\,3\,1)$ is a derangement. In all there are

$$n!\,(1 - (1/1!) + (1/2!) - \cdots + (-1)^n(1/n!))$$

derangements of n items. Design a parallel algorithm to generate derangements and analyze its running time, number of processors used, and cost.

6.18 Given an integer n, it is possible to represent it as the sum of one or more positive integers a_i:

$$n = a_1 + a_2 + \cdots + a_m.$$

This representation is called a *partition* if the order of the a_i is of no consequence. Thus two partitions of an integer n are distinct if they differ with respect to the a_i they contain.

For example, there are seven distinct partitions of the integer 5:

$$5, \ 4 + 1, \ 3 + 2, \ 3 + 1 + 1, \ 2 + 2 + 1, \ 2 + 1 + 1 + 1, \ 1 + 1 + 1 + 1 + 1.$$

Design a parallel algorithm for generating all partitions of an integer n.

6.19 For a given integer n, the representation

$$n = a_1 + a_2 + \cdots + a_m$$

is said to be a *composition* if the order of the a_i is important. Thus two compositions of an integer n are distinct if they differ with respect to the a_i they contain and the order in which the a_i are listed. For example, there are sixteen compositions of the integer 5:

$$5, \ 4 + 1, \ 1 + 4, \ 3 + 2, \ 2 + 3, \ 3 + 1 + 1, \ 1 + 3 + 1, \ 1 + 1 + 3, \ 2 + 2 + 1, \ 2 + 1 + 2,$$
$$1 + 2 + 2, \quad 2 + 1 + 1 + 1, \quad 1 + 2 + 1 + 1, \quad 1 + 1 + 2 + 1, \quad 1 + 1 + 1 + 2,$$
$$1 + 1 + 1 + 1 + 1.$$

Design a parallel algorithm for generating all compositions of an integer n.

6.20 A partition (or composition) $a_1 + a_2 + \cdots + a_m$ of an integer n is said to be *restricted* if the value of m is given. Thus, for $m = 2$, there are two partitions of the integer 5, namely, $4 + 1$ and $3 + 2$, and four compositions, namely, $4 + 1$, $1 + 4$, $3 + 2$, and $2 + 3$. Design parallel algorithms that, for given n and m, generate all restricted partitions and all restricted compositions, respectively.

6.6 BIBLIOGRAPHICAL REMARKS

The problem of generating permutations has a long history, and dozens of sequential algorithms exist for its solution. This history is traced in [Sedgewick] along with a review of the different approaches. A sequential algorithm, different from the one in section 6.2.1, for generating all m-permutations of n items is described in [Rohl]. The numbering system in section 6.2.2 is based on ideas from [Knott 2]. Many sequential algorithms have also been proposed for generating all m-combinations of n items. A number of these are compared in [Akl 2]. The combination generator (section 6.2.3) and numbering system (section 6.2.4) are based on ideas from [Mifsud] and [Knott 1], respectively.

There has been surprisingly little reported in the literature on fast generation of permutations and combinations in parallel. The algorithm in section 6.3.1 is based on that in section 6.2.1, and neither has appeared elsewhere. Both procedures ADAPTIVE PERMUTATIONS and FULL PERMUTATIONS are from [Akl 3]. An adaptive but not cost-optimal parallel algorithm for generating all ^nP_m permutations is described in [Gupta]. It runs on an EREW SM SIMD computer with N processors, $1 < N \leqslant {}^nP_m$, in $O(\lceil {}^nP_m/N \rceil m \log m)$ time. Other algorithms are described in [Chen] and [Mor].

Another approach to generating m-permutations is through the use of so-called *permutation networks*. Examples of such networks are provided in [Beneš], [Clos], [Golomb], [Lawrie], [Lenfant 1], [Lenfant 2], [Nassimi 2], [Nassimi 3], [Orcutt], [Siegel], and [Wu]. Some permutation generators are *application dependent*: They generate only those permutations that are needed to solve the problem at hand. Some of these are described in [Batcher], [Fraser], [Nassimi 1], and [Pease]. The two approaches mentioned in this paragraph are restricted in at least one of the following three ways:

1. They are based on a *hard-wired* interconnection of a predefined number of processors that can generate permutations for a fixed-size input only.

2. They are capable of generating *only a subset* of all possible permutations.

3. They typically require $O(n)$ processors and $O(\log^a n)$ steps, where $a \geqslant 1$, to generate *one* permutation of an input of length n: All permutations are therefore generated in $O(n! \log^a n)$ steps for a cost of $O(n! \, n \log^a n)$, which is *not optimal*.

By contrast the algorithms in sections 6.3.2 and 6.3.3 are

1. *adaptive*, that is, the number of available processors bears no relation to the size of the input to be permuted;

2. capable of generating *all possible* permutations of a given input; and

3. *cost optimal.*

Procedure PARALLEL COMBINATIONS is based on an algorithm in [Chan], while procedure ADAPTIVE COMBINATIONS is from [Akl 3]. Sequential algorithms for generating derangements, partitions, and compositions are given in [Akl 1] and [Page]. Other problems involving the generation of combinatorial objects for which no parallel algorithms are known are described in [Liu], [Nijenhuis], and [Reingold].

6.7 REFERENCES

[AKL 1]
   Akl, S. G., A new algorithm for generating derangements, *BIT*, Vol. 20, No. 1, 1980, pp. 2–7.

[AKL 2]
   Akl, S. G., A comparison of combination generation methods, *ACM Transactions on Mathematical Software*, Vol. 7, No. 1, March 1981, pp. 42–45.

[AKL 3]
   Akl, S. G., Adaptive and optimal parallel algorithms for enumerating permutations and combinations, *The Computer Journal*, Vol. 30, No. 5, 1987, pp. 433–436.

[BATCHER]
   Batcher, K. E., The flip network in STARAN, Proceedings of the 1976 International Conference on Parallel Processing, Detroit, Michigan, August 1976, pp. 65–71, IEEE Computer Society, Washington, D.C., 1976.

[BENEŠ]
   Beneš, V. E., *Mathematical Theory of Connecting Networks and Telephone Traffic*, Academic, New York, 1965.

[CHAN]
   Chan, B., and Akl, S. G., Generating combinations in parallel, *BIT*, Vol. 26, No. 1, 1986, pp. 2–6.

[CHEN]
   Chen, G. H., and Chern, M.-S., Parallel generation of permutations and combinations, *BIT*, Vol. 26, 1986, pp. 277–283.

[CLOS]

Clos, C., A study of non-blocking switching networks, *Bell System Technical Journal*, Vol. 32, 1953, pp. 406–424.

[FRASER]

Fraser, D., Array permutation by index digit permutation, *Journal of the ACM*, Vol. 23, No. 2, April 1976, pp. 298–308.

[GOLOMB]

Golomb, S. W., Permutations by cutting and shuffling, *SIAM Review*, Vol. 3, No. 4, October 1961, pp. 293–297.

[GUPTA]

Gupta, P., and Bhattacharjee, G. P., Parallel generation of permutations, *The Computer Journal*, Vol. 26, No. 2, 1983, pp. 97–105.

[KNOTT 1]

Knott, G. D., A numbering system for combinations, *Communications of the ACM*, Vol. 17, No. 1, January 1974, pp. 45–46.

[KNOTT 2]

Knott, G. D., A numbering system for permutations of combinations, *Communications of the ACM*, Vol. 19, No. 6, June 1976, pp. 355–356.

[LAWRIE]

Lawrie, D. H., Access and alignment of data in an array processor, *IEEE Transactions on Computers*, Vol. C-24, No. 12, December 1975, pp. 1145–1155.

[LENFANT 1]

Lenfant, J., Parallel permutations of data: A Benes network control algorithm for frequently used permutations, *IEEE Transactions on Computers*, Vol. 27, No. 7, July 1978, pp. 637–647.

[LENFANT 2]

Lenfant, J., and Tahé, S., Permuting data with the Omega network, *Acta Informatica*, Vol. 21, 1985, pp. 629–641.

[LIU]

Liu, C. L., *Introduction to Combinatorial Mathematics*, McGraw-Hill, New York, 1968.

[MIFSUD]

Mifsud, C. J., Algorithm 154: Combination in lexicographical order, *Communications of the ACM*, Vol. 6, No. 3, March 1963, p. 103.

[MOR]

Mor, M., and Fraenkel, A. S., Permutation generation on vector processors, *The Computer Journal*, Vol. 25, No. 4, 1982, pp. 423–428.

[NASSIMI 1]

Nassimi, D., and Sahni, S., Data broadcasting in SIMD computers, *IEEE Transactions on Computers*, Vol. C-30, No. 2, February 1981, pp. 282–288.

[NASSIMI 2]

Nassimi, D., and Sahni, S., A self-routing Benes network and parallel permutation algorithms, *IEEE Transactions on Computers*, Vol. C-30, No. 5, May 1981, pp. 332–340.

[NASSIMI 3]

Nassimi, D., and Sahni, S., Parallel permutation and sorting algorithms and a new generalized connection network, *Journal of the ACM*, Vol. 29, July 1982, pp. 642–677.

[NIJENHUIS]

Nijenhuis, A., and Wilf, H. S., *Combinatorial Algorithms*, Academic, New York, 1978.

[ORCUTT]

Orcutt, S. E., Implementation of permutation functions in Illiac IV-type computers, *IEEE Transactions on Computers*, Vol. C-25, No. 9, September 1976, pp. 929–936.

[PAGE]

Page, E. S., and Wilson, L. B., *An Introduction to Computational Combinatorics*, Cambridge University Press, Cambridge, England, 1979.

[PEASE]

Pease, M. C., The indirect binary *n*-cube microprocessor array, *IEEE Transactions on Computers*, Vol. C-26, No. 5, May 1977, pp. 458–473.

[REINGOLD]

Reingold, E. M., Nievergelt, J., and Deo, N., *Combinatorial Algorithms*, Prentice-Hall, Englewood Cliffs, N.J., 1977.

[ROHL]

Rohl, J. S., Generating permutations by choosing, *The Computer Journal*, Vol. 21, No. 4, 1978, pp. 302–305.

[SEDGEWICK]

Sedgewick, R., Permutation generation methods, *ACM Computing Surveys*, Vol. 19, No. 2, June 1977, pp. 137–164.

[SIEGEL]

Siegel, H. J., *Interconnection Networks for Large-Scale Parallel Processing*, Heath, Lexington, Mass., 1985.

[WU]

Wu, C.-L., and Feng, T.-Y., The universality of the shuffle-exchange network, *IEEE Transactions on Computers*, Vol. C-30, No. 5, May 1981, pp. 324–332.

7

Matrix Operations

7.1 INTRODUCTION

Problems involving matrices arise in a multitude of numerical and nonnumerical contexts. Examples range from the solution of systems of equations (see chapter 8) to the representation of graphs (see chapter 10). In this chapter we show how three operations on matrices can be performed in parallel. These operations are matrix transposition (section 7.2), matrix-by-matrix multiplication (section 7.3), and matrix-by-vector multiplication (section 7.4). Other operations are described in chapters 8 and 10. One particular feature of this chapter is that it illustrates the use of all the interconnection networks described in chapter 1, namely, the one-dimensional array, the mesh, the tree, the perfect shuffle, and the cube.

7.2 TRANSPOSITION

An $n \times n$ matrix A is given, for example:

$$A = \begin{bmatrix} a_{11} & a_{12} & a_{13} & a_{14} \\ a_{21} & a_{22} & a_{23} & a_{24} \\ a_{31} & a_{32} & a_{33} & a_{34} \\ a_{41} & a_{42} & a_{43} & a_{44} \end{bmatrix};$$

it is required to compute the *transpose* of A:

$$A^T = \begin{bmatrix} a_{11} & a_{21} & a_{31} & a_{41} \\ a_{12} & a_{22} & a_{32} & a_{42} \\ a_{13} & a_{23} & a_{33} & a_{43} \\ a_{14} & a_{24} & a_{34} & a_{44} \end{bmatrix}.$$

In other words, every *row* in matrix A is now a *column* in matrix A^T. The elements of A are any data objects; thus a_{ij} could be an integer, a real, a character, and so on.

Sequentially the transpose of a matrix can be computed very easily as shown in procedure TRANSPOSE. The procedure transposes A *in place*, that is, it returns A^T in the same memory locations previously occupied by A.

procedure TRANSPOSE (A)

> **for** $i = 2$ **to** n **do**
>> **for** $j = 1$ **to** $i - 1$ **do**
>>> $a_{ij} \leftrightarrow a_{ji}$
>> **end for**
> **end for.** $\square$

This procedure runs in $O(n^2)$ time, which is optimal in view of the $\Omega(n^2)$ steps required to simply read A.

In this section we show how the transpose can be computed in parallel on three different models of parallel computation, namely, the mesh-connected, shuffle-connected, and the shared-memory SIMD computers.

7.2.1 Mesh Transpose

The parallel architecture that lends itself most naturally to matrix operations is the mesh. Indeed, an $n \times n$ mesh of processors can be regarded as a matrix and is therefore perfectly fitted to accommodate an $n \times n$ data matrix, one element per processor. This is precisely the approach we shall use to compute the transpose of an $n \times n$ matrix A initially stored in an $n \times n$ mesh of processors, as shown in Fig. 7.1 for $n = 4$. Initially, processor $P(i, j)$ holds data element a_{ij}; at the end of the computation $P(i, j)$ should hold a_{ji}. Note that with this arrangement $\Omega(n)$ is a lower bound on the running time of any matrix transposition algorithm. This is seen by observing that a_{1n} cannot reach $P(n, 1)$ in fewer than $2n - 2$ steps.

The idea of our algorithm is quite simple. Since the diagonal elements are not affected during the transposition, that is, element a_{ii} of A equals element a_{ii} of A^T, the data in the diagonal processors will stay stationary. Those below the diagonal are sent to occupy symmetrical positions above the diagonal (solid arrows in Fig. 7.1). Simultaneously, the elements above the diagonal are sent to occupy symmetrical positions below the diagonal (dashed arrows in Fig. 7.1). Each processor $P(i, j)$ has three registers:

1. $A(i, j)$ is used to store a_{ij} initially and a_{ji} when the algorithm terminates;
2. $B(i, j)$ is used to store data received from $P(i, j + 1)$ or $P(i - 1, j)$, that is, from its right or top neighbors; and
3. $C(i, j)$ is used to store data received from $P(i, j - 1)$ or $P(i + 1, j)$, that is, from its left or bottom neighbors.

The algorithm is given as procedure MESH TRANSPOSE. Note that the contents of registers $A(i, i)$, initially equal to a_{ii}, $1 \leqslant i \leqslant n$, are not affected by the procedure.

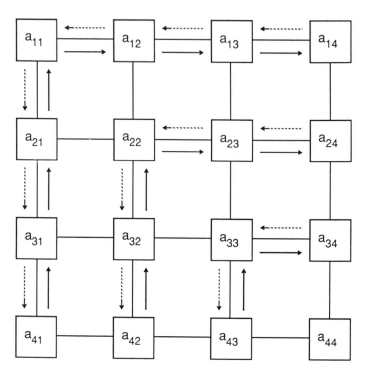

Figure 7.1   Matrix to be transposed, stored in mesh of processors.

procedure MESH TRANSPOSE (A)

Step 1:   **do** steps 1.1 and 1.2 **in parallel**
           (1.1) **for** $i = 2$ **to** n **do in parallel**
                   for $j = 1$ **to** $i - 1$ **do in parallel**
                      $C(i - 1, j) \leftarrow (a_{ij}, j, i)$
                   end for
                 end for
           (1.2) **for** $i = 1$ **to** $n - 1$ **do in parallel**
                   for $j = i + 1$ **to** n **do in parallel**
                      $B(i, j - 1) \leftarrow (a_{ij}, j, i)$
                   end for
                 end for.

Step 2:   **do** steps 2.1, 2.2, and 2.3 **in parallel**
           (2.1) **for** $i = 2$ **to** n **do in parallel**
                   for $j = 1$ **to** $i - 1$ **do in parallel**
                      while $P(i, j)$ receives input from its neighbors **do**
                        (i) **if** (a_{km}, m, k) is received from $P(i + 1, j)$
                            then send it to $P(i - 1, j)$
                            end if

(ii) **if** (a_{km}, m, k) is received from $P(i - 1, j)$
  then if $i = m$ **and** $j = k$
    then $A(i, j) \leftarrow a_{km}$ $\{a_{km}$ has reached its destination$\}$
    else send (a_{km}, m, k) to $P(i + 1, j)$
    end if
  end if
 end while
 end for
end for

(2.2) **for** $i = 1$ **to** n **do in parallel**
  while $P(i, i)$ receives input from its neighbors **do**
  (i) **if** (a_{km}, m, k) is received from $P(i + 1, i)$
    then send it to $P(i, i + 1)$
   end if
  (ii) **if** (a_{km}, m, k) is received from $P(i, i + 1)$
    then send it to $P(i + 1, i)$
   end if
  end while
 end for

(2.3) **for** $i = 1$ **to** $n - 1$ **do in parallel**
  for $j = i + 1$ **to** n **do in parallel**
   while $P(i, j)$ receives input from its neighbors **do**
   (i) **if** (a_{km}, m, k) is received from $P(i, j + 1)$
     then send it to $P(i, j - 1)$
    end if
   (ii) **if** (a_{km}, m, k) is received from $P(i, j - 1)$
     then if $i = m$ **and** $j = k$
       then $A(i, j) \leftarrow a_{km}$ $\{a_{km}$ has reached its destination$\}$
       else send (a_{km}, m, k) to $P(i, j + 1)$
      end if
     end if
    end while
   end for
  end for. $\square$

Analysis.   Each element a_{ij}, $i > j$, must travel up its column until it reaches $P(j, j)$ and then travel along a row until it settles in $P(j, i)$. Similarly for $a_{ij}, j > i$. The longest path is the one traversed by a_{n1} (or a_{1n}), which consists of $2(n - 1)$ steps. The running time of procedure MESH TRANSPOSE is therefore

$$t(n) = O(n),$$

which is the best possible for the mesh. Since $p(n) = n^2$, the procedure has a cost of $O(n^3)$, which is not optimal.

Example 7.1

 The behavior of procedure MESH TRANSPOSE is illustrated in Fig. 7.2 for the input matrix

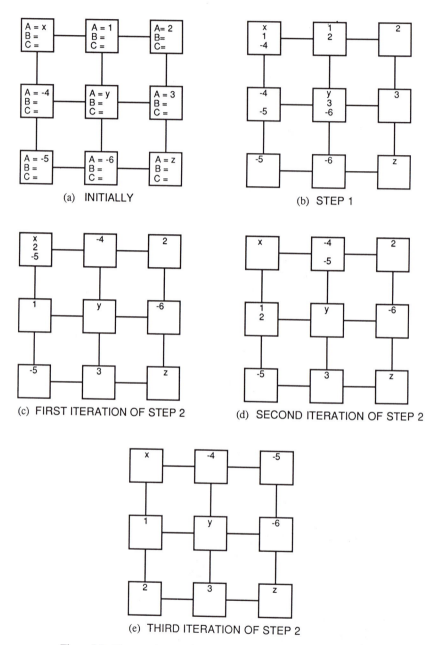

(a) INITIALLY

(b) STEP 1

(c) FIRST ITERATION OF STEP 2

(d) SECOND ITERATION OF STEP 2

(e) THIRD ITERATION OF STEP 2

Figure 7.2 Transposing matrix using procedure MESH TRANSPOSE.

$$A = \begin{bmatrix} x & 1 & 2 \\ -4 & y & 3 \\ -5 & -6 & z \end{bmatrix}.$$

The contents of registers A, B, and C in each processor are shown. Note that for clarity only the a_{ij} component of (a_{ij}, j, i) is shown for registers B and C. Also when either B or C receives no new input, it is shown empty. □

7.2.2 Shuffle Transpose

We saw in the previous section that procedure MESH TRANSPOSE computes the transpose of an $n \times n$ matrix in $O(n)$ time. We also noted that this running time is the fastest that can be obtained on a mesh with one data element per processor. However, since the transpose can be computed sequentially in $O(n^2)$ time, the speedup achieved by procedure MESH TRANSPOSE is only linear. This speedup may be considered rather small since the procedure uses a quadratic number of processors. This section shows how the same number of processors arranged in a different geometry can transpose a matrix in logarithmic time.

Let $n = 2^q$ and assume that an $n \times n$ matrix A is to be transposed. We use for that purpose a perfect shuffle interconnection with n^2 processors P_0, P_1, ..., $P_{2^{2q}-1}$. Element a_{ij} of A is initially stored in processor P_k, where $k = 2^q(i-1) + (j-1)$, as shown in Fig. 7.3 for $q = 2$.

We claim that after exactly q shuffle operations processor P_k contains element a_{ji}. To see this, recall that if P_k is connected to P_m, then m is obtained from k by cyclically shifting to the left by one position the binary representation of k. Thus P_{0000} is connected to itself, P_{0001} to P_{0010}, P_{0010} to P_{0100}, ..., P_{1001} to P_{0011}, P_{1010} to

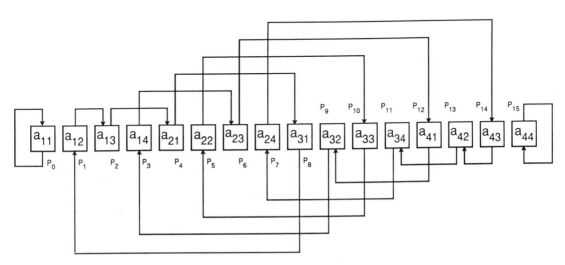

Figure 7.3 Matrix to be transposed, stored in perfect shuffle-connected computer.

$P_{0101}, \ldots$, and P_{1111} to itself. Now consider a processor index k consisting of $2q$ bits. If $k = 2^q(i-1) + (j-1)$, then the q most significant bits of k represent $i-1$ while the q least significant bits represent $j-1$. This is illustrated in Fig. 7.4(a) for $q = 5$, $i = 5$, and $j = 12$. After q shuffles (i.e., q cyclic shifts to the left), the element originally held by P_k will be in the processor whose index is

$$s = 2^q(j-1) + (i-1),$$

as shown in Fig. 7.4(b). In other words a_{ij} has been moved to the position originally occupied by a_{ji}. The algorithm is given as procedure SHUFFLE TRANSPOSE. In it we use the notation $2k \bmod (2^{2q} - 1)$ to represent the remainder of the division of $2k$ by $2^{2q} - 1$.

procedure SHUFFLE TRANSPOSE (A)

    for $i = 1$ **to** q **do**
        for $k = 1$ **to** $2^{2q} - 2$ **do in parallel**
            P_k sends the element of A it currently holds to $P_{2k \bmod(2^{2q}-1)}$
        end for
    end for.   □

Analysis.   There are q constant time iterations and therefore the procedure runs in $t(n) = O(\log n)$ time. Since $p(n) = n^2$, $c(n) = O(n^2 \log n)$, which is not optimal. Interestingly, the shuffle interconnection is faster than the mesh in computing the transpose of a matrix. This is contrary to our original intuition, which suggested that the mesh is the most naturally suited geometry for matrix operations.

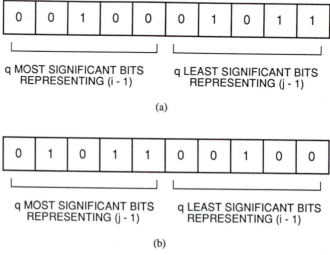

Figure 7.4   Derivation of number of shuffles required to transpose matrix.

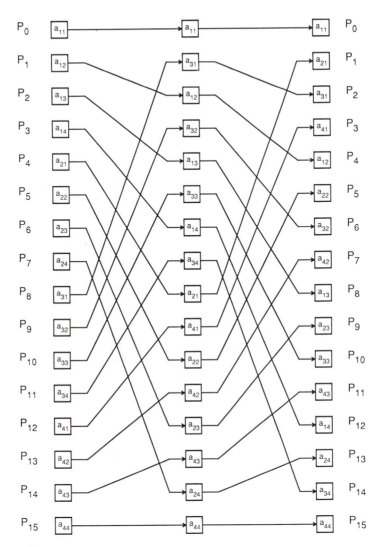

Figure 7.5   Transposing matrix using procedure SHUFFLE TRANSPOSE.

Example 7.2

   The behavior of procedure SHUFFLE TRANSPOSE is illustrated in Fig. 7.5 for the case
   where $q = 2$. For clarity, the shuffle interconnections are shown as a mapping from the set
   of processors to itself.   □

7.2.3 EREW Transpose

Although faster than procedure MESH TRANSPOSE, procedure SHUFFLE
TRANSPOSE is not cost optimal. We conclude this section by describing a cost-

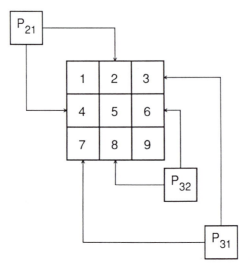

Figure 7.6 Transposing matrix using procedure EREW TRANSPOSE.

optimal algorithm for transposing an $n \times n$ matrix A. The algorithm uses $(n^2 - n)/2$ processors and runs on an **EREW SM SIMD** computer. Matrix A resides in the shared memory. For ease of exposition, we assume that each processor has two indices i and j, where $2 \leqslant i \leqslant n$ and $1 \leqslant j \leqslant i - 1$. With all processors operating in parallel, processor P_{ij} swaps two elements of A, namely, a_{ij} and a_{ji}. The algorithm is given as procedure EREW TRANSPOSE.

procedure EREW TRANSPOSE (A)

for $i = 2$ **to** n **do in parallel**
  for $j = 1$ **to** $i - 1$ **do in parallel**
    $a_{ij} \leftrightarrow a_{ji}$
  end for
end for. □

Analysis. It takes constant time for each processor to swap two elements. Thus the running time of procedure **EREW TRANSPOSE** is $t(n) = O(1)$. Since $p(n) = O(n^2)$, $c(n) = O(n^2)$, which is optimal.

Example 7.3

The behavior of procedure EREW TRANSPOSE is illustrated in Fig. 7.6 for $n = 3$. The figure shows the two elements swapped by each processor. □

7.3 MATRIX-BY-MATRIX MULTIPLICATION

In this section we assume that the elements of all matrices are numerals, say, integers. The product of an $m \times n$ matrix A by an $n \times k$ matrix B is an $m \times k$ matrix C whose elements are given by

$$c_{ij} = \sum_{s=1}^{n} a_{is} \times b_{sj}, \qquad 1 \leqslant i \leqslant m, \quad 1 \leqslant j \leqslant k.$$

A straightforward sequential implementation of the preceding definition is given by procedure MATRIX MULTIPLICATION.

procedure MATRIX MULTIPLICATION (A, B, C)

    for $i = 1$ **to** m **do**
      for $j = 1$ **to** k **do**
      (1) $c_{ij} \leftarrow 0$
      (2) **for** $s = 1$ **to** n **do**
            $c_{ij} \leftarrow c_{ij} + (a_{is} \times b_{sj})$
      end for
    end for
    end for. □

Assuming that $m \leqslant n$ and $k \leqslant n$, it is clear that procedure MATRIX MULTIPLICATION runs in $O(n^3)$ time. As indicated in section 7.6, however, there exist several sequential matrix multiplication algorithms whose running time is $O(n^x)$, where $2 < x < 3$. It is not known at the time of this writing whether the fastest of these algorithms is optimal. Indeed, the only known lower bound on the number of steps required for matrix multiplication is the *trivial* one of $\Omega(n^2)$. This lower bound is obtained by observing that n^2 outputs are to be produced, and therefore any algorithm must require at least that many steps. In view of this gap between n^2 and n^x, $2 < x < 3$, we will find ourselves unable to exhibit cost-optimal parallel algorithms for matrix multiplication. Rather, we present algorithms whose cost is matched against the running time of procedure MATRIX MULTIPLICATION.

7.3.1 Mesh Multiplication

As with the problem of transposition, again we feel compelled to use a mesh-connected parallel computer to perform matrix multiplication. Our algorithm uses $m \times k$ processors arranged in a mesh configuration to multiply an $m \times n$ matrix A by an $n \times k$ matrix B. Mesh rows are numbered $1, \ldots, m$ and mesh columns $1, \ldots, k$. Matrices A and B are fed into the *boundary* processors in column 1 and row 1, respectively, as shown in Fig. 7.7 for $m = 4, n = 5$, and $k = 3$. Note that row i of matrix A lags one time unit behind row $i - 1$ for $2 \leqslant i \leqslant m$. Similarly, column j of matrix B lags one time unit behind column $j - 1$ for $2 \leqslant j \leqslant k$. This ensures that a_{is} meets b_{sj} in processor $P(i, j)$ at the right time. At the end of the algorithm, element c_{ij} of the product matrix C resides in processor $P(i, j)$. Initially c_{ij} is zero. Subsequently, when $P(i, j)$ receives two inputs a and b, it

  (i) multiplies them,
  (ii) adds the result to c_{ij},

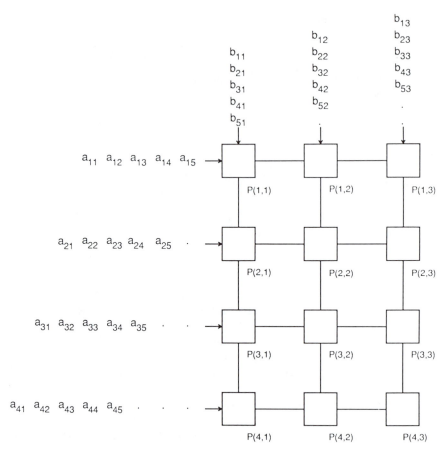

Figure 7.7   Two matrices to be multiplied, being fed as input to mesh of processors.

(iii) sends a to $P(i, j + 1)$ unless $j = k$, and

(iv) sends b to $P(i + 1, j)$ unless $i = m$.

The algorithm is given as procedure MESH MATRIX MULTIPLICATION.

procedure MESH MATRIX MULTIPLICATION (A, B, C)

    for $i = 1$ **to** m **do in parallel**
    for $j = 1$ **to** k **do in parallel**
        (1) $c_{ij} \leftarrow 0$
        (2) **while** $P(i, j)$ receives two inputs a and b **do**
            (i) $c_{ij} \leftarrow c_{ij} + (a \times b)$
            (ii) **if** $i < m$ **then** send b to $P(i + 1, j)$
                end if

(iii) **if** $j < k$ **then** send a to $P(i, j + 1)$
    end if
  end while
 end for
 end for.   □

Analysis.   Elements a_{m1} and b_{1k} take $m + k + n - 2$ steps from the beginning of the computation to reach $P(m, k)$. Since $P(m, k)$ is the last processor to terminate, this many steps are required to compute the product. Assuming that $m \leq n$ and $k \leq n$, procedure MESH MATRIX MULTIPLICATION therefore runs in time $t(n) = O(n)$. Since $p(n) = O(n^2)$, $c(n) = O(n^3)$, which matches the running time of the sequential procedure MATRIX MULTIPLICATION. It should be noted that the running time of procedure MESH MATRIX MULTIPLICATION is the fastest achievable for matrix multiplication on a mesh of processors assuming that only boundary processors are capable of handling input and output operations. Indeed, under this assumption $\Omega(n)$ steps are needed for the input to be read (by the processors in row 1 and column 1, say) and/or for the output to be produced (by the processors in row m and column k, say).

Example 7.4

The behavior of procedure MESH MATRIX MULTIPLICATION is illustrated in Fig. 7.8 for

$$A = \begin{bmatrix} 1 & 2 \\ 3 & 4 \end{bmatrix} \quad \text{and} \quad B = \begin{bmatrix} -5 & -6 \\ -7 & -8 \end{bmatrix}.$$

The value of c_{ij} after each step is shown inside $P(i, j)$.   □

7.3.2 Cube Multiplication

The running time of procedure MESH MATRIX MULTIPLICATION not only is the best achievable on the mesh, but also provides the highest speedup over the sequential procedure MATRIX MULTIPLICATION using n^2 processors. Nevertheless, we seek to obtain a faster algorithm, and as we did in section 7.2.2, we shall turn to another architecture for that purpose. Our chosen model is the cube-connected SIMD computer introduced in chapter 1 and that we now describe more formally.

Let $N = 2^g$ processors $P_0, P_1, \ldots, P_{2^g - 1}$ be available for some $g \geq 1$. Further, let i and $i^{(b)}$ be two integers, $0 \leq i, i^{(b)} \leq 2^g - 1$, whose binary representations differ only in position b, $0 \leq b < g$. In other words, if $i_{g-1} \ldots i_{b+1} i_b i_{b-1} \ldots i_1 i_0$ is the binary representation of i, then $i_{g-1} \ldots i_{b+1} i'_b i_{b-1} \ldots i_1 i_0$ is the binary representation of $i^{(b)}$, where i'_b is the binary complement of bit i_b. The cube connection specifies that every processor P_i is connected to processor $P_{i^{(b)}}$ by a two-way link for all $0 \leq b < g$. The g processors to which P_i is connected are called P_i's *neighbors*. An example of such a connection is illustrated in Fig. 7.9 for the case $g = 4$. Now let $n = 2^q$. We use a cube-connected SIMD computer with $N = n^3 = 2^{3q}$ processors to multiply two $n \times n$ matrices A and B. (We assume for simplicity of presentation that the two matrices

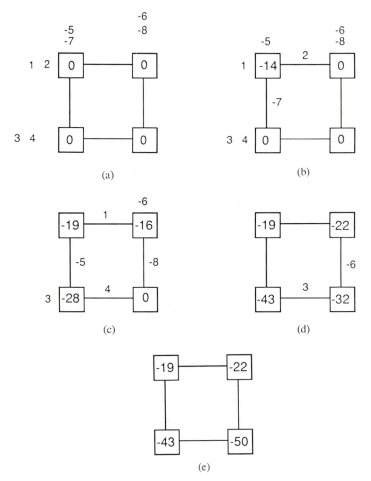

Figure 7.8 Multiplying two matrices using procedure MESH MATRIX MULTIPLICATION.

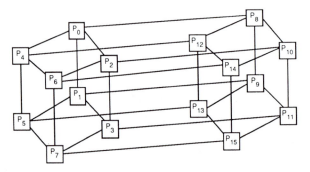

Figure 7.9 Cube-connected computer with sixteen processors.

have the same number of rows and columns.) It is helpful to visualize the processors as being arranged in an $n \times n \times n$ array pattern. In this array, processor P_r occupies position (i, j, k), where $r = in^2 + jn + k$ and $0 \leqslant i, j, k \leqslant n - 1$ (this is referred to as *row-major order*). Thus if the binary representation of r is $r_{3q-1} r_{3q-2} \ldots r_0$, then the binary representations of i, j, and k are $r_{3q-1} \ldots r_{2q}$, $r_{2q-1} \ldots r_q$, and $r_{q-1} \ldots r_0$, respectively. Each processor P_r has three registers A_r, B_r, and C_r, also denoted $A(i, j, k)$, $B(i, j, k)$, and $C(i, j, k)$, respectively. Initially, processor P_s in position $(0, j, k)$, $0 \leqslant j < n$, $0 \leqslant k < n$, contains a_{jk} and b_{jk} in its registers A_s and B_s, respectively. The registers of all other processors are initialized to zero. At the end of the computation, C should contain c_{jk}, where

$$c_{jk} = \sum_{i=0}^{n-1} a_{ji} \times b_{ik}.$$

The algorithm is designed to perform the n^3 multiplications involved in computing the n^2 entries of C simultaneously. It proceeds in three stages.

Stage 1: The elements of matrices A and B are distributed over the n^3 processors. As a result, $A(i, j, k) = a_{ji}$ and $B(i, j, k) = b_{ik}$.

Stage 2: The products $C(i, j, k) = A(i, j, k) \times B(i, j, k)$ are computed.

Stage 3: The sums $\sum_{i=0}^{n-1} C(i, j, k)$ are computed.

The algorithm is given as procedure CUBE MATRIX MULTIPLICATION. In it we denote by $\{N, r_m = d\}$ the set of integers r, $0 \leqslant r < N - 1$, whose binary representation is $r_{3q-1} \ldots r_{m+1} \, d \, r_{m-1} \ldots r_0$.

procedure CUBE MATRIX MULTIPLICATION (A, B, C)

Step 1:   **for** $m = 3q - 1$ **downto** $2q$ **do**
  for all r **in** $\{N, r_m = 0\}$ **do in parallel**
    (1.1) $A_{r^{(m)}} = A_r$
    (1.2) $B_{r^{(m)}} = B_r$
  end for
end for.

Step 2:   **for** $m = q - 1$ **downto** 0 **do**
  for all r **in** $\{N, r_m = r_{2q+m}\}$ **do in parallel**
    $A_{r^{(m)}} \leftarrow A_r$
  end for
end for.

Step 3:   **for** $m = 2q - 1$ **downto** q **do**
  for all r **in** $\{N, r_m = r_{q+m}\}$ **do in parallel**
    $B_{r^{(m)}} \leftarrow B_r$
  end for
end for.

Step 4:   **for** $r = 1$ **to** N **do in parallel**
    $C_r \leftarrow A_r \times B_r$
  end for.

Step 5: **for** $m = 2q$ **to** $3q - 1$ **do**
 for $r = 1$ **to** N **do in parallel**
 $C_r \leftarrow C_r + C_{r^{(m)}}$
 end for
 end for. ☐

Stage 1 of the algorithm is implemented by steps 1–3. During step 1, the data initially in $A(0, j, k)$ and $B(0, j, k)$ are copied into the processors in positions (i, j, k), where $1 \leq i < n$, so that at the end of this step $A(i, j, k) = a_{jk}$ and $B(i, j, k) = b_{jk}$ for $0 \leq i < n$. Step 2 copies the contents of $A(i, j, i)$ into the processors in position (i, j, k), so that at the end of this step $A(i, j, k) = a_{ji}$, $0 \leq k < n$. Similarly, step 3 copies the contents of $B(i, i, k)$ into the processors in position (i, j, k), so that at the end of this step $B(i, j, k) = b_{ik}$, $0 \leq j < n$. In step 4 the product $C(i, j, k) = A(i, j, k) \times B(i, j, k)$ is computed by the processors in position (i, j, k) for all $0 \leq i, j, k < n$ simultaneously. Finally, in step 5, the n^2 sums

$$C(0, j, k) = \sum_{i=0}^{n-1} C(i, j, k)$$

are computed simultaneously.

Analysis. Steps 1, 2, 3, and 5 consist of q constant time iterations, while step 4 takes constant time. Thus procedure CUBE MATRIX MULTIPLICATION runs in $O(q)$ time, that is, $t(n) = O(\log n)$. We now show that this running time is the fastest achievable by any parallel algorithm for multiplying two $n \times n$ matrices on the cube. First note that each c_{ij} is the sum of n elements. It takes $\Omega(\log n)$ steps to compute this sum on any interconnection network with n (or more) processors. To see this, let s be the smallest number of steps required by a network to compute the sum of n numbers. During the final step, at most one processor is needed to perform the last addition and produce the result. During step $s - 1$ at most two processors are needed, during step $s - 2$ at most four processors, and so on. Thus after s steps, the maximum number of useful additions that can be performed is

$$\sum_{i=0}^{s-1} 2^i = 2^s - 1.$$

Given that exactly $n - 1$ additions are needed to compute the sum of n numbers, we have $n - 1 \leq 2^s - 1$, that is, $s \geq \log n$.

Since $p(n) = n^3$, procedure CUBE MATRIX MULTIPLICATION has a cost of $c(n) = O(n^3 \log n)$, which is higher than the running time of sequential procedure MATRIX MULTIPLICATION. Thus, although matrix multiplication on the cube is faster than on the mesh, its cost is higher due to the large number of processors it uses.

Example 7.5

Let $n = 2^2$ and assume that the two 4×4 matrices to be multiplied are

$$A = \begin{bmatrix} 17 & 23 & 27 & 3 \\ 9 & 1 & 14 & 16 \\ 31 & 26 & 22 & 8 \\ 15 & 4 & 10 & 29 \end{bmatrix} \quad \text{and} \quad B = \begin{bmatrix} -7 & -25 & -19 & -5 \\ -18 & -30 & -28 & -12 \\ -13 & -21 & -11 & -32 \\ -20 & -2 & -6 & -24 \end{bmatrix}$$

There are $N = 2^6$ processors available on a cube-connected SIMD computer $P_0, P_1, \ldots, P_{63}$. The processors are arranged in a three-dimensional array as shown in Fig. 7.10(a). (Note that this three-dimensional array is in fact a six-dimensional cube with connections omitted for simplicity.) Each of i, j, k contributes two bits to the binary representation $r_5 r_4 r_3 r_2 r_1 r_0$ of the index r of processor P_r: $i = r_5 r_4$, $j = r_3 r_2$, and $k = r_1 r_0$. Initially the matrices A and B are loaded into registers $P_0, \ldots, P_{15}$, as shown in Fig. 7.10(b).

Since $q = 2$, step 1 is iterated twice: once for $m = 5$ and once for $m = 4$. In the first iteration, all processors whose binary index $r_5 r_4 r_3 r_2 r_1 r_0$ is such that $r_5 = 0$ copy their contents into the processors with binary index $r_5' r_4 r_3 r_2 r_1 r_0$ (i.e., $r_5' = 1$). Thus $P_0, \ldots, P_{15}$ copy their initial contents into $P_{32}, \ldots, P_{47}$, respectively, and simultaneously $P_{16}, \ldots, P_{31}$ copy their initial contents (all zeros) into $P_{48}, \ldots, P_{63}$, respectively. In the second iteration, all processors whose binary index $r_5 r_4 r_3 r_2 r_1 r_0$ is such that $r_4 = 0$ copy their contents into the processors with binary index $r_5 r_4' r_3 r_2 r_1 r_0$ (i.e., $r_4' = 1$). Thus $P_0, \ldots, P_{15}$ copy their contents into $P_{16}, \ldots, P_{31}$, respectively, and simultaneously $P_{32}, \ldots, P_{47}$ copy their new contents (acquired in the previous iteration) into $P_{48}, \ldots, P_{63}$, respectively. At the end of step 1, the contents of the sixty-four processors are as shown in Fig. 7.10(c).

There are two iterations of step 2: one for $m = 1$ and one for $m = 0$. During the first iteration all processors with binary index $r_5 r_4 r_3 r_2 r_1 r_0$ such that $r_1 = r_5$ copy the contents of their A registers into those of processors with binary index $r_5 r_4 r_3 r_2 r_1' r_0$. Thus, for example, P_0 and P_1 copy the contents of their A registers into the A registers of P_2 and P_3, respectively. During the second iteration all processors with binary index $r_5 r_4 r_3 r_2 r_1 r_0$ such that $r_0 = r_4$ copy the contents of their A registers into the A registers of processors with binary index $r_5 r_4 r_3 r_2 r_1 r_0'$. Again, for example, P_0 and P_2 copy the contents of their A registers into the A registers of P_1 and P_3, respectively. At the end of this step one element of matrix A has been replicated across each "row" in Fig. 7.10(a). Step 3 is equivalent except that it replicates one element of matrix B across each "column." The contents of the sixty-four processors at the end of steps 2 and 3 are shown in Fig. 7.10(d). In step 4, with all processors operating simultaneously, each processor computes the product of its A and B registers and stores the result in its C register. Step 5 consists of two iterations: one for $m = 4$ and one for $m = 5$. In the first iteration the contents of the C registers of processor pairs whose binary indices differ in bit r_4 are added. Both processors keep the result. The same is done in the second iteration for processors differing in bit r_5. The final answer, stored in $P_0, \ldots, P_{15}$ is shown in Fig. 7.10(e).   □

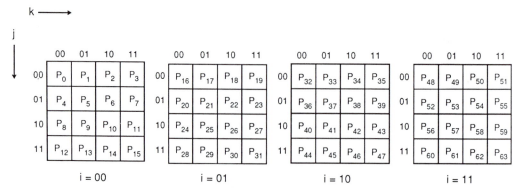

(a)

(b)

17 / -7	23 / -25	27 / -19	3 / -5
9 / -18	1 / -30	14 / -28	16 / -12
31 / -13	26 / -21	22 / -11	8 / -32
15 / -20	4 / -2	10 / -6	29 / -24

(c)

17 / -7	23 / -25	27 / -19	3 / -5
9 / -18	1 / -30	14 / -28	16 / -12
31 / -13	26 / -21	22 / -11	8 / -32
15 / -20	4 / -2	10 / -6	29 / -24

17 / -7	23 / -25	27 / -19	3 / -5
9 / -18	1 / -30	14 / -28	16 / -12
31 / -13	26 / -21	22 / -11	8 / -32
15 / -20	4 / -2	10 / -6	29 / -24

17 / -7	23 / -25	27 / -19	3 / -5
9 / -18	1 / -30	14 / -28	16 / -12
31 / -13	26 / -21	22 / -11	8 / -32
15 / -20	4 / -2	10 / -6	29 / -24

17 / -7	23 / -25	27 / -19	3 / -5
9 / -18	1 / -30	14 / -28	16 / -12
31 / -13	26 / -21	22 / -11	8 / -32
15 / -20	4 / -2	10 / -6	29 / -24

(d)

17 / -7	17 / -25	17 / -19	17 / -5
9 / -7	9 / -25	9 / -19	9 / -5
31 / -7	31 / -25	31 / -19	31 / -5
15 / -7	15 / -25	15 / -19	15 / -5

23 / -18	23 / -30	23 / -28	23 / -12
1 / -18	1 / -30	1 / -28	1 / -12
26 / -18	26 / -30	26 / -28	26 / -12
4 / -18	4 / -30	4 / -28	4 / -12

27 / -13	27 / -21	27 / -11	27 / -32
14 / -13	14 / -21	14 / -11	14 / -32
22 / -13	22 / -21	22 / -11	22 / -32
10 / -13	10 / -21	10 / -11	10 / -32

3 / -20	3 / -2	3 / -6	3 / -24
16 / -20	16 / -2	16 / -6	16 / -24
8 / -20	8 / -2	8 / -6	8 / -24
29 / -20	29 / -2	29 / -6	29 / -24

-944	-1688	-1282	-1297
-583	-581	-449	-889
-1131	-2033	-1607	-1363
-887	-763	-681	-1139

(e)

Figure 7.10 Multiplying two matrices using procedure CUBE MATRIX MULTIPLICATION.

7.3.3 CRCW Multiplication

We conclude this section by presenting a parallel algorithm for matrix multiplication that is faster and has lower cost than procedure CUBE MATRIX MULTIPLICATION. The algorithm is designed to run on a CRCW SM SIMD computer. We assume that *write conflicts* are resolved as follows: When several processors attempt to write in the same memory location, the *sum* of the numbers to be written is stored in that location. The algorithm is a direct parallelization of sequential procedure MATRIX MULTIPLICATION. It uses $m \times n \times k$ processors to multiply an $m \times n$ matrix A by an $n \times k$ matrix B. Conceptually the processors may be thought of as being arranged in a $m \times n \times k$ array pattern, each processor having three indices (i, j, s), where $1 \leqslant i \leqslant m$, $1 \leqslant j \leqslant n$, and $1 \leqslant s \leqslant k$. Initially matrices A and B are in shared memory; when the algorithm terminates, their product matrix C is also in shared memory. The algorithm is given as procedure CRCW MATRIX MULTIPLICATION.

    procedure CRCW MATRIX MULTIPLICATION (A, B, C)

     for $i = 1$ **to** m **do in parallel**
      for $j = 1$ **to** k **do in parallel**
       for $s = 1$ **to** n **do in parallel**
        (1) $c_{ij} \leftarrow 0$
        (2) $c_{ij} \leftarrow a_{is} \times b_{sj}$
       end for
      end for
     end for. □

  Analysis.   It is clear that procedure CRCW MATRIX MULTIPLICATION runs in constant time. Since $p(n) = n^3$,

$$c(n) = p(n) \times t(n)$$
$$= n^3 \times O(1)$$
$$= O(n^3),$$

which matches the running time of sequential procedure MATRIX MULTI-PLICATION.

Example 7.6

A CRCW SM SIMD computer with sixty-four processors can multiply the two matrices A and B of example 7.5 in constant time. All sixty-four products shown in Fig. 7.10(d) are computed simultaneously and stored (i.e., added) in groups of four in the appropriate position in C. Thus, for example, P_1, P_2, P_3, and P_4 compute $17 \times (-7)$, $23 \times (-18)$, $27 \times (-13)$, and $3 \times (-20)$, respectively, and store the results in c_{11}, yielding $c_{11} = -944$. □

7.4 MATRIX-BY-VECTOR MULTIPLICATION

The problem addressed in this section is that of multiplying an $m \times n$ matrix A by an $n \times 1$ vector U to produce an $m \times 1$ vector V, as shown for $m = 3$ and $n = 4$:

$$\begin{bmatrix} a_{11} & a_{12} & a_{13} & a_{14} \\ a_{21} & a_{22} & a_{23} & a_{24} \\ a_{31} & a_{32} & a_{33} & a_{34} \end{bmatrix} \times \begin{bmatrix} u_1 \\ u_2 \\ u_3 \\ u_4 \end{bmatrix} = \begin{bmatrix} v_1 \\ v_2 \\ v_3 \end{bmatrix}.$$

The elements of V are obtained from

$$v_i = \sum_{j=1}^{n} a_{ij} \times u_j, \qquad 1 \leqslant i \leqslant m.$$

This of course is a special case of matrix-by-matrix multiplication. We study it separately in order to demonstrate the use of two interconnection networks in performing matrix operations, namely, the linear (or one-dimensional) array and the tree. In addition, we show how a parallel algorithm for matrix-by-vector multiplication can be used to solve the problem of convolution.

7.4.1 Linear Array Multiplication

Our first algorithm for matrix-by-vector multiplication is designed to run on a linear array with m processors $P_1, P_2, \ldots, P_m$. Processor P_i is used to compute element v_i of V. Initially, v_i is zero. Matrix A and vector U are fed to the array, as shown in Fig. 7.11, for $n = 4$ and $m = 3$. Each processor P_i has three registers a, u, and v. When P_i receives two inputs a_{ij} and u_j, it

   (i) stores a_{ij} in a and u_j in u,
  (ii) multiplies a by u,
 (iii) adds the result to v_i, and
 (iv) sends u_j to P_{i-1} unless $i = 1$.

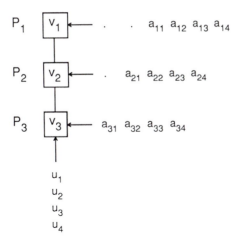

Figure 7.11 Matrix and vector to be multiplied, being fed as input to linear array.

Note that row i of matrix A lags one time unit behind row $i + 1$ for $1 \leqslant i \leqslant m - 1$. This ensures that a_{ij} meets u_j at the right time. The algorithm is given as procedure LINEAR MV MULTIPLICATION.

procedure LINEAR MV MULTIPLICATION (A, U, V)

   for $i = 1$ **to** m **do in parallel**
    (1) $v_i \leftarrow 0$
    (2) **while** P_i receives two inputs a and u **do**
      (2.1) $v_i \leftarrow v_i + (a \times u)$
      (2.2) **if** $i > 1$ **then** send u to P_{i-1}
         end if
      end while
   end for. $\square$

Analysis.   Element a_{1n} takes $m + n - 1$ steps to reach P_1. Since P_1 is the last processor to terminate, this many steps are required to compute the product. Assuming $m \leqslant n$, procedure LINEAR MV MULTIPLICATION therefore runs in time $t(n) = O(n)$. Since m processors are used, the procedure has a cost of $O(n^2)$, which is optimal in view of the $\Omega(n^2)$ steps required to read the input sequentially.

Example 7.7

   The behavior of procedure LINEAR MV MULTIPLICATION for

$$A = \begin{bmatrix} 1 & 2 \\ 3 & 4 \end{bmatrix} \quad \text{and} \quad U = \begin{bmatrix} 5 \\ 6 \end{bmatrix}$$

is illustrated in Fig. 7.12. $\square$

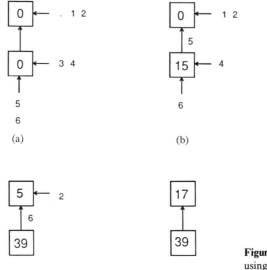

Figure 7.12 Multiplying matrix by vector using procedure LINEAR MV MULTI-PLICATION.

7.4.2 Tree Multiplication

As observed in the previous section, matrix-by-vector multiplication requires $m + n - 1$ steps on a linear array. It is possible to reduce this time to $m - 1 + \log n$ by performing the multiplication on a tree-connected SIMD computer. The arrangement is as shown in Fig. 7.13 for $m = 3$ and $n = 4$. The tree has n leaf processors $P_1, P_2, \ldots, P_n$, $n - 2$ intermediate processors $P_{n+1}, P_{n+2}, \ldots, P_{2n-2}$, and a root processor P_{2n-1}. Leaf processor P_i stores u_i throughout the execution of the algorithm. The matrix A is fed to the tree row by row, one element per leaf. When leaf processor P_i receives a_{ji}, it computes $u_i \times a_{ji}$ and sends the product to its parent. When intermediate or root processor P_k receives two inputs from its children, it adds them and sends the result to its parent. Eventually v_j emerges from the root. If the rows of A are input at the leaves in consecutive time units, then the elements of V are also produced as output from the root in consecutive time units. The algorithm is given as procedure TREE MV MULTIPLICATION.

> **procedure** TREE MV MULTIPLICATION (A, U, V)
>
>   **do** steps 1 and 2 **in parallel**
>   (1) **for** $i = 1$ **to** n **do in parallel**
>   **for** $j = 1$ **to** m **do**
>   (1.1) compute $u_i \times a_{ji}$
>   (1.2) send result to parent
>   **end for**
>   **end for**

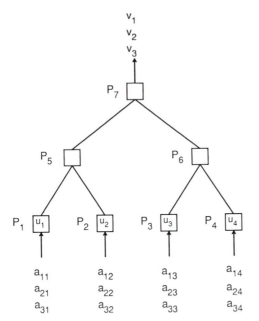

Figure 7.13   Tree-connected computer for matrix-by-vector multiplication.

(2) **for** $i = n + 1$ **to** $2n - 1$ **do in parallel**
    while P_i receives two inputs **do**
        (2.1) compute the sum of the two inputs
        (2.2) **if** $i < 2n - 1$ **then** send the result to parent
                             else produce the result as output
        end if
    end while
    end for.   □

Analysis.   It takes $\log n$ steps after the first row of A has been entered at the leaves for v_1 to emerge from the root. Exactly $m - 1$ steps later, v_m emerges from the root. Procedure TREE MV MULTIPLICATION thus requires $m - 1 + \log n$ steps for a cost of $O(n^2)$ when $m \leqslant n$. The procedure is therefore faster than procedure LINEAR MV MULTIPLICATION while using almost twice as many processors. It is cost optimal in view of the $\Omega(n^2)$ time required to read the input sequentially.

Example 7.8

The behavior of procedure TREE MV MULTIPLICATION is illustrated in Fig. 7.14 for the same data as in example 7.7.   □

7.4.3 Convolution

We conclude this section by demonstrating one application of matrix-by-vector multiplication algorithms. Given a sequence of constants $\{w_1, w_2, \ldots, w_n\}$ and an

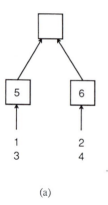

(a)

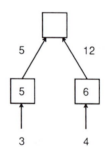

(b)

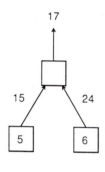

(c)

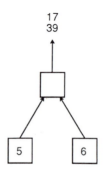

(d)

Figure 7.14   Multiplying matrix by vector using procedure TREE MV MULTIPLICATION.

input sequence $\{x_1, x_2, \ldots, x_n\}$, it is required to compute the output sequence $\{y_1, y_2, \ldots, y_{2n-1}\}$ defined by

$$y_i = \sum_{j=1}^{n} x_{i-j+1} \times w_j, \qquad 1 \leqslant i \leqslant 2n - 1.$$

This computation, known as *convolution*, is important in digital signal processing. It can be formulated as a matrix-by-vector multiplication. This is shown for the case $n = 3$:

$$\begin{bmatrix} x_1 & 0 & 0 \\ x_2 & x_1 & 0 \\ x_3 & x_2 & x_1 \\ 0 & x_3 & x_2 \\ 0 & 0 & x_3 \end{bmatrix} \times \begin{bmatrix} w_1 \\ w_2 \\ w_3 \end{bmatrix} = \begin{bmatrix} y_1 \\ y_2 \\ y_3 \\ y_4 \\ y_5 \end{bmatrix}.$$

7.5 PROBLEMS

7.1 Procedure MESH TRANSPOSE requires that the destination (j, i) of each element a_{ij} be sent along with it during the computation of the transpose of a matrix A. Design an algorithm for transposing a matrix on a mesh where it is not necessary for each element to carry its new destination along.

7.2 Is the running time of procedure SHUFFLE TRANSPOSE the smallest achievable when transposing a matrix on a shuffle-connected SIMD computer?

7.3 Can the transpose of an $n \times n$ matrix be obtained on an interconnection network, other than the perfect shuffle, in $O(\log n)$ time?

7.4 Is there an interconnection network capable of simulating procedure EREW TRANSPOSE in constant time?

7.5 Assume that every processor of an $n \times n$ mesh-connected computer contains one element of each of two $n \times n$ matrices A and B. Use a "distance" argument to show that, regardless of input and output considerations, this computer requires $\Omega(n)$ time to obtain the product of A and B.

7.6 Modify procedure MESH MULTIPLICATION so it can be used in a pipeline fashion to multiply several pairs of matrices. By looking at Fig. 7.7, we see that as soon as processor $P(1, 1)$ has multiplied a_{11} and b_{11}, it is free to receive inputs from a new pair of matrices. One step later, $P(1, 2)$ and $P(2, 1)$ are ready, and so on. The only problem is with the results of the previous computation: Provision must be made for c_{ij}, once computed, to vacate $P(i, j)$ before the latter becomes involved in computing the product of a new matrix pair.

7.7 Consider an $n \times n$ mesh of processors with the following additional links: (i) the rightmost processor in each row is directly connected to the leftmost, (ii) the bottommost processor in each column is directly connected to the topmost. These additional links are called *wraparound* connections. Initially, processor $P(i, j)$ stores elements a_{ij} and b_{ij} of two matrices A and B, respectively. Design an algorithm for multiplying A and B on this architecture so that at the end of the computation, $P(i, j)$ contains (in addition to a_{ij} and b_{ij}) element c_{ij} of the product matrix C.

7.8 Repeat problem 7.7 for the mesh under the same initial conditions but without the wraparound connections.

7.9 Design an algorithm for multiplying two $n \times n$ matrices on a mesh with fewer than n^2 processors.

7.10 Design an algorithm for multiplying two $n \times n$ matrices on an $n \times n$ *mesh of trees* architecture (as described in problem 4.2).

7.11 Extend the mesh of trees architecture to three dimensions. Show how the resulting architecture can be used to multiply two $n \times n$ matrices in $O(\log n)$ time using n^3 processors. Show also that m pairs of $n \times n$ matrices can be multiplied in $O(m + 2\log n)$ steps.

7.12 Assume that every processor of a cube-connected computer with n^2 processors contains one element of each of two $n \times n$ matrices A and B. Use a "distance" argument to show that, regardless of the number of steps needed to evaluate sums, this computer requires $\Omega(\log n)$ time to obtain the product of A and B.

7.13 Design an algorithm for multiplying two $n \times n$ matrices on a cube with n^2 processors in $O(n)$ time.

7.14 Combine procedure CUBE MATRIX MULTIPLICATION and the algorithm in problem 7.13 to obtain an algorithm for multiplying two $n \times n$ matrices on a cube with n^2m processors in $O((n/m) + \log m)$ time, where $1 \leqslant m \leqslant n$.

7.15 Design an algorithm for multiplying two matrices on a perfect shuffle-connected SIMD computer.

7.16 Repeat problem 7.15 for a tree-connected SIMD computer.

7.17 It is shown in section 7.3.2 that n processors require $\Omega(\log n)$ steps to add n numbers. Generalize this bound for the case of k processors, where $k < n$.

7.18 Modify procedure CRCW MATRIX MULTIPLICATION to run on an EREW SM SIMD computer. Can the modified procedure be made to have a cost of $O(n^3)$?

7.19 Design an MIMD algorithm for multiplying two matrices.

7.20 Given m $n \times n$ matrices $A_1, A_2, \ldots, A_m$, design algorithms for two different interconnection networks to compute the product matrix

$$C = A_1 \times A_2 \times \cdots \times A_m.$$

7.21 Let w be a *primitive nth root of unity*, that is, $w^n = 1$ and $w^i \neq 1$ for $1 \leqslant i < n$. The Discrete Fourier Transform (DFT) of the sequence $\{a_0, a_1, \ldots, a_{n-1}\}$ is the sequence $\{b_0, b_1, \ldots, b_{n-1}\}$ where

$$b_j = \sum_{i=0}^{n-1} a_i \times w^{ij} \quad \text{for } 0 \leqslant j < n.$$

Show how the DFT computation can be expressed as a matrix-by-vector product.

7.22 The *inverse* of an $n \times n$ matrix A is an $n \times n$ matrix A^{-1} such that $A \times A^{-1} = A^{-1} \times A = I$, where I is an $n \times n$ *identity* matrix whose entries are 1 on the main diagonal and 0 elsewhere. Design a parallel algorithm for computing the inverse of a given matrix.

7.23 A q-dimensional cube-connected SIMD computer with $n = 2^q$ processors $P_0, P_1, \ldots, P_{n-1}$ is given. Each processor P_i holds a datum x_i. Show that each of the following computations can be done in $O(\log n)$ time:
  (a) Broadcast x_0 to $P_1, P_2, \ldots, P_{n-1}$.
  (b) Replace x_0 with $x_0 + x_1 + \cdots + x_{n-1}$.
  (c) Replace x_0 with the smallest (or largest) of $x_0, x_1, \ldots, x_{n-1}$.

7.24 An *Omega network* is a multistage interconnection network with n inputs and n outputs. It consists of $k = \log n$ rows numbered $1, 2, \ldots, k$ with n processors per row. The processors in row i are connected to those in row $i + 1$, $i = 1, 2, \ldots, k - 1$, by a perfect shuffle interconnection. Discuss the relationship between the Omega network and a k-dimensional cube.

7.6 BIBLIOGRAPHICAL REMARKS

A mesh algorithm is described in [Ullman] for computing the transpose of a matrix that, unlike procedure MESH TRANSPOSE, does not depend directly on the number of processors on the mesh. Procedure SHUFFLE TRANSPOSE is based on an idea proposed in [Stone 1].

For references to sequential matrix multiplication algorithms with $O(n^x)$ running time, $2 < x < 3$, see [Gonnet], [Strassen], and [Wilf]. A lower bound on the number of parallel steps required to multiply two matrices is derived in [Gentleman]. Let $f(k)$ be the maximum number of processors to which a datum originally in a given processor can be transmitted in k or fewer routing steps. A mesh-connected computer, for example, has $f(k) = 2k^2 + 2k + 1$. It is shown in [Gentleman] that multiplying two $n \times n$ matrices requires at least s routing steps, where $f(2s) \geq n^2$. It follows that matrix multiplication on a mesh requires $\Omega(n)$ steps. Several mesh algorithms besides procedure MESH MATRIX MULTIPLICATION are proposed in the literature whose running time matches this bound. Such algorithms appear in [Flynn], [Preparata], [Ullman], and [Van Scoy 1]. Algorithms for the mesh with wraparound connections and two- and three-dimensional mesh of trees are described in [Cannon], [Nath], and [Leighton], respectively. The idea of procedure CUBE MATRIX MULTIPLICATION originated in [Dekel], where a number of other matrix multiplication algorithms for the cube and perfect shuffle interconnection networks are described. The $\Omega(\log n)$ lower bound on computing the sum of n numbers is adapted from [Munro]. Matrix multiplication algorithms for the cube and other interconnection networks and their applications are proposed in [Cheng], [Fox], [Horowitz], [Hwang 1], [Hwang 2], [Kung 2], [Mead], [Ramakrishnan], and [Varman]. Algorithms for shared-memory computers similar to procedure CRCW MATRIX MULTIPLICATION can be found in [Chandra], [Horowitz], [Savage 1], and [Stone 2]. A discussion of various implementation issues regarding parallel matrix multiplication algorithms is provided in [Clint].

Matrix-by-vector multiplication algorithms for a number of computational models appear in [Kung 1], [Mead], and [Nath]. Parallel algorithms and lower bounds for a variety of matrix operations arising in both numerical and nonnumerical problems are described in [Abelson], [Agerwala], [Borodin 1], [Borodin 2], [Chazelle], [Csanky], [Eberly], [Fishburn], [Fortes], [Guibas], [Hirschberg], [Kronsjö], [Kučera], [Kulkarni], [Kung 2], [Leiserson], [Lint], [Mead], [Navarro], [Pease 1], [Quinn], [Savage 2], and [Van Scoy 2].

The computational abilities of the Omega network [Lawrie] and its relationship to other interconnection networks such as the *generalized-cube* [Siegel 2], *indirect binary n-cube* [Pease 2], *Staran flip* [Batcher], and *SW-banyan* [Goke] are investigated in [Siegel 1].

7.7 REFERENCES

[ABELSON]
Abelson, H., Lower bounds on information transfer in distributed computations, Proceedings of the 19th Annual IEEE Symposium on Foundations of Computer Science, Ann Arbor, Michigan, October 1978, pp. 151–158, IEEE Computer Society, Washington, D.C., 1978.

[AGERWALA]
Agerwala, T., and Lint, B. J., Communication in parallel algorithms for Boolean matrix multiplication, Proceedings of the 1978 International Conference on Parallel Processing, Bellaire, Michigan, August 1978, pp. 146–153, IEEE Computer Society, Washington, D.C., 1978.

[BATCHER]
Batcher, K. E., The flip network in STARAN, Proceedings of the 1976 International Conference on Parallel Processing, Detroit, Michigan, August 1976, pp. 65–71, IEEE Computer Society, Washington, D.C., 1976.

[BORODIN 1]
Borodin, A., and Munro, J. I., *The Computational Complexity of Algebraic and Numeric Problems*, American Elsevier, New York, 1975.

[BORODIN 2]

Borodin, A., von zur Gathen, J., and Hopcroft, J. E., Fast parallel matrix and GCD computations, *Information and Control*, Vol. 52, 1982, pp. 241–256.

[CANNON]

Cannon, L. E., A cellular computer to implement the Kalman filter algorithm, Ph.D. thesis, Montana State University, Bozeman, Montana, 1969.

[CHANDRA]

Chandra, A. K., Maximal parallelism in matrix multiplication, IBM Technical Report RC6193, Thomas J. Watson Research Center, Yorktown Heights, N.Y., September 1976.

[CHAZELLE]

Chazelle, B., and Monier, L., Optimality in VLSI, Technical Report No. CMU-CS-81-141, Department of Computer Science, Carnegie-Mellon University, Pittsburgh, September 1981.

[CHENG]

Cheng, K. H. and Sahni, S., VLSI systems for band matrix multiplication, *Parallel Computing*, Vol. 4, 1987, pp. 239–258.

[CLINT]

Clint, M., Perrot, R. H., Holt, C. M., and Stewart, A., The influence of hardware and software considerations on the design of synchronous parallel algorithms, *Software Practice and Experience*, Vol. 13, No. 10, 1983, pp. 961–974.

[CSANKY]

Csanky, L., Fast parallel matrix inversion algorithms, *SIAM Journal on Computing*, Vol. 5, No. 4, December 1976, pp. 618–623.

[DEKEL]

Dekel, E., Nassimi, D., and Sahni, S., Parallel matrix and graph algorithms, *SIAM Journal on Computing*, Vol. 10, No. 4, November 1981, pp. 657–675.

[EBERLY]

Eberly, W., Very fast parallel matrix and polynomial arithmetic, Proceedings of the 25th Annual IEEE Symposium on Foundations of Computer Science, Singer Island, Florida, October 1984, pp. 21–30, IEEE Computer Society, Washington, D. C., 1984.

[FISHBURN]

Fishburn, J. P., Analysis of speedup in distributed algorithms, Ph.D. thesis, Computer Sciences Department, University of Wisconsin-Madison, Madison, May 1981.

[FLYNN]

Flynn, M. J., and Kosaraju, S. R., Processes and their interactions, *Kybernetics*, Vol. 5, 1976, pp. 159–163.

[FORTES]

Fortes, J. A. B., and Wah, B. W., Eds., Special Issue on Systolic Arrays, *Computer*, Vol. 20, No. 7, July 1987.

[FOX]

Fox, G. C., Otto, S. W., and Hey, A. J. G., Matrix algorithms on a hypercube I: Matrix multiplication, *Parallel Computing*, Vol. 4, 1987, pp. 17–31.

[GENTLEMAN]

Gentleman, W. M., Some complexity results for matrix computations on parallel processors, *Journal of the ACM*, Vol. 25, No. 1, January 1978, pp. 112–115.

[GOKE]

Goke, L. R., and Lipovski, G. J., Banyan networks for partitioning multiprocessor systems, Proceedings of the 1st Annual ACM International Symposium on Computer Architecture, Gainesville, Florida, December 1973, pp. 21–28, Association for Computing Machinery, New York, N.Y., 1973.

[GONNET]

Gonnet, G. H., *Handbook of Algorithms and Data Structures*, Addison-Wesley, Reading, Mass., 1984.

[GUIBAS]

Guibas, L. J., Kung, H. T., and Thompson, C. D., Direct VLSI implementation of combinatorial algorithms, Proceedings of the Conference on Very Large Scale Integration, California Institute of Technology, Pasadena, California, January 1979, pp. 509–525, California Institute of Technology, Pasadena, California, 1979.

[HIRSCHBERG]

Hirschberg, D. S., Parallel algorithms for the transitive closure and the connected components problems, Proceedings of the 8th Annual ACM Symposium on Theory of Computing, Hershey, Pennsylvania, May 1976, pp. 55–57, Association for Computing Machinery, New York, N.Y., 1976.

[HOROWITZ]

Horowitz, E., and Zorat, A., Divide-and-conquer for parallel processing, *IEEE Transactions on Computers*, Vol. C-32, No. 6, June 1983, pp. 582–585.

[HWANG 1]

Hwang, K., and Cheng, Y.-H., Partitioned matrix algorithms for VLSI arithmetic systems, *IEEE Transactions on Computers*, Vol. C-31, No. 12, December 1982, pp. 1215–1224.

[HWANG 2]

Hwang, K., and Briggs, F. A., *Computer Architecture and Parallel Processing*, McGraw-Hill, New York, 1984.

[KRONSJÖ]

Kronsjö, L., *Computational Complexity of Sequential and Parallel Algorithms*, Wiley, Chichester, England, 1985.

[KUČERA]

Kučera, L., Parallel computation and conflicts in memory access, *Information Processing Letters*, Vol. 14, No. 2, April 1982, pp. 93–96.

[KULKARNI]

Kulkarni, A. V., and Yen, D. W. L., Systolic processing and an implementation for signal and image processing, *IEEE Transactions on Computers*, Vol. C-31, No. 10, October 1982, pp. 1000–1009.

[KUNG 1]

Kung, H. T., Let's design algorithms for VLSI systems, Technical Report No. CMU-CS-79-151, Department of Computer Science, Carnegie-Mellon University, Pittsburgh, January 1979.

[KUNG 2]

Kung, H. T., The structure of parallel algorithms, in Yovits, M. C., Ed., *Advances in Computers*, Academic, New York, 1980, pp. 65–112.

[LAWRIE]

Lawrie, D. H., Access and alignment of data in an array processor, *IEEE Transactions on Computers*, Vol. C-24, No. 12, December 1975, pp. 1145–1155.

[LEIGHTON]
Leighton, F. T., *Complexity Issues in VLSI*, MIT Press, Cambridge, Mass., 1983.

[LEISERSON]
Leiserson, C. E., *Area-Efficient VLSI Computation*, MIT Press, Cambridge, Mass., 1983.

[LINT]
Lint, B. J., Communication issues in parallel algorithms and computers, Ph.D. thesis, University of Texas at Austin, Austin, Texas, May 1979.

[MEAD]
Mead, C. A., and Conway, L. A., *Introduction to VLSI Systems*, Addison-Wesley, Reading, Mass., 1980.

[MUNRO]
Munro, J. I., and Paterson, M., Optimal algorithms for parallel polynomial evaluation, *Journal of Computer and System Sciences*, Vol. 7, 1973, pp. 189–198.

[NATH]
Nath, D., Maheshwari, S. N., and Bhatt, P. C. P., Efficient VLSI networks for parallel processing based on orthogonal trees, *IEEE Transactions on Computers*, Vol. C-32, No. 6, June 1983, pp. 569–581.

[NAVARRO]
Navarro, J. J., Llaberia, J. M., and Valero, M., Solving matrix problems with no size restriction on a systolic array processor, Proceedings of the 1986 International Conference on Parallel Processing, St. Charles, Illinois, August 1986, pp. 676–683, IEEE Computer Society, Washington, D.C., 1986.

[PEASE 1]
Pease, M. C., Matrix inversion using parallel processing, *Journal of the ACM*, Vol. 14, No. 4, October 1967, pp. 757–764.

[PEASE 2]
Pease, M. C., The indirect binary *n*-cube microprocessor array, *IEEE Transactions on Computers*, Vol. C-26, No. 5, May 1977, pp. 458–473.

[PREPARATA]
Preparata, F. P., and Vuillemin, J. E., Area-time optimal VLSI networks for multiplying matrices, *Information Processing Letters*, Vol. 11, No. 2, October 1980, pp. 77–80.

[QUINN]
Quinn, M. J., *Designing Efficient Algorithms for Parallel Computers*, McGraw-Hill, New York, 1987.

[RAMAKRISHNAN]
Ramakrishnan, I. V., and Varman, P. J., Modular matrix multiplication on a linear array, *IEEE Transactions on Computers*, Vol. C-33, No. 11, November 1984, pp. 952–958.

[SAVAGE 1]
Savage, C., Parallel algorithms for graph theoretical problems, Ph.D. thesis, Department of Computer Science, University of Illinois, Urbana-Champaign, Illinois, August 1978.

[SAVAGE 2]
Savage, J. E., Area-time tradeoffs for matrix multiplication and related problems in VLSI models, Proceedings of the 17th Annual Allerton Conference on Communications, Control, and Computing, Monticello, Illinois, October 1979, pp. 670–676, University of Illinois, Urbana-Champaign, Illinois, 1979.

[SIEGEL 1]

Siegel, H. J., *Interconnection Networks for Large Scale Parallel Processing*, Lexington Books, Lexington, Mass., 1985.

[SIEGEL 2]

Siegel, H. J., and Smith, S. D., Study of multistage SIMD interconnection networks, Proceedings of the 5th Annual ACM International Symposium on Computer Architecture, Palo Alto, California, April 1978, pp. 223–229, Association for Computing Machinery, New York, N.Y., 1978.

[STONE 1]

Stone, H. S., Parallel processing with the perfect shuffle, *IEEE Transactions on Computers*, Vol. C-20, No. 2, February 1971, pp. 153–161.

[STONE 2]

Stone, H. S., Ed., *Introduction to Computer Architecture*, Science Research Associates, Chicago, 1980.

[STRASSEN]

Strassen, V., The asymptotic spectrum of tensors and the exponent of matrix multiplication, Proceedings of the 27th Annual IEEE Symposium on Foundations of Computer Science, Toronto, Canada, October 1986, pp. 49–54, IEEE Computer Society, Washington, D.C., 1986.

[ULLMAN]

Ullman, J. D., *Computational Aspects of VLSI*, Computer Science Press, Rockville, Md., 1984.

[VAN SCOY 1]

Van Scoy, F. L., Parallel algorithms in cellular spaces, Ph.D. thesis, University of Virginia, Charlotteville, Va., 1976.

[VAN SCOY 2]

Van Scoy, F. L., The parallel recognition of classes of graphs, *IEEE Transactions on Computers*, Vol. C-29, No. 7, July 1980, pp. 563–570.

[VARMAN]

Varman, P. J., Ramakrishnan, I. V., and Fussell, D. S., A robust matrix-multiplication array, *IEEE Transactions on Computers*, Vol. C-33, No. 10, October 1984, pp. 919–922.

[WILF]

Wilf, H. S., *Algorithms and Complexity*, Prentice-Hall, Englewood Cliffs, N.J., 1986.

8

Numerical Problems

8.1 INTRODUCTION

In any scientific or engineering application of computers, it is usually required to solve a mathematical problem. Such applications span a wide range, from modeling the atmosphere in weather prediction to modeling hot plasmas in theoretical physics and from the design of space stations, airplanes, automatic pilots and air-traffic control systems to the design of power stations, automobiles, and ground transportation networks. In these applications computers are used to find zeros of functions, solve systems of equations, calculate eigenvalues, and perform a variety of numerical tasks including differentiation, integration, interpolation, approximation, and Monte Carlo simulations. These problems have a number of distinguishing properties:

1. Because they typically involve physical quantities, their data are represented using *real* values, or in computer terminology, *floating-point numbers*. Sometimes the numbers to be manipulated are *complex*, that is, they are of the form $a + ib$, where a and b are real and

$$i = \sqrt{-1}.$$

2. Their solutions are obtained through algorithms derived from a branch of mathematics known as *numerical analysis* and are therefore based on mathematical theory.

3. Their algorithms usually consist of a number of *iterations*: Each iteration is based on the result of the previous one and is supposed, theoretically, to improve on it.

4. Generally, the results produced by numerical algorithms are *approximations* of exact answers that may or may not be possible to obtain.

5. There is an almost inevitable element of *error* involved in numerical computation: *round-off errors* (which arise when infinite precision real numbers are stored in a memory location of fixed size) and *truncation errors* (which arise when an infinite computation is approximated by a finite one).

200

In this chapter we describe parallel algorithms for the following numerical problems: solving a system of linear equations (section 8.2), finding roots of nonlinear equations (section 8.3), solving partial differential equations (section 8.4), and computing eigenvalues (section 8.5). We assume throughout this chapter that all problems involve real (as opposed to complex) numbers.

8.2 SOLVING SYSTEMS OF LINEAR EQUATIONS

Given an $n \times n$ matrix A and an $n \times 1$ vector b, it is required to solve $Ax = b$ for the unknown $n \times 1$ vector x. When $n = 4$, for example, we have to solve the following system of linear equations for x_1, x_2, x_3, and x_4:

$$a_{11}x_1 + a_{12}x_2 + a_{13}x_3 + a_{14}x_4 = b_1,$$

$$a_{21}x_1 + a_{22}x_2 + a_{23}x_3 + a_{24}x_4 = b_2,$$

$$a_{31}x_1 + a_{32}x_2 + a_{33}x_3 + a_{34}x_4 = b_3,$$

$$a_{41}x_1 + a_{42}x_2 + a_{43}x_3 + a_{44}x_4 = b_4.$$

8.2.1 An SIMD Algorithm

A well-known sequential algorithm for this problem is the Gauss–Jordan method. It consists in eliminating all unknowns but x_i from the ith equation. The solution is then obtained directly. A direct parallelization of the Gauss–Jordan method is now presented. It is designed to run on a CREW SM SIMD computer with $n^2 + n$ processors that can be thought of as being arranged in an $n \times (n + 1)$ array. The algorithm is given as procedure SIMD GAUSS JORDAN. In it we denote b_i by $a_{i,n+1}$.

procedure SIMD GAUSS JORDAN (A, b, x)

Step 1: **for** $j = 1$ **to** n **do**
      for $i = 1$ **to** n **do in parallel**
        for $k = j$ **to** $n + 1$ **do in parallel**
          if $(i \neq j)$
          then $a_{ik} \leftarrow a_{ik} - (a_{ij}/a_{jj})a_{jk}$
          end if
        end for
      end for
    end for.

Step 2: **for** $i = 1$ **to** n **do in parallel**
      $x_i \leftarrow a_{i,n+1}/a_{ii}$
    end for. $\square$

Note that the procedure allows concurrent-read operations since more than one processor will need to read a_{ij}, a_{jj}, and a_{jk} simultaneously.

Analysis.   Step 1 consists of n constant time iterations, while step 2 takes constant time. Thus $t(n) = O(n)$. Since $p(n) = O(n^2)$, $c(n) = O(n^3)$. Although this cost matches the number of steps required by a sequential implementation of the Gauss–Jordan algorithm, it is not optimal. To see this, note that the system $Ax = b$ can be solved by first computing the inverse A^{-1} of A and then obtaining x from

$$x = A^{-1}b.$$

The inverse of A can be computed as follows. We begin by writing

$$A = \begin{bmatrix} A_{11} & A_{12} \\ A_{21} & A_{22} \end{bmatrix} = \begin{bmatrix} I & 0 \\ A_{21}A_{11}^{-1} & I \end{bmatrix} \begin{bmatrix} A_{11} & 0 \\ 0 & B \end{bmatrix} \begin{bmatrix} I & A_{11}^{-1}A_{12} \\ 0 & I \end{bmatrix}$$

where the A_{ij} are $(n/2) \times (n/2)$ submatrices of A, and $B = A_{22} - A_{21}A_{11}^{-1}A_{12}$. The $(n/2) \times (n/2)$ matrices I and 0 are the *identity matrix* (whose main diagonal elements are 1 and all the rest are zeros) and *zero matrix* (all of whose elements are zero), respectively. The inverse of A is then given by the matrix product

$$A^{-1} = \begin{bmatrix} I & -A_{11}^{-1}A_{12} \\ 0 & I \end{bmatrix} \begin{bmatrix} A_{11}^{-1} & 0 \\ 0 & B^{-1} \end{bmatrix} \begin{bmatrix} I & 0 \\ -A_{21}A_{11}^{-1} & I \end{bmatrix}$$

where A_{11}^{-1} and B^{-1} are computed by applying the same process recursively. This requires two inversions, six multiplications, and two additions of $(n/2) \times (n/2)$ matrices. Denoting the time required by these operations by the functions $i(n/2)$, $m(n/2)$, and $a(n/2)$, respectively, we get

$$i(n) = 2i(n/2) + 6m(n/2) + 2a(n/2).$$

Since $a(n/2) = n^2/4$ and $m(n/2) = O((n/2)^x)$, where $2 < x < 2.5$ (as pointed out in example 1.11), we get $i(n) = O(n^x)$. Thus, in sequential computation the time required to compute the inverse of an $n \times n$ matrix matches, up to a constant multiplicative factor, the time required to multiply two $n \times n$ matrices. Furthermore, multiplying A^{-1} by b can be done in $O(n^2)$ steps. The overall running time of this sequential solution of $Ax = b$ is therefore $O(n^x)$, $2 < x < 2.5$.

Example 8.1

Let us apply procedure SIMD GAUSS JORDAN to the system

$$2x_1 + x_2 = 3,$$

$$x_1 + 2x_2 = 4.$$

In the first iteration of step 1, $j = 1$ and the following values are computed in parallel:

$$a_{21} = a_{21} - (a_{21}/a_{11})a_{11} = 1 - (\tfrac{1}{2})2 = 0,$$

$$a_{22} = a_{22} - (a_{21}/a_{11})a_{12} = 2 - (\tfrac{1}{2})1 = \tfrac{3}{2},$$

$$a_{23} = a_{23} - (a_{21}/a_{11})a_{13} = 4 - (\tfrac{1}{2})3 = \tfrac{5}{2}.$$

In the second iteration of step $1, j = 2$ and the following values are computed in parallel:

$$a_{12} = a_{12} - (a_{12}/a_{22})a_{22} = 1 - (1/\tfrac{3}{2})(\tfrac{3}{2}) = 0,$$

$$a_{13} = a_{13} - (a_{12}/a_{22})a_{23} = 3 - (1/\tfrac{3}{2})(\tfrac{5}{2}) = \tfrac{4}{3}.$$

In step 2, the answer is obtained as $x_1 = \tfrac{2}{3}$ and $x_2 = \tfrac{5}{3}$. $\square$

8.2.2 An MIMD Algorithm

A different sequential algorithm for solving the set of equations $Ax = b$ is the Gauss–Seidel method. We begin by writing

$$A = E + D + F$$

where E, D, and F are $n \times n$ matrices whose elements e_{ij}, d_{ij}, and f_{ij}, respectively, are given by

$$e_{ij} = \begin{cases} a_{ij} & \text{for } i > j, \\ 0 & \text{otherwise,} \end{cases} \qquad d_{ij} = \begin{cases} a_{ij} & \text{for } i = j, \\ 0 & \text{otherwise,} \end{cases} \qquad f_{ij} = \begin{cases} a_{ij} & \text{for } i < j, \\ 0 & \text{otherwise.} \end{cases}$$

Thus $(E + D + F)x = b$ and $Dx = b - Ex - Fx$. For $n = 3$, say, we have

$$\begin{bmatrix} a_{11} & 0 & 0 \\ 0 & a_{22} & 0 \\ 0 & 0 & a_{33} \end{bmatrix} \begin{bmatrix} x_1 \\ x_2 \\ x_3 \end{bmatrix} = b - \begin{bmatrix} 0 & 0 & 0 \\ a_{21} & 0 & 0 \\ a_{31} & a_{32} & 0 \end{bmatrix} \begin{bmatrix} x_1 \\ x_2 \\ x_3 \end{bmatrix} - \begin{bmatrix} 0 & a_{12} & a_{13} \\ 0 & 0 & a_{23} \\ 0 & 0 & 0 \end{bmatrix} \begin{bmatrix} x_1 \\ x_2 \\ x_3 \end{bmatrix}.$$

Starting with a vector x^0 (an arbitrary initial estimate of x), the solution vector is obtained through an iterative process where the kth iteration is given by

$$Dx^k = b - Ex^k - Fx^{k-1}.$$

In other words, during the kth iteration the current estimates of the unknowns are substituted in the right-hand sides of the equations to produce new estimates. Again for $n = 4$ and $k = 1$, we get

$$a_{11}x_1^1 = b_1 - 0 - (a_{12}x_2^0 + a_{13}x_3^0 + a_{14}x_4^0),$$

$$a_{22}x_2^1 = b_2 - (a_{21}x_1^1) - (a_{23}x_3^0 + a_{24}x_4^0),$$

$$a_{33}x_3^1 = b_3 - (a_{31}x_1^1 + a_{32}x_2^1) - (a_{34}x_4^0),$$

$$a_{44}x_4^1 = b_4 - (a_{41}x_1^1 + a_{42}x_2^1 + a_{43}x_3^1) - 0.$$

The method is said to converge if, for some k,

$$\sum_{i=1}^{n} \text{abs}(x_i^{k+1} - x_i^k) < c,$$

where abs denotes the absolute value function and c is a prespecified error tolerance.

The algorithm does not appear to be easily adapatable for an SIMD computer. Given N processors, we may assign each processor the job of computing the new iterates for n/N components of the vector x. At the end of each iteration, all processors must be synchronized before starting the next iteration. The cost of this synchronization may be high because of the following:

(i) The x_i^k cannot be computed until x_j^k is available, for all $j < i$; this forces the processor computing x_i to wait for those computing $x_j, j < i$, and then forces all processors to wait for the one computing x_n.

(ii) Some components may be possible to update faster than others depending on the values involved in its computation (some of which may be zero, say).

Typically, this would lead to an algorithm that is not significantly faster than its sequential counterpart.

There are two ways to remedy this situation:

1. The most recently available values are used to compute x_i^k (i.e., there is no need to wait for $x_j^k, j < i$).

2. No synchronization is imposed on the behavior of the processors.

Both of these changes are incorporated in an algorithm designed to run on a CREW SM MIMD computer with N processors, where $N \leq n$. The algorithm creates n processes, each of which is in charge of computing one of the components of x. These processes are executed by the N processors in an asynchronous fashion, as described in chapter 1. The algorithm is given in what follows as procedure MIMD MODIFIED GS. In it x_i^0, old_i, and new_i denote the initial value, the previous value, and the current value of component x_i, respectively. As mentioned earlier, c is the desired accuracy. Also note that the procedure allows concurrent-read operations since more than one process may need new_i simultaneously.

procedure MIMD MODIFIED GS (A, x, b, c)

Step 1: **for** $i = 1$ **to** n **do**
    (1.1) $old_i \leftarrow x_i^0$
    (1.2) $new_i \leftarrow x_i^0$
    (1.3) create process i
    end for.

Step 2: Process i
    (2.1) **repeat**
      (i) $old_i \leftarrow new_i$
      (ii) $new_i \leftarrow \left(b_i - \sum_{k=1}^{i-1} (a_{ik} \times old_k) - \sum_{k=i+1}^{n} (a_{ik} \times old_k) \right) \Big/ a_{ii}$

    until $\sum_{i=1}^{n} abs(new_i - old_i) < c$
    (2.2) $x_i \leftarrow new_i$. $\square$

Note that step 2 states one of the n identical processes created in step 1.

Discussion.   In an actual implementation of the preceding procedure, care must be taken to prevent a process from reading a variable while another process is updating it, as this would most likely result in the first process reading an incorrect value. There are many ways to deal with this problem. One approach uses special variables called *semaphores*. For each shared variable v_i there is a corresponding semaphore s_i whose value is set as

$$s_i = \begin{cases} 0 & \text{if } v_i \text{ is free,} \\ 1 & \text{if } v_i \text{ is currently being updated.} \end{cases}$$

When a process needs to read v_i, it first tests s_i: If $s_i = 0$, then the process reads v_i; otherwise it waits for it to be available. When a process needs to update v_i, it first sets s_i to 1 and then proceeds to update v_i.

As pointed out in chapter 1, MIMD algorithms in general are extremely difficult to analyze theoretically due to their asynchronous nature. In the case of procedure MIMD MODIFIED GS the analysis is further complicated by the use of semaphores and, more importantly, by the uncertainty regarding the number of iterations required for convergence. An accurate evaluation of the procedure's behavior is best obtained empirically.

Example 8.2

Consider the system of example 8.1 and assume that two processors are available on a CREW SM MIMD computer. Take $x_1^0 = \frac{1}{2}$, $x_2^0 = \frac{3}{2}$, and $c = 0.02$. Process 1 sets $old_1 = \frac{1}{2}$ and computes

$$new_1 = \tfrac{1}{2}(3 - \tfrac{3}{2}) = \tfrac{3}{4}.$$

Simultaneously, process 2 sets $old_2 = \frac{3}{2}$ and computes

$$new_2 = \tfrac{1}{2}(4 - \tfrac{1}{2}) = \tfrac{7}{4}.$$

The computation then proceeds as follows

(1) $new_1 = \frac{5}{8},$ $new_2 = \frac{13}{8},$

(2) $new_1 = \frac{11}{16},$ $new_2 = \frac{27}{16},$

(3) $new_1 = \frac{21}{32},$ $new_2 = \frac{53}{32},$

(4) $new_1 = \frac{43}{64},$ $new_2 = \frac{107}{64},$

(5) $new_1 = \frac{85}{128},$ $new_2 = \frac{213}{128}.$

Since $\text{abs}(\frac{43}{64} - \frac{85}{128}) + \text{abs}(\frac{107}{64} - \frac{213}{128}) < 0.02$, the procedure terminates.   □

8.3 FINDING ROOTS OF NONLINEAR EQUATIONS

In many science and engineering applications it is often required to find the root of an equation of one variable, such as

$$x^5 - x^3 + 7 = 0,$$

$$\sin x - e^x = 0,$$

$$x^2 - \cos x = 0.$$

Finding the root of an equation of this form analytically is usually impossible, and one must resort to numerical algorithms to obtain an approximate solution.

8.3.1 An SIMD Algorithm

A standard sequential algorithm for root finding is the *bisection method*. Let $f(x)$ be a continuous function and let a_0 and b_0 be two values of the variable x such that $f(a_0)$ and $f(b_0)$ have opposite signs, that is,

$$f(a_0)f(b_0) < 0.$$

A *zero* of f [i.e., a value z for which $f(z) = 0$] is guaranteed to exist in the interval (a_0, b_0). Now the interval (a_0, b_0) is *bisected*, that is, its middle point

$$m_0 = \tfrac{1}{2}(a_0 + b_0)$$

is computed. If $f(a_0)f(m_0) < 0$, then z must lie in the interval $(a_1, b_1) = (a_0, m_0)$; otherwise it lies in the interval $(a_1, b_1) = (m_0, b_0)$. We now repeat the process on the interval (a_1, b_1). This continues until an acceptable approximation of z is obtained, that is, until for some $n \geqslant 0$,

  (i) $\text{abs}(b_n - a_n) < c$ or
  (ii) $\text{abs}(f(m_n)) < c'$,

where c and c' are small positive numbers chosen such that the desired accuracy is achieved.

The algorithm using criterion (i) is given in what follows as procedure BISECTION. Initially, $a = a_0$ and $b = b_0$. When the procedure terminates, a zero is known to exist in (a, b).

procedure BISECTION (f, a, b, c)

  while $\text{abs}(b - a) \geqslant c$ **do**
  (1) $m \leftarrow \tfrac{1}{2}(a + b)$
  (2) **if** $f(a)f(m) < 0$ **then** $b \leftarrow m$
                             else $a \leftarrow m$
      end if
  end while. □

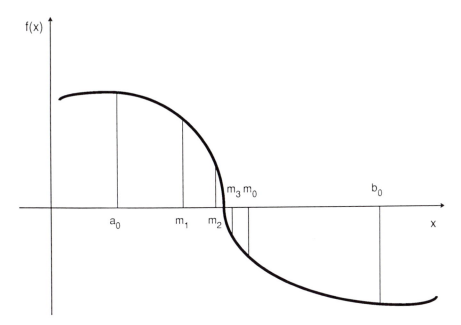

Figure 8.1   Finding root using procedure BISECTION.

Since the interval to be searched is halved at each iteration, the procedure runs in $O(\log w)$ time, where $w = \text{abs}(b_0 - a_0)$. When f is discrete rather than continuous, procedure BISECTION is equivalent to procedure BINARY SEARCH of chapter 3. The procedure's behavior is illustrated in Fig. 8.1 for some function f. After four iterations, a zero is known to lie in the interval (m_2, m_3).

In much the same way as we did with procedure BINARY SEARCH in section 5.2.2, we can implement procedure BISECTION on a parallel computer. Given N processors, the idea is to conduct an $(N + 1)$-*section search* on a CREW SM SIMD computer. The initial interval, known to contain *one* zero of a function f, is divided into $N + 1$ subintervals of equal length. Each processor evaluates the function at one of the division points, and based on these evaluations, one of the subintervals is chosen for further subdivision. As with the sequential case, this process is continued until the interval containing a root is narrowed to the desired width. The algorithm is given in what follows as procedure SIMD ROOT SEARCH. It takes the function f, the initial interval (a, b), and the accuracy c as input and returns an interval in which a zero of f lies and whose width is less than c. The procedure is designed to run on a CREW SM SIMD computer since at the end of each iteration all processors need to know the endpoints (a, b) of the new interval. Without loss of generality, we assume that $a < b$ at all times.

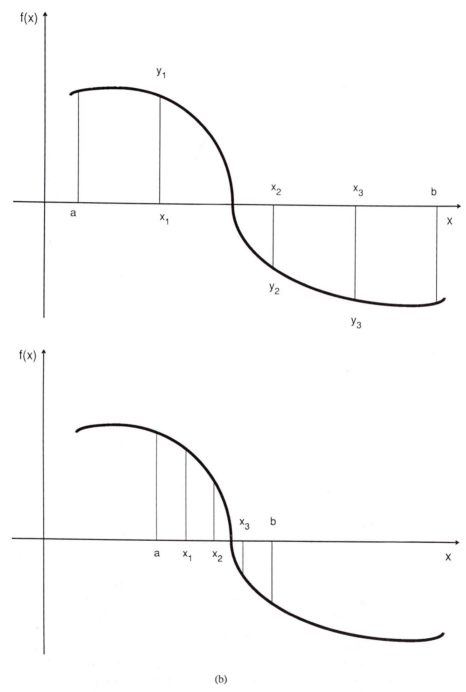

(b)

Figure 8.2 Finding root using procedure SIMD ROOT SEARCH.

procedure SIMD ROOT SEARCH (f, a, b, c)

   while $(b - a) \geqslant c$ **do**
     (1) $s \leftarrow (b - a)/(N + 1)$
     (2) $y_0 \leftarrow f(a)$
     (3) $y_{N+1} \leftarrow f(b)$
     (4) **for** $k = 1$ **to** N **do in parallel**
       (4.1) $y_k \leftarrow f(a + ks)$
       (4.2) **if** $y_{k-1} y_k < 0$ **then** (i) $a \leftarrow a + (k - 1)s$
                          (ii) $b \leftarrow a + ks$
        end if
      end for
     (5) **if** $y_N y_{N+1} < 0$ **then** $a \leftarrow a + Ns$
     end if
   end while. $\square$

Analysis.   Steps 1, 2, 3, and 5 may be executed by one processor, say, P_N, in constant time. In step 4, which also takes constant time, at most one processor P_k will discover that $y_{k-1} y_k < 0$ and hence update a and b. If no processor updates a and b in step 4, then the zero must be in the $(N + 1)$st interval, and only a is updated in step 5. The number of iterations is obtained as follows. Let w be the width of the initial interval, that is, $w = b - a$. After j iterations the interval width is $w/(N + 1)^j$. The procedure terminates as soon as $w/(N + 1)^j < c$. The number of iterations, and hence the running time, of procedure SIMD ROOT SEARCH is therefore $O(\log_{N+1} w)$. Its cost is $O(N \log_{N+1} w)$, which, as we know from chapter 5, is not optimal.

Example 8.3

   The behavior of procedure SIMD ROOT SEARCH on the function in Fig. 8.1 when three processors are used is illustrated in Fig. 8.2. After one iteration the interval containing the zero is (x_1, x_2), as shown in Fig. 8.2(a). After the second iteration the interval is (x_2, x_3) as shown in Fig. 8.2(b). $\square$

8.3.2 An MIMD Algorithm

Another sequential root-finding algorithm that is very commonly used is *Newton's method*. A continuously differentiable function $f(x)$ is given together with an initial approximation x_0 for one of its roots z. The method computes

$$x_{n+1} = x_n - f(x_n)/f'(x_n) \quad \text{for } n = 0, 1, 2, \ldots,$$

until $\text{abs}(x_{n+1} - x_n) < c$. Here $f'(x)$ is the derivative of $f(x)$ and c is the desired accuracy. A geometric interpretation of Newton's method is shown in Fig. 8.3. Note that the next approximation x_{n+1} is the intersection with the x axis of the tangent to the curve $f(x)$ at x_n.

   The main reason for this method's popularity is its rapid convergence when x_0 is

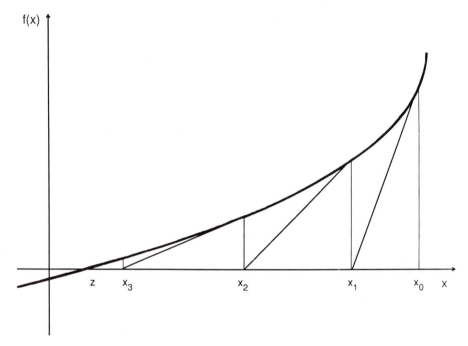

Figure 8.3   Newton's method for finding root.

sufficiently close to z. More precisely, if

   (i) $f(x)$ and its first and second derivatives $f'(x)$ and $f''(x)$, respectively, are continuous and bounded on an interval containing a root z, with $f'(x) \neq 0$, and
   (ii) $\mathrm{abs}(x_0 - z) < 1$,

then for large n, $\mathrm{abs}(x_{n+1} - z) = k(x_n - z)^2$, where k is a constant of proportionality that depends on $f'(z)$ and $f''(z)$. In other words, the error in x_{n+1} is proportional to the square of the error in x_n.

    The method is said to have *quadratic convergence* under the conditions stated in the preceding. In practice, this means that the number of correct digits in the answer doubles with each iteration. Therefore, if the answer is to be accurate to m digits, the method converges in $O(\log m)$ time.

    One difficulty with Newton's method is finding an initial approximation that is sufficiently close to the desired root. This difficulty is almost eliminated by implementing the method on a CRCW SM MIMD computer as follows. We begin with an interval (a, b), where $a < b$, known to contain *one* zero z of $f(x)$. The interval is divided into $N + 1$ subintervals of equal size, for some $N \geqslant 2$, and the division points are taken as initial approximations of z. The computation consists of N processes. Each process applies Newton's method beginning with one of the division points. The processes are executed concurrently, though asynchronously, depending on the availability of processors. As soon as a process converges, it indicates that by writing the value it found in a shared-memory location ROOT. Initially, ROOT is set to the value ∞. As soon as that value is changed by a process, all processes are terminated. If two (or more) processes converge at the same time and attempt to write in ROOT simultaneously, then only the smallest-numbered process is allowed access while the others are denied it. In case a process does not converge after a predefined number of iterations, it is suspended. The algorithm is given in what follows as procedure MIMD ROOT SEARCH. It takes as input the function f, its derivative f', the interval (a, b), the accuracy c, and the maximum allowable number of iterations r. It returns its answer in ROOT.

procedure MIMD ROOT SEARCH $(f, f', a, b, c, r, \text{ROOT})$

Step 1: $s \leftarrow (b - a)/(N + 1)$.

Step 2:   **for** $k = 1$ **to** N **do**
        create process k
       end for.

Step 3:   ROOT $\leftarrow \infty$.

Step 4:   Process k
       (4.1) $x_{\text{old}} \leftarrow a + ks$
       (4.2) iteration $\leftarrow 0$
       (4.3) **while** (iteration $< r$) **and** (ROOT $= \infty$) **do**
           (i) iteration $\leftarrow$ iteration $+ 1$
           (ii) $x_{\text{new}} \leftarrow x_{\text{old}} - f(x_{\text{old}})/f'(x_{\text{old}})$
           (iii) **if** $\text{abs}(x_{\text{new}} - x_{\text{old}}) < c$ **then** ROOT $\leftarrow x_{\text{new}}$
              end if
           (iv) $x_{\text{old}} \leftarrow x_{\text{new}}$
       end while.   □

Note that variables a, s, r, c, and ROOT used in process k are global. On the other hand, variables iteration, x_{old}, and x_{new} are local; they are not subscripted in order to simplify the notation.

Analysis.   Let N processors be available. If N is large, one of the starting points will be close enough to z. If in addition $f(x), f'(x)$, and $f''(x)$ are continuous and bounded on the interval (a, b), then one of the N processes will converge in $O(\log m)$ time, where m is the desired number of accurate digits in the answer.

Example 8.4

Let $f(x) = x^3 - 4x - 5$. Thus $f'(x) = 3x^2 - 4$. There is a zero of $f(x)$ in the interval $(-3, 3)$. Let $N = 5$; the interval is divided into six subintervals with division points at $x = -2, -1, 0, 1,$ and 2, and the corresponding five processes are created. Let $c = 10^{-10}$, and assume that five processors are available to execute the five processes simultaneously. In that case, process 5 is the fastest to converge to a root at 2.456678.   □

8.4 SOLVING PARTIAL DIFFERENTIAL EQUATIONS

Partial differential equations (PDEs) arise in such diverse applications as weather forecasting, modeling supersonic flow, and elasticity studies. A particularly important class of PDEs is that of linear equations of second order in two independent variables x and y. One representative of this class is Poisson's equation

$$u_{xx} + u_{yy} = G(x, y) \quad \text{where } u_{xx} = \frac{\partial^2 u(x, y)}{\partial x^2}, \qquad u_{yy} = \frac{\partial^2 u(x, y)}{\partial y^2},$$

$u(x, y)$ is the unknown function, and G is a given function of x and y. The solution of this equation is often needed in so-called *boundary-value problems,* a typical example of which is the *Model Problem* stated as follows.

Let R and S denote the interior and boundary, respectively, of a region in two-dimensional space, and let $f(x, y)$ be a continuous function defined on S. The desired function $u(x, y)$ must satisfy Poisson's equation on R and equal $f(x, y)$ on S. In sequential computation, the Model Problem is solved numerically by first deriving a *discrete* version of it. Here R and S are the interior and boundary, respectively, of the unit square, $0 \leqslant x \leqslant 1$, $0 \leqslant y \leqslant 1$. A uniform mesh of $n + 1$ horizontal and $n + 1$ vertical lines, where n is an arbitrary positive integer, is superimposed over the unit square, with a spacing of $d = 1/n$ between lines. The $(n + 1)^2$ intersections of these lines are called *mesh points.* For a mesh point (x, y) in R, u_{xx} and u_{yy} are approximated by *difference quotients* as follows:

$$u_{xx} = [u(x + d, y) + u(x - d, y) - 2u(x, y)]/d^2,$$

$$u_{yy} = [u(x, y + d) + u(x, y - d) - 2u(x, y)]/d^2.$$

This leads to the following form of Poisson's equation:

$$u(x, y) = [u(x + d, y) + u(x - d, y) + u(x, y + d) + u(x, y - d) - d^2 G(x, y)]/4,$$

known as a *difference equation.* An iterative process called *successive overrelaxation* is used to obtain an approximate value for $u(x, y)$ at each of the $(n - 1)^2$ interior mesh points. Beginning with an arbitrary value $u_0(x, y)$, the following iteration is used:

$$u_k(x, y) = u_{k-1}(x, y) + w[u'_k(x, y) - u_{k-1}(x, y)] \quad \text{for } k = 1, 2, \ldots,$$

where

$$u'_k(x, y) = [u_{k-1}(x + d, y) + u_k(x - d, y) + u_{k-1}(x, y + d)$$

$$+ u_k(x, y - d) - d^2 G(x, y)]/4$$

and

$$w = 2/[1 + \sin(\pi d)].$$

Let e_k denote the absolute value of the difference between $u_k(x, y)$ and the *exact* value of u at (x, y). The iterative process continues until

$$e_k \leqslant e_0/10^v$$

where v is a positive integer representing the desired accuracy. Neither e_0 nor e_k is known, of course. However, it can be shown that the process converges and the preceding inequality is true after $k = gn$ iterations, where $g = v/3$. Since there are $(n - 1)^2$ interior points, the entire process takes $O(n^3)$ time.

This approach to solving PDEs lends itself naturally to implementation on an $N \times N$ mesh-connected SIMD computer with $N = n - 1$, as shown in Fig. 8.4 for $N = 4$. Each processor $P(i, j)$, $1 \leqslant i, j \leqslant N$, is in charge of computing an approximation of the function u at point (id, jd). It does so beginning with the initial value $u_0(id, jd)$ and then iteratively using the values computed by its four neighbors as input. Boundary processors, of course, have fewer than four neighbors and use the values of $f(x, y)$ at $x = 0, 1$ and $y = 0, 1$ to replace the input from missing neighbors. One difficulty to overcome is the fact that $u_k(x, y)$ depends on $u_k(x - d, y)$ and $u_k(x, y - d)$. In sequential computation, this is no problem since the kth iterates are computed one at a time from $x = 0$ to $x = 1$ and from $y = 0$ to $y = 1$. By the time $u_k(x, y)$ is to be

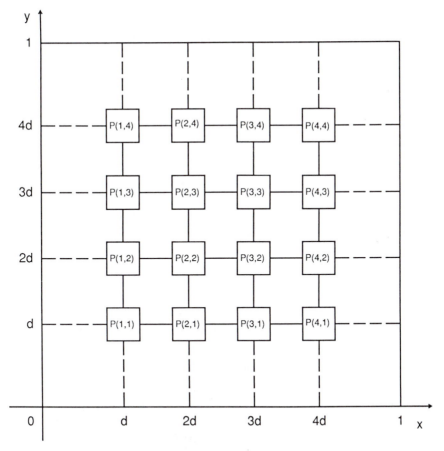

Figure 8.4 Mesh of processors for solving partial differential equations.

computed, $u_k(x - d, y)$ and $u_k(x, y - d)$ are available. In the parallel version each iteration will consist of two stages:

1. During the first stage one-half of the processors compute new values for u based on the values held by the other half.
2. During the second stage, the remaining processors update their values of u using the new values just computed in 1.

The two sets of processors in 1 and 2 are chosen to correspond to the red and black squares, respectively, on a checkerboard. Let $w_{k,1}$ and $w_{k,2}$ denote the value of w during stages 1 and 2, respectively, of iteration k, where

$$w_{1,1} = 1,$$
$$w_{1,2} = 1/(1 - \tfrac{1}{2}\cos^2 \pi d),$$

and for $k = 2, 3, \ldots,$

$$w_{k,1} = 1/[1 - \tfrac{1}{4}\cos^2 \pi d)w_{k-1,2}],$$
$$w_{k,2} = 1/[1 - \tfrac{1}{4}\cos^2 \pi d)w_{k,1}].$$

The equations for updating u are now as follows:

Stage 1: For all $1 \leqslant i, j \leqslant N$, such that $i + j$ is even,

$$u_k(id, jd) = u_{k-1}(id, jd) + w_{k,1}[u_k'(id, jd) - u_{k-1}(id, jd)],$$

where

$$u'(id, jd) = [u_{k-1}(id + d, jd) + u_{k-1}(id - d, jd)$$
$$+ u_{k-1}(id, jd + d) + u_{k-1}(id, jd - d) - d^2 G(x, y)]/4.$$

Stage 2: For all $1 \leqslant i, j \leqslant N$ such that $i + j$ is odd,

$$u_k(id, jd) = u_{k-1}(id, jd) + w_{k,2}[u_k'(id, jd) - u_{k-1}(id, jd)],$$

where

$$u_k'(id, jd) = [u_k(id + d, jd) + u_k(id - d, jd) + u_k(id, jd + d)$$
$$+ u_k(id, jd - d) - d^2 G(x, y)]/4.$$

The algorithm is given as procedure MESH PDE.

procedure MESH PDE (f, G, g)

Step 1:   {Compute boundary values}
      (1.1) **for** $i = 1$ **to** N **do in parallel**
          (i) $P(1, i)$ computes $f(0, id)$
          (ii) $P(N, i)$ computes $f(1, id)$
      end for

(1.2) **for** $i = 1$ **to** N **do in parallel**
    (i) $P(i, 1)$ computes $f(id, 0)$
    (ii) $P(i, N)$ computes $f(id, 1)$
end for.

Step 2:   {Input initial values}
    for $i = 1$ **to** N **do in parallel**
      for $j = 1$ **to** N **do in parallel**
       $P(i, j)$ reads $u_0(id, jd)$
      end for
    end for.

Step 3:   {Iterate until convergence}
    for $k = 1$ **to** gn **do**
      for $i = 1$ **to** N **do in parallel**
        for $j = 1$ **to** N **do in parallel**
          (3.1) **if** $(i + j)$ is even
             then $P(i, j)$ updates $u(id, jd)$
             end if
          (3.2) **if** $(i + j)$ is odd
             then $P(i, j)$ updates $u(id, jd)$
             end if

        end for
      end for
    end for.   □

Analysis.   Steps 1 and 2 take constant time. Step 3 consists of $O(n)$ constant time iterations. Thus $t(n) = O(n)$. Since $p(n) = O(n^2)$, $c(n) = O(n^3)$, which matches the running time of the sequential algorithm.

Example 8.5

Figure 8.5 illustrates the behavior of procedure MESH PDE for the processors in Fig. 8.4. Note that $d = 0.2$.   □

8.5 COMPUTING EIGENVALUES

The *algebraic eigenvalue problem* derives its importance from its relation to the problem of solving a system of n simultaneous linear differential equations of first order with constant coefficients. Such a system is written as

$$dx/dt = Ax$$

where A is an $n \times n$ matrix and x is an $n \times 1$ vector. For some vector $u \neq 0$, $x = ue^{\lambda t}$ is a solution of the preceding system if and only if $\lambda u = Au$. Here, λ is called an *eigenvalue* and u an *eigenvector*. The algebraic eigenvalue problem is to determine such λ and u. There are always n eigenvalues. To each eigenvalue, there corresponds at least one eigenvector.

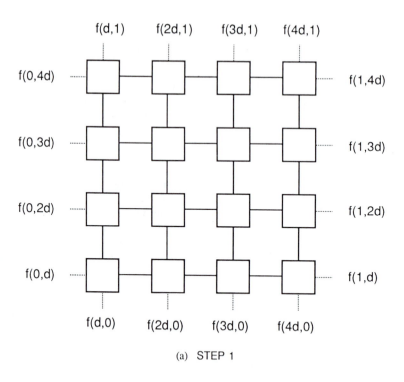

(a) STEP 1

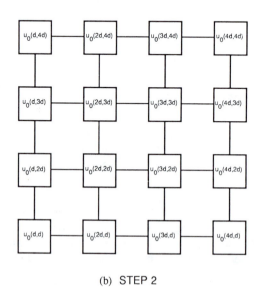

(b) STEP 2

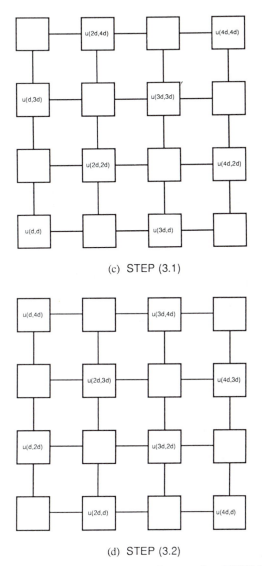

(c) STEP (3.1)

(d) STEP (3.2)

Figure 8.5 Solving Model Problem using procedure MESH PDE.

For an $n \times n$ matrix B and an $n \times 1$ vector y, if we apply the transformation $x = By$ to the system of differential equations, we get

$$dy/dt = (B^{-1}AB)y.$$

The eigenvalues of $B^{-1}AB$ are the same as those of A. We therefore choose B such that the eigenvalues of $B^{-1}AB$ are easily obtainable. For example, if $B^{-1}AB$ is a *diagonal* matrix (i.e., all elements are zero except on the diagonal), then the diagonal elements are the eigenvalues. One method of transforming a symmetric matrix A to diagonal form is *Jacobi's algorithm*. The method is an iterative one, where the kth iteration is defined by

$$A_k = R_k A_{k-1} R_k^T \quad \text{for } k = 1, 2, \ldots,$$

with

$$A_0 = A.$$

The $n \times n$ matrices R_k are known as *plane rotations*. Let a_{ij}^k denote the elements of A_k. The purpose of R_k is to reduce the two elements a_{pq}^{k-1} and a_{qp}^{k-1} to zero (for some $p < q$ depending on k). In reality, each iteration decreases the sum of the squares of the nondiagonal elements so that A_k converges to a diagonal matrix. The process stops when the sum of the squares is sufficiently small, or more specifically, when

$$d_k = \left(\sum_{\substack{i=1 \\ i \neq j}}^{n} \sum_{j=1}^{n} (a_{ij}^k)^2 \right)^{1/2} < c$$

for some small tolerance c. At that point, the columns of the matrix $R_1^T R_2^T \cdots R_k^T$ are the eigenvectors.

The plane rotations are chosen as follows. If a_{pq}^{k-1} is a nonzero off-diagonal element of A_{k-1}, we wish to define R_k so that $a_{pq}^k = a_{qp}^k = 0$. Denote the elements of R_k by r_{ij}^k. We take

$$r_{pp}^k = r_{qq}^k = \cos \theta_k,$$

$$r_{pq}^k = -r_{qp}^k = \sin \theta_k,$$

$$r_{ii}^k = 1 \quad \text{for } i \neq p \text{ or } q,$$

$$r_{ij}^k = 0 \quad \text{otherwise},$$

where $\cos \theta_k$ and $\sin \theta_k$ are obtained as follows. Let

$$\alpha_k = (a_{qq}^{k-1} - a_{pp}^{k-1})/2a_{pq}^{k-1}$$

and

$$\beta_k = 1/[\text{sign}(\alpha_k)][\text{abs}(\alpha_k) + (1 + \alpha_k^2)^{1/2}],$$

where $\text{sign}(\alpha_k)$ is $+1$ or -1 depending on whether α_k is positive or negative, respectively. Then

$$\cos \theta_k = 1/(1 + \beta_k^2)^{1/2} \quad \text{and} \quad \sin \theta_k = \beta_k \cos \theta_k.$$

The only question remaining is: Which nonzero element a_{pq}^{k-1} is selected for reduction to zero during the kth iteration? Many approaches are possible, one of which is to choose the element of greatest magnitude since this would lead to the greatest reduction in d_k.

As described in the preceding, the algorithm converges in $O(n^2)$ iterations. Since each iteration consists of two matrix multiplications, the entire process takes $O(n^5)$

time, assuming that the (sequential) procedure MATRIX MULTIPLICATION is used.

Jacobi's method lends itself naturally to parallel implementation. Let $n = 2^s$, for some positive integer s. In what follows we give a parallel algorithm designed to run on a cube-connected SIMD computer with $n^3 = 2^{3s}$ processors, as we did in section 7.3.2. We visualize the processors of this $3s$-dimensional cube as being arranged in an $n \times n \times n$ array pattern, with processor P_r occupying position (i, j, m), $0 \leqslant i, j,$ $m \leqslant n - 1$. The processors are arranged in row-major order, that is, $r = in^2 + jn + m$. The matrix A (i.e., A_0) is initially stored in the n^2 processors occupying positions $(0, j, m)$, $0 \leqslant j, m \leqslant n - 1$, one element per processor. In other words, A_0 is stored in the processors of a $2s$-dimensional cube. At the beginning of iteration k, $k = 1, 2, \ldots,$ these same processors contain A_{k-1}. They find its largest off-diagonal element and create R_k and R_k^T. All n^3 processors are then used to obtain $C_k = R_k A_{k-1}$ and $A_k = C_k R_k^T$. At the end of the iteration, if $d_k < c$, the process terminates.

The algorithm is given in what follows as procedure CUBE EIGENVALUES. The subscript k is omitted from A_k, R_k, R_k^T, and d_k since new values replace old ones.

> **procedure** CUBE EIGENVALUES (A, c)
>
> > **while** $d > c$ **do**
> > > (1) Find the off-diagonal element in A with largest absolute value
> > > (2) Create R
> > > (3) $A \leftarrow RA$
> > > (4) Create R^T
> > > (5) $A \leftarrow AR^T$
> > **end while.**   □

Analysis.   As pointed out earlier, the n^2 processors holding A form a $2s$-dimensional cube. From problem 7.23 we know therefore that they can compute d_k in $O(\log n)$ time. By the same reasoning, step 1 takes $O(\log n)$ time. Steps 2 and 4 take constant time since each of the n^2 processors in positions $(0, j, m)$, $0 \leqslant j, m \leqslant n - 1$, creates one element of R_k and one of R_k^T. Procedure CUBE MATRIX MULTIPLICATION of chapter 7 whose running time is $O(\log n)$ is then applied in steps 3 and 5 to compute $R_k A R_k^T$. The time per iteration is thus $O(\log n)$. Since convergence is attained after $O(n^2)$ iterations, the overall running time is $O(n^2 \log n)$. Given that $p(n) = n^3$, $c(n) = O(n^5 \log n)$, which is by a factor of $\log n$ larger than the sequential running time.

Example 8.6

Let $n = 2$ (i.e., $s = 1$),

$$A = \begin{bmatrix} 1 & 1 \\ 1 & 1 \end{bmatrix} \quad \text{and} \quad c = 10^{-5}.$$

Procedure CUBE EIGENVALUES in this case requires eight processors forming a three-dimensional cube. Figure 8.6(a) shows the elements of A_0 inside the processors to which they are assigned.

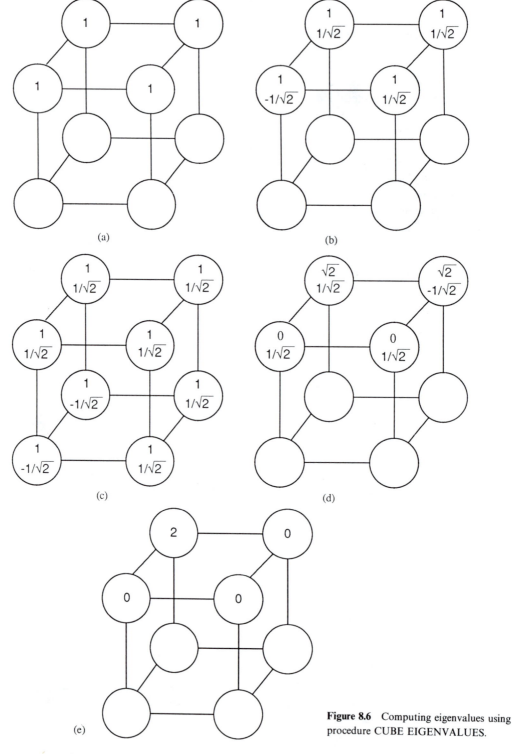

(a)

(b)

(c)

(d)

(e)

Figure 8.6 Computing eigenvalues using procedure CUBE EIGENVALUES.

In the first iteration, the off-diagonal element $a_{12} = 1$ is chosen for reduction to zero (i.e., $p = 1$ and $q = 2$). Thus

$$R_1 = \begin{bmatrix} \cos\theta_1 & \sin\theta_1 \\ -\sin\theta_1 & \cos\theta_1 \end{bmatrix} = \begin{bmatrix} 1/\sqrt{2} & 1/\sqrt{2} \\ -1/\sqrt{2} & 1/\sqrt{2} \end{bmatrix},$$

as shown in Fig. 8.6(b). Now

$$R_1 A_0 = \begin{bmatrix} 1/\sqrt{2} & 1/\sqrt{2} \\ -1/\sqrt{2} & 1/\sqrt{2} \end{bmatrix}\begin{bmatrix} 1 & 1 \\ 1 & 1 \end{bmatrix} = \begin{bmatrix} \sqrt{2} & \sqrt{2} \\ 0 & 0 \end{bmatrix}$$

is computed using all eight processors to execute the eight multiplications involved simultaneously, as shown in Fig. 8.6(c).

The elements of $R_1 A_0$ replace those of A_0 and R_1^T replaces R_1, as shown in Fig. 8.6(d). Finally $A R_1^T$ is computed and the value of A_1 at the end of the first iteration is shown in Fig. 8.6(e). Since the two off-diagonal elements are both zero, the procedure terminates. The eigenvalues are 2 and 0, and the eigenvectors are

$$(1/\sqrt{2} \quad 1/\sqrt{2})^T \quad \text{and} \quad (-1/\sqrt{2} \quad 1/\sqrt{2})^T. \quad \square$$

8.6 PROBLEMS

8.1 In procedure SIMD GAUSS JORDAN the elements a_{jj} are called the *pivots*. If at any point a pivot equals zero, then the procedure obviously fails since a_{jj} is a denominator. In fact, if the values of one or more pivots are near zero, then the errors of computation grow exponentially as they propagate, and the procedure is said to be *numerically unstable*. To avoid these problems, a method called *pivoting* is used: A pair of rows and columns are interchanged so that the new element used as a pivot is not too close to zero. Modify procedure SIMD GAUSS JORDAN to include pivoting.

8.2 *Gaussian elimination* is a standard method for solving the system of equations $Ax = b$. It begins by transforming the given system to the equivalent form $Ux = c$, where U is an $n \times n$ upper triangular matrix (i.e., all elements below the diagonal are zero) and c is an $n \times 1$ vector. The transformation is performed in $n - 1$ steps. During step j, variable x_j is eliminated from equations $i = j + 1, j + 2, \ldots, n$ by subtracting from each of these equations the product $(a_{ij}/a_{jj}) \times$ (equation j). The triangular system $Ux = c$ is now solved by *back substitution*, computing x_n from the nth equation, x_{n-1} from the $(n - 1)$st, and finally x_1 from the first. Design a parallel version of Gaussian elimination for a SM SIMD computer and analyze its running time and cost.

8.3 Modify the parallel algorithm derived in problem 8.2 to include pivoting as described in problem 8.1.

8.4 Another method for solving $Ax = b$ is known as *LU decomposition*. The matrix A is decomposed into two matrices L and U such that $LU = A$, where U is upper triangular ($u_{kj} = 0$ if $k > j$) and L is lower triangular ($l_{ik} = 0$ if $i < k$) with diagonal elements equal to 1 ($l_{ik} = 1$ if $i = k$). The solution of $Ax = b$ is now achieved by solving $Ly = b$ and $Ux = y$ using forward and back substitution, respectively. Consider the special case where A is *positive definite*, that is,

(i) $a_{ij} = a_{ji}$ for all i and j, $1 \leqslant i, j \leqslant n$, meaning that A is *symmetric*;
(ii) $v^T A v > 0$ for all $n \times 1$ nonzero vectors v.

In this case the elements of L and U are obtained as follows:

$$l_{ik} = a_{ik}^k / u_{kk}, \qquad i > k,$$

$$u_{kj} = a_{kj}^k, \qquad k \leqslant j,$$

where

$$a_{ij}^1 = a_{ij} \quad \text{and} \quad a_{ij}^{k+1} = a_{ij}^k - (l_{ik} \times u_{kj}).$$

(a) Show how the matrices L and U can be computed on an interconnection network SIMD computer in which the processors form a *hexagonal array* as shown in Fig. 8.7.

(b) Show how both systems $Ly = b$ and $Ux = y$ can be solved on an interconnection-network SIMD computer in which the processors form a linear array.

8.5 A matrix Q is said to be *orthogonal* if $QQ^T = Q^TQ = I$. The system $Ax = b$ can also be solved using a method known as *QR factorization*. Here two matrices Q and R are obtained such that

$$QA = R$$

where Q is orthogonal and R upper triangular. Thus the system $Rx = Qb$ can be solved directly by back substitution. Matrix Q is formed as the product of plane rotations, that is, matrices $P_{i+1,j}$ identical to I except in positions p_{ii}, $p_{i,i+1}$, $p_{i+1,i}$, and $p_{i+1,i+1}$. Let $b_{ij} = (a_{ij}^2 + a_{i+1,j}^2)^{1/2}$, $c_i = a_{ij}/b_{ij}$, and $s_i = a_{i+1,j}/b_{ij}$. We take $p_{ii} = p_{i+1,i+1} = c_i$, and $p_{i,i+1} = -p_{i+1,i} = s_i$. Each plane rotation therefore annihilates one element of A below the diagonal. Show how the matrix R can be computed on an $n \times n$ mesh-connected SIMD computer.

8.6 Let two processors be available on an MIMD computer, and assume that procedure MIMD MODIFIED GS is used to solve the system of equations

$$4x_1 - x_2 - x_3 - x_4 = 0,$$

$$-x_1 + 4x_2 - x_3 - x_4 = 0,$$

$$-x_1 - x_2 + 10x_3 + 4x_4 = 22,$$

$$-x_1 - x_2 + 4x_3 + 10x_4 = 16,$$

with $c = 0.1$ and starting from the initial estimates $x_1^0 = x_2^0 = x_3^0 = x_4^0 = 0$. Processors P_1 and P_2 begin by executing processes 1 and 2, respectively, and halt after one iteration with $x_1 = x_2 = 0$. Processes 3 and 4 are now executed. After a few iterations, the values of x_3 and x_4 eventually converge to approximately $\frac{13}{7}$ and $\frac{6}{7}$, respectively. The procedure therefore returns an incorrect answer since the solution to the system is $x_1 = 1$, $x_2 = 1$, $x_3 = 2$, and $x_4 = 1$. The error is due to the fact that the values computed for one pair of unknowns are not revised once new values for the other pair have been obtained. Suggest changes to the procedure to allow for this revision.

8.7 Derive MIMD algorithms for the methods described in problems 8.2, 8.4, and 8.5.

8.8 Unlike procedure BISECTION, procedure SIMD ROOT SEARCH assumes that the initial interval contains exactly one zero of the input function. Modify the procedure so that it returns exactly one of possibly several roots in the initial interval. Analyze the running time and cost of the new procedure.

8.9 An old method for solving $f(x) = 0$ is based on linear interpolation between two previous approximations to a root in order to obtain an improved approximation. Let (x_l, x_r) be an

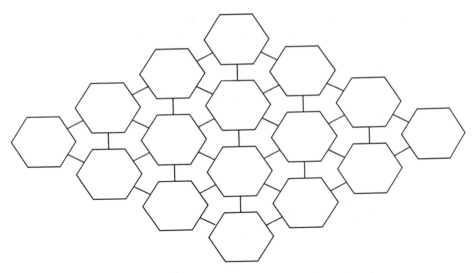

Figure 8.7 Hexagonal array connection.

interval containing a root. The method is called *regula falsi* and uses the iteration

$$x_{\text{new}} = x_l - f(x_l)(x_r - x_l)/[f(x_r) - f(x_l)]$$

to obtain a new interval. Derive a parallel version of this algorithm.

8.10 Procedure MIMD ROOT SEARCH begins with an interval (a, b) known to contain a root z of $f(x) = 0$. The interval is divided into $N + 1$ subintervals and the division points are taken as initial approximations of z. Each of N processes applies Newton's method beginning with one of these approximations. Discuss the possibility of one of these processes converging to a zero outside (a, b) before any other process converges to z. Can the procedure be modified to include this possibility?

8.11 Our analysis of procedure MIMD ROOT SEARCH assumes that N processors are available to execute the N processes involved. What can be said about the procedure's cost? Analyze the procedure's running time and cost for the case where fewer than N processors are available.

8.12 One disadvantage of Newton's method is that it requires that $f'(x)$ be computable. In some applications $f'(x)$ may not be known. The *secant method* solves $f(x) = 0$ using essentially the same approach but without requiring any knowledge of $f'(x)$. Instead the difference equation

$$f'(x_n) = [f(x_n) - f(x_{n-1})]/(x_n - x_{n-1})$$

is used. Thus

$$x_{n+1} = x_n - (x_n - x_{n-1})f(x_n)/[f(x_n) - f(x_{n-1})].$$

The method derives its name from the fact that x_{n+1} is the intersection with the x axis of the secant passing through the points $(x_n, f(x_n))$ and $(x_{n-1}, f(x_{n-1}))$. Discuss various approaches to implementing this algorithm in parallel.

8.13 Show that the solution to the discrete Model Problem can be obtained by solving a system of $(n-1)^2$ linear equations in $(n-1)^2$ unknowns using the methods of section 8.2.

8.14 Procedure MESH PDE assumes the existence of $(n-1)^2$ processors on the mesh. Show how the algorithm can be modified for the case where fewer processors are available. Analyze the running time and cost of the new algorithm.

8.15 What changes should procedure MESH PDE undergo to handle the case where R is not the unit square but an arbitrary plane region?

8.16 Jacobi's method is another iterative approach to solving the Model Problem. Given "old" values $u_{k-1}(x, y)$ at mesh points, the following equation is used to generate "new" values:

$$u_k(x, y) = [u_{k-1}(x + d, y) + u_{k-1}(x - d, y) + u_{k-1}(x, y + d)$$
$$+ u_{k-1}(x, y - d) - d^2 G(x, y)]/4.$$

Although slow in its convergence, requiring $O(n^2)$ iterations, this method is easier to implement in parallel than successive overrelaxation. Show how this can be done.

8.17 Modify procedure CUBE EIGENVALUES to produce the eigenvectors as well as eigenvalues.

8.18 Implement Jacobi's method for computing eigenvalues on a mesh-connected SIMD computer and analyze its performance.

8.19 Can you implement Jacobi's method for computing eigenvalues on a parallel model of computation with a cost of $O(n^5)$?

8.20 Jacobi's method for computing eigenvalues can be modified so that more than just one off-diagonal element is annihilated in each iteration, thus providing greater parallelism. Show how this can be done.

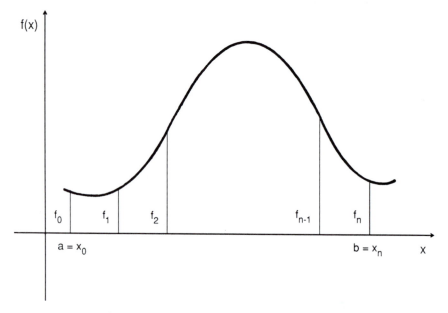

Figure 8.8 Numerical integration by trapezoidal rule.

8.21 As we saw in this chapter, many numerical algorithms are inherently parallel. One further example is provided by *numerical integration*, that is, the computation of an approximation to the definite integral

$$D = \int_a^b f(s)\, dx.$$

As shown in Fig. 8.8, this problem can be interpreted as that of computing the area between the curve for $f(x)$ and the x axis on the interval (a, b). One very simple formula for approximating D is the *trapezoidal rule*. The interval (a, b) is divided into N subintervals of equal size $h = (b - a)/N$. With $x_0 = a$, $x_1 = a + h, \ldots, x_N = b$ and $f_i = f(x_i)$, the approximate value of D is given by

$$(h/2)(f_0 + 2f_1 + 2f_2 + \cdots + 2f_{N-1} + f_N).$$

Discuss various parallel implementations of this rule.

8.7 BIBLIOGRAPHICAL REMARKS

References to sequential numerical algorithms, including the ones described in this chapter, are found in [Conte], [Hamming], [Ralston], [Stewart], [Wilkinson], and [Young]. Parallel numerical algorithms are either described or reviewed in [Heller 2], [Hockney], [Hwang], [ICPP], [Kronsjö], [Kuck 2], [Kung], [Miranker], [Poole], [Quinn], [Rodrigue], [Sameh 2], [Schendel], and [Traub].

There is a vast literature on SIMD algorithms for solving systems of linear equations; we simply mention [Bojanczyk], [Fortes], [Heller 2], [Mead], [Sameh 2], [Sameh 5], and [Traub]. In our analysis of procedure SIMD GAUSS JORDAN, we showed that matrix inversion can be reduced to matrix multiplication. Our argument ignored a number of rare special cases. A thorough treatment is provided in [Bunch] and [Schönhage]. In fact, the converse is also true: It is shown in [Munro] that the product AB of two $n \times n$ matrices A and B can be obtained by inverting a $3n \times 3n$ matrix as follows:

$$\begin{bmatrix} I & A & 0 \\ 0 & I & B \\ 0 & 0 & I \end{bmatrix}^{-1} = \begin{bmatrix} I & -A & AB \\ 0 & I & -B \\ 0 & 0 & I \end{bmatrix}.$$

We conclude therefore that inverting an $n \times n$ matrix is equivalent to multiplying two $n \times n$ matrices. Procedure MIMD MODIFIED GS is based on ideas from [Baudet], where results of experiments with the method are reported. It should be noted that many situations are known in which the Gauss–Seidel method is guaranteed to converge. For example, let A be an $n \times n$ symmetric matrix all of whose diagonal elements are positive. The Gauss–Seidel method converges when applied to the system $Ax = b$ if and only if A is positive definite. Other MIMD algorithms for solving linear systems are presented in [Arnold], [Evans], [Lord], and [Wing].

The development of procedure SIMD ROOT SEARCH was inspired by [Kung], where an MIMD algorithm is also described. Other approaches are proposed in [Eriksen], [Gal], [Heller 1], and [Schendel].

Parallel algorithms for solving partial differential equations are discussed in [Buzbee 1], [Buzbee 2], [Fishburn], [Heller 2], [Jones], [Karp], [Rosenfeld], [Saltz], [Sameh 3], [Swarztrauber], [Sweet], and [Traub].

Methods for accelerating the convergence of procedure CUBE EIGENVALUES, as well as other algorithms for computing eigenvalues in parallel, are the subject of [Kuck 1], [Sameh 1], and [Sameh 2]. Parallel algorithms for special cases of the eigenvalue problem are studied in [Heller 2] and [Sameh 4].

Parallel solutions to a variety of other numerical problems can be found in [Borodin 1], [Borodin 2], [Csanky], [Devreese], [Eberly], [Haynes], [Numrich], [Pan], [Valiant], and [von zur Gathen].

8.8 REFERENCES

[ARNOLD]

Arnold, C. P., Parr, M. I., and Dewe, M. B., An efficient parallel algorithm for the solution of large sparse linear matrix equations, *IEEE Transactions on Computers*, Vol. C-32, No. 3, March 1983, pp. 265–273.

[BAUDET]

Baudet, G. M., Asynchronous iterative methods for multiprocessors, *Journal of the ACM*, Vol. 25, No. 2, April 1978, pp. 226–244.

[BOJANCZYK]

Bojanczyk, A., Brent, R. P., and Kung, H. T., Numerically stable solution of dense systems of linear equations using mesh-connected processors, Technical Report CMU-CS-81-119, Department of Computer Science, Carnegie-Mellon University, Pittsburgh, May 1981.

[BORODIN 1]

Borodin A., and Munro, J. I., *The Computational Complexity of Algebraic and Numeric Problems*, American Elsevier, New York, 1975.

[BORODIN 2]

Borodin, A., von zur Gathen, J., and Hopcroft, J. E., Fast parallel matrix and gcd computations, *Information and Control*, Vol. 52, 1982, pp. 241–256.

[BUNCH]

Bunch, J., and Hopcroft, J. E., Triangular factorization and inversion by fast matrix multiplication, *Mathematics of Computation*, Vol. 28, No. 125, 1974, pp. 231–236.

[BUZBEE 1]

Buzbee, B. L., A fast Poisson solver amenable to parallel computation, *IEEE Transactions on Computers*, Vol. C-22, No. 8, August 1973, pp. 793–796.

[BUZBEE 2]

Buzbee, B. L., Golub, G. H., and Nielson, C. W., On direct methods for solving Poisson's equations, *SIAM Journal on Numerical Analysis*, Vol. 7, No. 4, December 1970, pp. 627–656.

[CONTE]

Conte, S. D., and de Boor, C. J., *Elementary Numerical Analysis: An Algorithmic Approach*, McGraw-Hill, New York, 1972.

[CSANKY]

Csanky, L., Fast parallel matrix inversion algorithms, *SIAM Journal on Computing*, Vol. 5, No. 4, December 1976, pp. 618–623.

[DEVREESE]

Devreese, J. T., and Camp, P. T., Eds., *Supercomputers in Theoretical and Experimental Science*, Plenum, New York, 1985.

[EBERLY]

Eberly, W., Very fast parallel matrix and polynomial arithmetic, Proceedings of the 25th Annual IEEE Symposium on Foundations of Computer Science, Singer Island, Florida, October 1984, pp. 21–30, IEEE Computer Society, Washington, D.C., 1984.

[ERIKSEN]

Eriksen, O., and Staunstrup, J., Concurrent algorithms for root searching, *Acta Informatica*, Vol. 18, No. 4, 1983, pp. 361–376.

[EVANS]

Evans, D. J., and Dunbar, R. C., The parallel solution of triangular systems of equations, *IEEE Transactions on Computers*, Vol. C-32, No. 2, February 1983, pp. 201–204.

[FISHBURN]

Fishburn, J. P., Analysis of speedup in distributed algorithms, Ph.D. thesis, Computer Sciences Department, University of Wisconsin–Madison, Madison, Wisconsin, May 1981.

[FORTES]

Fortes, J. A. B., and Wah, B. W., Eds., Special Issue on Systolic Arrays, *Computer*, Vol. 20, No. 7, July 1987.

[GAL]

Gal, S., and Miranker, W. L., Optimal sequential and parallel search for finding a root, *Journal of Combinatorial Theory (A)*, Vol. 23, 1977, pp. 1–4.

[HAMMING]

Hamming, R. W., *Numerical Methods for Scientists and Engineers*, McGraw-Hill, New York, 1973.

[HAYNES]

Haynes, L. S., Ed., Special Issue on Highly Parallel Computing, *Computer*, Vol. 15, No. 1, January 1982.

[HELLER 1]

Heller, D., A determinant theorem with applications to parallel algorithms, Technical Report, Department of Computer Science, Carnegie-Mellon University, Pittsburgh, March 1973.

[HELLER 2]

Heller, D., A survey of parallel algorithms in numerical linear algebra, *SIAM Review*, Vol. 20, No. 4, October 1978, pp. 740–777.

[HOCKNEY]

Hockney, R. W., and Jesshope, C. R., *Parallel Computers*, Adam Hilger, Bristol, England, 1981.

[HWANG]

Hwang, K., and Briggs, F. A., *Computer Architecture and Parallel Processing*, McGraw-Hill, New York, 1984.

[ICPP]

Proceedings of the International Conference on Parallel Processing, Annual, 1972–, IEEE Computer Society, Washington, D.C.

[JONES]

Jones, A. K., and Gehringer, E. F., Eds., The Cm* multiprocessor project: A research review, Technical Report CMU-CS-80-131, Department of Computer Science, Carnegie-Mellon University, Pittsburgh, July 1980.

[KARP]
Karp, R. M., Miller, R. E., and Winograd, S., The organization of computations for uniform recurrence relations, *Journal of the ACM*, Vol. 14, No. 3, July 1967, pp. 563–590.

[KRONSJÖ]
Kronsjö, L., *Computational Complexity of Sequential and Parallel Algorithms*, Wiley, Chichester, England, 1985.

[KUCK 1]
Kuck, D. J., and Sameh, A. H., Parallel computation of eigenvalues of real matrices, Proceedings of IFIP Congress 71, Ljubljana, Yugoslavia, August 1971, in *Information Processing 71*, North-Holland, Amsterdam, 1972, pp. 1266–1272.

[KUCK 2]
Kuck, D. J., Lawrie, D. H., and Sameh, A. H., Eds., *High Speed Computer and Algorithm Organization*, Academic, New York 1977.

[KUNG]
Kung, H. T., Synchronized and asynchronous parallel algorithms for multiprocessors, in Traub, J. F., Ed., *Algorithms and Complexity: New Directions and Recent Results*, Academic, New York, 1976, pp. 153–200.

[LORD]
Lord, R. E., Kowalik, J. S., and Kumar, S. P., Solving linear algebraic equations on an MIMD computer, *Journal of the ACM*, Vol. 30, No. 1, January 1983, pp. 103–117.

[MEAD]
Mead, C. A., and Conway, L. A., *Introduction to VLSI Systems*, Addison-Wesley, Reading, Mass., 1980.

[MIRANKER]
Miranker, W. L., A survey of parallelism in numerical analysis, *SIAM Review*, Vol. 13, No. 4, October 1971, pp. 524–547.

[MUNRO]
Munro, J. I., Problems related to matrix multiplication, in Rustin, R., Ed., *Courant Institute Symposium on Computational Complexity*, Algorithmics Press, New York, 1973, pp. 137–152.

[NUMRICH]
Numrich, R. W., Ed., *Supercomputer Applications*, Plenum, New York, 1985.

[PAN]
Pan, V., and Reif, J. H., Fast and efficient parallel linear programming and linear least squares computations, in Makedon, F., Mehlhorn, K., Papatheodorou, T., and Spirakis, P., *VLSI Algorithms and Architectures*, Lecture Notes in Computer Science, Vol. 227, Springer-Verlag, Berlin, 1986, pp. 283–295.

[POOLE]
Poole, W. G., Jr., and Voight, R. G., Numerical Algorithms for parallel and vector computers: An annotated bibliography, *Computing Reviews*, Vol. 15, No. 10, October 1974, pp. 379–388.

[QUINN]
Quinn, M. J., *Designing Efficient Algorithms for Parallel Computers*, McGraw-Hill, New York, 1987.

[RALSTON]
Ralston, A., and Rabinowitz, P., *A First Course in Numerical Analysis*, McGraw-Hill, New York, 1978.

[RODRIGUE]

Rodrigue, G., Ed., *Parallel Computations*, Academic, New York, 1982.

[ROSENFELD]

Rosenfeld, J. L., A case study in programming for parallel processors, *Communications of the ACM*, Vol. 12, No. 12, December 1969, pp. 645–655.

[SALTZ]

Saltz, J. H., Naik, V. K., and Nicol, D. M., Reduction of the effects of the communication delays in scientific algorithms on message passing MIMD architectures, *SIAM Journal on Scientific and Statistical Computing*, Vol. 8, No. 1, January 1987, pp. s118–s134.

[SAMEH 1]

Sameh, A. H., On Jacobi and Jacobi-like algorithms for a parallel computer, *Mathematics of Computation*, Vol. 25, No. 115, July 1971, pp. 579–590.

[SAMEH 2]

Sameh, A. H., Numerical parallel algorithms: A survey, in Kuck, D. J., Lawrie, D. H., and Sameh, A. H., Eds., *High Speed Computer and Algorithm Organization*, Academic, New York, 1977, pp. 207–228.

[SAMEH 3]

Sameh, A. H., Chen, S. C., and Kuck, D. J., Parallel Poisson and biharmonic solvers, *Computing*, Vol. 17, 1976, pp. 219–230.

[SAMEH 4]

Sameh, A. H., and Kuck, D. J., A parallel QR algorithm for symmetric tridiagonal matrices, *IEEE Transactions on Computers*, Vol. C-26, No. 2, February 1977, pp. 147–153.

[SAMEH 5]

Sameh, A. H., and Kuck, D. J., On stable parallel linear system solvers, *Journal of the ACM*, Vol. 25, No. 1, January 1978, pp. 81–91.

[SCHENDEL]

Schendel, U., *Introduction to Numerical Methods for Parallel Computers*, Ellis Horwood, Chichester, England, 1984.

[SCHÖNHAGE]

Schönhage, A., Fast Schmidt orthogonalization and unitary transformations of large matrices, in Traub, J. F., Ed., *Complexity of Sequential and Parallel Numerical Algorithms*, Academic, New York, 1973, pp. 283–291.

[STEWART]

Stewart, G. W., *Introduction to Matrix Computations*, Academic, New York, 1973.

[SWARZTRAUBER]

Swarztrauber, P. N., A direct method for the discrete solution of separable elliptic equations, *SIAM Journal on Numerical Analysis*, Vol. 11, No. 6, December 1974, pp. 1136–1150.

[SWEET]

Sweet, R. A., A generalized cyclic reduction algorithm, *SIAM Journal on Numerical Analysis*, Vol. 11, No. 3, June 1974, pp. 506–520.

[TRAUB]

Traub, J. F., Ed., *Complexity of Sequential and Parallel Numerical Algorithms*, Academic, New York, 1973.

[VALIANT]

Valiant, L. G., Computing multivariate polynomials in parallel, *Information Processing Letters*, Vol. 11, No. 1, August 1980, pp. 44–45.

[VON ZUR GATHEN]

Von zur Gathen, J., Parallel algorithms for algebraic problems, Proceedings of the 15th Annual ACM Symposium on Theory of Computing, Boston, Massachusetts, April 1983, pp. 17–23, Association for Computing Machinery, New York, N.Y., 1983.

[WILKINSON]

Wilkinson, J. H., and Reinsch, C., Eds., *Handbook for Automatic Computation*, Vol. II, *Linear Algebra*, Springer-Verlag, New York, 1971.

[WING]

Wing, O., and Huang, J. W., A computation model of parallel solution of linear equations, *IEEE Transactions on Computers*, Vol. C-29, No. 7, July 1980, pp. 632–638.

[YOUNG]

Young, D. M., *Iterative Solution of Large Linear Systems*, Academic, New York, 1971.

9

Computing Fourier Transforms

9.1 INTRODUCTION

This chapter is about one of the most important computations arising in engineering and scientific applications, namely, the discrete Fourier transform (DFT). Given a sequence of numbers $\{a_0, a_1, \ldots, a_{n-1}\}$, its DFT is the sequence $\{b_0, b_1, \ldots, b_{n-1}\}$, where

$$b_j = \sum_{k=0}^{n-1} a_k \times w^{kj} \quad \text{for } j = 0, 1, \ldots, n-1.$$

In the preceding expression, w is a primitive nth root of unity, that is, $w = e^{2\pi i/n}$, where

$$i = \sqrt{-1}.$$

9.1.1 The Fast Fourier Transform

Sequentially, a straightforward computation of b_j requires n multiplications and $n-1$ additions of complex numbers. This leads to an $O(n^2)$ computation time to obtain the entire sequence $\{b_0, b_1, \ldots, b_{n-1}\}$. Such time is prohibitive for very large values of n, particularly in applications where several sequences of this kind must be computed successively. Fortunately, a better algorithm exists. Let $n = 2^s$ for some positive integer s. Thus the expression for b_j can be rewritten as

$$b_j = \sum_{m=0}^{2^{s-1}-1} a_{2m} w^{2mj} + \sum_{m=0}^{2^{s-1}-1} a_{2m+1} w^{(2m+1)j}$$

$$= \sum_{m=0}^{2^{s-1}-1} a_{2m} e^{2\pi ijm/2^{s-1}} + w^j \sum_{m=0}^{2^{s-1}-1} a_{2m+1} e^{2\pi ijm/2^{s-1}}$$

for $j = 0, 1, \ldots, n-1$. This leads to a recursive algorithm for computing b_j since each of the two sums in the last expression is itself a DFT. This algorithm, known as the fast Fourier transform (FFT), is given in what follows as procedure SEQUENTIAL FFT. The procedure takes as input the sequence $A = \{a_0, a_1, \ldots, a_{n-1}\}$ and returns its transform $B = \{b_0, b_1, \ldots, b_{n-1}\}$.

procedure SEQUENTIAL FFT (A, B)

if $n = 1$ then $b_0 \leftarrow a_0$
  else (1) SEQUENTIAL FFT $(a_0, a_2, \ldots, a_{n-2}, u_0, u_1, \ldots, u_{(n/2)-1})$
     (2) SEQUENTIAL FFT $(a_1, a_3, \ldots, a_{n-1}, v_0, v_1, \ldots, v_{(n/2)-1})$
     (3) $z \leftarrow 1$
     (4) for $j = 0$ to $n - 1$ do
         (4.1) $b_j \leftarrow u_{j \bmod (n/2)} + z(v_{j \bmod (n/2)})$
         (4.2) $z \leftarrow z \times w$
     end for
  end if. □

As can be easily verified, the procedure runs in $O(n \log n)$ time.

9.1.2 An Application of the FFT

The efficiency of the FFT has made it an extremely popular computational technique in such applications as digital signal processing, coding theory, computerized axial tomography scanning, speech transmission, weather prediction, statistics, image processing, multiplication of very large integers, and polynomial multiplication. In order to illustrate its use, we show how the FFT accelerates the computation of the product of two polynomials. Consider the polynomial

$$a_0 + a_1 x + a_2 x^2 + \cdots + a_{n-2} x^{n-2} + a_{n-1} x^{n-1}$$

whose coefficients form the sequence $\{a_0, a_1, \ldots, a_{n-1}\}$. Then element b_j of the sequence $\{b_0, b_1, \ldots, b_{n-1}\}$ defined in the preceding is the value of this polynomial at $x = w^j$, where $w^0, w^1, \ldots, w^{n-1}$ are the nth roots of unity. Conversely, the value of the polynomial

$$b_0 + b_1 x + \cdots + b_{n-2} x^{n-2} + b_{n-1} x^{n-1}$$

at $x = (w^{-1})^k$ is given by

$$a_k = \frac{1}{n} \sum_{j=0}^{n-1} b_j (w^{-1})^{jk} \quad \text{for } k = 0, 1, \ldots, n - 1.$$

The sequence $\{a_0, a_1, \ldots, a_{n-1}\}$ is the *inverse* DFT of $\{b_0, b_1, \ldots, b_{n-1}\}$ and can be computed in $O(n \log n)$ time through minor modifications to procedure SEQUENTIAL FFT.

Assume now that we want to multiply the two polynomials

$$f(x) = \sum_{j=0}^{n-1} a_j x^j \quad \text{and} \quad g(x) = \sum_{k=0}^{n-1} c_k x^k$$

to obtain the product polynomial $h = fg$. The straightforward product requires $O(n^2)$ time. By using the FFT, we can reduce this to an $O(n \log n)$ time computation. This is done as follows:

Step 1: Let N be the smallest integer that is a power of 2 and is greater than $2n - 1$. Each of the two sequences $\{a_0, a_1, \ldots, a_{n-1}\}$ and $\{c_0, c_1, \ldots, c_{n-1}\}$ is padded with $N - n$ zeros.

Step 2: Compute the FFT of $\{a_0, a_1, \ldots, a_{n-1}, 0, 0, \ldots, 0\}$. This yields the values of polynomial f at the Nth roots of unity.

Step 3: Compute the FFT of $\{c_0, c_1, \ldots, c_{n-1}, 0, 0, \ldots, 0\}$. This yields the values of polynomial g at the Nth roots of unity.

Step 4: Compute the product $f(w^j) \times g(w^j)$ for $j = 0, 1, \ldots, N - 1$, where $w = e^{2\pi i/N}$. The resulting numbers are the values of the product polynomial h at the Nth roots of unity.

Step 5: Compute the inverse DFT of the sequence $\{f(w^0)g(w^0), f(w^1)g(w^1), \ldots, f(w^{N-1})g(w^{N-1})\}$. The resulting sequence of numbers are the *coefficients* of the product polynomial h.

Step 1 takes $O(N)$ time. Each of steps 2, 3, and 5 is known to require $O(N \log N)$ operations while step 4 consists of N multiplications. Since $N < 4n$, the overall product takes $O(n \log n)$ time.

9.1.3 Computing the DFT in Parallel

There is a considerable amount of inherent parallelism in computing the DFT of a sequence $\{a_0, a_1, \ldots, a_{n-1}\}$. Two general approaches can be adopted in order to exploit this parallelism.

1. In the first approach, the sequence $\{b_0, b_1, \ldots, b_{n-1}\}$ is computed directly from the definition

$$b_j = \sum_{k=0}^{n-1} a_k \times w^{kj}$$

using N processors, where typically $N \geq n$. This results in algorithms whose running times are *at most* linear in n and whose costs are *at least* quadratic in n. We illustrate this approach in section 9.2.

2. In the second approach, parallel versions of the FFT are derived. Among the best of these are algorithms using n processors and running in $O(\log n)$ time for a cost of $O(n \log n)$. This cost matches the running time of procedure SEQUENTIAL FFT. We illustrate this approach in sections 9.3 and 9.4.

9.2 DIRECT COMPUTATION OF THE DFT

This approach to the parallel computation of the DFT is based on the observation that the sequence

$$b_j = \sum_{k=0}^{n-1} a_k \times w^{kj}$$

can be expressed as the following matrix-by-vector product

$$
\begin{bmatrix}
b_0 \\
b_1 \\
b_2 \\
\vdots \\
b_{n-1}
\end{bmatrix}
=
\begin{bmatrix}
1 & 1 & 1 & 1 & \cdots & 1 \\
1 & w & w^2 & w^3 & \cdots & w^{n-1} \\
1 & w^2 & w^4 & w^6 & \cdots & w^{2(n-1)} \\
\vdots & \vdots & \vdots & \vdots & \ddots & \vdots \\
1 & w^{n-1} & w^{2(n-1)} & w^{3(n-1)} & \cdots & w^{(n-1)(n-1)}
\end{bmatrix}
\begin{bmatrix}
a_0 \\
a_1 \\
a_2 \\
\vdots \\
a_{n-1}
\end{bmatrix},
$$

or $b = Wa$, where W is an $n \times n$ matrix and b and a are $n \times 1$ vectors.

Consequently, any of the algorithms developed in chapter 7 for matrix-by-matrix multiplication or matrix-by-vector multiplication can be used to compute the preceding product. Regardless of which algorithm is used, however, an efficient way must be specified for generating the matrix W, or more precisely for obtaining the various powers of w. Our purpose in this section is twofold:

1. We first describe a simple algorithm for computing the matrix W, which runs in $O(\log n)$ time and uses n^2 processors.

2. We then show how the processors of 1, with an appropriate interconnection network, can be used to compute the DFT.

9.2.1 Computing the Matrix W

Assume that an SIMD computer is available that consists of n^2 processors. The processors are arranged in an $n \times n$ array pattern with n rows numbered $1, \ldots, n$, and n columns numbered $1, \ldots, n$. Processor $P(k, j)$, $1 \leqslant k, j \leqslant n$, is required to compute $w^{(k-1)(j-1)}$. This computation can be accomplished by repeated squaring and multiplication. For example, w^{13} is obtained from $[(w^2)^2 \times w] \times [(w^2)^2]^2$. The algorithm is given in what follows as procedure COMPUTE W. Each processor $P(k, j)$ is assumed to have three registers: M_{kj}, X_{kj}, and Y_{kj}. Register M_{kj} stores the power to which w is to be raised, while registers X_{kj} and Y_{kj} store intermediate results. When the procedure terminates, $Y_{kj} = w^{(k-1)(j-1)}$.

procedure COMPUTE W (k, j)

Step 1: $M_{kj} \leftarrow (k-1)(j-1)$.

Step 2: $X_{kj} \leftarrow w$.

Step 3: $Y_{kj} \leftarrow 1$.

Step 4:   **while** $M_{kj} \neq 0$ **do**
      (4.1) **if** M_{kj} is odd
            then $Y_{kj} \leftarrow X_{kj} \times Y_{kj}$
            end if
      (4.2) $M_{kj} \leftarrow \lfloor M_{kj}/2 \rfloor$
      (4.3) $X_{kj} \leftarrow X_{kj}^2$
      end while.   □

Analysis.   Steps 1, 2, and 3 of the preceding procedure take constant time. There are $O(\log[(k-1)(j-1)])$ iterations of step 4, each requiring constant time. Procedure COMPUTE W therefore runs in $O(\log n)$ time. In fact, the procedure's actual running time can be slightly reduced by noting that $w^{n/2} = -1$, and therefore $w^{j+(n/2)} = -w^j$. Consequently, only powers of w smaller than $n/2$ need be computed.

Discussion.   The preceding description does not specify whether or not the n^2 processors on the SIMD computer share a common memory or are linked by an interconnection network. Indeed, procedure COMPUTE W requires no communication among the processors since each processor produces a power of w independently of all other processors. In the next section we show that when a particular network connects the processors, the DFT of a sequence can be computed in the same amount of time required to generate the matrix W.

9.2.2 Computing the DFT

The n^2 processors of the SIMD computer in the previous section are now interconnected as follows:

1. The processors in row k are interconnected to form a binary tree, that is, for $j = 1, \ldots, \lfloor n/2 \rfloor$, processor $P(k, j)$ is linked directly to processors $P(k, 2j)$ and $P(k, 2j+1)$, with $P(k, 2\lfloor n/2 \rfloor + 1)$ nonexistent if n is even.
2. The processors in column j are interconnected to form a binary tree, that is, for $k = 1, \ldots, \lfloor n/2 \rfloor$, processor $P(k, j)$ is linked directly to processors $P(2k, j)$ and $P(2k+1, j)$, with $P(2\lfloor n/2 \rfloor + 1, j)$ nonexistent if n is even.

This configuration, called the *mesh of trees* in problem 4.2, is illustrated in Fig. 9.1 for $n = 4$. We assume that the processors in row 1 and column 1 are in charge of input and output operations, respectively. Thus, for example, processor $P(1, j)$ can read a datum a_j. It is then possible, using the binary tree connections, to propagate a_j to all processors in column j. The algorithm is given as procedure PROPAGATE.

> **procedure** PROPAGATE (a_j)
>
>   **for** $m = 1$ **to** $(\log n) - 1$ **do**
>   **for** $k = 2^{m-1}$ **to** $2^m - 1$ **do in parallel**
> $P(k, j)$ sends a_j to $P(2k, j)$ and $P(2k+1, j)$
>   **end for**
>   **end for.** $\square$

This procedure (which is essentially procedure BROADCAST of chapter 2 implemented on a tree) requires $O(\log n)$ time.

Similarly, assume that each processor in row k contains a number d_{kj} and that the sum of these numbers is required. Again, using the binary tree connections, the sum can be computed and produced as output by $P(k, 1)$. The algorithm is given as procedure SUM.

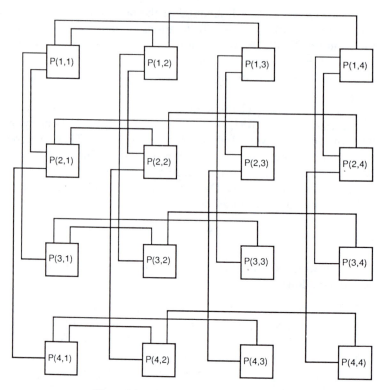

Figure 9.1   Mesh of trees connection.

procedure SUM (k)

   for $m = (\log n) - 1$ **downto** 1 **do**
     for $j = 2^{m-1}$ **to** $2^m - 1$ **do in parallel**
        $d_{kj} \leftarrow d_{k,2j} + d_{k,2j+1}$
     end for
   end for.   □

This procedure is a formal statement of the algorithm in example 1.5 and runs in $O(\log n)$ time.

We are now ready to show how the product

$$b = Wa$$

is obtained. There are four stages to this computation. Initially, the elements of matrix W are created one element per processor. In the second stage, the elements of the vector a are read. Each processor in row 1 reads a different element of vector a and propagates it down its column. At this point, processor $P(k, j)$ contains $w^{(k-1)(j-1)}$ and a_{j-1}: All the products $a_{j-1} \times w^{(k-1)(j-1)}$ are computed simultaneously. Finally, the sums of these products are obtained for each row and the results produced by the processors in column 1. The algorithm is given as procedure SIMD DFT.

procedure SIMD DFT (A, B)

Step 1: **for** $k = 1$ **to** n **do in parallel**
  for $j = 1$ **to** n **do in parallel**
    COMPUTE W (k, j)
  end for
end for.

Step 2: **for** $j = 1$ **to** n **do in parallel**
  (2.1) $P(1, j)$ receives a_{j-1} as input
  (2.2) PROPAGATE (a_{j-1})
end for.

Step 3: **for** $k = 1$ **to** n **do in parallel**
  for $j = 1$ **to** n **do in parallel**
    $d_{kj} \leftarrow Y_{kj} \times a_{j-1}$
  end for
end for.

Step 4: **for** $k = 1$ **to** n **do in parallel**
  (4.1) SUM (k)
  (4.2) $b_{k-1} \leftarrow d_{k1}$
  (4.3) $P(k, 1)$ produces b_{k-1} as output
end for. □

Analysis.   Steps 1, 2, and 4 require $O(\log n)$ time, while step 3 takes constant time. The overall running time of procedure SIMD DFT is therefore

$$t(n) = O(\log n).$$

This represents a speedup of $O(n)$ with respect to produce SEQUENTIAL FFT (the fastest sequential algorithm for computing the DFT). In fact, this running time is the best possible for any network that computes the DFT. To see this, note that each b_j is the sum of n quantities, and we know from section 7.3.2 that computing such a sum requires $\Omega(\log n)$ parallel time.

Since $p(n) = n^2$, the procedure's cost is $c(n) = O(n^2 \log n)$ for an efficiency of $O(1/n)$ with respect to procedure SEQUENTIAL FFT.

Example 9.1

The four steps of procedure SIMD DFT are illustrated in Fig. 9.2 for the case $n = 4$. □

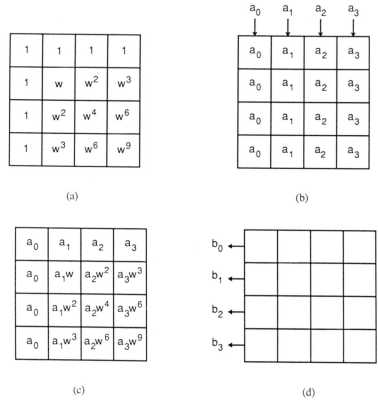

Figure 9.2   Computing discrete Fourier transform using procedure SIMD DFT.

9.3 A PARALLEL FFT ALGORITHM

With a running time of $O(\log n)$ procedure SIMD DFT is quite fast, and as was just shown, it achieves the best possible speedup over the fastest sequential algorithm for computing the DFT. The procedure's efficiency, however, is very low due to the large number of processors it uses.

In this section a parallel algorithm with better efficiency is described. The algorithm implements in parallel a nonrecursive version of procedure SEQUENTIAL FFT. It is designed to run on a mesh-connected SIMD computer with n processors $P_0, P_1, \ldots, P_{n-1}$ arranged in a $2^s \times 2^s$ array, where $n = 2^{2s}$. The processors are organized in row-major order, as shown in Fig. 9.3 for $n = 16$.

Let k be a $\log n$-bit binary integer. We denote by $r(k)$ the $\log n$-bit binary integer obtained by reversing the bits of k. Thus, for example, if the binary representation of k is 01011, then the binary representation of $r(k)$ is 11010. The algorithm is given in what follows as procedure MESH FFT. The input sequence $\{a_0, a_1, \ldots, a_{n-1}\}$ is initially

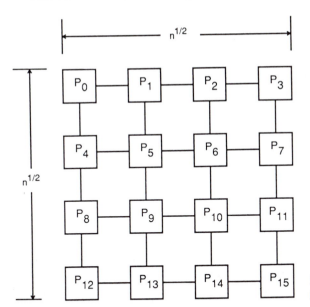

Figure 9.3 Mesh of processors for computing fast Fourier transform.

held by the processors in the mesh, one element per processor; specifically P_k holds a_k for $k = 0, 1, \ldots, n - 1$. When the procedure terminates the output sequence, $\{b_0, b_1, \ldots, b_{n-1}\}$ is held by the processors such that P_k holds b_k for $k = 0, 1, \ldots, n - 1$.

procedure MESH FFT (A, B)

Step 1:   **for** $k = 0$ **to** $n - 1$ **do in parallel**
$$c_k \leftarrow a_k$$
end for.

Step 2:   **for** $h = (\log n) - 1$ **downto** 0 **do**
  for $k = 0$ **to** $n - 1$ **do in parallel**
  (2.1) $p \leftarrow 2^h$
  (2.2) $q \leftarrow n/p$
  (2.3) $z \leftarrow w^p$
  (2.4) **if** $(k \bmod p) = (k \bmod 2p)$
      then (i) $c_k \leftarrow c_k + c_{k+p} \times z^{r(k)\bmod q}$
         (ii) $c_{k+p} \leftarrow c_k - c_{k+p} \times z^{r(k)\bmod q}$
      end if
  end for
end for.

Step 3:   **for** $k = 0$ **to** $n - 1$ **do in parallel**
$$b_k \leftarrow c_{r(k)}$$
end for. □

Note that part (ii) in step 2.4 used the *old* value of c_k rather than the new value computed in part (i), that is, c_k and c_{k+p} may be thought of as being updated simultaneously.

Analysis.   The purpose of step 1 is to save the values of the input sequence; it is performed locally by each processor and takes constant time. Step 2 comprises both routing and computational operations, while step 3 consists of routing operations only. We analyze the time required by these two kinds of operations separately.

Computational Operations.   There are $\log n$ iterations in step 2. During each iteration, processor P_k performs a fixed number of computations, the most time consuming of which is exponentiation, which (as shown in section 9.2.1) takes $O(\log n)$ time. The time required for computational operations is therefore $O(\log^2 n)$.

Routing Operations.   One time unit is required to communicate a datum from one processor to an immediate neighbor. In step 2.4, if $k \bmod p = k \bmod 2p$, then processor P_k needs to receive c_{k+p} from P_{k+p} (in order to update c_k and c_{k+p}) and then return c_{k+p} to P_{k+p}. The time required by this routing depends on the value of h. When $h = 0$, $p = 1$ and communication is between processors on the same row or column whose indices differ by 1 (i.e., processors that are directly connected on the mesh): The routing takes one time unit. When $h = 1$, $p = 2$ and communication is between processors on the same row or column whose indices differ by 2: The routing takes two time units. Continuing with the same reasoning, when $h = \log n - 1$, $p = n/2$ and communication is between processors on the same column whose indices differ by $n/2$: The routing takes $n^{1/2}/2$ time units. In general, for $p = 2^h$, $h = 2s - 1$, $2s - 2, \ldots, 0$, the number of time units required for routing is $2^{h \bmod s}$. The total number of time units required for routing in step 2 is therefore

$$2(1 + 2 + 4 + \cdots + 2^{s-1}) = 2(2^s - 1).$$

In step 3, $c_{r(k)}$ is to be routed from $P_{r(k)}$ to P_k. The two processors that are the furthest apart are $P_{2^s - 1}$ (northeast corner) and $P_{2^s(2^s - 1)}$ (southwest corner). These two processes are separated by $2(2^s - 1)$ edges, that is, $2(2^s - 1)$ time units are needed to communicate a datum from one of them to the other. This means that the routing operations performed in steps 2 and 3 require $O(2^s)$ time units, that is, $O(n^{1/2})$ time.

For sufficiently large values of n, the time needed for routing dominates that consumed by computations. Therefore, the overall running time of procedure MESH FFT is $t(n) = O(n^{1/2})$. Since $p(n) = n$, $c(n) = O(n^{3/2})$. It follows that the procedure provides a speedup of $O(n^{1/2} \log n)$ with an efficiency of $O(\log n/n^{1/2})$.

Compared with procedure SIMD DFT, procedure MESH FFT is slower and thus provides a smaller speedup with respect to procedure SEQUENTIAL FFT. On the other hand, it uses fewer processors and has a lower cost and a higher efficiency. Furthermore, the architecture for which it is designed uses constant-length wires and is modular and regular.

Example 9.2

Let $n = 4$. The contents of the four processors after step 1 of procedure MESH FFT are shown in Fig. 9.4(a). During the first iteration of step 2, $h = 1$. All processors simultaneously compute $p = 2$, $q = 2$, and $z = w^2$. The condition

$$k \bmod p = k \bmod 2p$$

holds for $k = 0, 1$ but not for $k = 2, 3$. Therefore processor P_0 computes

$$c_0 = c_0 + (w^2)^0 c_2$$
$$= a_0 + a_2,$$

and

$$c_2 = c_0 - (w^2)^0 c_2$$
$$= a_0 - a_2,$$

while P_1 computes

$$c_1 = c_1 + (w^2)^0 c_3$$
$$= a_1 + a_3,$$

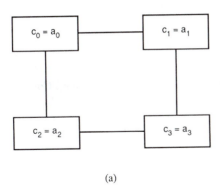

(a)

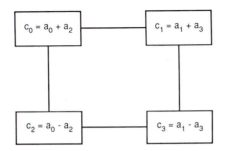

(b)

Figure 9.4   Computing fast Fourier transform using procedure MESH FFT.

and

$$c_3 = c_1 - (w^2)^0 c_3$$
$$= a_1 - a_3.$$

The contents of the four processors at the end of this iteration are shown in Fig. 9.4(b).

During the second iteration of step 2, $h = 0$, $p = 1$, $q = 4$, and $z = w$. This time the condition $k \bmod p = k \bmod 2p$ holds for $k = 0, 2$ but not for $k = 1, 3$. Therefore P_0 computes

$$c_0 = c_0 + w^0 c_1$$
$$= a_0 + a_2 + a_1 + a_3,$$

and

$$c_1 = c_0 - w^0 c_1$$
$$= a_0 + a_2 - (a_1 + a_3),$$

while P_2 computes

$$c_2 = c_2 + w^1 c_3$$
$$= a_0 - a_2 + w(a_1 - a_3),$$

and

$$c_3 = c_2 - w^1 c_3$$
$$= a_0 - a_2 - w(a_1 - a_3).$$

During step 3, $b_0 = c_0$, $b_1 = c_2$, $b_2 = c_1$, and $b_3 = c_3$. Consequently,

$$b_0 = a_0 + a_1 + a_2 + a_3,$$
$$b_1 = a_0 + wa_1 - a_2 - wa_3$$
$$= a_0 + wa_1 + w^2 a_2 + w^3 a_3,$$
$$b_2 = a_0 - a_1 + a_2 - a_3$$
$$= a_0 + w^2 a_1 + w^4 a_2 + w^6 a_3,$$
$$b_3 = a_0 - wa_1 - a_2 + wa_3$$
$$= a_0 + w^3 a_1 + w^6 a_2 + w^9 a_3,$$

as required. □

9.4 PROBLEMS

9.1 Suppose that the DFT of *several* sequences of the form $\{a_0, a_1, \ldots, a_{n-1}\}$ is to be computed directly from the definition, that is, as a matrix-by-vector product (see section 9.2). One approach would be to *pipeline* the computation on a mesh with $O(n^2)$ processors. Another is to take the input sequences n at a time and regard the computation as a matrix-by-matrix product; any of the solutions to this problem given in chapter 7 can then be used. Propose a precise algorithm for each of these two approaches and analyze the running time and number of processors used by each.

9.2 Give the iterative sequential algorithm for computing the FFT upon which procedure MESH FFT is based, and prove that it is equivalent to the recursive procedure SEQUENTIAL FFT of section 9.1.

9.3 Show how the algorithm derived in problem 9.2 can be implemented on a linear array of processors.

9.4 A special-purpose parallel architecture for implementing the algorithm derived in problem 9.2 may consist of $\log n$ rows of $n/2$ processors each. The processors in a row execute the computations required by one iteration of the algorithm's main loop (step 2 in procedure MESH FFT). This is illustrated for $n = 8$ in Fig. 9.5, where the two values in $\{c_0, c_1, \ldots, c_{n-1}\}$ updated by each processor are shown. Compare this implementation to the one in section 9.3 in terms of number of processors, running time, period, architecture regularity, and modularity.

9.5 Routing operations take place in steps 2.4 and 3 of procedure MESH FFT. As stated in section 9.3, however, the procedure does not specify how this routing is to be performed. Give a formal description of the routing process.

9.6 Modify procedure MESH FFT for the case where N processors are available to compute the FFT of the sequence $\{a_0, a_1, \ldots, a_{n-1}\}$ when $N < n$.

9.7 The following sequential procedure is another iterative way of computing the FFT.

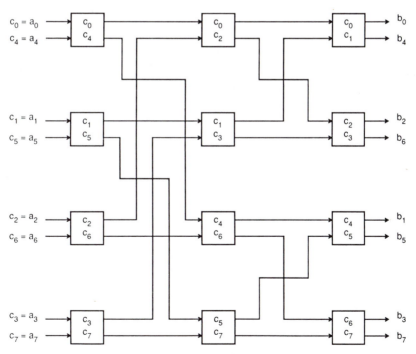

Figure 9.5 Architecture for problem 9.4.

procedure ITERATIVE FFT (A, B)

Step 1:   **for** $k = 0$ **to** $n - 1$ **do**
$$c_k \leftarrow a_k$$
end for.

Step 2:   **for** $h = (\log n) - 1$ **downto** 0 **do**
(2.1) $p \leftarrow 2^h$
(2.2) $q \leftarrow n/p$
(2.3) $z \leftarrow w^{q/2}$
(2.4) **for** $k = 0$ **to** $n - 1$ **do**
if $(k \bmod p) = (k \bmod 2p)$
then (i) $c_k \leftarrow c_k + c_{k+p}$
(ii) $c_{k+p} \leftarrow (c_k - c_{k+p})z^{k \bmod p}$
end if
end for
end for.

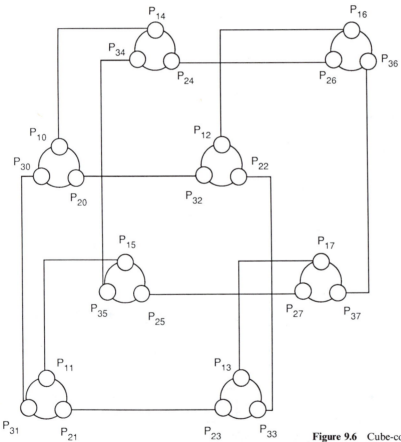

Figure 9.6 Cube-connected cycles network.

Step 3:   **for** $k = 0$ **to** $n - 1$ **do**
$$b_{r(k)} \leftarrow c_k$$
end for.   □

Note that part (ii) of step 2.4 uses the *old* value of c_k [not the value computed in (i)]. Show how this procedure can be implemented to run on a shuffle-exchange-connected SIMD computer using $O(n)$ processors and $O(\log n)$ constant time iterations (not counting the time required to compute $z^{k \bmod p}$ during each iteration).

9.8 An interconnection-network SIMD model known as the *cube-connected cycles* (CCC) network is described as follows. Consider a d-dimensional cube. Each of the 2^d corners of the cube is a cycle of d processors. Each processor in a cycle is connected to a processor in a neighboring cycle in the same dimension. A CCC network with twenty-four processors is shown in Fig. 9.6. Note that P_{ij} is connected to P_{ik} when j and k differ only in their ith most

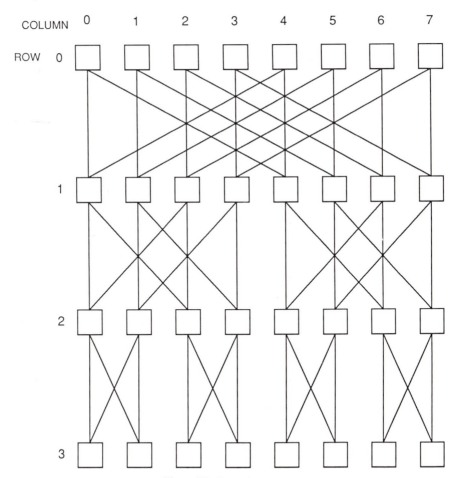

Figure 9.7 Butterfly network.

significant bit. Describe an algorithm for computing the FFT of an n-element input sequence on an n-processor CCC network.

9.9 Show that the CCC network is essentially the network in problem 9.4 with wraparound connections (as defined in problem 7.7) between the first and last rows.

9.10 An interconnection-network SIMD model known as *the butterfly network* consists of $d + 1$ rows and 2^d columns, as shown in Fig. 9.7 for $d = 3$. Let $P(i, j)$ represent the processor in row i and column j. For $i > 0$, $P(i, j)$ is connected to $P(i - 1, j)$ and $P(i - 1, k)$ where the binary representations of k and j differ only in their ith most significant bit. Relate the butterfly network to the cube and cube-connected cycles networks.

9.11 Show how the FFT of an input sequence of length $n = 2^d$ can be computed on a butterfly network.

9.12 Repeat problem 9.11 for a d-dimensional cube interconnection network.

9.13 Repeat problem 9.6 for the parallel algorithms derived in problems 9.7, 9.8, 9.11, and 9.12.

9.14 Relate the process of computing the FFT to that of bitonic merging as discussed in problem 3.9.

9.15 Two numbers x and n are given. It is required to raise x to the power n. Assuming that one is not allowed to use a concurrent-write shared-memory computer (SIMD or MIMD), how fast can this computation be performed in parallel? Compare the running time of your parallel algorithm with that of the sequential procedure COMPUTE W in section 9.2.1.

9.5 BIBLIOGRAPHICAL REMARKS

Various descriptions of the sequential FFT and its applications can be found in [Burrus], [Cochran], [Cooley 1], [Cooley 2], [Cooley 3], [Horowitz], [Schönhage], and [Wilf]. Parallel algorithms for the direct computation of the DFT are described in [Ahmed], [Mead], and [Thompson 2]. The mesh of trees architecture was originally proposed for the problem of sorting in [Muller] and then rediscovered in [Leighton] and [Nath]. Parallel algorithms for implementing the FFT on a mesh-connected SIMD computer appear in [Stevens], [Thompson 1], and [Thompson 2].

Other architectures for implementing the FFT in parallel are the linear array ([Thompson 2]), the perfect shuffle ([Heller], [Pease 1], [Stone], and [Thompson 1]), the cube ([Pease 2] and [Quinn]), the butterfly ([Hwang], [Kronsjö], and [Ullman]), the tree ([Ahmed]), and the cube-connected cycles ([Preparata]). It is shown in [Fishburn] and [Hwang] how to implement the parallel FFT algorithms for the perfect shuffle and butterfly networks, respectively, when the number of processors is smaller than the size of the input.

Other parallel algorithms for Fourier transforms and related computations can be found in [Bergland], [Bhuyan], [Briggs], [Brigham], [Chow], [Corinthios], [Cyre], [Dere], [Despain 1], [Despain 2], [Evans], [Flanders], [Hockney], [Jesshope], [Korn], [Kulkarni], [Lint], [Parker], [Ramamoorthy], [Redinbo], [Swarztrauber], [Temperton], [Wang], [Wold], and [Zhang]. The problem of parallel exponentiation is discussed in [Kung].

9.6 REFERENCES

[AHMED]
Ahmed, H., Delosme, J.-M., and Morf, M., Highly concurrent computing structures for matrix arithmetic and signal processing, *Computer*, Vol. 15, No. 1, January 1982, pp. 65–82.

[BERGLAND]
Bergland, G. D., A parallel implementation of the fast Fourier transform algorithm, *IEEE Transactions on Computers*, Vol. C-21, No. 4, April 1972, pp. 366–370.

[BHUYAN]
Bhuyan, L. N., and Agrawal, D. P., Performance analysis of FFT algorithms on multiprocessor systems, *IEEE Transactions on Software Engineering*, Vol. SE-9, No. 4, July 1983, pp. 512–521.

[BRIGGS]
Briggs, W. L., Hart, L. B., Sweet, R. A., and O'Gallagher, A., Multiprocessor FFT methods, *SIAM Journal on Scientific and Statistical Computing*, Vol. 8, No. 1, January 1987, pp. s27–s42.

[BRIGHAM]
Brigham, E. O., *The Fast Fourier Transform*, Prentice-Hall, Englewood Cliffs, N.J., 1973.

[BURRUS]
Burrus, C. S., and Parks, T. W., *DFT/FFT and Convolution Algorithms*, Wiley, New York, 1985.

[CHOW]
Chow, P., Vranesic, Z. G., and Yen, J. L., A pipeline distributed arithmetic PFFT processor, *IEEE Transactions on Computers*, Vol. C-32, No. 12, December 1983, pp. 1128–1136.

[COCHRAN]
Cochran, W. T., Cooley, J. W., Favin, D. L., Helms, H. D., Kaenel, R. A., Lang, W. W., Maling, G. C., Jr., Nelson, D. E., Rader, C. M., and Welch, P. D., What is the fast Fourier transform? *IEEE Transactions on Audio and Electroacoustics*, Vol. AU-15, No. 2, June 1967, pp. 45–55.

[COOLEY 1]
Cooley, J. W., and Tukey, T. W., An algorithm for the machine calculation of complex Fourier series, *Mathematics of Computation*, Vol. 19, No. 90, April 1965, pp. 297–301.

[COOLEY 2]
Cooley, J. W., Lewis, P. A., and Welch, P. D., Historical notes on the fast Fourier transform, *Proceedings of the IEEE*, Vol. 55, No. 10, October 1967, pp. 1675–1679.

[COOLEY 3]
Cooley, J. W., Lewis, P. A., and Welch, P. D., The fast Fourier transform and its application to time series analysis, in Enslein, K., Ralston, A., and Wilf, H. S., Eds., *Statistical Methods for Digital Computers*, Wiley, New York, 1977, pp. 377–423.

[CORINTHIOS]
Corinthios, M. J., and Smith, K. C., A parallel radix-4 fast Fourier transform computer, *IEEE Transactions on Computers*, Vol. C-24, No. 1, January 1975, pp. 80–92.

[CYRE]
Cyre, W. R., and Lipovski, G. J., On generating multipliers for a cellular fast Fourier transform processor, *IEEE Transactions on Computers*, Vol. C-21, No. 1, January 1972, pp. 83–87.

[DERE]
Dere, W. Y., and Sakrison, D. J., Berkeley array processor, *IEEE Transactions on Computers*, Vol. C-19, No. 5, May 1970, pp. 444–447.

[DESPAIN 1]
Despain, A. M., Fourier transform computers using CORDIC iterations, *IEEE Transactions on Computers*, Vol. C-23, No. 10, October 1974, pp. 993–1001.

[DESPAIN 2]

Despain, A. M., Very fast Fourier transform algorithms for hardware implementation, *IEEE Transactions on Computers*, Vol. C-28, No. 5, May 1979, pp. 333–341.

[EVANS]

Evans, D. J., and Mai, S., A parallel algorithm for the fast Fourier transform, in Cosnard, M., Quinton, P., Robert, Y., and Tchuente, M., Eds., *Parallel Algorithms and Architectures*, North-Holland, Amsterdam, 1986, pp. 47–60.

[FISHBURN]

Fishburn, J. P., An analysis of speedup in distributed algorithms, Ph.D. thesis, Computer Sciences Department, University of Wisconsin–Madison, Madison, Wisconsin, May 1981.

[FLANDERS]

Flanders, P. M., A unified approach to a class of data movements on an array processor, *IEEE Transactions on Computers*, Vol. C-31, No. 9, September 1982, pp. 809–819.

[HELLER]

Heller, D., A survey of parallel algorithms in numerical linear algebra, *SIAM Review*, Vol. 20, No. 4, October 1978, pp. 740–777.

[HOCKNEY]

Hockney, R. W., and Jesshope, C. R., *Parallel Computers*, Adam Higler, Bristol, England, 1981.

[HOROWITZ]

Horowitz, E., and Sahni, S., *Fundamentals of Computer Algorithms*, Computer Science Press, Rockville, Md, 1978.

[HWANG]

Hwang, K., and Briggs, F. A., *Computer Architecture and Parallel Processing*, McGraw-Hill, New York, 1984.

[JESSHOPE]

Jesshope, C. R., Implementation of fast RADIX 2 transforms on array processors, *IEEE Transactions on Computers*, Vol. C-29, No. 1, January 1980, pp. 20–27.

[KORN]

Korn, D. G., and Lambiotte, J. J., Jr., Computing the fast Fourier transform on a vector computer, *Mathematics of Computation*, Vol. 33, No. 147, July 1979, pp. 977–992.

[KRONSJÖ]

Kronsjö, L., *Computational Complexity of Sequential and Parallel Algorithms*, Wiley, Chichester, England, 1985.

[KULKARNI]

Kulkarni, A. V., and Yen, D. W. L., Systolic processing and an implementation for signal and image processing, *IEEE Transactions on Computers*, Vol. C-31, No. 10, October 1982, pp. 1000–1009.

[KUNG]

Kung, H. T., New algorithms and lower bounds for the parallel evaluation of certain rational expressions and recurrences, *Journal of the ACM*, Vol. 23, No. 2, April 1976, pp. 252–261.

[LEIGHTON]

Leighton, F. T., *Complexity Issues in VLSI*, MIT Press, Cambridge, Mass., 1983.

[LINT]

Lint, B. J., and Agerwala, T., Communication issues in the design and analysis of parallel algorithms, *IEEE Transactions on Software Engineering*, Vol. SE-7, No. 2, March 1981, pp. 174–188.

[MEAD]

Mead, C. A., and Conway, L. A., *Introduction to VLSI Systems*, Addison-Wesley, Reading, Mass., 1980.

[MULLER]

Muller, D. E., and Preparata, F. P., Bounds to complexities of networks for sorting and for switching, *Journal of the ACM*, Vol. 22, No. 2, April 1975, pp. 195–201.

[NATH]

Nath, D., Maheshwari, S. N., and Bhatt, P. C. P., Efficient VLSI networks for parallel processing based on orthogonal trees, *IEEE Transactions on Computers*, Vol. C-32, No. 6, June 1983, pp. 569–581.

[PARKER]

Parker, D. S., Jr., Notes on shuffle/exchange-type switching networks, *IEEE Transactions on Computers*, Vol. C-29, No. 3, March 1980, pp. 213–222.

[PEASE 1]

Pease, M. C., An adaptation of the fast Fourier transform for parallel processing, *Journal of the ACM*, Vol. 15, No. 2, April 1968, pp. 252–264.

[PEASE 2]

Pease, M. C., The indirect binary n-cube microprocessor array, *IEEE Transactions on Computers*, Vol. C-26, No. 5, May 1977, pp. 458–473.

[PREPARATA]

Preparata, F. P., and Vuillemin, J. E., The cube-connected cycles: A versatile network for parallel computation, *Communications of the ACM*, Vol. 24, No. 5, May 1981, pp. 300–309.

[QUINN]

Quinn, M. J., *Designing Efficient Algorithms for Parallel Computers*, McGraw-Hill, New York, 1987.

[RAMAMOORTHY]

Ramamoorthy, C. V., and Chang, L.-C., System segmentation for the parallel diagnosis of computers, *IEEE Transactions on Computers*, Vol. C-20, No. 3, March 1971, pp. 261–270.

[REDINBO]

Redinbo, G. R., Finite field arithmetic on an array processor, *IEEE Transactions on Computers*, Vol. C-28, No. 7, July 1979, pp. 461–471.

[SCHÖNHAGE]

Schönhage, A., and Strassen, V., Schnelle Multiplikation grosser Zahlen, *Computing*, Vol. 7, 1971, pp. 281–292.

[STEVENS]

Stevens, J. E., A fast Fourier transform subroutine for Illiac IV, Technical Report, Center for Advanced Computation, University of Illinois, Urbana-Champaign, Illinois, 1971.

[STONE]

Stone, H. S., Parallel processing with the perfect shuffle, *IEEE Transactions on Computers*, Vol. C-20, No. 2, February 1971, pp. 153–161.

[SWARZTRAUBER]

Swarztrauber, P. N., Vectorizing the FFTs, in Rodrigue, G., Ed., *Parallel Computations*, Academic, New York, 1982, pp. 51–83.

[TEMPERTON]

Temperton, C., Fast Fourier transform for numerical prediction models on vector computers, *EDF–Bulletin de la Direction des Études et des Recherches*, Série C, Vol. 1, 1983, pp. 159–162.

[THOMPSON 1]

Thompson, C. D., A complexity theory for VLSI, Ph.D. thesis, Computer Science Department, Carnegie-Mellon University, Pittsburgh, August 1980.

[THOMPSON 2]

Thompson, C. D., Fourier transforms in VLSI, *IEEE Transactions on Computers*, Vol. C-32, No. 11, November 1983, pp. 1047–1057.

[ULLMAN]

Ullman, J. D., *Computational Aspects of VLSI*, Computer Science Press, Rockville, Md., 1984.

[WANG]

Wang, H. H., On vectorizing the fast Fourier transform, Technical Report No. G320-3392-1, IBM Palo Alto Scientific Centre, Palo Alto, California, March 1980.

[WILF]

Wilf, H. S., *Algorithms and Complexity*, Prentice-Hall, Englewood Cliffs, N.J., 1986.

[WOLD]

Wold, E. H., and Despain, A. M., Pipeline and parallel-pipeline FFT processors for VLSI implementations, *IEEE Transactions on Computers*, Vol. C-33, No. 5, May 1984, pp. 414–426.

[ZHANG]

Zhang, C. N., and Yun, D. Y. Y., Multi-dimensional systolic networks for discrete Fourier transform, Proceedings of the 11th Annual ACM International Symposium on Computer Architecture, Ann Arbor, Michigan, June 1984, pp. 215–222, Association for Computing Machinery, New York, N.Y., 1984.

10

Graph Theory

10.1 INTRODUCTION

In virtually all areas of computer science, graphs are used to organize data, to model algorithms, and generally as a powerful tool to represent computational concepts. Trees, in particular, are omnipresent. Many branches of engineering and science rely on graphs for representing a wide variety of objects from electrical circuits, chemical compounds, and crystals to genetical processes, sociological structures, and economic systems. The same is true for operations research, where graphs play a crucial role in modeling and solving numerous optimization problems such as scheduling, routing, transportation, and network flow problems. It is therefore important for these applications to develop efficient algorithms to manipulate graphs and answer questions about them. As a consequence, a large body of literature exists today on computational graph-theoretic problems and their solutions.

This chapter is concerned with parallel graph algorithms. We begin in section 10.2 by defining some terms from graph theory. Section 10.3–10.6 are devoted to the problems of computing the connectivity matrix, the connected components, the shortest paths, and minimum spanning tree of a graph, respectively.

10.2 DEFINITIONS

A graph consists of a finite set of *nodes* and a finite set of *edges* connecting pairs of these nodes. A graph with six nodes and nine edges is shown in Fig. 10.1(a). Here the nodes (also called *vertices*) are labeled a, b, c, d, e, and f. The edges are $(a, b), (a, c), (b, c),$ $(b, e), (c, d), (c, f), (d, e), (d, f),$ and (e, f). A graph is *directed* when its edges (also called *arcs*) have an orientation and thus provide a one-way connection as indicated by the arrow heads in Fig. 10.2(a). Here node a is connected to b, node b is connected to c and d, and node d is connected to c. The notation $G = (V, E)$ is used to represent a graph G whose vertex set is V and edge set is E.

A matrix representation can be used for computer storage and manipulation of a graph. Let G be a graph whose vertex set is $V = \{v_0, v_1, \ldots, v_{n-1}\}$. This graph can be

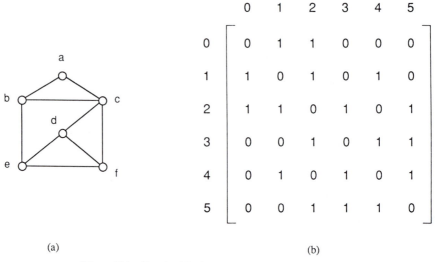

(a)   (b)

Figure 10.1   Graph with six nodes and its adjacency matrix.

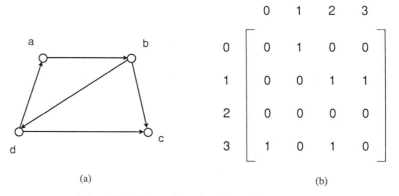

(a)   (b)

Figure 10.2   Directed graph and its adjacency matrix.

uniquely represented by an $n \times n$ *adjacency matrix* A whose entries a_{ij}, $0 \leqslant i$, $j \leqslant n - 1$, are defined as follows:

$$a_{ij} = \begin{cases} 1 & \text{if } v_i \text{ is connected to } v_j, \\ 0 & \text{otherwise.} \end{cases}$$

The adjacency matrices for the graphs in Figs. 10.1(a) and 10.2(a) are shown in Figs. 10.1(b) and 10.2(b), respectively, where $v_0 = a$, $v_1 = b$, and so on. Note that since the graph in Fig. 10.1(a) is undirected, the matrix in Fig. 10.1(b) is symmetric.

When each edge of a graph is associated with a real number, called its *weight*, the graph is said to be *weighted*. A weighted graph may be directed or undirected. Figure

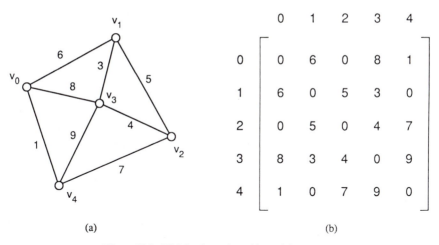

(a)   (b)

Figure 10.3   Weighted graph and its weight matrix.

10.3(a) shows an undirected weighted graph. The meaning of an edge's weight varies from one application to another; it may represent distance, cost, time, probability, and so on. A *weight matrix W* is used to represent a weighted graph, as shown in Fig. 10.3(b). Here, entry w_{ij} of W represents the weight of edge (v_i, v_j). If v_i and v_j are not connected by an edge, then w_{ij} may be equal to zero, or infinity or any appropriate value, according to the application.

A *path* from an *origin* vertex v_i to a *destination* vertex v_j in a graph $G = (V, E)$, is a sequence of edges $(v_i, v_k), (v_k, v_l), \ldots, (v_m, v_j)$ from E, where no vertex appears more than once. In Fig. 10.1, for example, $(a, c), (c, d), (d, e)$ is a path from a to e. A *cycle* is a path in which the origin and destination are the same. The sequence $(a, b), (b, d), (d, a)$ in Fig. 10.2 forms a cycle. In an unweighted graph, the length of a path or cycle is equal to the number of edges forming it.

A *subgraph* $G' = (V', E')$ of a graph $G = (V, E)$ is a graph such that $V' \subseteq V$ and $E' \subseteq E$, that is, a graph whose vertices and edges are in G. Figure 10.4 shows two subgraphs of the graph in Fig. 10.1.

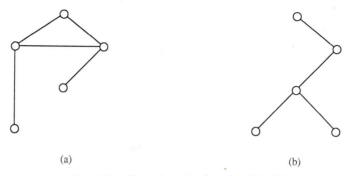

(a)   (b)

Figure 10.4   Two subgraphs of graph in Fig. 10.1.

10.3 COMPUTING THE CONNECTIVITY MATRIX

The *connectivity matrix* of an n-node graph G is an $n \times n$ matrix C whose elements are defined as follows:

$$c_{jk} = \begin{cases} 1 & \text{if there is a path of length 0 or more from } v_j \text{ to } v_k, \\ 0 & \text{otherwise,} \end{cases}$$

for $j, k = 0, 1, \ldots, n - 1$. Note that a path of length 0 begins and ends at a vertex without using any edges, while a path of length 1 consists of one edge. The matrix C is also known as the *reflexive and transitive closure* of G. Given the adjacency matrix A of a graph G, it is required to compute C. The approach that we take uses *Boolean matrix multiplication*, which differs from regular matrix multiplication in that

    (i) the matrices to be multiplied as well as the product matrix are all binary, that is, each of their entries is either 0 or 1;

    (ii) the Boolean (or logical) **and** operation replaces regular multiplication, that is, 0 **and** 0 = 0, 0 **and** 1 = 0, 1 **and** 0 = 0, and 1 **and** 1 = 1; and

    (iii) the Boolean (or logical) **or** operation replaces regular addition, that is, 0 **or** 0 = 0, 0 **or** 1 = 1, 1 **or** 0 = 1, and 1 **or** 1 = 1.

Thus if X, Y, and Z are $n \times n$ Boolean matrices where Z is the Boolean product of X and Y, then

$$z_{ij} = (x_{i1} \textbf{ and } y_{1j}) \textbf{ or } (x_{i2} \textbf{ and } y_{2j}) \textbf{ or} \ldots \textbf{or } (x_{in} \textbf{ and } y_{nj}) \quad \text{for } i, j = 0, 1, \ldots, n - 1.$$

The first step in the computation of the connectivity matrix C is to obtain the $n \times n$ matrix B from A as follows:

$$b_{jk} = a_{jk} \quad (\text{for } j \neq k) \quad \text{and} \quad b_{jj} = 1$$

for $j, k = 0, 1, \ldots, n - 1$. Matrix B therefore represents all paths in G of length less than 2; in other words

$$b_{jk} = \begin{cases} 1 & \text{if there is a path of length 0 or 1 from } v_j \text{ to } v_k, \\ 0 & \text{otherwise.} \end{cases}$$

Similarly, B^2 (i.e., the Boolean product of B by itself) represents paths of length 2 or less, B^4 represents paths of length 4 or less, and B^n represents paths of length n or less. We now observe that if there is a path from v_i to v_j, it cannot have length more than $n - 1$. Consequently, $C = B^{n-1}$, that is, the connectivity matrix is obtained after $\lceil \log(n - 1) \rceil$ Boolean matrix multiplications. Note that when $n - 1$ is not a power of 2, C is obtained from B^m, where $m = 2^{\lceil \log(n-1) \rceil}$. This is correct since $B^m = B^{n-1}$ for $m > n - 1$.

In order to implement this algorithm in parallel, we can use any of the matrix multiplication algorithms described in chapter 7 adapted to perform Boolean matrix multiplication. In particular, procedure CUBE MATRIX MULTIPLICATION can be used. The resulting algorithm is given in what follows as procedure CUBE

CONNECTIVITY. The procedure takes the adjacency matrix A as input and returns the connectivity matrix C as output. It runs on a cube-connected SIMD computer with $N = n^3$ processors $P_1, P_2, \ldots, P_N$. The processors can be thought of as being arranged in an $n \times n \times n$ array pattern. In this array, P_r occupies position (i, j, k), where $r = in^2 + jn + k$ and $0 \leqslant i, j, k \leqslant n - 1$. It has three registers $A(i, j, k)$, $B(i, j, k)$, and $C(i, j, k)$. Initially, the processors in positions $(0, j, k)$, $0 \leqslant j, k \leqslant n - 1$, contain the adjacency matrix, that is, $A(0, j, k) = a_{jk}$. At the end of the computation, these processors contain the connectivity matrix, that is, $C(0, j, k) = c_{jk}$, $0 \leqslant j, k \leqslant n - 1$.

procedure CUBE CONNECTIVITY (A, C)

Step 1: {The diagonal elements of the adjacency matrix are made equal to 1}
    for $j = 0$ **to** $n - 1$ **do in parallel**
        $A(0, j, j) \leftarrow 1$
    end for.

Step 2: {The A registers are copied into the B registers}
    for $j = 0$ **to** $n - 1$ **do in parallel**
      for $k = 0$ **to** $n - 1$ **do in parallel**
        $B(0, j, k) \leftarrow A(0, j, k)$
      end for
    end for.

Step 3: {The connectivity matrix is obtained through repeated Boolean multiplication}
    for $i = 1$ **to** $\lceil \log(n - 1) \rceil$ **do**
      (3.1) CUBE MATRIX MULTIPLICATION (A, B, C)
      (3.2) **for** $j = 0$ **to** $n - 1$ **do in parallel**
          for $k = 0$ **to** $n - 1$ **do in parallel**
            (i) $A(0, j, k) \leftarrow C(0, j, k)$
            (ii) $B(0, j, k) \leftarrow C(0, j, k)$
          end for
        end for
    end for. □

Analysis.   Steps 1, 2, and 3.2 take constant time. In step 3.1 procedure CUBE MATRIX MULTIPLICATION requires $O(\log n)$ time. This step is iterated $\log n$ times. It follows that the overall running time of this procedure is $t(n) = O(\log^2 n)$. Since $p(n) = n^3$, $c(n) = O(n^3 \log^2 n)$.

Example 10.1

Consider the adjacency matrix in Fig. 10.2(b). After steps 1 and 2 of procedure CUBE CONNECTIVITY, we have computed

$$B = \begin{bmatrix} 1 & 1 & 0 & 0 \\ 0 & 1 & 1 & 1 \\ 0 & 0 & 1 & 0 \\ 1 & 0 & 1 & 1 \end{bmatrix}.$$

The first iteration of step 3 produces

$$B^2 = \begin{bmatrix} 1 & 1 & 1 & 1 \\ 1 & 1 & 1 & 1 \\ 0 & 0 & 1 & 0 \\ 1 & 1 & 1 & 1 \end{bmatrix}$$

while the second yields $B^4 = B^2$.   □

10.4 FINDING CONNECTED COMPONENTS

An undirected graph is said to be *connected* if for every pair v_i and v_j of its vertices there is a path from v_i to v_j. A *connected component* of a graph G is a subgraph G' of G that is connected. The problem we consider in this section is the following. An undirected n-node graph G is given by its adjacency matrix, and it is required to decompose G into the smallest possible number of connected components. We can solve the problem by first computing the connectivity matrix C of G. Using C, we can now construct an $n \times n$ matrix D whose entries are defined by

$$d_{jk} = \begin{cases} v_k & \text{if } c_{jk} = 1, \\ 0 & \text{otherwise,} \end{cases}$$

for $0 \leqslant j, k \leqslant n - 1$. In other words, row j of D contains the names of the vertices to which v_j is connected by a path, that is, those vertices in the same connected components as v_j. Finally, the graph G can be decomposed into the smallest number of connected components by assigning each vertex to a component as follows: v_j is assigned to component l if l is the smallest index for which $d_{jl} \neq 0$.

A parallel implementation of this approach uses procedure CUBE CONNECTIVITY developed in the previous section to compute the connectivity matrix C. The algorithm is given in what follows as procedure CUBE COMPONENTS. The procedure runs on a cube-connected SIMD computer with $N = n^3$ processors, each with three registers A, B, and C. The processors are arranged in an $n \times n \times n$ array pattern as explained earlier. Initially, $A(0, j, k) = a_{jk}$ for $0 \leqslant j$, $k \leqslant n - 1$, that is, the processors in positions $(0, j, k)$ contain the adjacency matrix of G. When the procedure terminates, $C(0, j, 0)$ contains the component number for vertex v_j, where $j = 0, 1, \ldots, n - 1$.

procedure CUBE COMPONENTS (A, C)

Step 1:   {Compute the connectivity matrix}
            CUBE CONNECTIVITY (A, C).

Step 2:   {Construct the matrix D}
            for $j = 0$ **to** $n - 1$ **do in parallel**
                for $k = 0$ **to** $n - 1$ **do in parallel**

if $C(0, j, k) = 1$ **then** $C(0, j, k) = v_k$
   end if
  end for
end for.

Step 3:   {Assign a component number to each vertex}
     for $j = 0$ **to** $n - 1$ **do in parallel**
       (3.1) the n processors in row j (forming a log n-dimensional cube) find the smallest
          l for which $C(0, j, l) \neq 0$
       (3.2) $C(0, j, 0) \leftarrow l$
     end for.   □

Analysis. As shown in the previous section, step 1 requires $O(\log^2 n)$ time. Steps 2 and 3.2 take constant time. From problem 7.23, we know that step 3.1 can be done in $O(\log n)$ time. The overall running time of procedure CUBE COMPONENTS is $t(n) = O(\log^2 n)$. Since $p(n) = n^3$, $c(n) = O(n^3 \log^2 n)$.

Example 10.2

Consider the graph in Fig. 10.5(a) whose adjacency and connectivity matrices are given in Figs. 10.5(b) and (c), respectively. Matrix D is shown in Fig. 10.5(d). The component assignment is therefore:

$$\text{component 0:} \quad v_0, v_3, v_6, v_8$$

$$\text{component 1:} \quad v_1, v_4, v_7$$

$$\text{component 2:} \quad v_2, v_5. \quad □$$

10.5 ALL-PAIRS SHORTEST PATHS

A directed and weighted graph $G = (V, E)$ is given, as shown, for example, in Fig. 10.6. For convenience, we shall refer in this section to the weight of edge (v_i, v_j) as its *length*.

For every pair of vertices v_i and v_j in V, it is required to find the *shortest path* from v_i to v_j along edges in E. Here the length of a path or cycle is the sum of the lengths of the edges forming it. In Fig. 10.6, the shortest path from v_0 to v_4 is along edges (v_0, v_2), (v_2, v_3), (v_3, v_6), (v_6, v_5), and (v_5, v_4) and has length 6.

Formally, the *all-pairs shortest paths problem* is stated as follows: An n-vertex graph G is given by its $n \times n$ weight matrix W; construct an $n \times n$ matrix D such that d_{ij} is the length of the shortest path from v_i to v_j in G for all i and j. We shall assume that W has positive, zero, or negative entries as long as there is no cycle of negative length in G.

Let d_{ij}^k denote the length of the shortest path from v_i to v_j that goes through at most $k - 1$ intermediate vertices. Thus $d_{ij}^1 = w_{ij}$, that is, the weight of the edge from v_i to v_j. In particular, if there is no edge from v_i to v_j, where i and j are distinct, $d_{ij}^1 = \infty$. Also $d_{ii}^1 = 0$. Given that G has no cycles of negative length, there is no advantage in visiting any vertex more than once in a shortest path from v_i to v_j (even if our

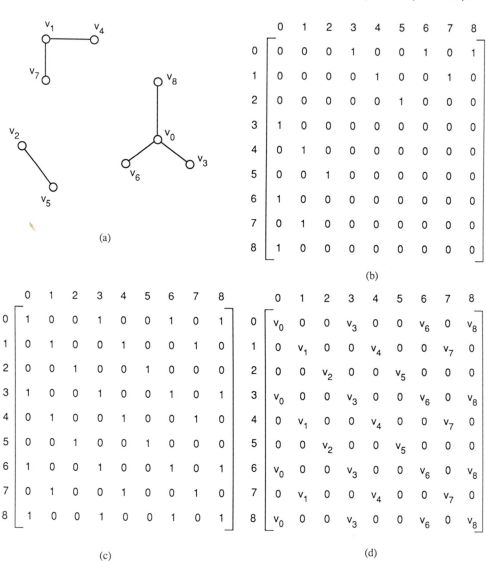

Figure 10.5 Computing connected components of graph.

definition of a path allowed for a vertex to appear more than once on a path). It follows that $d_{ij} = d_{ij}^{n-1}$.

In order to compute d_{ij}^k for $k > 1$ we can use the fact that

$$d_{ij}^k = \min_l \{d_{il}^{k/2} + d_{lj}^{k/2}\},$$

that is, d_{ij}^k is equal to the *smallest* $d_{il}^{k/2} + d_{lj}^{k/2}$, over all values of l. Therefore matrix D

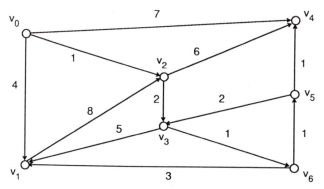

Figure 10.6 Directed and weighted graph.

can be generated from D^1 by computing $D^2, D^4, \ldots, D^{n-1}$ and then taking $D = D^{n-1}$. In order to obtain D^k from $D^{k/2}$ by the preceding expression, we can use a special form of matrix multiplication in which the standard operations of matrix multiplication, that is, $\times$ and $+$ are replaced by $+$ and min, respectively. Hence if a matrix multiplication procedure is available, it can be modified to generate D^{n-1} from D^1. Exactly $\lceil \log(n-1) \rceil$ such matrix products are required.

The algorithm is implemented in parallel using any of the matrix multiplication procedures described in section 7.3 adapted to perform $(+, \min)$ multiplication. Once again, as we did in the previous two sections, we shall invoke procedure CUBE MATRIX MULTIPLICATION. The resulting algorithm is given in what follows as procedure CUBE SHORTEST PATHS. The procedure runs on a cube-connected SIMD computer with $N = n^3$ processors, each with three registers A, B, and C. As before, the processors can be regarded as being arranged in an $n \times n \times n$ array pattern. Initially, $A(0, j, k) = w_{jk}$ for $0 \leqslant j$, $k \leqslant n - 1$, that is, the processors in positions $(0, j, k)$ contain the weight matrix of G. If v_j is not connected to v_k or if $j = k$, then $w_{jk} = 0$. When the procedure terminates, $C(0, j, k)$ contains the length of the shortest path from v_j to v_k for $0 \leqslant j$, $k \leqslant n - 1$.

procedure CUBE SHORTEST PATHS (A, C)

Step 1: {Construct the matrix D^1 and store it in registers A and B}
  for $j = 0$ **to** $n - 1$ **do in parallel**
   for $k = 0$ **to** $n - 1$ **do in parallel**
   (1.1) **if** $j \neq k$ **and** $A(0, j, k) = 0$
      then $A(0, j, k) \leftarrow \infty$
      end if
   (1.2) $B(0, j, k) \leftarrow A(0, j, k)$
   end for
  end for.

Step 2:   {Construct the matrices $D^2, D^4, \ldots, D^{n-1}$ through repeated matrix multiplication}
          for $i = 1$ **to** $\lceil \log(n-1) \rceil$ **do**
              (2.1) CUBE MATRIX MULTIPLICATION (A, B, C)
              (2.2) **for** $j = 0$ **to** $n - 1$ **do in parallel**
                      for $k = 0$ **to** $n - 1$ **do in parallel**
                          (i) $A(0, j, k) \leftarrow C(0, j, k)$
                          (ii) $B(0, j, k) \leftarrow C(0, j, k)$
                      end for
                  end for
          end for.   □

Analysis.   Steps 1 and 2.2 take constant time. There are $\lceil \log(n-1) \rceil$ iterations of step 2.1 each requiring $O(\log n)$ time. The overall running time of

$$
\begin{array}{c|ccccccc}
 & 0 & 1 & 2 & 3 & 4 & 5 & 6 \\
\hline
0 & 0 & 4 & 1 & \infty & 7 & \infty & \infty \\
1 & \infty & 0 & 8 & \infty & \infty & \infty & \infty \\
2 & \infty & \infty & 0 & 2 & 6 & \infty & \infty \\
3 & \infty & 5 & \infty & 0 & \infty & \infty & 1 \\
4 & \infty & \infty & \infty & \infty & 0 & \infty & \infty \\
5 & \infty & \infty & \infty & 2 & 1 & 0 & \infty \\
6 & \infty & 3 & \infty & \infty & \infty & 1 & 0 \\
\end{array}
$$

(a)

$$
\begin{array}{c|ccccccc}
 & 0 & 1 & 2 & 3 & 4 & 5 & 6 \\
\hline
0 & 0 & 4 & 1 & 3 & 7 & \infty & \infty \\
1 & \infty & 0 & 8 & 10 & 14 & \infty & \infty \\
2 & \infty & 7 & 0 & 2 & 6 & \infty & 3 \\
3 & \infty & 4 & 13 & 0 & \infty & 2 & 1 \\
4 & \infty & \infty & \infty & \infty & 0 & \infty & \infty \\
5 & \infty & 7 & \infty & 2 & 1 & 0 & 3 \\
6 & \infty & 3 & 11 & 3 & 2 & 1 & 0 \\
\end{array}
$$

(b)

$$
\begin{array}{c|ccccccc}
 & 0 & 1 & 2 & 3 & 4 & 5 & 6 \\
\hline
0 & 0 & 4 & 1 & 3 & 7 & 5 & 4 \\
1 & \infty & 0 & 8 & 10 & 14 & 12 & 11 \\
2 & \infty & 6 & 0 & 2 & 5 & 4 & 3 \\
3 & \infty & 4 & 12 & 0 & 3 & 2 & 1 \\
4 & \infty & \infty & \infty & \infty & 0 & \infty & \infty \\
5 & \infty & 6 & 14 & 2 & 1 & 0 & 3 \\
6 & \infty & 3 & 11 & 3 & 2 & 1 & 0 \\
\end{array}
$$

(c)

$$
\begin{array}{c|ccccccc}
 & 0 & 1 & 2 & 3 & 4 & 5 & 6 \\
\hline
0 & 0 & 4 & 1 & 3 & 6 & 5 & 4 \\
1 & \infty & 0 & 8 & 10 & 13 & 12 & 11 \\
2 & \infty & 6 & 0 & 2 & 5 & 4 & 3 \\
3 & \infty & 4 & 12 & 0 & 3 & 2 & 1 \\
4 & \infty & \infty & \infty & \infty & 0 & \infty & \infty \\
5 & \infty & 6 & 14 & 2 & 1 & 0 & 3 \\
6 & \infty & 3 & 11 & 3 & 2 & 1 & 0 \\
\end{array}
$$

(d)

Figure 10.7   Computing all-pairs shortest paths for graph in Fig. 10.6.

procedure CUBE SHORTEST PATHS is therefore $t(n) = O(\log^2 n)$. Since $p(n) = n^3$, $c(n) = O(n^3 \log^2 n)$.

Example 10.3

   Matrices D^1, D^2, D^4, and D^8 for the graph in Fig. 10.6 are shown in Fig. 10.7. $\Box$

10.6 COMPUTING THE MINIMUM SPANNING TREE

A *tree* is a connected (undirected) graph with no cycles. Given an undirected and connected graph $G = (V, E)$, a *spanning tree* of G is a subgraph $G' = (V', E')$ of G such that

(i) G' is a tree, and

(ii) $V' = V$.

If the graph G is weighted, then a *minimum spanning tree* (MST) of G has the smallest edge-weight sum among all spanning trees of G. These definitions are illustrated in Fig. 10.8. Three spanning trees of the weighted graph in Fig. 10.8(a) are shown in Figs.

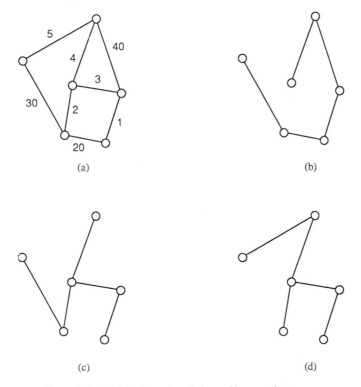

(a)

(b)

(c)

(d)

Figure 10.8   Weighted graph and three of its spanning trees.

10.8(b)–(d). The tree in Fig. 10.8(d) has minimum weight. Note that when all the edges of the graph have distinct weights, the MST is unique.

If $V = \{v_0, v_1, \ldots, v_{n-1}\}$, then the MST has $n - 1$ edges. These edges must be chosen among potentially $n(n - 1)/2$ candidates. This gives an $\Omega(n^2)$ lower bound on the number of operations required to compute the MST since each edge must be examined at least once. For convenience, we henceforth refer to the weight of edge (v_i, v_j) as the *distance* separating v_i and v_j and denote it by dist(v_i, v_j).

A sequential algorithm for computing the MST based on the *greedy* approach to problem solving proceeds in stages. Beginning with an arbitrarily chosen vertex, each stage adds one vertex and an associated edge to the tree. If v_i is a vertex that is *not yet in the tree*, let $c(v_i)$ denote a vertex *already in the tree* that is closest to v_i. The algorithm therefore consists of two steps:

Step 1: Include vertex v_0 in the MST and let $c(v_i) = v_0$ for $i = 1, 2, \ldots, n - 1$.

Step 2: This step is repeated as long as there are vertices not yet in the MST:

(2.1) Include in the tree the closest vertex not yet in the tree; that is, for all v_i not in the MST find the edge $(v_i, c(v_i))$ for which dist$(v_i, c(v_i))$ is smallest and add it to the tree.

(2.2) For all v_i not in the MST, update $c(v_i)$; that is, assuming that v_j was the most recently added vertex to the tree, then $c(v_i)$ can be updated by determining the smaller of dist$(v_i, c(v_i))$ and dist(v_i, v_j).

Step 1 requires n constant time operations. Step 2 is executed once for each of $n - 1$ vertices. If there are already k vertices in the tree, then steps 2.1 and 2.2 consist of $n - k - 1$ and $n - k$ comparisons, respectively. Thus step 2, and hence the algorithm, require time proportional to $\sum_{k=1}^{n-1} (n - k)$, which is $O(n^2)$. This sequential running time is therefore optimal in view of the lower bound stated previously.

We now show how this algorithm can be adapted to run in parallel on an EREW SM SIMD computer. The parallel implementation uses N processors P_0, $P_1, \ldots, P_{N-1}$. The number of processors is independent of the number of vertices in G except that we assume $1 < N < n$. As we did in earlier chapters, we find it convenient to write $N = n^{1-x}$, where $0 < x < 1$. Each processor P_i is assigned a distinct subsequence V_i of V of size n^x. In other words, P_i is "in charge" of the vertices in V_i. Note that P_i needs only to store the indices of the first and last vertices in V_i. During the process of constructing the MST and for each vertex v_p in V_i that is not yet in the tree, P_i also keeps track of the closest vertex in the tree, denoted $c(v_p)$.

The weight matrix W of G is stored in shared memory, where $w_{ij} = $ dist(v_i, v_j) for $i, j = 0, 1, \ldots, n - 1$. If $i = j$ or if v_i and v_j are not directly connected by an edge, then $w_{ij} = \infty$. The algorithm initially includes an arbitrary vertex in the tree. The computation of the MST then proceeds in $n - 1$ stages. During each stage, a new vertex and hence a new edge are added to the existing partial tree. This is done as follows. With all processors operating in parallel, each processor finds among its vertices not yet in the tree the vertex closest to (a vertex in) the tree. Among the n^{1-x}

vertices thus found, the vertex closest to (a vertex in) the tree is found and added to the tree along with the associated edge. This vertex, call it v_h, is now made known to all processors. The following step is then performed in parallel by all processors, each for its n^x vertices: For each vertex v_p not yet in the tree, if $\text{dist}(v_p, v_h) < \text{dist}(v_p, c(v_p))$, then $c(v_p)$ is made equal to v_h.

The algorithm is given in what follows as procedure EREW MST. The procedure uses procedures BROADCAST and MINIMUM described in sections 2.5.1 and 6.3.1, respectively. It produces an array TREE in shared memory containing the $n - 1$ edges of the MST. When two distances are equal, the procedure breaks the tie arbitrarily.

procedure EREW MST (W, TREE)

Step 1:   (1.1) Vertex v_0 in V_0 is labeled as a vertex already in the tree
          (1.2) **for** $i = 0$ **to** $N - 1$ **do in parallel**
                for each vertex v_j in V_i **do**
                      $c(v_j) \leftarrow v_0$
                end for
              end for.

Step 2:   **for** $i = 1$ **to** $n - 1$ **do**
          (2.1) **for** $j = 0$ **to** $N - 1$ **do in parallel**
              (i) P_j finds the smallest of the quantities $\text{dist}(v_p, c(v_p))$, where v_p is a vertex in V_j that is not yet in the tree
              (ii) Let the smallest quantity found in (i) be $\text{dist}(v_r, v_t)$: P_j delivers a triple (d_j, a_j, b_j), where
                      $d_j = \text{dist}(v_r, v_t)$,
                      $a_j = v_r$, and
                      $b_j = v_t$
              end for
          (2.2) Using procedure MINIMUM the smallest of the distances d_j and its associated vertices a_j and b_j, for $0 \leqslant j \leqslant N - 1$, are found; let this triple be (d_s, a_s, b_s), where a_s is some vertex v_h not in the tree and b_s is some vertex v_k already in the tree
          (2.3) P_0 assigns (v_h, v_k) to $\text{TREE}(i)$, the ith entry of array TREE
          (2.4) Using BROADCAST, v_h is made known to all N processors
          (2.5) **for** $j = 0$ **to** $N - 1$ **do in parallel**
              (i) **if** v_h is in V_j
                then P_j labels v_h as a vertex already in the tree
                end if
              (ii) **for** each vertex v_p in V_j that is not yet in the tree **do**
                    if $\text{dist}(v_p, v_h) < \text{dist}(v_p, c(v_p))$
                      then $c(v_p) \leftarrow v_h$
                    end if
                end for
              end for
          end for. □

Analysis. Step 1.1 is done in constant time. Since each processor is in charge of n^x vertices, step 1.2 requires n^x assignments. Therefore step 1 runs in $O(n^x)$ time. In step 2.1, a processor finds the smallest of n^x quantities (sequentially) using $n^x - 1$ comparisons. Procedures MINIMUM and BROADCAST both involve $O(\log N)$ constant time operations. Since $N = n^{1-x}$, steps 2.2 and 2.4 are done in $O(\log n)$ time. Clearly steps 2.3 and 2.5 require constant time and $O(n^x)$ time, respectively. Hence each iteration of step 2 takes $O(n^x)$ time. Since this step is iterated $n + 1$ times, it is completed in $O(n^{1+x})$ time. Consequently, the overall running time of the procedure is $O(n^{1+x})$. The procedure is therefore *adaptive*. Its cost is

$$c(n) = p(n) \times t(n)$$
$$= n^{1-x} \times O(n^{1+x})$$
$$= O(n^2).$$

This means that the procedure is also *cost optimal*. Note that, for sufficiently large n, $n^x > \log n$ for any x and $N = n^{1-x} = n/n^x < n/\log n$. The procedure's optimality is therefore limited to the range $N < n/\log n$.

Example 10.4

Let G be a weighted nine-node graph whose weight matrix is given in Fig. 10.9. Also assume that an EREW SM SIMD computer with three processors is available. Thus

	0	1	2	3	4	5	6	7	8
0	∞	5	6	1	∞	6	10	∞	5
1	5	∞	3	9	2	5	4	12	∞
2	6	3	∞	7	3	9	11	∞	14
3	1	9	7	∞	10	∞	∞	9	8
4	∞	2	3	10	∞	1	5	3	15
5	6	5	9	∞	1	∞	6	13	∞
6	10	4	11	∞	5	6	∞	4	16
7	∞	12	∞	9	3	13	4	∞	7
8	5	∞	14	8	15	∞	16	7	∞

Figure 10.9 Weight matrix for example 10.4.

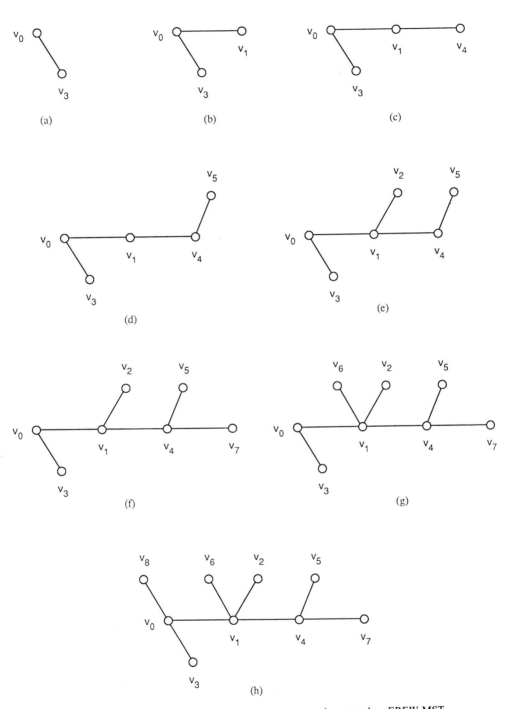

Figure 10.10 Computing minimum spanning tree using procedure EREW MST.

$3 = 9^{1-x}$, that is, $x = 0.5$. Processors P_0, P_1, and P_2 are assigned sequences $V_0 = \{v_0, v_1, v_2\}$, $V_1 = \{v_3, v_4, v_5\}$, and $V_2 = \{v_6, v_7, v_8\}$. In step 1.1, v_0 is included in the tree and is assigned as the closest vertex in the tree to all remaining vertices.

During the first iteration of step 2, P_0 determines that $\text{dist}(v_1, v_0) < \text{dist}(v_2, v_0)$ and returns the triple $(5, v_1, v_0)$. Similarly, P_1 and P_2 return $(1, v_3, v_0)$ and $(5, v_8, v_0)$, respectively. Procedure MINIMUM is then used to determine $v_h = v_3$ and hence TREE(1) $= (v_3, v_0)$. Now v_3 is made known to all processors using BROADCAST and P_1 labels it as a vertex in the tree. In step 2.5, P_0 keeps $c(v_1)$ and $c(v_2)$ equal to v_0, P_2 updates $c(v_4)$ to v_3 but keeps $c(v_5) = v_0$, and P_3 keeps $c(v_6) = v_0$ and $c(v_8) = 0$ while updating $c(v_7) = v_3$. The process continues until the tree (v_3, v_0), (v_1, v_0), (v_4, v_1), (v_5, v_4), (v_2, v_1), (v_7, v_4), (v_6, v_1), (v_8, v_0) is generated. This is illustrated in Fig. 10.10. □

10.7 PROBLEMS

10.1 Show that procedure CUBE CONNECTIVITY is not cost optimal. Can the procedure's cost be reduced?

10.2 Derive a parallel algorithm to compute the connectivity matrix of an n-vertex graph in $O(n)$ time on an $n \times n$ mesh-connected SIMD computer.

10.3 Consider a CRCW SM SIMD computer with n^3 processors. Simultaneous write operations to the same memory location are allowed provided that all the values to be written are the same. Give an algorithm to compute the connectivity matrix of an n-vertex graph on this computer in $O(\log n)$ time.

10.4 Let A be the adjacency matrix of an n-vertex graph G. Another way of computing the connectivity matrix C of G sequentially is given by the following algorithm. Initially C is set equal to A.

> Step 1: **for** $i = 0$ **to** $n - 1$ **do**
> $\qquad c_{ii} \leftarrow 1$
> **end for.**

> Step 2: **for** $k = 0$ **to** $n - 1$ **do**
> $\qquad$ **for** $i = 0$ **to** $n - 1$ **do**
> $\qquad\qquad$ **for** $j = 0$ **to** $n - 1$ **do**
> $\qquad\qquad\qquad$ **if** $c_{ik} = 1$ **and** $c_{kj} = 1$
> $\qquad\qquad\qquad$ **then** $c_{ij} \leftarrow 1$
> $\qquad\qquad\qquad$ **end if**
> $\qquad\qquad$ **end for**
> $\qquad$ **end for**
> **end for.**

Derive a parallel version of this algorithm for an interconnection-network SIMD computer.

10.5 Show that if the connected components of a graph are given, then its connectivity matrix can be obtained trivially.

10.6 Repeat problem 10.1 for procedure CUBE COMPONENTS.

10.7 Another approach to computing the connected components of a graph is based on the idea of *breadth-first search*. Beginning with a vertex, its *neighbors* (i.e., all the vertices to which it is connected by an edge) are visited. The neighbors of each of these vertices are now visited, and the process continues until no unvisited neighbor is left. This gives one connected component. We now pick a vertex (outside of this component) and find its connected component. Continuing in this fashion, all the connected components can be found. Derive a parallel implementation of this approach.

10.8 Consider the following approach to computing the connected components of a graph, which in a sense is symmetric to the one described in problem 10.7. Here vertices are *collapsed* instead of *expanded*. Pairs of vertices that are connected by an edge are combined into *supervertices*. Supervertices are now themselves combined into new (and larger) supervertices. The process continues until all the vertices in a given connected component have been combined into one supervertex. Derive a parallel implementation of this approach.

10.9 Establish the validity of the relation

$$d_{ij}^k = \min_l \{d_{il}^{k/2} + d_{lj}^{k/2}\}$$

upon which procedure CUBE SHORTEST PATHS is based.

10.10 Repeat problem 10.1 for procedure CUBE SHORTEST PATHS.

10.11 Modify procedure CUBE SHORTEST PATHS to provide a list of the edges on the shortest path from v_j to v_k for all $0 \leqslant j, k \leqslant n - 1$.

10.12 Derive an algorithm for the model of computation in problem 10.3 to compute all-pairs shortest paths in $O(\log n)$ time.

10.13 Let W be the weight matrix of an n-vertex graph G, with $w_{ii} = 0$ and $w_{ij} = \infty$ if there is no edge from v_i to v_j. Consider the following sequential method for computing the all-pairs shortest paths matrix D. Initially, D is set equal to W.

> **for** $k = 0$ **to** $n - 1$ **do**
>   **for** $i = 0$ **to** $n - 1$ **do**
>   **for** $j = 0$ **to** $n - 1$ **do**
> $d_{ij} \leftarrow \min\{d_{ij}, d_{ik} + d_{kj}\}$
>   **end for**
>   **end for**
> **end for.**

Design a parallel implementation of this algorithm on an interconnection-network SIMD computer.

10.14 Discuss the feasibility of the following approach to computing the MST of a weighted graph G: All spanning trees of G are examined and the one with minimum weight is selected.

10.15 Procedure EREW MST is cost optimal when $N < n/\log n$. Can this range of optimality be widened?

10.16 Adapt procedure EREW MST to run on an interconnection-network SIMD computer.

10.17 Derive a parallel algorithm based on the following approach to computing the MST of a weighted n-vertex graph G.

> Step 1: The edges of G are sorted in order of increasing weight.
>
> Step 2: The $n - 1$ edges with smallest weight *that do not include a cycle* are selected as the edges of the MST.

10.18 Consider the following approach to computing the MST of an n-vertex weighted graph G.

Step 1:   **for** $i = 0$ **to** $n - 1$ **do**
   (1.1) Determine for vertex v_i its closest neighbor v_j; if two or more vertices are equidistant from v_i, then v_j is the one with the smallest index
   (1.2) The edge (v_i, v_j) is designated as an edge of the MST
   end for.

Step 2:   (2.1) $k \leftarrow$ number of distinct edges designated in step 1
   (2.2) Each collection of vertices and edges selected in step 1 and forming a connected component is called a subtree of the MST.

Step 3:   **while** $k < n - 1$ **do**
   (3.1) Let $T_1, T_2, \ldots, T_m$ be the distinct subtrees formed so far
   (3.2) **for** $i = 1$ **to** m **do**
      (i) Using an appropriate tie-breaking rule, select for T_i an edge of smallest weight connecting a vertex in T_i to a vertex in any other subtree T_j
      (ii) This edge is designated as an MST edge and the two subtrees it connects are coalesced into one subtree
   end for
   (3.3) $k \leftarrow k +$ number of distinct edges selected in 3.2
   end while.

Applying this approach to the weight matrix in Fig. 10.9, we get the following edges after step 1: (v_0, v_3), (v_1, v_4), (v_2, v_1), (v_4, v_5), (v_6, v_1), (v_7, v_4), and (v_8, v_0). These form two subtrees $T_1 = \{(v_0, v_3), (v_8, v_0)\}$ and $T_2 = \{(v_1, v_4), (v_2, v_1), (v_4, v_5), (v_6, v_1), (v_7, v_4)\}$. Since $k = 7$, we execute step 3 and find that the edge of smallest weight connecting T_1 to T_2 is (v_0, v_1). Design a parallel algorithm based on the preceding approach for the problem of determining the MST and analyze its performance.

10.19 Assume that the n vertices of an undirected weighted graph G are points in k-dimensional Euclidean space, $k \geqslant 2$, with $w_{ij} =$ Euclidean distance separating v_i and v_j. The graph is therefore fully defined by a list of n vertices, each vertex being represented by its k coordinates. This means that the weight matrix is not required as part of the input since w_{ij} can be computed when needed. Implement the MST algorithm in section 10.6 on a tree-connected SIMD computer with n leaves to run in $O(n \log n)$ time.

10.20 Show that by reducing the number of leaves in the tree-connected SIMD computer of problem 10.19, a cost-optimal algorithm can be obtained.

10.21 An undirected n-vertex graph is said to be *sparse* if it has m edges, where m is much smaller than the maximum possible $n(n - 1)/2$ edges. Design a CREW algorithm for computing the MST of a weighted sparse n-vertex graph in $O(m \log n/N)$ time using N processors, where $N \leqslant \log n$, and the approach described in problem 10.17.

10.22 Can the algorithm in problem 10.21 be modified to have a cost of $O(m \log m)$?

10.23 Repeat problem 10.21 for the approach in problem 10.18 with $N \leqslant m/\log n$.

10.24 Repeat problem 10.21 for the approach in section 10.6 with $N \log N \leqslant (m \log n)/n$.

10.25 Can the algorithms in problems 10.23 and 10.24 be modified to have a cost of $O(m)$?

10.26 Repeat problems 10.21–10.25 for the EREW SM SIMD model.

10.27 Let $G = (V, E)$ be a directed graph. A *strong component* of G is a subgraph $G' = (V', E')$ of G such that there is a path from every vertex in V' to every other vertex in V' along edges in E'. Design a parallel algorithm for decomposing a given directed graph into the smallest possible number of strong components.

10.28 A *weak component* of a directed graph G is a subgraph G' of G where every two vertices are joined by a path in which the direction of each edge is ignored. Design a parallel algorithm for decomposing a given directed graph into the smallest number of weak components.

10.29 A *biconnected component* of an undirected graph $G = (V, E)$ is a connected component $G' = (V', E')$ such that the deletion of any vertex of V' does not disconnect G'. Design a parallel algorithm for decomposing a given undirected graph into the smallest possible number of biconnected components.

10.30 Let G be an undirected graph. A *bridge* in G is an edge whose removal divides one connected component into two. Design a parallel algorithm for finding the bridges of a given graph.

10.31 An *articulation point* of a connected undirected graph G is a vertex whose removal splits G into two or more connected components. Design a parallel algorithm to determine all the articulation points of a given graph.

10.32 Consider the following variant of the all-pairs shortest paths problem: Given a specified vertex in a weighted directed graph, it is required to find the shortest path from that vertex to every other vertex in the graph. This is known as the *single-source shortest path problem*. Design a parallel algorithm for this problem and analyze its running time and cost.

10.33 Let G be an unweighted undirected graph. It is desired to obtain a spanning tree of G. Use the parallel algorithm designed in problem 10.32 to solve this problem.

10.34 Another variant of the all-pairs shortest path problem is the all-pairs *longest* path problem. Derive a parallel algorithm for this problem.

10.35 Let G be a directed graph with no cycles. It is required to sort the vertices of G into a sequence $v_0, v_1, \ldots, v_n$ such that (v_i, v_j) may be an arc of G only if $i < j$. Suggest two parallel solutions to this problem known as *topological sorting*. One solution may be based on the reflexive and transitive closure of G, the other on the matrix of all-pairs shortest paths.

10.36 The *diameter* of a weighted graph G is the length of the shortest path separating the farthest two vertices of G. The *center* of G is the vertex for which the length of the shortest path to the farthest vertex is smallest. This distance is called the *radius* of G. Show how the diameter, center, and radius of an n-vertex weighted graph can be obtained in $O(\log^2 n)$ time on a cube-connected computer with n^3 processors.

10.37 The *median* of a weighted graph is the vertex for which the sum of the shortest paths to all other vertices is smallest. Derive a parallel algorithm to find the median.

10.38 Let G be a directed and weighted graph with no cycles. We assume that $w_{ij} = 0$ in the weight matrix W if the arc (v_i, v_j) is not present. The *gain* on a path from v_k to v_m is the product of the arc weights on that path. A maximum gain matrix H is such that h_{ij} equals the maximum gain for every i and j. Derive a parallel algorithm for computing the matrix H from W.

10.39 Let G be an n-vertex undirected graph, and define the *length* of a cycle as the number of edges it contains (as in section 10.2).

   (i) Derive a parallel algorithm for determining the shortest cycle in $O(n)$ time on an $n \times n$ mesh-connected SIMD computer.

   (ii) Repeat part (i) for an undirected graph.

10.40 The *cyclic index* of a directed graph G is the greatest common divisor of the lengths of all the cycles in G. Design a parallel algorithm for computing the cyclic index.

10.41 An undirected graph is *bipartite* if and only if it has no cycle of odd length. Show that it is possible to determine whether an n-vertex graph is bipartite in $O(n)$ time on an $n \times n$ mesh-connected SIMD computer.

10.42 Let $G = (V, E)$ be a connected undirected graph. Further, let $H = (V_H, E_H)$ and $K = (V_K, E_K)$ be two subgraphs of G. The *symmetric difference* of H and K, written $H \oplus K$, is the subgraph $G' = (V', E')$ of G where E' is the set of edges in $E_H \cup E_K$ but not in $E_H \cap E_K$, and V' is the set of vertices connected by edges in E'. A set of *fundamental cycles* of G is a collection F of cycles of G with the property that any cycle C of G can be written as $C = C_1 \oplus C_2 \oplus \cdots \oplus C_m$ for some subcollection of cycles $C_1, C_2, \ldots, C_m$ of F. Design a CREW algorithm for determining the set of fundamental cycles of an n-vertex graph in $O(\log^2 n)$ time using $O(n^3)$ processors.

10.43 A *matching* in an undirected graph $G = (V, E)$ is a subset M of E such that no two edges in M share a vertex. A matching has *maximum cardinality* if no other matching in G contains more edges. Design a parallel algorithm for finding a maximum-cardinality matching.

10.44 Repeat problem 10.43 for the case where G is bipartite.

10.45 A matching of $G = (V, E)$ is said to be *perfect* if it includes all the vertices in V. Assume that G is a $2n$-vertex graph that is weighted and *complete* (i.e., every two vertices are connected by an edge). Design a parallel algorithm for finding a perfect matching of G that has minimum weight.

10.46 Let G be a directed and weighted graph where each edge weight is positive. Two vertices of G are distinguished as the *source* and the *sink*. Each edge may be thought of as a conduit for fluid, and the edge's weight determines how much fluid it can carry. The *network flow problem* asks for the maximum quantity of fluid that could flow from source to sink. Design a parallel algorithm for this problem.

10.47 The *dead-end path problem* is defined as follows: Given a graph $G = (V, E)$ and a distinguished vertex v, find a path starting from v that cannot be extended without going to a vertex that is already on the path. A *greedy* sequential algorithm for this problem is to start at v and always go to the lowest numbered unvisited neighbor. Can this algorithm be implemented efficiently in parallel? Is there a fast parallel algorithm that computes the *same* dead-end path as the sequential algorithm?

10.48 Let G be a directed graph with no cycles. We say that G is *layered* if its nodes are laid out in levels, its edges going only between consecutive layers. The *maximal set of disjoint paths problem* is to find the largest set possible of paths from the first level to the last with no vertices in common. Describe a greedy algorithm for this problem and determine whether it can be implemented efficiently in parallel.

10.49 A *Hamilton cycle* of an undirected graph $G = (V, E)$ is a cycle that includes all the elements of V. Design a parallel algorithm for determining whether a given graph has a Hamilton cycle.

10.50 An undirected and weighted graph G is given where all the edge weights are positive integers. A positive integer B is also given. It is required to determine whether G possesses a Hamilton cycle whose weight is no larger than *B*. This is known as the *traveling salesman problem*, where the vertices represent cities and the edge weights distances separating them. Design a parallel algorithm for solving this problem.

10.8 BIBLIOGRAPHICAL REMARKS

Descriptions of many sequential graph algorithms can be found in [Christofides], [Deo 1], [Even], and [Papadimitriou]. Graph-theoretic algorithms for parallel computers are surveyed in [Quinn 2]. Textbook treatment of parallel graph algorithms is provided in [Kronsjö], [Quinn 1], and [Ullman].

Parallel algorithms for computing the connectivity matrix are given in [Chin], [Guibas], [Hirschberg 1], [Hirschberg 2], [Kučera], [Levitt], and [Van Scoy]. In particular, it is shown in [Hirschberg 1] how an n^3-processor CRCW SM SIMD computer can be used to compute the reflexive and transitive closure of an n-vertex graph in $O(\log n)$ time.

Various approaches to solving the connected-components problem in parallel are proposed in [Chin], [Hirschberg 1], [Hirschberg 2], [Hochschild 1], [Hochschild 2], [Kučera], [Lakhani], [Nassimi], [Nath 1], [Nath 2], [Reghbati], and [Shiloach 1]. Notably, it is shown in [Chin] how a CREW SM SIMD computer with $O(n^2/\log^2 n)$ processors can be used to find the connected components of an n-vertex graph in $O(\log^2 n)$ time.

Parallel algorithms for solving the all-pairs shortest path problem on a number of different models of computation are described in [Dekel 1], [Deo 2], and [Hirschberg 1]. The algorithm in [Hirschberg 1] uses an n^4-processor CRCW SM SIMD computer and runs in $O(\log n)$ time. The idea of procedure CUBE SHORTEST PATHS originated in [Dekel 1].

Several approaches for computing the minimum spanning tree in parallel are described in [Atallah], [Bentley], [Chin], [Deo 3], [Doshi], [Gallager], [Hirschberg 1], [Hirschberg 3], [Hochschild 1], [Hochschild 2], [Kučera], [Kwan], [Nath 1], [Nath 2], [Santoro], [Savage 1], and [Savage 2]. In particular, it is shown in [Doshi] how the approach in problem 10.18 can be used to compute the MST of an n-vertex weighted graph on a linear array of N processors, where $1 \leq N \leq n$. The algorithm runs in $O(n^2/N)$ time for an optimal cost of $O(n^2)$. This algorithm is superior to procedure EREW MST in two respects:

1. It achieves the same performance on a much weaker model of computation.
2. It has a wider range of optimality.

Procedure EREW MST is from [Akl], where a number of references to parallel MST algorithms are provided.

Other graph-theoretic problems that were solved in parallel include finding biconnected components ([Hirschberg 1], [Hochschild 1], [Hochschild 2], and [Savage 2]), triconnected components ([Ja'Ja']), strongly connected components ([Hochschild 2], [Kosaraju], and [Levitt]), and weakly connected components ([Chin]); single-source shortest paths ([Chandy], [Crane], [Deo 2], and [Mateti]); all-pairs longest paths ([Hirschberg 1]); topological sorting ([Er], [Hirschberg 1], and [Kučera]); constructing spanning trees and forests ([Bhatt], [Chin], [Dekel 1], and [Levitt]); contracting trees ([Leiserson]); determining the radius, diameter, center, median, articulation points, and bridges ([Atallah], [Dekel 1], [Doshi], and [Savage 2]); computing maximum gains ([Dekel 1]); searching and traversing graphs ([Chang], [Kalra], [Kosaraju], [Reghbati], and [Wyllie]); testing planarity ([Hochschild 2], and [Ja'Ja']); computing matchings ([Dekel 2], and [Hembold]); finding the cyclic index ([Atallah]), fundamental cycles ([Levitt] and Savage 2]), cycles of shortest length ([Atallah]), and maximal sets of disjoint paths ([Anderson]); computing flows in networks ([Chen 1], [Chen 2], [Goldberg], and [Shiloach 2]); and testing whether a graph is bipartite ([Atallah]).

The *cellular array* model of parallel computation was first proposed in [Kautz] and then used in [Levitt] for solving graph-theoretic problems. It consists of a large number of simple processors interconnected to form a two-dimensional array. The concept of a cellular array was later rediscovered and renamed *systolic array* in [Foster].

The dead-end path problem and the maximal set of disjoint paths problem belong to the class of *P-complete* problems. These problems are believed not to have fast parallel solutions. Furthermore, if a fast parallel algorithm is found for one of these problems, then all the problems in the class are amenable to fast parallel solution ([Anderson] and [Cook]). Note that, according to this theory, a parallel algorithm is *fast* if it uses $O(n^c)$ processors for some $c \geq 0$ and runs in $O(\log^k n)$ time for some constant $k \geq 0$. The class of problems solved by such fast algorithms is nicknamed in the literature as *NC* ([Cook]).

Let π be a problem of *size n*, where n may be the number of vertices in a graph, rows in a matrix, or elements of a sequence. An algorithm for solving π is said to be *polynomial* if its running time is of $O(n^k)$ for some constant $k \geq 0$. An algorithm is *exponential* if it runs in $O(c^n)$ for some constant $c \geq 2$. The Hamilton cycle and traveling salesman problems belong to the class of *NP-complete* problems. A problem π in this class has the following characteristics:

(i) no sequential algorithm with polynomial running time is known for solving π and, furthermore, it is not known whether such an algorithm exists;

(ii) all known sequential algorithms for solving π have exponential running time and it is not known whether this is optimal;

(iii) if a solution to π is given, it can be verified in polynomial time; and

(iv) if a sequential polynomial time algorithm is found for solving π, it can be used to solve all NP-complete problems in polynomial time.

A good reference to NP-complete problems is [Garey]. Parallel algorithms for NP-complete problems help only a little in mitigating the exponential growth in the running time. To have a truly fast parallel algorithm that is based on our current state of knowledge, one needs an exponential number of processors. This is prohibitive, to say the least, and we must await a better understanding of the nature of NP-complete problems before embarking in the design of parallel algorithms for large-problem instances. Parallel algorithms for NP-complete graph problems are described in [Mead] and [Mohan].

10.9 REFERENCES

[AKL]
Akl, S. G., An adaptive and cost-optimal parallel algorithm for minimum spanning trees, *Computing*, Vol. 36, 1986, pp. 271–277.

[ANDERSON]
Anderson, R., and Mayr, E. W., Parallelism and greedy algorithms, Technical Report No. STAN-CS-84-1003, Department of Computer Science, Stanford University, Stanford, California, 1984.

[ATALLAH]
Atallah, M. J., and Kosaraju, S. R., Graph problems on a mesh-connected processor array, *Journal of the ACM*, Vol. 31, No. 3, July 1984, pp. 649–667.

[BENTLEY]
Bentley, J. L., A parallel algorithm for constructing minimum spanning trees, *Journal of Algorithms*, Vol. 1, No. 1, March 1980, pp. 51–59.

[BHATT]
Bhatt, P. C. P., A parallel algorithm to generate all sink trees for directory routing, Proceedings of the 1984 International Conference on Parallel Processing, Bellaire, Michigan, August 1984, pp. 425–430, IEEE Computer Society, Washington, D.C., 1984.

[CHANDY]
Chandy, K. M., and Misra, J., Distributed computation on graphs: Shortest path algorithms, *Communications of the ACM*, Vol. 25, No. 11, November 1982, pp. 833–837.

[CHANG]
Chang, E. J. H., Echo algorithms: Depth-first parallel operations on general graphs, *IEEE Transactions on Software Engineering*, Vol. SE-8, No. 4, July 1982, pp. 391–401.

[CHEN 1]
Chen, I. N., A new parallel algorithm for network flow problems, in Feng, T.-Y., Ed., *Parallel Processing*, Lecture Notes in Computer Science, Vol. 24, Springer-Verlag, New York, 1975, pp. 306–307.

[CHEN 2]
Chen, Y. K., and Feng, T.-Y., A parallel algorithm for maximum flow problem, Proceedings of the 1973 International Conference on Parallel Processing, Sagamore, New York, August 1973, p. 60, IEEE Computer Society, Washington, D.C., 1973.

[CHIN]
Chin, F. Y., Lam, J., and Chen, I. N., Efficient parallel algorithms for some graph problems, *Communications of the ACM*, Vol. 25, No. 9, September 1982, pp. 659–665.

[CHRISTOFIDES]
Christofides, N., *Graph Theory: An Algorithmic Approach*, Academic, London, England, 1975.

[CRANE]
Crane, B. A., Path finding with associative memory, *IEEE Transactions on Computers*, Vol. C-17, No. 7, July 1968, pp. 691–693.

[COOK]
Cook, S. A., A taxonomy of problems with fast parallel algorithms, *Information and Control*, Vol. 64, 1985, pp. 2–22.

[DEKEL 1]
Dekel, E., Nassimi, D., and Sahni, S., Parallel matrix and graph algorithms, *SIAM Journal on Computing*, Vol. 10, No. 4, November 1981, pp. 657–675.

[DEKEL 2]
Dekel, E., and Sahni, S., A parallel matching algorithm for convex bipartite graphs, Proceedings of the 1982 International Conference on Parallel Processing, Bellaire, Michigan, August 1982, pp. 178–184, IEEE Computer Society, Washington, D.C., 1982.

[DEO 1]
Deo, N., *Graph Theory with Applications to Engineering and Computer Science*, Prentice-Hall, Englewood-Cliffs, N.J., 1974.

[DEO 2]

Deo, N., Pang, C. Y., and Lord, R. E., Two parallel algorithms for shortest path problems. Proceedings of the 1980 International Conference on Parallel Processing, Harbor Springs. Michigan, August 1980, pp. 244–253, IEEE Computer Society, Washington, D.C., 1980.

[DEO 3]

Deo, N., and Yoo, Y. B., Parallel algorithms for the minimum spanning tree problem, Proceedings of the 1981 International Conference on Parallel Processing, Bellaire, Michigan, August 1981, pp. 188–189, IEEE Computer Society, Washington, D.C., 1981.

[DOSHI]

Doshi, K. A., and Varman, P. J., Optimal graph algorithms on a fixed size linear array, *IEEE Transactions on Computers*, Vol. C-36, No. 4, April 1987, pp. 460–470.

[ER]

Er, M. C., A parallel computation approach to topological sorting, *The Computer Journal*, Vol. 26, No. 4, 1983, pp. 293–295.

[EVEN]

Even, S., *Graph Algorithms*, Computer Science Press, Rockville, Md., 1979.

[FOSTER]

Foster, M. J., and Kung, H. T., The design of special purpose VLSI chips, *Computer*, Vol. 13, No. 1, January 1980, pp. 26–40.

[GALLAGER]

Gallager, R. G., Humblet, P. A., and Spira, P. M., A distributed algorithm for minimum weight spanning trees, *ACM Transactions on Programming Languages and Systems*, Vol. 5, No. 1, January 1983, pp. 66–77.

[GAREY]

Garey, M. R., and Johnson, D. S., *Computers and Intractability: A Guide to the Theory of NP-Completeness*, W. H. Freeman, San Francisco, 1979.

[GOLDBERG]

Goldberg, A. V., Efficient graph algorithms for sequential and parallel computers, Technical Report No. MIT/LCS/TR-374, Laboratory for Computer Science, Massachusetts Institute of Technology, Cambridge, Mass., February 1987.

[GUIBAS]

Guibas, L. J., Kung, H. T., and Thompson, C. D., Direct VLSI implementation of combinatorial problems, Proceedings of the Conference on Very Large Scale Integration, California Institute of Technology, Pasadena, California, January 1979, pp. 509–525, California Institute of Technology, Pasadena, California, 1979.

[HEMBOLD]

Hembold, D., and Mayr, E. W., Two processor scheduling is in NC, in Makedon, F., Mehlhorn, K., Papatheodorou, T., and Spirakis, P., *VLSI Algorithms and Architectures*, Lecture Notes in Computer Science, Vol. 227, Springer-Verlag, Berlin, 1986, pp. 12–25.

[HIRSCHBERG 1]

Hirschberg, D. S., Parallel graph algorithms without memory conflicts, Proceedings of the 20th Annual Allerton Conference on Communication, Control and Computing, Monticello, Illinois, October 1982, pp. 257–263, University of Illinois, Urbana-Champaign, Illinois, 1982.

[HIRSCHBERG 2]

Hirschberg, D. S., and Volper, D. J., A parallel solution for the minimum spanning tree problem, Proceedings of the 17th Annual Conference on Information Science and Systems, Baltimore, Maryland, March 1983, pp. 680–684, The Johns Hopkins University, Baltimore, Maryland, 1983.

[HIRSCHBERG 3]
Hirschberg, D. S., Chandra, A. K., and Sarwate, D. V., Computing connected components on parallel computers, *Communications of the ACM*, Vol. 22, No. 8, August 1979, pp. 461–464.

[HOCHSCHILD 1]
Hochschild, P. H., Mayr, E. W., and Siegel, A. R., Techniques for solving graph problems in parallel environments, Proceedings of the 24th Annual IEEE Symposium on Foundations of Computer Science, Tucson, Arizona, November 1983, pp. 351–359, IEEE Computer Society, Washington, D.C., 1983.

[HOCHSCHILD 2]
Hochschild, P. H., Mayr, E. W., and Siegel, A. R., Parallel graph algorithms, Technical Report No. STAN-CS-84-1028, Department of Computer Science, Stanford University, Stanford, California, December 1984.

[JA'JA']
Ja'Ja', J., and Simon, J., Parallel algorithms in graph theory: Planarity testing, *SIAM Journal on Computing*, Vol. 11, No. 2, May 1982, pp. 314–328.

[KALRA]
Kalra, N. C., an ! Bhatt, P. C. P., Parallel algorithms for tree traversals, *Parallel Computing*, Vol. 2, 1985, pp. 163–171.

[KAUTZ]
Kautz, W. H., Levitt, K. N., and Waksman, A., Cellular interconnection arrays, *IEEE Transactions on Computers*, Vol. C-17, No. 5, May 1968, pp. 443–451.

[KOSARAJU]
Kosaraju, S. R., Fast parallel processing array algorithms for some graph problems, Proceedings of the 11th Annual ACM Symposium on Theory of Computing, Atlanta, Georgia, April 30–May 2, 1979, pp. 231–236, Association for Computing Machinery, New York, N.Y., 1979.

[KRONSJÖ]
Kronsjö, L., *Computational Complexity of Sequential and Parallel Algorithms*, Wiley, Chichester, England, 1985.

[KUČERA]
Kučera, L., Parallel computation and conflicts in memory access, *Information Processing Letters*, Vol. 14, No. 2, April 1982, pp. 93–96.

[KWAN]
Kwan, S. C., and Ruzzo, W. L., Adaptive parallel algorithms for finding minimum spanning trees, Proceedings of the 1984 International Conference on Parallel Processing, Bellaire, Michigan, August 1984, pp. 439–443, IEEE Computer Society, Washington, D.C., 1984.

[LAKHANI]
Lakhani, G. D., A parallel computation of connected components, Proceedings of the 19th Annual Allerton Conference on Communication, Control and Computing, Monticello, Illinois, October 1981, pp. 211–213, University of Illinois, Urbana-Champaign, Illinois, 1981.

[LEISERSON]
Leiserson, C. E., and Maggs, B. M., Communication-efficient parallel graph algorithms, Proceedings of the 1986 International Conference on Parallel Processing, St. Charles, Illinois, August 1986, pp. 861–868, IEEE Computer Society, Washington, D.C., 1986.

[LEVITT]
Levitt, K. N., and Kautz, W. H., Cellular arrays for the solution of graph problems, *Communications of the ACM*, Vol. 15, No. 9, September 1972, pp. 789–801.

[MATETI]

Mateti, P., and Deo, N., Parallel algorithms for the single source shortest path problem, *Computing*, Vol. 29, 1982, pp. 31–49.

[MEAD]

Mead, C. A., and Conway, L. A., *Introduction to VLSI Systems*, Addison-Wesley, Reading, Massachusetts, 1980.

[MOHAN]

Mohan, J., A study in parallel computation—the traveling salesman problem, Technical Report CMU-CS-82-136, Department of Computer Science, Carnegie-Mellon University, Pittsburgh, August 1982.

[NASSIMI]

Nassimi, D., and Sahni, S., Finding connected components and connected ones on a mesh-connected parallel computer, *SIAM Journal on Computing*, Vol. 9, No. 4, November 1980, pp. 744–757.

[NATH 1]

Nath, D., and Maheshwari, S. N., Parallel algorithms for the connected components and minimal spanning tree problems, *Information Processing Letters*, Vol. 14, No. 1, March 1982, pp. 7–11.

[NATH 2]

Nath, D., Maheshwari, S. N., and Bhatt, P. C. P., Efficient VLSI networks for parallel processing based on orthogonal trees, *IEEE Transactions on Computers*, Vol. C-32, No. 6, June 1983, pp. 569–581.

[PAPADIMITRIOU]

Papadimitriou, C. H., and Steiglitz, K., *Combinatorial Optimization*, Prentice-Hall, Englewood Cliffs, N.J., 1982.

[QUINN 1]

Quinn, M. J., *Designing Efficient Algorithms for Parallel Computers*, McGraw-Hill, New York, 1987.

[QUINN 2]

Quinn, M. J., and Deo, N., Parallel graph algorithms, *Computing Surveys*, Vol. 16, No. 3, September 1984, pp. 319–348.

[REGHBATI]

Reghbati (Arjomandi), E., and Corneil, D. G., Parallel computations in graph theory, *SIAM Journal on Computing*, Vol. 7, No. 2, May 1978, pp. 230–237.

[SANTORO]

Santoro, N., On the message complexity of distributed problems, Technical Report No. SCS-TR-13, School of Computer Science, Carleton University, Ottawa, Ontario, December 1982.

[SAVAGE 1]

Savage, C., A systolic data structure chip for connectivity problems, in Kung, H. T., Sproull, R., and Steele, G., Eds., *VLSI Systems and Computations*, Computer Science Press, Rockville, Md., 1981, pp. 296–300.

[SAVAGE 2]

Savage, C., and Ja'Ja', J., Fast, efficient parallel algorithms for some graph problems, *SIAM Journal on Computing*, Vol. 10, No. 4, November 1981, pp. 682–691.

[SHILOACH 1]

Shiloach, Y., and Vishkin, U., An $O(\log n)$ parallel connectivity algorithm, *Journal of Algorithms*, Vol. 3, 1982, pp. 57–67.

[SHILOACH 2]

Shiloach, Y., and Vishkin, U., An $O(n^2 \log n)$ parallel MAX-FLOW algorithm, *Journal of Algorithms*, Vol. 3, 1982, pp. 128–146.

[ULLMAN]

Ullman, J. D., *Computational Aspects of VLSI*, Computer Science Press, Rockville, Md., 1984.

[VAN SCOY]

Van Scoy, F. L., The parallel recognition of classes of graphs, *IEEE Transactions on Computers*, Vol. C-29, No. 7, July 1980, pp. 563–570.

[WYLLIE]

Wyllie, J., The complexity of parallel computations, Ph.D. thesis, Cornell University, Ithaca, N.Y., 1979.

11

Computational Geometry

11.1 INTRODUCTION

Computational geometry is a branch of computer sicence concerned with the study of efficient algorithms for problems involving geometric objects. Examples of such problems include:

1. *Inclusion problems:* locating a point in a planar subdivision, reporting which points among a given set are contained in a specified domain, and so on.
2. *Intersection problems:* finding intersections of line segments, polygons, circles, rectangles, polyhedra, half spaces, and so on.
3. *Proximity problems:* determining the closest pair among a set of given points or among the vertices of a polygon; computing the smallest distance from one set of points to another; and so on.
4. *Construction problems:* identifying the convex hull of a polygon, obtaining the smallest box that includes a set of points, and so on.

These problems arise naturally, not only in the obvious application areas such as image analysis, pattern recognition, pattern classification, computer graphics, computer-aided design, and robotics, but also in statistics, operations research, and database search.

There is a wealth of sequential and parallel algorithms for computational geometry developed mainly over the last fifteen years. The overwhelming majority of these algorithms address well-understood problems in the Euclidean plane, that is, problems involving points, lines, polygons, and circles. Problems in higher dimensions are largely unexplored and remain as the major challenge for researchers in the field.

In this chapter we describe a number of parallel algorithms for fundamental problems in computational geometry. With only one exception, all our algorithms are for the two-dimensional case. In section 11.2 we begin by examining the problem of how to determine whether a point falls inside a polygon. Our solution is then used to address the more general problem of locating a point in a planar subdivision. Section

11.3 deals with the problem of finding out whether two polygons intersect. In section 11.4 we show how to identify the closest pair among a given set of points in d dimensions, where $d \geqslant 1$. Finally, section 11.5 is devoted to the problem of computing the convex hull of a finite set of points in the plane.

For each problem addressed in this chapter, a parallel algorithm is described that runs on an interconnection-network SIMD computer where the processors are linked to form a mesh of trees. This architecture is particularly suited to exhibit the parallelism inherent in geometric problems. Since the mesh of trees solutions use the same basic ideas, we present only the first of these in detail and give high-level descriptions of the remaining three. Our solutions are generally simple and fast. Perhaps their only disadvantage is the relatively large number of processors they require. Therefore, we show in section 11.5 that a more powerful model, such as the shared-memory SIMD computer, may be needed to achieve cost optimality and a sublinear running time while using only a sublinear number of processors.

11.2 AN INCLUSION PROBLEM

A graph is said to be *planar* if it can be drawn in the plane so that no two of its edges intersect. If the edges are drawn as straight-line segments, the resulting drawing of the graph is called a *planar subdivision*. As shown in Fig. 11.1, a planar subdivision consists of a collection of adjacent polygons. These polygons are said to be *simple*, meaning that no two edges of a polygon intersect, except at a vertex. The problem we

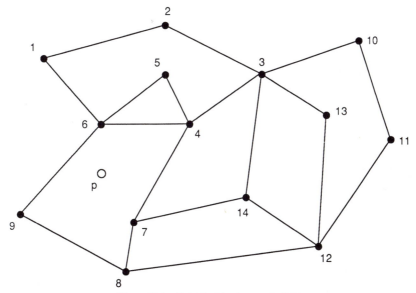

Figure 11.1   Point inside planar subdivision.

address in this section is the following: Given a planar subdivision and a point p, determine which polygon (if any) contains p; otherwise report that p falls outside the planar subdivision. A situation in which this problem needs to be solved is *pattern recognition*, where it is required to assign a given object to one of several classes. For example, a robot may wish to determine whether an object it is facing is a chair, a person, a dog, or a plant. Each class is described by a region in some space, and the points inside the region represent objects in that class. Points are given by their coordinates in space, each coordinate being the value of an object *feature*. In order to classify a new object, it suffices to identify the region in which the point representing the object falls. In Fig. 11.1 the space is two-dimensional and the regions are polygons.

In order to solve the point location problem stated in the preceding, we begin by considering the more fundamental question: Given a simple polygon Q with $n \geqslant 3$ edges and a point p, does p fall inside Q?

11.2.1 Point in Polygon

The basic idea behind our first parallel algorithm is illustrated in Fig. 11.2. Assume that a vertical line is drawn through point p. Next, the intersection points between this line and the edges of Q are found. If the number of such intersection points above p is odd, then p is inside Q; otherwise it is outside Q. This test can be performed

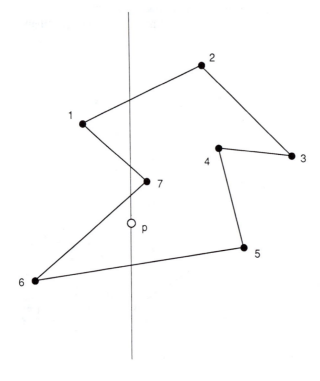

Figure 11.2 Test for point inclusion inside polygon.

sequentially in $O(n)$ steps for a polygon with n edges, and this is clearly optimal since $\Omega(n)$ steps are needed to read the input.

We can implement this test on a tree-connected SIMD computer as follows. Since Q has n edges, the tree consists of n processors $P_1, P_2, \ldots, P_n$. The processors are numbered beginning from the root and proceeding, level by level, from left to right. Thus the root is P_1, its children P_2 and P_3, and so on. Each processor stores an edge of Q given by the Cartesian coordinates of its two endpoints. Initially the root reads the x and y coordinates of p, namely, (x_p, y_p), and broadcasts them to all the other processors. When a processor P_j receives the coordinates of p, it determines whether

(i) a vertical line through p (call it L_p) intersects the edge of Q it stores (call it e_j) and

(ii) the intersection point is located above p.

If these two conditions hold, the processor produces a 1 as output. Otherwise it produces a 0. The processors' outputs are now added, and if the sum is odd, p is declared to be inside Q. The algorithm is given in what follows as procedure POINT IN POLYGON. It is assumed that each processor P_j already contains e_j. Two additional variables a_j and s_j in P_j serve in computing the total number of intersections above p. At the end of the procedure P_1 produces an answer equal to 1 if p is inside Q and equal to 0 otherwise.

procedure POINT IN POLYGON $(x_p, y_p, \text{answer})$

Step 1:   (1.1) P_1 reads (x_p, y_p)
            (1.2) **if** L_p intersects e_1 above p
                     then $s_1 \leftarrow 1$
                     else $s_1 \leftarrow 0$
                     end if
            (1.3) P_1 sends (x_p, y_p, s_1) to P_2 and $(x_p, y_p, 0)$ to P_3.

Step 2:   **for** $i = \log(n+1) - 2$ **downto** 1 **do**
                for $j = 2^{\log(n+1)-1-i}$ **to** $2^{\log(n+1)-i} - 1$ **do in parallel**
                     (2.1) P_j receives (x_p, y_p, s) from its parent
                     (2.2) **if** L_p intersects e_j above p
                              then $s_j \leftarrow 1$
                              else $s_j \leftarrow 0$
                              end if
                     (2.3) P_j sends $(x_p, y_p, s_j + s)$ to P_{2j} and $(x_p, y_p, 0)$ to P_{2j+1}
                end for
            end for.

Step 3:   **for** $j = 2^{\log(n+1)-1}$ **to** $2^{\log(n+1)} - 1$ **do in parallel**
                (3.1) P_j receives (x_p, y_p, s) from its parent
                (3.2) **if** L_p intersects e_j above p
                         then $a_j \leftarrow s + 1$
                         else $a_j \leftarrow s$
                         end if
            end for.

Step 4:   **for** $i = 1$ **to** $\log(n + 1) - 1$ **do**
              for $j = 2^{\log(n + 1) - 1 - i}$ **to** $2^{\log(n + 1) - i} - 1$ **do in parallel**
                  $a_j \leftarrow a_{2j} + a_{2j+1}$
              end for
            end for.

Step 5:   **if** a_1 is odd
            then answer $\leftarrow 1$
            else answer $\leftarrow 0$
            end if.   □

Analysis.   The procedure consists of two stages: the *descent* stage (steps 1–3), where all the intersection tests are performed, and the *ascent* stage (steps 4 and 5), where the total number of intersections above p is computed. It takes a constant number of operations to test whether a straight line and a straight-line segment intersect. Given that the tree has n processors, both the descent and ascent stages take $O(\log n)$ time. Since $p(n) = n$, $c(n) = O(n \log n)$, which is not optimal.

Example 11.1

    The edges of the polygon in Fig. 11.2 are stored in a tree-connected computer with seven processors, as shown in Fig. 11.3. For the input point p of Fig. 11.2, only processors P_1, P_2, and P_4 produce a 1 as output, and the root declares p to be inside Q.   □

Three points are worth noting:

  1. Several points p can be tested for inclusion in a polygon Q by pipelining procedure POINT IN POLYGON. Indeed, once a processor has performed its test (*and sent to its left child the partial total of the number of intersections above p*) it is free to receive the next point. It is with this pipelining in mind that the procedure was designed, so that partial totals never stay in a given processor

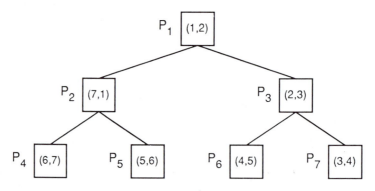

Figure 11.3   Testing point inclusion using procedure POINT IN POLYGON.

but are constantly moving either downward or upward. The *period* is therefore constant.

2. The procedure can be easily modified to handle the case where there are more (or fewer) processors than polygon edges.

3. It is possible to modify the procedure to achieve optimal cost. The idea is to use $n/\log n$ processors each storing $\log n$ edges of Q. It takes $O(\log(n/\log n))$ time to broadcast the coordinates of p to all processors. Each processor now performs the intersection test for all $\log n$ edges it stores and adds up the number of intersections above p in $O(\log n)$ time. The total number of intersections above p is computed in $O(\log(n/\log n))$ time. The overall running time is $O(\log n)$ as before. However, the period is no longer constant.

11.2.2 Point in Planar Subdivision

We are now ready to address the more general problem of locating a point in a planar subdivision. Our parallel algorithm uses the *mesh of trees* architecture (introduced in problem 4.2 and first used in section 9.2.2). Assume that the planar subdivision consists of m polygons, each with at most n edges. We use an $m \times n$ mesh. Each of the m rows, numbered $1, \ldots, m$, is a binary tree of processors storing the edges of one polygon, one edge per processor. Each of the n columns, numbered $1, \ldots, n$, is also a binary tree (although in this context we shall only make use of the tree in column 1).

The idea of the algorithm is to feed the coordinates of the query point p to the root processor of every row tree. This can be done using the tree connections in column 1. Procedure POINT IN POLYGON is now performed simultaneously by all rows. The procedure is slightly modified so that

(i) when it starts, the root processor in every row already contains (x_p, y_p), and

(ii) when it terminates, the root processor in row i produces the pair $(1, i)$ as output if p is inside the associated polygon; otherwise it produces $(0, i)$.

By using the tree connections in column 1 and the logical **or** operation on the first components of the output pairs, either

(i) the (unique) polygon containing p can be identified or

(ii) the fact that p is not inside any of the polygons can be established.

The algorithm is given in what follows as procedure POINT IN SUBDIVISION. The processor in row i and column j is denoted $P(i, j)$. The output pair for root processor $P(i, 1)$ is denoted (a_i, b_i), where a_i is either 0 or 1 and b_i is a row number.

procedure POINT IN SUBDIVISION (x_p, y_p, a_1, b_1)

Step 1: $P(1, 1)$ reads (x_p, y_p).

Step 2:   **for** $i = \log(m + 1) - 1$ **downto** 1 **do**
            for $j = 2^{\log(m+1)-1-i}$ **to** $2^{\log(m+1)-i} - 1$ **do in parallel**
              $P(j, 1)$ sends (x_p, y_p) to $P(2j, 1)$ and $P(2j + 1, 1)$
            end for
          end for.

Step 3:   **for** $i = 1$ **to** m **do in parallel**
            Processors $P(i, 1)$ to $P(i, n)$ execute POINT IN POLYGON
          end for.

Step 4:   **for** $i = 1$ **to** $\log(m + 1) - 1$ **do**
            for $j = 2^{\log(m+1)-1-i}$ **to** $2^{\log(m+1)-i} - 1$ **do in parallel**
              if $a_{2j} = 1$
              then $(a_j, b_j) \leftarrow (a_{2j}, b_{2j})$
              else if $a_{2j+1} = 1$
                then $(a_j, b_j) \leftarrow (a_{2j+1}, b_{2j+1})$
                end if
              end if
            end for
          end for.

Step 5: $P(1, 1)$ produces (a_1, b_1) as output.   □

Note that when the procedure terminates, if $a_1 = 1$, then this means that the polygon numbered b_1 contains p. Otherwise $a_1 = 0$, in which case p is outside of the planar subdivision.

Example 11.2

The subdivision in Fig. 11.1 requires a 7×6 mesh of trees, as shown in Fig. 11.4 (where the tree connections are omitted for simplicity). When the coordinates of point p in Fig. 11.1 are given as input to the mesh of trees, row 3 produces $(1, 3)$ while all other rows produce $(0, i)$, $i \neq 3$. Thus $(1, 3)$ is the mesh's output.   □

Analysis.   Steps 1 and 5 run in constant time. Steps 2 and 3 take $O(\log m)$ and $O(\log n)$ time, respectively. Step 4 also requires $O(\log m)$ time. Assuming that m is $O(n)$, $t(n) = O(\log n)$. Since $p(n) = n^2$, the procedure's cost is $c(n) = O(n^2 \log n)$. This cost is not optimal given that a sequential algorithm that applies the $O(n)$ polygon inclusion test to each of the m polygons runs in $O(n^2)$ time.

If k points p are queued for processing, they can be pipelined and the procedure would require $O(k + \log n)$ time to answer all k queries. Finally, using the same

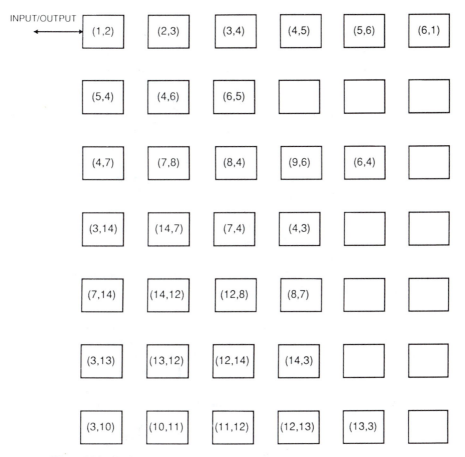

Figure 11.4   Testing point inclusion using procedure POINT IN SUBDIVISION.

approach as with procedure **POINT IN POLYGON**, procedure **POINT IN SUBDIVISION** can be made to have a cost of $O(n^2)$. This is illustrated in the next section.

11.3 AN INTERSECTION PROBLEM

In many applications, it is required to determine whether a set of geometric objects intersect. Thus, for example,

(i) in *pattern classification* it is necessary to determine whether different regions in space representing different classes have common subregions;

    (ii) in *integrated circuit design* it is important to avoid crossing wires and overlapping components; and

    (iii) in *computer graphics* it is required to remove hidden lines and hidden surfaces from two-dimensional representations of three-dimensional scenes.

In this section we examine one such intersection problem.

    Two polygons Q and R are said to *intersect* if an edge of Q crosses an edge of R. Note that the two polygons need not be simple, that is, two or more edges of Q (or two or more edges of R) may cross. Figure 11.5 illustrates two intersecting polygons. Let Q and R be two polygons, each given by a list of its edges. It is required to determine whether Q and R intersect. Our parallel solution to this problem is based on a straightforward approach: For each edge of Q we determine whether it crosses one of the edges of R. Assume that Q and R have m and n edges, respectively, each being given by the coordinates of its two endpoints. We use a mesh of trees with m rows and $n/\log n$ columns. Each processor is loaded with $\log n$ edges of R so that

    (i) the set of edges contained in a row is the set of edges of R and

    (ii) the processors in each column contain the same subset of $\log n$ edges of R.

Loading the processors in each column is done by pipelining the $\log n$ edges assigned to that column through its root processor. When a processor receives an edge, it stores it in its own memory and sends a copy of it to each of its two children using the tree connections in that column. It therefore takes $O(\log m) + O(\log n)$ time to load a column. If all columns are loaded simultaneously, then this would also be the time taken to load the entire mesh. In addition, each processor receives an edge of Q so that

    (i) the set of edges contained in a column is the set of edges of Q and

    (ii) the processors in each row contain the same edge of Q.

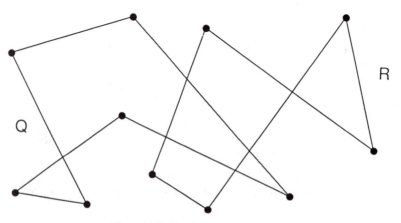

Figure 11.5 Two intersecting polygons.

The edges of Q are fed into the mesh, one edge per row, through the root processor in each row. When a processor in a given row receives the edge assigned to that row, it stores it in its own memory and sends a copy of it to each of its two children, using the tree connections in that row. It takes $\log(n/\log n)$ steps to load a row. If all rows are loaded simultaneously, then this would also be the time taken to load the entire mesh.

Now each processor tests whether the edge of Q assigned to it crosses one of the $\log n$ edges of R it also contains. If this is the case, it produces a 1 as output; otherwise it produces a 0. With all processors operating simultaneously, this step takes $O(\log n)$ time.

The outputs in each row are combined level by level, beginning from the leaves and all the way to the row's root processor. This is accomplished by requiring each processor to compute the logical **or** of three quantities: the two inputs received from its children and its own output. The processor then sends the result of this operation to its parent. After $\log(n/\log n)$ steps the root processor in each row would have computed the logical **or** of all outputs in that row, which it retains. These processors combine their results in the same way using the tree connections in column 1. This requires another $\log m$ steps.

Assuming that $m \leqslant n$, the overall running time of the algorithm is

$$t(n) = O(\log n).$$

Since $p(n) = O(n^2/\log n)$, the algorithm's cost is $O(n^2)$. The only known lower bound on the number of steps required to solve this problem is the *trivial* one of $\Omega(n)$ operations performed while reading the input. Furthermore, it is not known whether a sequential algorithm exists with a smaller than quadratic running time. The algorithm's cost optimality is therefore an open question.

11.4 A PROXIMITY PROBLEM

Proximity problems arise in many applications where physical or mathematical objects are represented as points in space. Examples include the following:

(i) *clustering:* a number of entities are grouped together if they are sufficiently close to one another;

(ii) *classification:* a new pattern to be classified is assigned to the class of its closest (classified) neighbor; and

(iii) *air-traffic control:* the two airplanes that are closest are the two most in danger.

One such proximity problem, that of finding the closest pair among a set of points, is addressed in this section.

Let S be a set of n points in d-dimensional space, where each point is given by its d coordinates $(x_1, x_2, \ldots, x_d)$. The distance between two points $(x_1, x_2, \ldots, x_d)$ and $(x'_1,$

$x'_2, \ldots, x'_d$) of S is defined as

$$\left(\sum_{i=1}^{d} \text{abs}(x_i - x'_i)^q \right)^{1/q},$$

where q is a positive integer. The value of q depends on the application. Thus, $q = 2$ corresponds to the usual Euclidean distance. For a given q, it is required to determine the closest pair of points in S.

A parallel solution to this problem can be modeled after the algorithm in the previous section. We use a mesh of trees with $n/\log n$ columns and n rows. Each processor holds the coordinates of $\log n$ points. All the processors in a column hold the same $\log n$ points. The n points held by a row of processors are equal to the set S. In addition, the coordinates of the ith point of S, call it p_i, are fed to the processors in the ith row. A processor in the ith row computes the distance between p_i and each of the $\log n$ points it was first assigned. It then reports the closest pair and the distance separating them. By using the row trees and then the tree in column 1, the overall closest pair of points are finally determined. The algorithm runs in $O(\log n)$ time. Since $p(n) = n^2/\log n$, $c(n) = O(n^2)$. It is not known whether the algorithm is optimal with arbitrary d and/or q for the same reasons given in the previous section.

11.5 A CONSTRUCTION PROBLEM

Given a set $S = \{p_1, p_2, \ldots, p_n\}$ of points in the plane, the *convex hull* of S, denoted $CH(S)$, is the smallest convex polygon that includes all the points of S. A set of points is shown in Fig. 11.6(a); its convex hull is illustrated in Fig. 11.6(b). Note that the vertices of $CH(S)$ are points of S. Thus every point of S is either a vertex of $CH(S)$ or lies inside $CH(S)$. The following analogy is useful. Assume that the points of S are nails driven halfway into a wooden board. A rubber band is now stretched around the set of

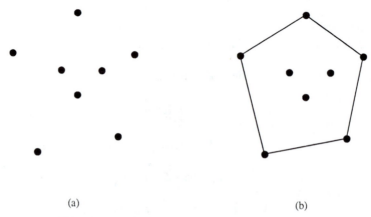

(a)   (b)

Figure 11.6 Set of points in plane and its convex hull.

nails and then released. When the band settles, it has the shape of a polygon: Those nails touching the band at the corners of that polygon are the vertices of the convex hull.

Applications of convex hulls abound. They include:

(i) *statistics* (e.g., when estimating the *mean* of a set of points, the convex hull of the set allows a robust estimate to be obtained since the vertices of the hull may represent outliers that can be ignored);

(ii) *picture processing* (e.g., the *concavities* in a digitized picture are found by constructing the convex hull);

(iii) *pattern recognition* (e.g., the convex hull of a visual pattern serves as a *feature* describing the shape of the pattern);

(iv) *classification* (e.g., the convex hull of a set of objects delineates the *class* to which these objects belong);

(v) *computer graphics* (e.g., *clusters* of points are displayed using their convex hull); and

(vi) *geometric problems* [e.g., the *farthest* two points of a set S are vertices of CH(S)].

In this section we are concerned with developing parallel algorithms for the problem of identifying the vertices of CH(S). We begin by deriving a lower bound on the number of steps required to solve the problem. This is followed by a brief outline of a sequential algorithm whose running time matches the lower bound and is therefore optimal. Two parallel algorithms are then presented, one for the mesh of trees and the other for the EREW SM SIMD computer.

11.5.1 Lower Bound

A powerful technique for proving lower bounds on the number of steps required to solve computational problems is that of *problem reduction*. Let A and B be two computational problems. A lower bound is known for B; it is required to prove a lower bound for A. If we can show that an algorithm for solving A—along with a transformation on problem instances—could be used to construct an algorithm to solve B, then the lower bound on B also applies to A. This is illustrated in Fig. 11.7.

We now use problem reduction to derive a lower bound on computing the convex hull. Let problems A and B be defined

A = find the convex hull CH(S) of a set S of n points in the plane;

B = sort a sequence of n numbers in nondecreasing order.

Note that problem A requires us to find the convex hull of S and not merely its vertices. More specifically, an algorithm to solve A must return a *polygon*, that is, a list of vertices in the order in which they appear on the perimeter of CH(S).

Let CONVEX HULL be an algorithm for solving A. We also know from

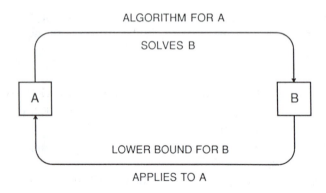

ALGORITHM FOR A

SOLVES B

A

B

LOWER BOUND FOR B

APPLIES TO A

Figure 11.7 Method of problem reduction for proving lower bounds.

example 1.10 that a lower bound on the number of steps required to solve B in the worst case is $\Omega(n \log n)$. Now, say that the input to B is the sequence $X = \{x_1, x_2, \ldots, x_n\}$. In order for X to become an input to CONVEX HULL, the following transformation is used. First, the elements of X are mapped, each in constant time, into the semiopen interval $[0, 2\pi)$ using a one-to-one function f. Thus, for $i = 1, 2, \ldots, n$, $\theta_i = f(x_i)$ represents an angle. For every θ_i a planar point is created whose polar coordinates are $(1, \theta_i)$. The resulting set of points

$$S = \{(1, \theta_1), (1, \theta_2), \ldots, (1, \theta_n)\}$$

has all its members on the circumference of a circle of unit radius, and CH(S) includes all the points of S, as shown in Fig. 11.8. If CONVEX HULL is applied to S, its output

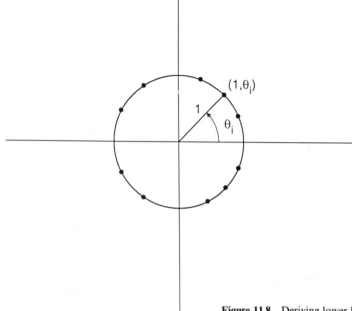

Figure 11.8 Deriving lower bound on convex hull computation.

would be a list of the members of S sorted on the θ_i, that is, in angular order. A sorted sequence X can now be obtained in linear time using the inverse transformation $x_i = f^{-1}(\theta_i)$. Since sorting n numbers requires $\Omega(n \log n)$ steps in the worst case, we are forced to conclude that the same lower bound applies to computing the convex hull of n points.

11.5.2 Sequential Solution

Our purpose in this section is to show that the $\Omega(n \log n)$ lower bound just derived is tight. To this purpose we briefly sketch a sequential algorithm for computing the convex hull of a set of n points. The algorithm runs in $O(n \log n)$ time and is therefore optimal. It is based on the algorithm design technique of *divide and conquer*. The algorithm is given in what follows as procedure SEQUENTIAL CONVEX HULL. The procedure takes $S = \{p_1, p_2, \ldots, p_n\}$ as input and returns a list CH(S) containing the vertices of the convex hull of S.

procedure SEQUENTIAL CONVEX HULL (S, CH(S))

    if S contains less than four points
      then CH(S) ← S
      else (1) {Divide}
             Divide S arbitrarily into two subsets S_1 and S_2 of approximately equal size
          (2) {Conquer}
             (2.1) SEQUENTIAL CONVEX HULL (S_1, CH(S_1))
             (2.2) SEQUENTIAL CONVEX HULL (S_2, CH(S_2))
          (3) {Merge}
             Merge CH(S_1) and CH(S_2) into one convex polygon to obtain CH(S)
    end if.   □

The most important step in the algorithm is the *merge* operation. Here we have two convex polygons CH(S_1) and CH(S_2) that are to be combined into one convex polygon CH(S). An example is illustrated in Fig. 11.9. In this case, the two polygons can be merged in three steps:

1. find an *upper tangent* (a, b) and a *lower tangent* (c, d);

2. delete points e and f of CH(S_1) and g of CH(S_2); and

3. return CH(S) as the list (i, a, b, h, d, c).

In general, if CH(S_1) and CH(S_2) contain $O(n)$ vertices in all, then CH(S) can be computed in $O(n)$ time.

    We now analyze the running time $t(n)$ of procedure SEQUENTIAL CONVEX HULL. Each of the *conquer* steps 2.1 and 2.2 is recursive, thus requiring $t(n/2)$ time. Steps 1 and 3 are linear. Therefore,

$$t(n) = 2t(n/2) + cn$$

where c is a constant. It follows that $t(n) = O(n \log n)$, which is optimal.

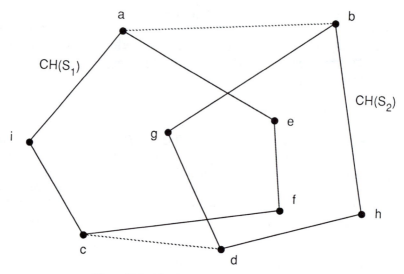

Figure 11.9 Merging two convex polygons into one.

11.5.3 Mesh of Trees Solution

Assume that a set $S = \{p_1, p_2, \ldots, p_n\}$ of points in the plane is given, where each point is represented by its Cartesian coordinates, that is, $p_i = (x_i, y_i)$. Our first parallel algorithm for computing CH(S) is designed to run on a mesh of trees SIMD computer. In order to avoid cluttering our presentation with "hairy" details, we make the following two simplifying assumptions.

(i) no two points have the same x or y coordinates and

(ii) no three points fall on the same straight line.

Once we have described the approach upon which our algorithm is based, it will become obvious how to modify it to deal with situations where the preceding assumptions do not hold. We begin by explaining three ideas that are central to our solution.

1. Identifying Extreme Points.   Assume that the *extreme* points, that is, the points with maximum x coordinate, maximum y coordinate, minimum x coordinate, and minimum y coordinate in S, have been determined as shown in Fig. 11.10. Call these points XMAX, YMAX, XMIN, and YMIN, respectively.

Three facts are obvious:

(i) The extreme points are vertices of CH(S);

(ii) any points falling inside the quadrilateral formed by the extreme points is definitely *not* a vertex of CH(S); and

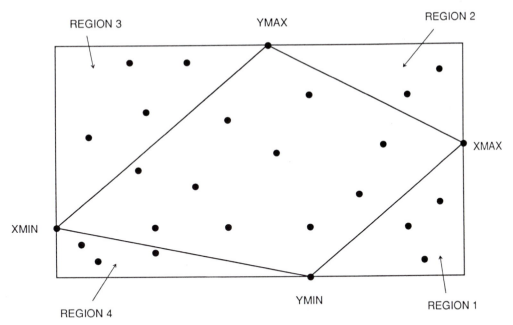

Figure 11.10   Extreme points of planar set.

(iii) the problem of identifying CH(S) has been reduced to finding a *convex polygonal path* joining two extreme points in each of the regions 1, 2, 3, and 4; CH(S) is obtained by linking these four paths.

2. Identifying Hull Edges.   A segment (p_i, p_j) is an edge of CH(S) if and only if all the $n - 2$ remaining points of S fall on the same side of an infinite straight line drawn through p_i and p_j. This property is illustrated in Fig. 11.11, where (a, b) is a convex hull edge while (c, d) and (e, f) are not. Note that this allows us to conclude that both a and b are vertices of CH(S).

3. Identifying the Smallest Angle.   Let p_i and p_j be consecutive vertices of CH(S) and assume that p_i is taken as the origin of coordinates. Then, among all points of S, p_j forms the smallest angle with p_i with respect to the (either positive or negative) x axis. This is illustrated in Fig. 11.12.

We are now ready to present our algorithm. Assume that a mesh of trees is available consisting of n rows and n columns of processors. The processor in row i and column j is denoted $P(i, j)$. For $i = 1, 2, \ldots, n$, $P(i, j)$ contains the coordinates (x_j, y_j). Thus,

(i) all the processors in a column contain the coordinates of the same point of S and
(ii) the coordinates contained in a row form the set $S = \{(x_1, y_1), (x_2, y_2), \ldots, (x_n, y_n)\}$.

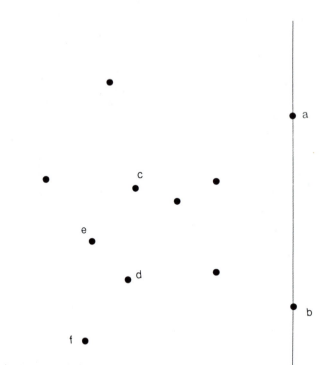

Figure 11.11 Property of convex hull edges.

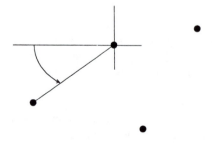

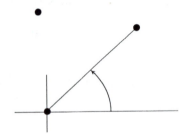

Figure 11.12 Property of consecutive convex hull vertices.

The algorithm consists of the following stages.

Stage 1

(i) The processors in rows 1, 2, 3, and 4 compute XMAX, YMAX, XMIN, and YMIN and store their coordinates in $P(1, 1)$, $P(2, 1)$, $P(3, 1)$, and $P(4, 1)$, respectively.

(ii) Using the tree connections, first in column 1 and then in row 1, the coordinates of the four extreme points are made known to all processors in row 1.

Stage 2

(i) The four processors in row 1 corresponding to the extreme points produce a 1 as output [indicating these points are vertices of CH(S)].

(ii) All processors in row 1 corresponding to points *inside* the quadrilateral formed by the extreme points produce a 0 [indicating these points are not vertices of CH(S) and should therefore be removed from further consideration].

(iii) Each of the remaining processors $P(1, j)$ in row 1 identifies the region (1, 2, 3, or 4) in which point p_j falls and communicates this information to all processors $P(i, j)$ in column j.

(iv) XMAX is assigned to region 1, YMAX to region 2, XMIN to region 3, and YMIN to region 4.

Stage 3

If processor $P(1, i)$ corresponding to point p_i of S produced neither a 1 nor a 0 in stage 2, then the following steps are executed by the processors in row i:

(i) The point p_j (in the same region as p_i) is found such that (p_i, p_j) forms the smallest angle with respect to
  (a) the positive x axis if p_i is in regions 1 or 2 or
  (b) the negative x axis if p_i is in regions 3 or 4.

(ii) If all remaining points (in the same region as p_i and p_j) fall on the same side of an infinite straight line through p_i and p_j, then p_i is a vertex of CH(S).

Stage 4

(i) If p_i was identified as a vertex of CH(S) in stage 3, then $P(1, i)$ produces a 1 as output; otherwise it produces a 0.

(ii) An arbitrary point in the plane is chosen inside the quadrilateral whose corners are the extreme points. This point (which need not be a point of S) is designated as an origin for polar coordinates. The polar angles formed by all points identified as vertices of CH(S) are computed.

(iii) The angles computed in (ii) are sorted in increasing order using the mesh of trees (see problem 4.2). This gives the convex hull vertices listed in counterclockwise order, exactly in the sequence in which they appear along the boundary of CH(S).

Analysis. Each of the four stages requires $O(\log n)$ operations. Thus $t(n) = O(\log n)$. Since $p(n) = n^2$, the algorithm's cost is $O(n^2 \log n)$, which is not optimal. As in previous sections the cost can be reduced to $O(n^2)$ by using n rows of $n/\log n$ processors each. This cost is still not optimal in view of the $O(n \log n)$ sequential algorithm described in section 11.5.2.

11.5.4 Optimal Solution

In this section we describe an optimal parallel algorithm for computing the convex hull. The algorithm is designed to run on an EREW SM SIMD computer with $N = n^{1-z}$ processors, $0 < z < 1$. As before, each point p_i of $S = \{p_1, p_2, \ldots, p_n\}$ is given by its Cartesian coordinates (x_i, y_i), and we continue to assume for clarity of presentation that no two points have the same x or y coordinates and that no three points fall on a straight line. A high-level description of the algorithm is first presented.

Let XMIN and XMAX denote, as before, the points with minimum and maximum x coordinates, respectively. As Fig. 11.13 illustrates, CH(S) consists of two parts: an *upper* convex polygonal path from XMIN to XMAX (solid lines) and a *lower* one from XMAX to XMIN (broken lines). Given these two polygonal paths, they can be concatenated to yield CH(S). The algorithm is given in what follows as procedure EREW CONVEX HULL. It takes the points of S as input and returns a list CH(S) of the vertices of CH(S) in the order in which they appear on the convex hull of S.

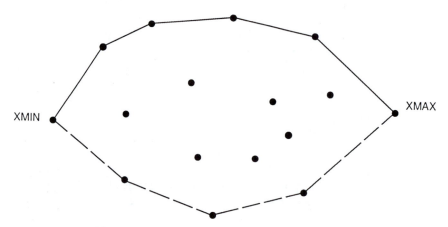

Figure 11.13   Upper and lower convex polygonal paths.

procedure EREW CONVEX HULL $(S, CH(S))$

Step 1:   (1.1) xmin ← index of XMIN in S
          (1.2) xmax ← index of XMAX in S.

Step 2: $UP(S)$ ← list of vertices on the upper convex polygonal path from p_{xmin} to p_{xmax}.

Step 3: $LP(S)$ ← list of vertices on the lower convex polygonal path from p_{xmax} to p_{xmin}.

Step 4:   (4.1) $LP(S)$ ← list $LP(S)$ with p_{xmax} and p_{xmin} removed
          (4.2) $CH(S)$ ← list $UP(S)$ followed by list $LP(S)$.   □

This procedure as described is rather vague and requires a good deal of refinement. We can dispose immediately to steps 1 and 4. Step 1 can be implemented using procedure PARALLEL SELECT, which, as we know from chapter 2, uses n^{1-z} processors and runs in $O(n^z)$ time. There are two operations in step 4: deleting the first and last elements of $LP(S)$ and linking the remaining ones with $UP(S)$. Both can be performed in constant time by a single processor. This leaves us with steps 2 and 3. Clearly, any algorithm for step 2 can be easily modified to carry out step 3. We therefore concentrate on refining step 2.

Finding the Upper Hull.   An algorithm for constructing the upper convex polygonal path (upper path, for short) can be obtained by making use of the following property: If a vertical line is drawn somewhere between p_{xmin} and p_{xmax} so that it does not go through a convex hull vertex, then this line crosses *exactly one* edge of the upper path. The algorithm first places a vertical line L dividing S into two sets S_{left} and S_{right} of approximately the same size. The unique edge of the upper path intersecting L is now determined as shown in Fig. 11.14. This edge is called a *bridge* (from S_{left} to S_{right}). The algorithm is then applied recursively to S_{left} and S_{right}. It is interesting to note here that like procedure SEQUENTIAL CONVEX HULL this algorithm is based on the *divide-and-conquer* principle for algorithm design. However, while procedure SEQUENTIAL CONVEX HULL divides, conquers, and then merges, this algorithm divides (into S_{left} and S_{right}), merges (by finding the bridge), and *then conquers* (by recursing on S_{left} and S_{right}).

Ideally, in a parallel implementation of this idea, the two recursive steps should be executed simultaneously since each of the two subproblems S_{left} and S_{right} has the same structure as the original problem S. Unfortunately, this is impossible since the number of available processors is not sufficient to provide a proper recursive execution of the algorithm. To see this, note that each of S_{left} and S_{right} contains approximately $n/2$ points and thus requires $(n/2)^{1-z}$ processors. This is larger than the $n^{1-z}/2$ processors that would be assigned to each of S_{left} and S_{right} if the two recursive steps were to be executed simultaneously. Therefore, we resort instead to a solution similar to the one used in the case of EREW SORT in chapter 4. Let $k = 2^{\lceil 1/z \rceil - 1}$. First, $2k - 1$ vertical lines $L_1, L_2, \ldots, L_{2k-1}$ are found that divide S into $2k$ subsets $S_i, i = 1, 2, \ldots, 2k$ of size $n/2k$ each. These subsets are such that

$$S_{left} = S_1 \cup S_2 \cup \cdots \cup S_k \quad \text{and} \quad S_{right} = S_{k+1} \cup S_{k+2} \cup \cdots \cup S_{2k}.$$

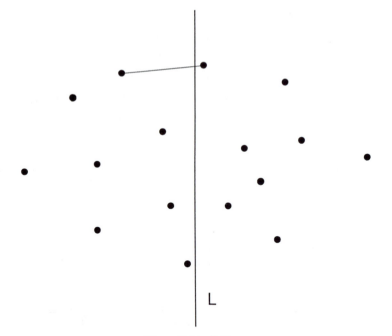

Figure 11.14 Bridge.

In the next step, edge (a_i, b_i) of the upper path that crosses vertical line L_i, $i = 1$, $2, \ldots, 2k - 1$, is obtained. (Here both a_i and b_i are elements of S; we use a and b instead of p to avoid multiple subscripts.) The algorithm is now applied recursively and in parallel to $S_1, S_2, \ldots, S_k$ using $(n^{1-z})/k$ processors per subset. The same is then done for $S_{k+1}, S_{k+2}, \ldots, S_{2k}$. The algorithm is given in what follows as procedure UPPER HULL. The procedure takes the set S and two points p_l and p_m as input. It produces the upper path from p_l to p_m as output. Initially, it is called from procedure EREW CONVEX HULL with $p_l = p_{\text{xmin}}$ and $p_m = p_{\text{xmax}}$.

procedure UPPER HULL (S, p_l, p_m)

    if $|S| \leqslant 2k$

    then find the upper path from p_l to p_m using SEQUENTIAL CONVEX HULL

    else (1) find $2k-1$ vertical lines $L_1, L_2, \ldots, L_{2k-1}$ that divide S into $S_1, S_2, \ldots, S_{2k}$

         (2) **for** $i = 1$ **to** $2k-1$ **do**

             find edge (a_i, b_i) of the upper path intersecting line L_i

         end for

         (3) {Construct upper path for S_{left}}

             (3.1) **if** $p_l = a_1$

                 then p_l is produced as output

                 else UPPER HULL (S_1, p_l, a_1)

                 end if

(3.2) **for** $j = 2$ **to** k **do in parallel**
$\quad$ **if** $b_{j-1} = a_j$
$\quad$ **then** b_{j-1} is produced as output
$\quad$ **else if** $a_{j-1} \neq a_j$
$\quad\quad\quad$ **then** UPPER HULL (S_j, b_{j-1}, a_j)
$\quad\quad$ **end if**
$\quad$ **end if**
$\quad$ **end for**
(4) {Construct upper path for S_{right}}
$\quad$ (4.1) **for** $j = k + 1$ **to** $2k - 1$ **do in parallel**
$\quad\quad$ **if** $b_{j-1} = a_j$
$\quad\quad$ **then** b_{j-1} is produced as output
$\quad\quad$ **else if** $a_{j-1} \neq a_j$
$\quad\quad\quad\quad$ **then** UPPER HULL (S_j, b_{j-1}, a_j)
$\quad\quad\quad$ **end if**
$\quad\quad$ **end if**
$\quad\quad$ **end for**
$\quad$ (4.2) **if** $b_{2k-1} = p_m$
$\quad\quad$ **then** b_{2k-1} is produced as output
$\quad\quad$ **else** UPPER HULL (S_{2k}, b_{2k-1}, p_m)
$\quad\quad$ **end if**
end if. $\square$

Step 1 can be implemented using procedure PARALLEL SELECT. Steps 3 and 4 are recursive. It remains to show how step 2 is performed. The following procedure BRIDGE (S, A) takes a set S of n points and a real number A as input and returns two points a_i and b_i where (a_i, b_i) is the unique edge of the upper path intersecting the vertical line L_i whose equation is $x = A$.

procedure BRIDGE (S, A)

Step 1:   The points of S are paired up into couples (p_u, p_v) such that $x_u < x_v$. The ordered pairs define $\lfloor n/2 \rfloor$ straight lines whose slopes are $\{s_1, s_2, \ldots, s_{\lfloor n/2 \rfloor}\}$.

Step 2:   Find the median K of the set $\{s_1, s_2, \ldots, s_{\lfloor n/2 \rfloor}\}$.

Step 3:   Find a straight line Q of slope K that contains at least one point of S but has no point of S above it.

Step 4:   **if** Q contains two points of S, one on each side of L_i
$\quad$ **then** return these as (a_i, b_i)
$\quad$ **else if** Q contains no points of S_{right}
$\quad\quad$ **then** for every straight line through (p_u, p_v) with slope larger than or equal to K
$\quad\quad\quad$ $S \leftarrow S - \{p_u\}$
$\quad\quad$ **else if** Q contains no points of S_{left}
$\quad\quad\quad$ **then** for every straight line through (p_u, p_v) with slope less than or equal to
$\quad\quad\quad\quad$ K
$\quad\quad\quad\quad$ $S \leftarrow S - \{p_v\}$
$\quad\quad$ **end if**
$\quad$ **end if**
end if.

Step 5:   BRIDGE (S, A). $\square$

We now describe how this procedure is implemented in parallel and analyze its running time, which we denote by $B(n)$. Step 1 is performed in parallel by assigning different subsets of S of size n^z to the n^{1-z} processors, each of which creates $\lfloor n^z/2 \rfloor$ pairs of points (p_u, p_v) and computes the slopes of the straight lines they form. Step 1 thus requires $O(n^z)$ time. Step 2 can be implemented using procedure PARALLEL SELECT in $O(n^z)$ time. Step 3 is executed by finding the (at most two) points maximizing the quantity $y_j - Kx_j$. This quantity can be obtained for all values of j by having each processor compute it for the points in its assigned subset of S. The maximum of these quantities is found using procedure PARALLEL SELECT. Hence step 3 also runs in $O(n^z)$ time. Finally, in step 4, determining whether Q contains the required edge can be done by one processor in constant time. Otherwise, the value of K is broadcast to all n^{1-z} processors in $O(\log n^{1-z})$ time using procedure BROADCAST. Each processor compares K to the $\lfloor n^z/2 \rfloor$ slopes it has computed in step 1 and updates S accordingly; this requires $O(n^z)$ time. Step 4 therefore runs in $O(n^z)$ time. Since one-quarter of the points are discarded in step 4, the complexity of step 5 is $B(3n/4)$. Thus, for some constant c_1,

$$B(n) = c_1 n^z + B(3n/4)$$

whose solution is $B(n) = O(n^z)$.

Analysis.   We are now in a position to analyze procedure EREW CONVEX HULL. As mentioned earlier, steps 1 and 4 run in $O(n^z)$ and $O(1)$ time, respectively. Let h_U and h_L be the number of edges of the upper and lower convex polygonal paths, respectively. We denote the running times of steps 2 and 3 by $F_U(n, h_U)$ and $F_L(n, h_L)$, respectively. Thus, the running time of procedure EREW CONVEX HULL is given by

$$t(n) = c_2 n^z + F_U(n, h_U) + F_L(n, h_L) + c_3$$

for two constants c_2 and c_3. From our discussion of procedure UPPER HULL, we have

$$F_U(n, h_U) = c_4 n^z + \max_{h_l + h_r = h_U} \left\{ \max_{1 \leqslant j \leqslant k} [F_U(|S_j|, h_j)] + \max_{k+1 \leqslant j \leqslant 2j} [F_U(|S_j|, h_j)] \right\}$$

where h_l, h_r, and h_j are the number of edges on the upper path associated with S_{left}, S_{right}, and S_j, respectively, and c_4 is a constant. Therefore

$$F_U(n, h_U) = O(n^z \log h_U),$$

and similarly

$$F_L(n, h_L) = O(n^z \log h_L).$$

It follows that $t(n) = O(n^z \log h)$, where $h = h_U + h_L$. Thus the procedure's running time not only adapts to the number of available processors, but is also sensitive to h, the number of edges on the convex hull. In the worst case, of course, $h = n$, and

$t(n) = O(n^z \log n)$. Since $p(n) = n^{1-z}$, the procedure has a cost of

$$c(n) = O(n \log n),$$

which is optimal in view of the $\Omega(n \log n)$ lower bound derived in section 11.5.1. Since $n^z > \log n$ for all z and sufficiently large n, optimality is achieved when $N < n/\log n$.

Example 11.3

Assume that four processors are available on an EREW SM SIMD computer. We apply procedure EREW CONVEX HULL to the set of points in Fig. 11.13. Since $n = 16$ and $N = 4$, $N = n^{1-x}$ yields $x = 0.5$. Furthermore, $k = 2^{\lceil 1/x \rceil - 1} = 2$. In step 1, p_{xmin} and p_{xmax} are determined. In step 2, procedure UPPER HULL is invoked to find the upper path.

Procedure UPPER HULL begins by placing $2k - 1$ (i.e., three) vertical lines L_1, L_2, and L_3 dividing the set into four subsets S_1, S_2, S_3, and S_4, as shown in Fig. 11.15.

The bridge crossing each vertical line is now computed by procedure BRIDGE. This is shown in Fig. 11.16.

Since $p_{xmin} \neq a_1$, procedure UPPER HULL is called recursively to obtain the upper path from p_{xmin} to a_1. Given that $|S_1| \leqslant 4$, the path is found sequentially (and the recursion terminates). Similarly, since $b_1 = a_2$, there is no need to recurse with S_2. Continuing in this fashion, b_2 is found equal to a_3, and the upper path from b_3 to p_{xmax} is

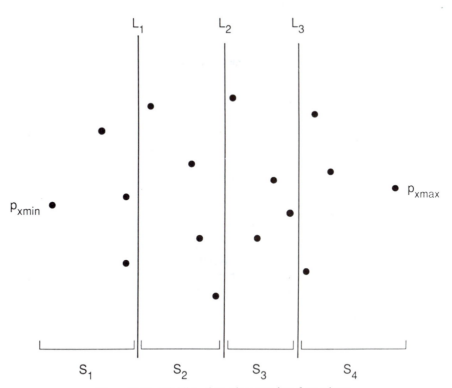

Figure 11.15 Dividing given planar set into four subsets.

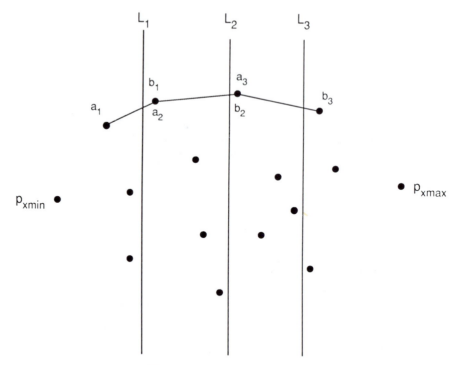

Figure 11.16   Finding three bridges.

obtained sequentially. This yields the upper path from p_{xmin} to p_{xmax} depicted in Fig. 11.13.

In step 3, the lower convex polygonal path is found in the same way, and the two paths are linked to produce the convex hull as shown in Fig. 11.13. □

11.6 PROBLEMS

11.1 Describe formally a (constant-time) sequential algorithm for determining whether a straight-line segment (given by the coordinates of its endpoints) and a vertical straight line (through a given point) intersect.

11.2 Procedure POINT IN POLYGON ignores the following degenerate situations:
  (i) the vertical line through point p passes through vertices of polygon Q,
  (ii) the vertical line through p coincides with edges of Q (i.e., Q has vertical edges), and
  (iii) p coincides with a vertex of Q [this is a special case of (ii)].
  Suggest how the procedure can be modified to handle these situations.

11.3 A planar subdivision with n polygons of $O(n)$ edges each is given. Show that once a preprocessing step requiring $O(n^2 \log n)$ time is performed, the location of an arbitrary data point in the subdivision can be determined in $O(\log n)$ time. Adapt this algorithm to run on a parallel computer.

11.4 Does procedure POINT IN SUBDIVISION extend to subdivisions of spaces in dimensions higher than 2? What about the algorithm in problem 11.3?

11.5 Describe formally a (constant-time) sequential algorithm for determining whether two straight-line segments (given by the coordinates of their endpoints) cross.

11.6 Give a formal statement of the parallel algorithm in section 11.3 for determining whether two polygons intersect.

11.7 Modify the algorithm in problem 11.6 so it produces *one* pair of crossing edges in case the two input polygons intersect.

11.8 Modify the algorithm in problem 11.6 so it produces *all* pairs of crossing edges in case the two input polygons intersect. What is the running time of your algorithm?

11.9 Two *simple* polygons of n edges each are said to intersect if either
(i) one of the two contains the other or
(ii) an edge of one crosses an edge of the other.
Show that it is possible to determine sequentially whether two simple polygons intersect in $O(n \log n)$ time.

11.10 Derive a parallel algorithm based on the approach in problem 11.9.

11.11 Give a formal statement of the parallel algorithm in section 11.4 for determining the closest pair of a set.

11.12 The algorithm in problem 11.11 uses $(n^2/\log n)$ processors. Show that this number can be reduced to $n(n-1)/2 \log n$ without any increase in the algorithm's running time.

11.13 Show that if the Euclidean distance is used, then the closest pair can be determined sequentially in $O(n \log n)$ time.

11.14 Derive a parallel algorithm based on the approach in problem 11.13.

11.15 In section 11.5.2 we stated without proof that two convex polygons with a total of $O(n)$ vertices can be merged sequentially into one convex polygon in $O(n)$ time. Show how this can be done.

11.16 Propose a parallel implementation of procedure SEQUENTIAL CONVEX HULL.

11.17 Give a formal statement of the parallel algorithm in section 11.5.3 for determining the convex hull of a set of planar points.

11.18 Show how to modify the algorithm in problem 11.17 to handle the following special cases:
(i) two points have the same x or y coordinates and
(ii) three or more points fall on the same straight line.

11.19 Show how to modify the algorithm in problem 11.17 to handle the cases where there are fewer than four extreme points, that is, when two or more extreme points coincide (e.g., XMAX = YMAX).

11.20 As stated in section 11.5.3, the algorithm for computing the convex hull relies heavily on the ability to measure angles. Show how to implement the algorithm so that no angle computation is necessary.

11.21 The mesh of trees architecture was used to solve all problems in this chapter. One characteristic of this architecture is that the edges of the trees (linking the rows and the columns) grow in length as they move further from the root. This has two potential disadvantages:
(i) The architecture is neither regular nor modular (in the sense of section 1.3.4.2).

(ii) If the propagation time for a datum along a wire is taken to be linearly proportional to the length of that wire, then our running time analyses (which assume constant propagation time) no longer hold. (For a similar discussion see the conclusion of section 5.3.2.)

Suggest other architectures for solving the problems in sections 11.2–11.5 that enjoy the efficiency of the mesh of trees but do not share its disadvantages.

11.22 Given a set S of points in the plane, design a parallel algorithm for computing CH(S) based on the following property of convex hull vertices: A point P_i of S belongs to CH(S) if p_i does not fall inside the triangle (p_j, p_k, p_m) formed by any three points of S.

11.23 Given a set S of points in the plane, design a parallel algorithm for computing CH(S) based on the following property of convex hull edges: A segment (p_i, p_j) is a convex hull edge if all the remaining $n - 2$ points fall in the same of the two half planes defined by the infinite straight line through p_i and p_j.

11.24 Describe in detail how the linking of UP(S) and LP(S) to obtain CH(S) is performed in step 4 of procedure EREW CONVEX HULL.

11.25 Describe in detail how the $2k - 1$ vertical lines $L_1, L_2, \ldots, L_{2k-1}$ that divide S into $S_1, S_2, \ldots, S_{2k}$ are obtained in step 1 of procedure UPPER HULL.

11.26 Describe formally how procedure UPPER HULL produces its output. Specifically, show how UP(S) is formed.

11.27 Modify procedure UPPER HULL to include the following refinement: Once a bridge (a_i, b_i) is found, all points falling between the two vertical lines through a_i and b_i can be discarded from further consideration as potential upper hull vertices.

11.28 Derive a CREW SM SIMD algorithm for computing the convex hull of a set of n points in the plane in $O(\log n)$ time using n processors.

11.29 Can you design an EREW SM SIMD algorithm with the same properties as the algorithm in problem 11.28?

11.30 Design a parallel algorithm for computing the convex hull of a set of points in a three-dimensional space.

11.31 Two sets of points in the plane are said to be *linearly separable* if a straight line can be found such that the two sets are on different sides of the line. Design a parallel algorithm for testing linear separability.

11.32 Given a set S of n points, design a parallel algorithm for computing a Euclidean minimum spanning tree of S (i.e., a minimum spanning tree, as defined in chapter 10, linking the points of S with rectilinear edges such that the weight of an edge is the Euclidean distance between its endpoints).

11.33 Given a set S of $2n$ points in the plane, design a parallel algorithm for computing a Euclidean minimum-weight perfect matching of S (i.e., a minimum-weight perfect matching, as defined in chapter 10, whose edges are straight-line segments linking pairs of points of S and the weight of an edge is the Euclidean distance between its endpoints).

11.34 A simple polygon Q and two points s and d inside Q are given. The *interior shortest path problem* is to determine the shortest path from s to d that lies completely inside Q. Give a parallel algorithm for solving this problem.

11.35 In problem 3.16 we defined a parallel architecture called the *pyramid*, which is a *binary tree* with the processors at each level connected to form a *linear array*. We may refer to this as a *one-dimensional* pyramid and extend the concept to higher dimensions. For

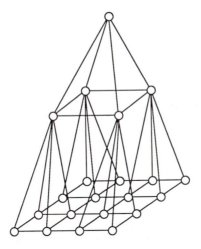

Figure 11.17 Two-dimensional pyramid.

example, a *two-dimensional* pyramid consists of $\frac{4}{3}n - \frac{1}{3}$ processors distributed among $1 + \log_4 n$ levels, where n is a power of 4. All processors at the same level are connected to form a *mesh*. There are n processors at level 0 (also called the *base*) arranged in an $n^{1/2} \times n^{1/2}$ mesh. There is only one processor at level $\log_4 n$ (also called the *apex*). In general, at level i, $0 \leqslant i \leqslant \log_4 n$, the mesh consists of $n/4^i$ processors. A processor at level i, in addition to being connected to its four neighbors at the same level, also has connections to

(i) four children at level $i - 1$ provided $i \geqslant 1$ and

(ii) one parent at level $i + 1$, provided $i \leqslant (\log_4 n) - 1$.

A two-dimensional pyramid for $n = 16$ is shown in Fig. 11.17. As described in example 1.7, a picture can be viewed as a two-dimensional array of *pixels*. For example, each pixel may be given a value representing the color of a corresponding (small) area in the picture. The *position* of a pixel is given by its coordinates (i, j), where i and j are row and column numbers, respectively. A set S of pixels is said to be *convex* if CH(S) does not contain any pixel not belonging to S. Figure 11.18 shows two sets of pixels (identified by an ×); the set in Fig. 11.18(a) is convex, while the one in Fig. 11.18(b) is not. Design a parallel algorithm for the two-dimensional pyramid to determine whether a set of pixels is convex.

11.36 This problem is about *general polygons*, that is, polygons two or more of whose edges *may* cross. We refer to these as *polygons* for short. This class includes simple polygons as a subclass.

(i) Give a definition of the *interior* of a polygon.

(ii) Design a test for *point inclusion* in a polygon.

```
•  •  •  •  •            •  •  •  •  •
•  ×  ×  •  •            •  ×  ×  ×  •
•  ×  ×  •  •            •  ×  •  ×  ×
•  •  ×  ×  •            •  ×  •  ×  ×
•  •  ×  ×  •            •  ×  •  •  •
•  •  •  •  •            •  •  •  •  •
•  •  •  •  •            •  •  •  •  •
```

Figure 11.18 Two sets of pixels.

(iii) Design a test for *polygon inclusion* in a polygon.

(iv) Design a test for *polygon intersection* (of which inclusion is a special case).

(v) Are there efficient parallel versions of (ii)–(iv)?

(vi) Are there applications where nonsimple polygons arise?

11.7 BIBLIOGRAPHICAL REMARKS

Good introductions to sequential algorithms for computational geometry are provided in [Lee], [Mehlhorn], and [Preparata]. Several parallel algorithms for the four problem classes discussed in this chapter have been proposed. They include

(i) algorithms for inclusion problems, in [Atallah 2], [Boxer], and [Chazelle];

(ii) algorithms for intersection problems, in [Aggarwal], [Atallah 2], [Chazelle], [Miller 5], and [Shih];

(iii) algorithms for proximity problems in [Aggarwal], [Atallah 1], [Boxer], [Chazelle], [Dehne 2], [Dyer], [Miller 1], [Miller 3], and [Miller 5]; and

(iv) algorithms for construction problems, in [Aggarwal], [Akl 1], [Akl 2], [Akl 3], [Atallah 2], [Boxer], [Chang], [Chazelle], [Chow 1], [Chow 2], [Dadoun], [Dehne 1], [ElGindy], [Miller 1], [Miller 2], [Miller 3], [Miller 5], and [Nath].

A branch of computer science known as *pattern recognition* studies how computers can be made to recognize visual patterns. It covers a wide range of concerns from the processing of digital pictures to the analysis of patterns that leads eventually to their classification. The role computational geometry can play in pattern recognition is recognized in [Toussaint]. Parallel architectures and algorithms for pattern recognition are described in [Dehne 2], [Dehne 3], [Holt], [Ibrahim], [Kung 1], [Kung 2], [Li], [Miller 2], [Miller 3], [Miller 4], [Preston], [Reeves], [Sankar], [Siegel 1], [Siegel 2], [Siegel 3], [Sklansky], and [Snyder].

11.8 REFERENCES

[AGGARWAL]

Aggarwal, A., Chazelle, B., Guibas, L. J., Ó'Dúnlaing, C., and Yap, C. K., Parallel computational geometry, Proceedings of the 26th Annual IEEE Symposium on Foundations of Computer Science, Portland, Oregon, October 1985, pp. 468–477, IEEE Computer Society, Washington, D.C., 1985.

[AKL 1]

Akl, S. G., A constant-time parallel algorithm for computing convex hulls, *BIT*, Vol. 22, No. 2, 1982, pp. 130–134.

[AKL 2]

Akl, S. G., Optimal parallel algorithms for computing convex hulls and for sorting, *Computing*, Vol. 33, No. 1, 1984, pp. 1–11.

[AKL 3]

Akl, S. G., Optimal parallel algorithms for selection, sorting, and computing convex hulls, in Toussaint, G. T., Ed., *Computational Geometry*, North-Holland, Amsterdam, 1985, pp. 1–22.

[ATALLAH 1]

Atallah, M. J., and Goodrich, M. T., Efficient parallel solutions to some geometric problems, *Journal of Parallel and Distributed Computing*, Vol. 3, 1986, pp. 492–507.

[ATALLAH 2]

Atallah, M. J., and Goodrich, M. T., Efficient plane sweeping in parallel, Proceedings of the 2nd Annual ACM Symposium on Computational Geometry, Yorktown Heights, N.Y., June 1986, pp. 216–225, Association for Computing Machinery, New York, N.Y., 1986.

[BOXER]

Boxer, L., and Miller, R., Parallel dynamic computational geometry, Technical Report No. 87–11, Department of Computer Science, State University of New York, Buffalo, N.Y., August 1987.

[CHANG]

Chang, R. C., and Lee, R. C. T., An $O(N \log N)$ minimal spanning tree algorithm for N points in the plane, *BIT*, Vol. 26, No. 1, 1986, pp. 7–16.

[CHAZELLE]

Chazelle, B., Computational geometry on a systolic chip, *IEEE Transactions on Computers*, Vol. C-33, No. 9, September 1984, pp. 774–785.

[CHOW 1]

Chow, A. L., Parallel algorithms for geometric problems, Ph.D. thesis, Department of Computer Science, University of Illinois, Urbana–Champaign, Illinois, 1980.

[CHOW 2]

Chow, A. L., A parallel algorithm for determining convex hulls of sets of points in two dimensions, Proceedings of the 19th Allerton Conference on Communication, Control and Computing, Monticello, Illinois, October 1981, pp. 214–223, University of Illinois, Urbana–Champaign, Illinois, 1981.

[DADOUN]

Dadoun, N., and Kirkpatrick, D. G., Parallel processing for efficient subdivision search, Proceedings of the 3rd Annual ACM Symposium on Computational Geometry, Waterloo, Ontario, Canada, June 1987, pp. 205–214, Association for Computing Machinery, New York, N.Y., 1987.

[DEHNE 1]

Dehne, F., $O(n^{1/2})$ algorithms for the maximal elements and ECDF searching problem on a mesh-connected parallel computer, *Information Processing Letters*, Vol. 22, No. 6, May 1986, pp. 303–306.

[DEHNE 2]

Dehne, F., Parallel computational geometry and clustering methods, Technical Report No. SCS-TR-104, School of Computer Science, Carleton University, Ottawa, Ontario, December 1986.

[DEHNE 3]

Dehne, F., Sack, J.-R., and Santoro, N., Computing on a systolic screen: Hulls, contours and applications, Technical Report No. SCS-TR-102, School of Computer Science, Carleton University, Ottawa, Ontario, October 1986.

[DYER]

Dyer, C. R., A fast parallel algorithm for the closest pair problem, *Information Processing Letters*, Vol. 11, No. 1, August 1980, pp. 49–52.

[ELGINDY]

ElGindy, H., A parallel algorithm for the shortest-path problem in monotonic polygons, Technical Report No. MS-CIS-86-49, Department of Computer and Information Science, University of Pennsylvania, Philadelphia, June 1986.

[HOLT]

Holt, C. M., Stewart, A., Clint, M., and Perrott, R. H., An improved parallel thinning algorithm, *Communications of the ACM*, Vol. 30, No. 2, February 1987, pp. 156–160.

[IBRAHIM]

Ibrahim, H. A. H., Kender, J. R., and Shaw, D. E., On the application of massively parallel SIMD tree machines to certain intermediate-level vision tasks, *Computer Vision, Graphics, and Image Processing*, Vol. 36, 1986, pp. 53–75.

[KUNG 1]

Kung, H. T., Special-purpose devices for signal and image processing: An opportunity in VLSI, Technical Report No. CMU-CS-80-132, Department of Computer Science, Carnegie-Mellon University, Pittsburgh, July 1980.

[KUNG 2]

Kung, H. T., and Webb, J. A., Mapping image processing operations onto a linear systolic machine, Technical Report No. CMU-CS-86-137, Department of Computer Science, Carnegie-Mellon University, Pittsburgh, March 1986.

[LEE]

Lee, D. T., and Preparata, F. P., Computational geometry: A survey, *IEEE Transactions on Computers*, Vol. C-33, No. 12, December 1984, pp. 1072–1101.

[LI]

Li, Z.-N., and Uhr, L., A pyramidal approach for the recognition of neurons using key features, *Pattern Recognition*, Vol. 19, No. 1, 1986, pp. 55–62.

[MEHLHORN]

Mehlhorn, K., *Multi-dimensional Searching and Computational Geometry*, Springer-Verlag, Berlin, 1984.

[MILLER 1]

Miller, R., and Stout, Q. F., Computational Geometry on a mesh-connected computer, Proceedings of the 1984 International Conference on Parallel Processing, Bellaire, Michigan, August 1984, pp. 66–73, IEEE Computer Society, Washington, D.C., 1984.

[MILLER 2]

Miller, R., and Stout, Q. F., Convexity algorithms for pyramid computers, Proceedings of the 1984 International Conference on Parallel Processing, Bellaire, Michigan, August 1984, pp. 177–184, IEEE Computer Society, Washington, D.C., 1984.

[MILLER 3]

Miller, R., and Stout, Q. F., Geometric algorithms for digitized pictures on a mesh-connected computer, *IEEE Transactions on Pattern Analysis and Machine Intelligence*, Vol. PAMI-7, No. 2, March 1985, pp. 216–228.

[MILLER 4]

Miller, R., and Stout, Q. F., Varying diameter and problem size in mesh connected computers, Proceedings of the 1985 International Conference on Parallel Processing, St. Charles, Illinois, August 1985, pp. 697–699, IEEE Computer Society, Washington, D.C., 1985.

[MILLER 5]

Miller, R., and Stout, Q. F., Mesh computer algorithms for computational geometry, Technical Report No. 86-18, Department of Computer Science, State University of New York, Buffalo, N.Y., July 1986.

[NATH]

Nath, D., Maheshwari, S. N., and Bhatt, P. C. P., Parallel algorithms for the convex hull problem in two dimensions, Technical Report No. EE-8005, Department of Electrical Engineering, Indian Institute of Technology, Delhi, India, October 1980.

[PREPARATA]

Preparata, F. P., and Shamos, M. I., *Computational Geometry*, Springer-Verlag, New York, 1985.

[PRESTON]

Preston, K., and Uhr, L., *Multicomputers and Image Processing*, Academic, New York, 1982.

[REEVES]

Reeves, A. P., Parallel computer architectures for image processing, *Computer Vision, Graphics, and Image Processing*, Vol. 25, 1984, pp. 68–88.

[SANKAR]

Sankar, P. V., and Sharma, C. U., A parallel procedure for the detection of dominant points on a digital curve, *Computer Graphics and Image Processing*, Vol. 7, 1978, pp. 403–412.

[SHIH]

Shih, Z.-C., Chen, G.-H., and Lee, R. C. T., Systolic algorithms to examine all pairs of elements, *Communications of the ACM*, Vol. 30, No. 2, February 1987, pp. 161–167.

[SIEGEL 1]

Siegel, H. J., Siegel, L. J., Kemmerer, F. C., Mueller, P. T. Smalley, H. E., and Smith, S. D., PASM: A partitionable SIMD/MIMD system for image processing and pattern recognition, *IEEE Transactions on Computers*, Vol. C-30, No. 12, December 1981, pp. 934–947.

[SIEGEL 2]

Siegel, L. J., Image processing on a partitionable SIMD machine, in Duff, M. J. B., and Levialdi, S., Eds., *Languages and Architectures for Image Processing*, Academic, London, 1981, pp. 293–300.

[SIEGEL 3]

Siegel, L. J., Siegel, H. J., and Feather, A. E., Parallel processing approaches to image correlation, *IEEE Transactions on Computers*, Vol. C-31, No. 3, March 1982, pp. 208–218.

[SKLANSKY]

Sklansky, J. Cordella, L. P., and Levialdi, S., Parallel detection of concavities in cellular blobs, *IEEE Transactions on Computers*, Vol. C-25, No. 2, February 1976, pp. 187–195.

[SNYDER]

Snyder, L., Jamieson, L. H., Gannon, D. B., and Siegel, H. J., Eds., *Algorithmically Specialized Parallel Computers*, Academic, Orlando, Florida, 1985.

[TOUSSAINT]

Toussaint, G. T., Pattern recognition and geometrical complexity, Proceedings of the 5th International Conference on Pattern Recognition, Vol. 2, Miami Beach, Florida, December 1980, pp. 1324–1347, IEEE Computer Society, Washington, D.C., 1980.

12

Traversing Combinatorial Spaces

12.1 INTRODUCTION

Many combinatorial problems can be solved by generating and searching a special graph known as a *state-space graph*. This method, aptly called *state-space traversal*, differs from the searching algorithms discussed in chapter 5 in that the data structure searched is not a list but rather a *graph*. Furthermore, state-space traversal differs from the graph search techniques of chapter 10 in that the graph is generated *while* it is being searched. There are two reasons for not generating a state-space graph in full and *then* searching it. First, a state space is typically very large and there may not be enough memory to store it. Second, assuming we can afford it, generating a full state space would be wasteful (both in terms of space and time), as only a small subgraph is usually needed to obtain a solution to the problem.

There are three types of nodes in a state-space graph:

1. the *origin* (or *start*) node(s) representing the initial conditions of the problem to be solved;
2. the *goal* (or *final*) node(s) representing the desired state of the problem; and
3. *intermediate* nodes representing states of the problem arrived at by applying some transformation to the origin.

Each edge in the graph is a transition that transforms one state of the problem to another. A solution to the problem is given by a path from an origin to a goal. The processes of generating and searching the state-space graph are governed by problem-dependent rules.

Example 12.1

A set of integers $S = \{s_1, s_2, \ldots, s_n\}$ is given along with an integer B. It is required to determine whether a subset S' of S exists such that

$$\sum_{s_i \in S'} s_i = B.$$

This problem, known as the *subset sum problem*, can be solved by traversing a state-space graph. The origin represents the empty set. Intermediate nodes represent subsets of *S*. A goal node represents a subset the sum of whose elements equals *B*.

For concreteness, let $S = \{15, 7, 19, 3, 6\}$ and $B = 16$. The state-space graph that is actually traversed for this instance of the subset sum problem is shown in Fig. 12.1. Intermediate nodes that cannot possibly lead to a goal node are marked with an ×. There is only one goal node, marked with a *G*.   □

Our purpose in this chapter is to show how a state space can be traversed in parallel. We choose one particular problem for illustration, namely, state spaces

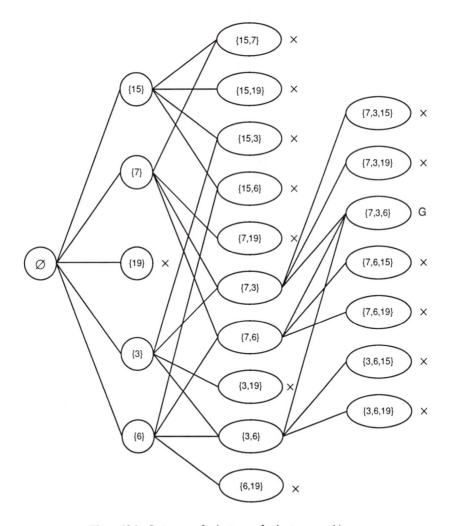

Figure 12.1   State space for instance of subset sum problem.

generated and searched by programs that play games with clear rules and goals, that is, *games of strategy*. In particular, we are concerned with games that

1. are played on a *board* on which pieces are placed and moved;
2. are played by exactly *two* players;
3. are *zero-sum* games, in the sense that one player's gain equals the other player's loss—the outcome for a player is either a win, a loss, or a draw;
4. involve no element of *chance*;
5. are *perfect-information* games, in the sense that at any point during the game each player knows everything there is to know about the current status of both players and no detail is hidden.

Examples of games satisfying these properties are *checkers*, *chess*, and *go*. Examples of games that do not satisfy one or more of these properties are *backgammon* (which violates the fourth property) and *poker* (which may violate all properties). In the remainder of this chapter we use the term *game* to refer to a game of strategy satisfying these five properties. Most computer programs that play games generate and search state spaces that have the characteristic of being *trees*. We shall refer to these as *game trees*.

In section 12.2 a brief introduction is provided to a sequential algorithm for traversing game trees and the associated terminology. The basic principles used in the design of a parallel implementation of this algorithm are given in section 12.3. The parallel algorithm itself is described in section 12.4. In section 12.5 various aspects of the algorithm are analyzed.

12.2 SEQUENTIAL TREE TRAVERSAL

Assume that we want to program a computer to play a game. The computer is given

(i) a representation of the board and pieces;
(ii) a description of the initial configuration, that is, the locations of the various pieces on the board when the game begins;
(iii) a procedure for generating all legal moves from a given position of the game;
(iv) an algorithm for selecting one of the (possibly many) available moves;
(v) a method for *making* the selected move from the current position, that is, a method for updating a given board configuration; and
(vi) a way of recognizing a winning, losing, or drawing position.

All of these ingredients of a game-playing program are usually straightforward, with the exception of (iv). It is the move selection algorithm that in general makes the difference between a program that plays well and one that plays poorly. For example, a program that selects every one of its moves at random cannot possibly perform well in a consistent way. The better game-playing programs utilize sophisticated techniques for choosing their moves. One such technique is based on generating and searching a game tree, an example of which is shown in Fig. 12.2. The figure illustrates the game tree generated for the game of *tic-tac-toe* from some configuration.

In a game tree, *nodes* correspond to board *positions* and *branches* correspond to *moves*. The *root node* represents the board position from which the program (whose turn it is to play) is required to make a move. A node is at *ply* (or *depth*) k if it is at a distance of k branches from the root. A node at ply k, which has branches leaving it and entering nodes at ply $k + 1$, is called a *nonterminal* node; otherwise the node is *terminal*. A nonterminal node at ply k is connected by branches to its *offspring* at ply $k + 1$. Thus the offspring of the root represent positions reached by moves from the initial board; offspring of these represent positions reached by the opponent's replies, offspring of these represent positions reached by replies to the replies, and so on. The number of branches leaving a nonterminal node is the *fan-out* of that node.

A *complete* game tree represents all possible plays of the game. Each path from the root to a terminal node corresponds to a complete game with the root representing the initial configuration and each terminal node representing an *end-*

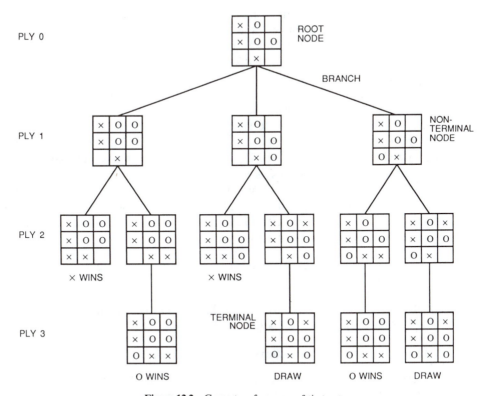

Figure 12.2 Game tree for game of tic-tac-toe.

game configuration, that is, a win for player 1, a win for player 2, or a draw. It has been estimated that a complete game tree of checkers, for example, contains approximately 10^{40} nonterminal nodes. Assuming that a program is capable of generating 10^9 such nodes per second, it would still require in the vicinity of 10^{21} centuries in order to generate the whole tree. Trees for chess and go would require even longer times to generate in full.

The observation made in the previous paragraph is generally true, even starting from a position other than the initial configuration. A tree whose root represents a position near the middle of a chess game, for example, would have approximately 10^{75} terminal nodes representing all end-game configurations. Instead, game-playing programs search an *incomplete* tree. The depth of such a tree is limited and, in addition, it is often the case that not all paths are explored. In an incomplete tree, terminal nodes are those appearing at some predefined ply k or less and do not necessarily represent positions for which the game ends. An *evaluation function* is used to assign a *score* to each of the positions represented by terminal nodes. This score is an estimate of the "goodness" of the position from the program's viewpoint and is obtained by computing and then combining a number of parameters. For most board games, *center control* and *mobility* of certain pieces are examples of such parameters.

An algorithm, known as the *alpha–beta algorithm*, is then used to move these scores back up the tree. In doing so, the alpha–beta algorithm may also eliminate some nodes of the game tree without assigning scores to them, as explained in what follows. When all the offspring of the root have been assigned back-up scores, the program chooses the move that appears to be best (in light of this incomplete information).

Once this move is made and the opponent has replied, the program generates and searches a new tree from the current position to determine its next move. Note that game trees, like all state spaces, are generated while they are searched, as mentioned in the beginning of this chapter. A so-called *depth-first search* is usually followed to traverse game trees: It starts by generating a complete path from the root to the leftmost terminal node; search then resumes from the latest nonterminal node on the path whose offspring have not all been generated or eliminated by the alpha–beta algorithm. Search continues (in this left-to-right manner) until all nodes—up to some depth k— have been either generated or eliminated. It remains to describe how the alpha–beta algorithm works.

The Alpha–Beta Algorithm. The alpha–beta algorithm performs a dual role:

(i) moving scores up the tree from the terminal nodes and, in doing so,
(ii) eliminating parts of the tree by determining that they need not be generated.

In backing up scores from terminal nodes, the *minimax principle* is invoked:

(i) Nodes at even ply (corresponding to positions from which the program is to select a move) attempt to *maximize* the program's gain while

(ii) nodes at odd ply (corresponding to positions from which the program's opponent is to select a move) attempt to minimize the program's gain.

Initially, every nonterminal node generated is assigned an *initial alpha–beta score* of $-\infty$ $(+\infty)$ if the node is at even (odd) ply. As mentioned earlier, every terminal node generated is assigned a *static score* obtained from an evaluation function. A *temporary alpha–beta score* is assigned to a nonterminal node while its offspring are being explored. If the node is at even (odd) ply, then its temporary score is equal to the maximum (minimum) of the *final* scores that have so far been assigned to its offspring. Final scores are defined as follows:

1. A static score assigned to a terminal node is final and
2. the final score of a nonterminal node is the score it receives when each of its offspring has either been assigned a final score or been eliminated (as explained in the following).

The process of backing up scores from terminal nodes is illustrated in Fig. 12.3. The figure shows the portion of a game tree that has already been generated. Square and

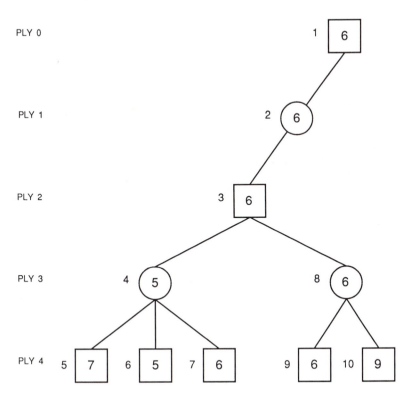

Figure 12.3 Backing up scores from terminal nodes.

circle nodes represent positions from which the first and second players are to make a move, respectively. The number beside each node indicates the order in which the node was generated by the algorithm. Also shown inside the nodes are temporary and final scores. Static scores are obtained using some evaluation function. Assuming that the nodes at plies 1, 2, and 3 have no further offspring, all scores at plies 1, 2, 3, and 4 are final. The score associated with the nonterminal node at ply 0 is temporary, assuming that further offspring of this node need to be generated and assigned final scores.

The scores are stored in a *score table*: Entry i of this table holds the score for a node under consideration at ply i. Figure 12.4 illustrates the contents of the score table as the tree in Fig. 12.3 is being traversed.

By its nature, the alpha–beta algorithm makes it unnecessary to obtain scores for all nodes in the game tree in order to assign a final score to the root. In fact, whole subtrees can be removed from further consideration by means of so-called *cutoffs*. To illustrate this point, consider the two portions of game trees shown in Fig. 12.5. In both trees some of the nodes have received a final score (and are labeled with that score), whereas the remaining nodes (labeled with a letter) are still waiting for a final score to be assigned to them. From the preceding discussion, the final score of the root node in Fig. 12.5(a) is obtained from

$$u = \max\{5, v\}, \quad \text{where } v = \min\{4, \dots\}.$$

Clearly $u = 5$ regardless of the value of v. It follows that the remaining offspring of the

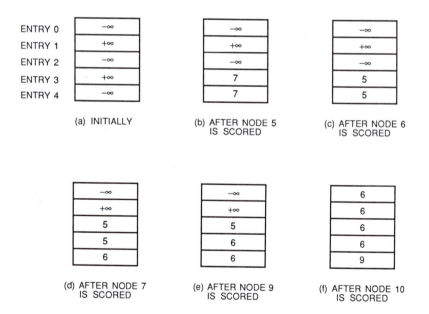

Figure 12.4 Contents of score table while tree in Fig. 12.3 is traversed.

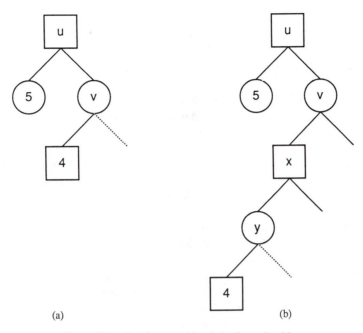

(a)   (b)

Figure 12.5   Cutoffs created by alpha–beta algorithm.

node labeled v need not be explored any further. We say that a *shallow cutoff* has occurred. A similar reasoning applies to the tree in Fig. 12.5(b), where the value of u can be obtained regardless of the exact value of y. Again it follows that the remaining offspring of the node labeled y can be ignored: This is called a *deep cutoff*.

When a final score is eventually assigned to the root, the search terminates. By definition, the score was backed up during the search from one of the root's offspring to the root. Thus the branch leading from the root to that offspring corresponds to the move chosen by the alpha–beta algorithm. Note that, upon termination of the traversal, the algorithm in fact determines the *principal continuation*, that is, the best sequence of moves found for both players to follow based on searching a tree of limited depth.

The preceding concepts constitute the foundation upon which our parallel algorithm is constructed. In the following section we show how an interesting property of the sequential alpha–beta algorithm is used profitably in the parallel version.

12.3 BASIC DESIGN PRINCIPLES

In this section we describe the main ideas behind

    (i) the parallel algorithm,
    (ii) the model of computation to be used,

(iii) the objectives motivating the design, and

(iv) the methods adopted to achieve these objectives.

12.3.1 The Minimal Alpha–Beta Tree

A game tree is said to be *uniform* if all of its nonterminal nodes have the same number of offspring and all of its terminal nodes are at the same distance from the root. Since the number of offspring is equal for all nonterminal nodes, it is referred to as the *fan-out of the tree*. Similarly, the distance of terminal nodes to the root is called the *depth of the tree*. The uniform tree of Fig. 12.6, for example, has a fan-out of 3 and a depth of 2.

    A game tree is *perfectly ordered* if the best move for each player from any position is always provided by the leftmost branch leaving the node representing that position. In such a tree it is guaranteed that only a subset of the nodes needs to be generated in order to determine the principal continuation. Consider, for example, the uniform tree in Fig. 12.7, which has a fan-out f equal to 3 and a depth d also equal to 3.

    In this tree, the terminal nodes shown with a score (and only these terminal nodes) must be examined by the alpha–beta algorithm to reach a decision about the best move for the player at the root. The tree shown in bold lines and called the *minimal tree* is the one actually generated by the algorithm. The remaining nodes and branches (drawn with thin lines) are cut off (i.e., they are not generated). Note that for this tree

(i) the scores shown for nonterminal nodes are final and

(ii) the principal continuation is given by the sequence of branches leading from the root to the terminal node labeled 30.

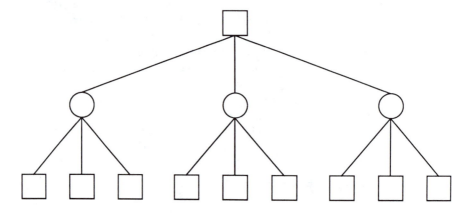

Figure 12.6   Uniform tree.

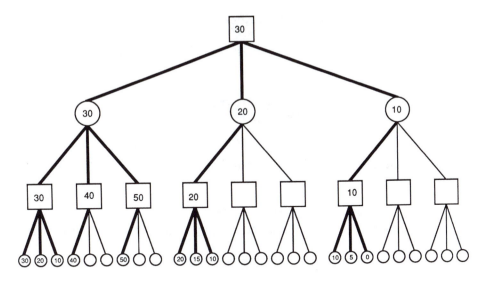

Figure 12.7   Perfectly ordered game tree.

In general, for a perfectly ordered uniform tree, the number of terminal nodes generated and assigned a score by the alpha–beta algorithm is equal to

$$M(f, d) = f^{\lceil d/2 \rceil} + f^{\lfloor d/2 \rfloor} - 1.$$

Thus $M(f, d)$ represents a lower bound on the number of nodes scored by the alpha–beta algorithm for a uniform tree that is not necessarily perfectly ordered. This fact represents the basis of our parallel implementation of the alpha–beta algorithm: Assuming that the tree to be traversed is perfectly ordered, those nodes that *have* to be scored are visited first *in parallel*. Once all cutoffs have taken place, the remaining subtrees are again searched in parallel.

12.3.2 Model of Computation

The algorithm is designed to run on an EREW SM MIMD computer with a number of processors operating asynchronously. A processor can initiate another processor, send a message to another processor, or wait for a message from another processor. Apart from these interactions, all of which take place through shared memory, processors proceed independently. As usual, the MIMD algorithm is viewed as a collection of processes. A process is created for each node generated. Its job is to traverse the tree rooted at that node. The number of processors is independent of the number of processes.

12.3.3 Objectives and Methods

The algorithm is designed with two objectives in mind:

1. to minimize the running time of the search and
2. to perform as many cutoffs as possible, thereby minimizing the cost of the search (total number of operations).

In order to achieve these goals, a distinction is made among the offspring of a node. The leftmost offspring of a node is called the *left offspring*. The subtree containing the left offspring is called the *left subtree*, and the process that traverses this subtree is the *left process*. All other offspring of a node are called *right offspring* and are contained in *right subtrees* that are searched by *right processes*. This is illustrated in Fig. 12.8, where L and R indicate left and right offspring, respectively. Note that the root is labeled with an L.

A high-level description of the algorithm consists of two stages.

Stage 1: The tree is traversed recursively by

(i) traversing recursively the left subtree of the root and
(ii) traversing the left subtree only of each right offspring of the root.

This stage assigns

(i) a final score to every left offspring and
(ii) a temporary score to every right offspring (which is the final score of its left offspring).

Stage 2: If the temporary score of a node cannot create a cutoff, then the right subtrees of this node are traversed one at a time until they all have been either visited or cut off.

The preceding description is now refined by explaining the mechanism of process creation. We mentioned earlier that a process is associated with every node generated. The tree traversal and process creation proceed as follows. The process associated with a node z spawns a left process to traverse the left subtree of z. This process is associated with the left offspring of z. In turn it spawns left and right processes to search all of the left offspring's subtrees. This continues until a final score is assigned to the left offspring of z and backed up, as a temporary score, to z. Concurrently to the traversal of the left subtree of z, a temporary value is obtained for each of the right offspring of z. These scores are then compared to the final score of the left offspring and cutoffs are made where appropriate.

The temporary score for a right offspring w is obtained as follows. The process associated with w spawns a process to traverse its left subtree. This new process

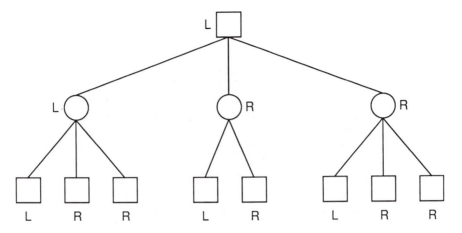

Figure 12.8   Distinction between left and right offspring of node.

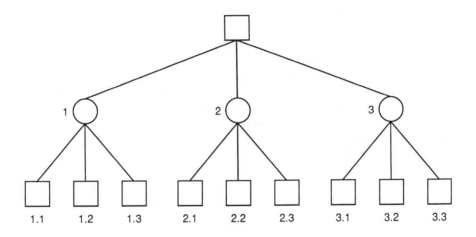

Figure 12.9   Process creation during tree traversal.

traverses the subtree, backs up a score to w, and terminates. If after a cutoff check the traversal of the right subtree rooted at w is to continue, then a process is generated to traverse the next subtree of w. This procedure continues until either the subtree rooted at w is exhaustively traversed or the search is cut off.

The foregoing description is illustrated in Fig. 12.9. Here the process associated with the root generates processes 1, 2, and 3. Process 1 being a left process generates processes 1.1, 1.2, and 1.3 to traverse all of the subtrees of the left offspring of the root. Processes 2 and 3 are right processes and therefore generate only processes to search the left subtrees of the right offspring of the root, namely, processes 2.1 and 3.1, respectively. This concludes stage 1. Only if necessary, (one or both) processes 2.2 and

3.2 followed by (one or both) processes 2.3 and 3.3 are created in stage 2. Note that after generating other processes, a process suspends itself and waits for these to back up a value.

It is clear that by applying this method those nodes that must be examined by the alpha–beta algorithm will be visited first. This ensures that needless work is not done in stage 1 of the algorithm. Also, a cutoff check is performed before processes are generated in stage 2 to search subtrees that may be cut off.

As mentioned earlier, game trees are typically very large, and it is reasonable to assume that there will be more processes created than there are processors available on the MIMD computer. However, let us assume for the sake of argument that there are more processors than processes. It may be possible in this case to reduce the running time of the tree traversal by generating processes to traverse the subtrees of a right offspring in parallel using the idle processors. This brute-force approach is not used since it conflicts with the other aim of our design, namely, minimizing the cost of the search. The cost of any tree traversal consists mainly in the cost of updating the board in moving from parent to offspring and in the cost of assigning a temporary or final value to a node. Therefore, even though our algorithm may leave some processors idle in this hypothetical situation, the overall cost in operations is minimized by not traversing subtrees that may not have to be traversed.

Process Priority.   We conclude this section by describing how processes are assigned priorities when deciding which is to be executed by an available processor. As already explained, left subtrees are searched exhaustively by the parallel algorithm, while initially only a single temporary value is obtained from each right subtree. In order to accomplish this, left processes should be given higher priority than right processes. Also, since scores must be obtained from terminal nodes, processes associated with the deepest nodes in the tree should be given preference. Any formula

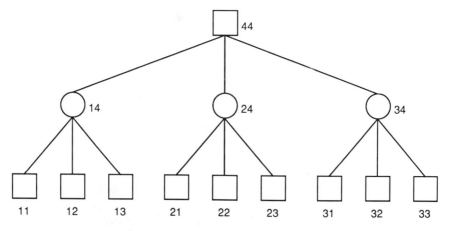

Figure 12.10   Assigning priorities to processes.

for labeling nodes that assigns all offspring a higher priority than their parent and left offspring a higher priority than their right siblings can be used. A process then adopts the priority of the node with which it is associated. One example of such a formula for uniform trees follows. It assigns a priority to a newly generated node as a function of the priority of its parent:

$$\text{priority(offspring)} = \text{priority(parent)} - (f + 1 - i) \times 10^{a(d - \text{ply} - 1)},$$

where

$\quad f$ = fan-out of the tree,

$\quad d$ = depth of the tree,

$\quad i$ = offspring's position among its siblings in a left-to-right order, $1 \leqslant i \leqslant f$,

ply = ply of parent,

and a is such that $10^{a-1} < f < 10^a$. The priority of the root is given by

$$\text{priority(root)} = \sum_{j=1}^{d} (f + 1) \times 10^{a(d - j)}.$$

Note that the smaller the integer returned by this formula, the higher the priority. An example of this priority assignment is shown in Fig. 12.10.

12.4 THE ALGORITHM

This section provides a formal description of the parallel alpha–beta algorithm as implemented on an EREW SM MIMD computer. We begin by defining three aspects of the implementation.

12.4.1 Procedures and Processes

An MIMD algorithm is a collection of procedures and processes. Syntactically, a process is the same as a procedure. Furthermore, both a procedure and a process can call other procedures and create other processes. Where the two differ is in the semantics. In the parallel alpha–beta algorithm, we shall distinguish between processes and procedures in the following way:

(i) When a procedure is called, control is transferred from the calling context to the procedure.

(ii) When a process is invoked, it is initiated to run asynchronously, and the invoking context continues execution.

12.4.2 Semaphores

Semaphores are used by the algorithm for process communication and synchronization. Here a semaphore consists of an integer value and a queue of processes.

When a semaphore is declared, it is initialized to have a value 0 and a null queue. There are two operations allowed on semaphores, denoted by U and V.

1. Operation U examines the integer value:
   (i) If it is greater than zero, it decrements it by 1, and the process doing the U operation proceeds.
   (ii) If the value is zero, the process doing the U operation suspends itself and enters the queue.
2. Operation V examines the queue:
   (i) If it is nonempty, it lets the first waiting process continue.
   (ii) If no processes are waiting, the integer value is incremented by 1.
   Both U and V are indivisible operations.

12.4.3 Score Tables

In the parallel alpha–beta algorithm, many parts of the tree are traversed simultaneously. Therefore, a single global score table cannot be used as in the sequential case. Instead, an individual score table is assigned to each node when a process is generated to search the subtree rooted at that node. This table is initialized to the values in the score table of the node's parent.

   We are now ready to state the parallel alpha–beta algorithm. The algorithm is given in what follows as procedure MIMD ALPHA BETA together with the procedures and processes it uses. Some of the procedures are entirely game dependent and therefore are not fully specified.

procedure MIMD ALPHA BETA (Board, Depth, Principal Continuation)

{This procedure uses three variables
   Board: a description of the board configuration from which a move is to be made,
   Depth: the depth to which the tree is to be traversed,
   Root Table: the root's score table;
and three semaphores
   RootTableFree, RootHandled, and LeftOffspringDone.}

Step 1:   (1.1) Read Board and Depth
          (1.2) Initialize RootTable
          (1.3) V(RootTableFree).

Step 2:   {Create a process to begin the search}
          HANDLE (Board, **true**, **true**, **false**, 0, RootTable, RootHandled,
               LeftOffspringDone).

Step 3:   {Has the root been assigned a final score?}
          U (RootHandled).

Step 4:   Output the Principal Continuation.   □

process HANDLE (Board, MyTurn, Left, ParentLeft, Ply, ParentTable, Done, LeftSiblingDone)

{This process uses the following variables
  MyTurn: **true** if ply is even, **false** otherwise,
  Left: **true** if the process is a left process, **false** otherwise,
  ParentLeft: **true** if the parent process is a left process, **false** otherwise,
  Ply: the ply number,
  ParentTable: the parent's score table,
  MyTable: the score table created automatically when this process was invoked, and initialized to the parent's core table;
and three semaphores
  Done, LeftSiblingDone, and MyTableFree.}

  Step 1: {If this is a terminal node, score it; otherwise, generate its offspring}
        (1.1) V(MyTableFree)
        (1.2) **if** Ply = Depth
            then SCORE (Board, MyTable)
            else GENERATE (Board)
            end if.

  Step 2: {Update parent's score table}
        UPDATE (ParentTable).

  Step 3: **if** Left **and** ParentLeft
        then V (LeftSiblingDone)
        end if.

  Step 4: V(Done).   □

procedure SCORE (Board, Table)

    {This procedure evaluates the given board configuration (Board) associated with a terminal node and puts the resulting static score in the given score table (Table). The evaluation function is game dependent and is left unspecified.}   □

procedure GENERATE (Board)

    {This procedure searches a subtree rooted at a nonterminal node. It calls procedure GENERATE MOVES to produce a list of moves from the current position. The moves are stored in an array Moves whose ith location is denoted Moves [i]. The number of moves is kept in the variable NumberMoves. OffspringDone and LeftOffspringDone are semaphores. Procedure APPLY is then used to apply each of the generated moves to the given Board thereby producing board configurations for its offspring. Variable NewBoard is used to store each new configuration. The variable Cutoff is assigned the value **true** if a cutoff is to occur, **false** otherwise.}

    Step 1: GENERATE MOVES (Board, Moves, NumberMoves).

    Step 2: {If the root of the subtree to be searched is a left node, then process HANDLE is invoked once for each offspring. The processes thus created run concurrently and procedure GENERATE waits until they all terminate}
            if Left

then (2.1) **for** $l = 1$ **to** NumberMoves **do**

      (i) APPLY (Board, Moves[l], NewBoard)

      (ii) HANDLE (NewBoard, **not** MyTurn, $l = 1$, Left, Ply $+ 1$, MyTable,
                        OffspringDone, LeftOffspringDone)

    end for

(2.2) **for** $l = 1$ **to** NumberMoves **do**

    U (OffspringDone)

end for

{If the root of the subtree to be searched is a right node, then its offspring are searched in sequence by calling process HANDLE for one of them, waiting for it to complete, and performing a cutoff check before handling the next offspring}

else (2.3) Cutoff $\leftarrow$ **false**

(2.4) $l \leftarrow 1$

(2.5) **while** ($l \leqslant$ NumberMoves **and not** Cutoff) **do**

      (i) APPLY (Board, Moves[l], NewBoard)

      (ii) HANDLE (NewBoard, **not** MyTurn, $l = 1$, Left, Ply $+ 1$, MyTable,
                         OffspringDone, LeftOffspringDone)

      (iii) U (OffspringDone)

      (iv) {Has the leftmost sibling received a final score?}
           U (LeftSiblingDone)

      (v) V (LeftSiblingDone)

      (vi) **if** (Ply is odd) **and** (offspring's score $\leqslant$ parent's score)
           then Cutoff $\leftarrow$ **true**
           else if (Ply is even) **and** (offspring's score $\geqslant$ parent's score)
               then Cutoff $\leftarrow$ **true**
               end if
           end if

      (vii) $l \leftarrow l + 1$

    end while

end if. □

procedure UPDATE (ParentTable)

{This procedure waits until the parent's score table is free. Then, if the score calculated for the current node improves on the parent's score, it is copied into the parent's score table. The semaphore ParentTableFree is used. This semaphore is created and initialized simultaneously with variable ParentTable.}

Step 1: U (ParentTableFree).

Step 2:   Copy value if applicable.

Step 3: V (ParentTableFree). □

procedure GENERATE MOVES (Board, Moves, NumberMoves)

{This procedure produces all the legal moves from a position given by variable Board, stores them in array Moves, and sets variable NumberMoves to their number. The procedure is game dependent and is therefore left unspecified.} □

procedure APPLY (Board, Moves, NewBoard)

{This procedure changes the current position given by variable Board by making the move received in variable Moves. The result is a new board configuration NewBoard. The procedure is game dependent and is therefore left unspecified.}   □

12.5 ANALYSIS AND EXAMPLES

As it is the case with most MIMD algorithms, the running time of procedure MIMD ALPHA BETA is best analyzed empirically. In this section we examine two other aspects of the procedure's performance.

1. One of the design objectives stated in section 12.3.3 is to increase the number of cutoffs as much as possible. How does the parallel implementation perform in this respect compared with the sequential version?
2. What amount of shared memory is needed by the algorithm?

In answering these two questions, we also present some examples that illustrate the behavior of procedure MIMD ALPHA BETA.

12.5.1 Parallel Cutoffs

In order to answer the first question, we shall invoke the distinction made in section 12.2 between shallow and deep cutoffs. In the following discussion we use "sequential search" and "parallel search" to refer to the sequential alpha–beta algorithm and procedure MIMD ALPHA BETA, respectively.

Shallow Cutoffs

1. All shallow cutoffs that would occur in a sequential search due to the (temporary) score backed up to a node from its left offspring are also caused by procedure MIMD ALPHA BETA. This is because all (temporary) scores obtained for the right offspring of the node are compared to the score backed up from its left offspring for a cutoff check before the right subtree traversal continues. An example illustrating this situation is shown in Fig. 12.11. During stage 1 of the parallel algorithm,

(i) the left subtree of the root is searched exhaustively resulting in the root being assigned (temporarily) the final score of its left offspring (i.e., 8) and

(ii) the two right subtrees are partially searched resulting in temporary scores of 3 and 5 being assigned to the first and second right offspring of the root, respectively.

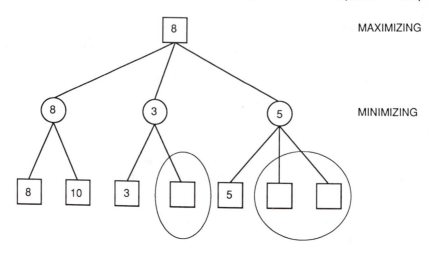

Figure 12.11 Shallow cutoff detected by both sequential search and procedure MIMD ALPHA BETA.

At the beginning of stage 2 it is determined that the circled sections of the two right subtrees are cut off in exactly the same way as in sequential traversal.

A right subtree that is exhaustively searched during stage 2 without cutoff compares its final score to the temporary score of the parent and changes the parent's score if necessary. Consequently, any cutoff that would have occurred in other right subtrees due to the score originally backed up to the parent from its left offspring will also occur with the new score backed up to the parent from a right offspring.

2. Some shallow cutoffs that would occur in a sequential search can be missed by procedure MIMD ALPHA BETA due to the way in which processes are generated. In the example of Fig. 12.12, a sequential search would cut off the circled portion of the tree. Parallel search misses the cutoff since a process is created to search that subtree before the right subtree of the root completes its search and updates the root's score to 7.

3. Some cutoffs that are missed in a sequential search may occur in procedure MIMD ALPHA BETA due to the way in which processes are generated. A right subtree search that terminates early and causes a change in the parent's score may cause cutoffs in other right subtrees that would not occur in a sequential search. This situation is illustrated in Fig. 12.13, where both right offspring of the root compare their initial scores of 6 and 7, respectively, to the final score of the left offspring, that is, 5. Neither right subtree search is cut off, so processes are generated to continue that search. But since the second right offspring of the root has no further offspring of its own to be examined, its score of 7 is final, and because 7 > 5, that score is backed up to the root. Now, when the terminal node labeled 8 has been scored and the process at the first right offspring of the root performs a cutoff check before proceeding, this time a cutoff occurs. The portion of the tree that is cut off is shown circled in Fig. 12.13; this portion is not cut off during a sequential search.

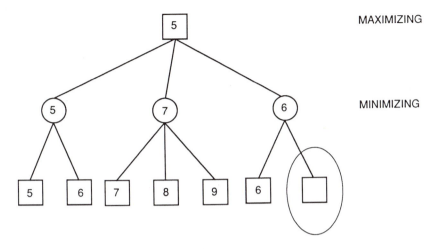

MAXIMIZING

MINIMIZING

Figure 12.12 Shallow cutoff missed by procedure MIMD ALPHA BETA.

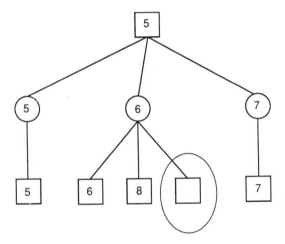

Figure 12.13 Shallow cutoff missed in sequential search and discovered by procedure MIMD ALPHA BETA.

Deep Cutoffs.   In order for deep cutoffs to occur at a node, scores from searches of other parts of the tree must be available. In a sequential search the scores at each ply are known to every node and are stored in a single global score table. In procedure MIMD ALPHA BETA this is impossible, as stated in the previous section. We now show briefly why this is the case. Assume that a single global score table was used. In Fig. 12.14(a) nodes 1 and 2 are scored simultaneously. Suppose that node 2 receives its score first, as shown in Fig. 12.14(c). This means that the right offspring of the root is backed up the score 9 at ply 1 and *then* the left offspring is backed up the score 6 (overwriting the score table value of 9 at ply 1). Now when node 3 is scored, the value 8 will not be recorded in the table at ply 1 (since 8 > 6 and we are minimizing at ply 1). Therefore, the value of 8 will not be backed up to the root as it would be in the

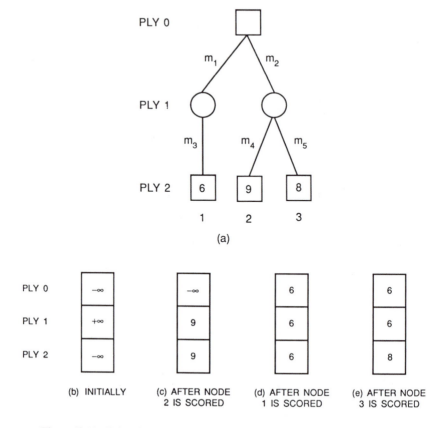

Figure 12.14   Using single score table in parallel search leads to incorrect results.

sequential search. As a result, the best sequence of moves from the root, namely, (m_2, m_5), is not returned; instead (m_1, m_3) is returned.

We conclude from the discussion that having a single score table is impossible in parallel search as it would lead to incorrect results. The alternative adopted by procedure MIMD ALPHA BETA is to assign to each node created its own score table; this, however, means that the information necessary for a deep cutoff to occur is not available in general, as shown in the following example.

Example 12.2

Figure 12.15 illustrates a deep cutoff occurring in a sequential search: The circled portion is cut off due to the score of the root's left subtree being available in the score table, while the root's right subtree is searched.

This deep cutoff cannot occur in procedure MIMD ALPHA BETA, as shown in Fig. 12.16: Each node of the right subtree has a score table initialized to the score table of its parent and not containing the score of the root's left offspring.

□

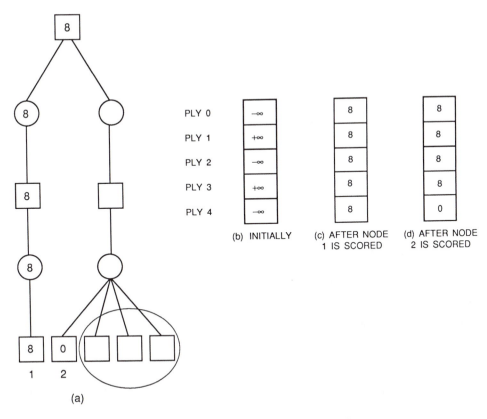

Figure 12.15   Deep cutoff in sequential search.

12.5.2 Storage Requirements

This section presents an analysis of the storage requirements of procedure **MIMD ALPHA BETA**. We begin by deriving an upper bound on the amount of storage needed by the procedure under the assumption that an infinite number of processors is available. A more realistic estimate of the storage requirements is then derived by fixing the number of processors used during the search.

Unlimited Processors.   Recall that the procedure makes a crucial distinction between the leftmost offspring of a node and the remaining offspring of that node. During stage 1, knowledge about the behavior of the sequential version is used to explore several paths in parallel. During each iteration of stage 2, several subtrees are searched in parallel, each subtree, however, being searched sequentially. This is illustrated in Figs. 12.17 and 12.18.

In Fig. 12.17 a uniform tree is shown whose depth and fan-out are both equal to 3. The paths explored in parallel during stage 1 are indicated by bold lines. Calling the

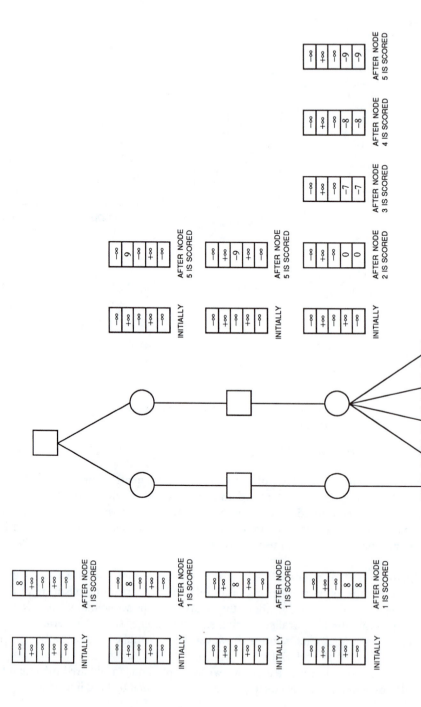

Figure 12.16 Deep cutoff missed by procedure MIMD ALPHA BETA.

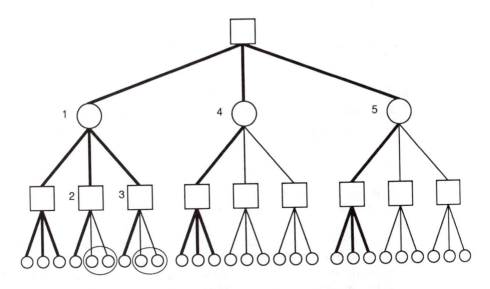

Figure 12.17   Subtrees traversed during stage 1 and first iteration of stage 2.

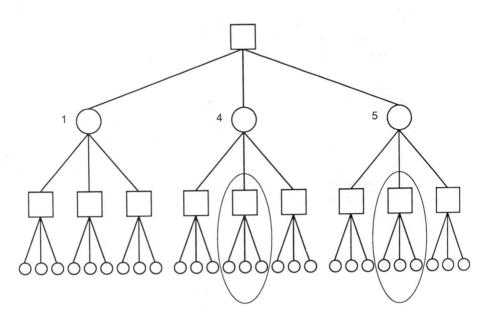

Figure 12.18   Subtrees traversed during second iteration of stage 2.

root a left node, it is clear that *left offspring* and their *right offspring* are given priority by the procedure. Nodes explored during stage 1 will therefore be known as *primary* nodes, that is, nodes at which a process is created during stage 1 to do the search. Formally:

1. The root is a primary left offspring,
2. a primary left offspring at ply k is the left offspring of a primary (left or right) offspring at ply $k - 1$, and
3. a primary right offspring at ply k is a right offspring of a primary left offspring at ply $k - 1$.

Following stage 1, the temporary score backed up at node 1 is compared with the ones at nodes 2 and 3; if the former is smaller, then the unexplored portions of the subtrees rooted at 2 and 3 need not be considered at all. Otherwise, one or both of these two portions, shown circled in Fig. 12.17, are searched simultaneously (each sequentially) during the first iteration of stage 2.

When the subtrees rooted at nodes 2 and 3 have been fully searched, the final score backed up at node 1 is compared with the temporary scores at nodes 4 and 5 for a cutoff. If the former is larger, the cutoff check is successful and the unexplored subtrees of 4 and 5 need not be considered. Otherwise, one or both of the subtrees shown circled in Fig. 12.18 are searched simultaneously (each sequentially) during the second iteration of stage 2, and so on.

To study the storage requirements of the procedure, we note that for every node being explored during the search at least one storage location is needed to hold the temporary score of that node. When an explored node is discarded from further consideration, its storage locations are reallocated to another unexplored node that the procedure decides to examine. Therefore, in order to determine how much storage is needed, it is necessary to derive the maximum number of nodes simultaneously explored at any time during the search. This number is precisely the number of primary nodes (during stage 1 where the maximum degree of parallelism occurs).

To see this, note that any tree searched sequentially during stage 2 is rooted at a node that was primary, that is, explored during stage 1. This subtree is isomorphic to the leftmost subtree rooted at the same primary node. The leftmost subtree has at least as many primary nodes as a subtree searched in stage 2. Therefore, the number of nodes searched in parallel during stage 2 cannot exceed the number of primary nodes.

This latter number is now derived (keeping in mind that an infinite number of processors is available and therefore no bound exists on the number of processes to be created). Let

$$L(k) = \text{number of primary left offspring at ply } k$$

and

$$R(k) = \text{number of primary right offspring at ply } k.$$

In Fig. 12.16, $L(3) = 5$ and $R(3) = 6$. From our definition of primary nodes it follows that for a uniform tree with fan-out f we have

$$L(k) = L(k - 1) + R(k - 1), \qquad k \geqslant 1,$$

$$R(k) = L(k - 1) \times (f - 1), \qquad k \geqslant 1,$$

$$L(0) = 1 \quad \text{and} \quad R(0) = 0.$$

For a uniform tree of depth d, the total number of primary nodes is therefore given by

$$S = \sum_{k=0}^{d} [L(k) + R(k)],$$

and the storage requirements of the algorithm are clearly of $O(S)$.

Solving the preceding recurrence, we get

$$L(k) = \frac{1}{x \times 2^{k+1}} [(1 + x)^{k+1} - (1 - x)^{k+1}]$$

and

$$R(k) = \frac{1}{x \times 2^{k}} [(1 + x)^{k} - (1 - x)^{k}] \times (f - 1)$$

where

$$x = [1 + 4(f - 1)]^{1/2}.$$

Limited Processors.   It is already clear that our assumption about the availability of an unlimited number of processors can now be somewhat relaxed. Indeed, the maximum number of processors the algorithm will ever need to search a uniform tree of depth d will be

$$P(f, d) = L(d) + R(d).$$

In Fig. 12.16, $P(f, d) = 11$. Even though $P(f, d)$ establishes an upper bound on the number of processors that will ever be needed by the algorithm to search a uniform tree, it is still a very large number of order $f^{d/2}$, as one should have expected. In practice, however, only a small number of processors is available and we are led to reconsider our definition of primary nodes. The actual number of primary nodes is in fact determined by the number of processors available. If N processors are used to search a uniform tree of fan-out f, then the actual number of primary nodes at level k is equal to

$$\min\{L(k) + R(k), N\},$$

and the total number of primary nodes for a tree of depth d is given by the function

$$s(N) = \sum_{k=0}^{d} \min\{L(k) + R(k), N\}.$$

Under these conditions the storage requirements of the algorithm are clearly of $O(s(N))$. Note that $S = s(P(f, d))$, and that for $N \leqslant f$ we have

$$s(N) = 1 + Nd.$$

12.6 PROBLEMS

12.1 The state-space graph in Fig. 12.1 contains twenty-three nodes. Graphs for other values of B may contain more or less nodes. In the worst case, 2^n nodes may have to be generated to solve the subset sum problem, where n is the number of elements of S. A sequential algorithm for traversing such a state-space graph requires exponential time in n in the worst case. Derive a parallel algorithm for the subset sum problem. What is the running time of your algorithm?

12.2 Prove the equality

$$M(f, d) = f^{\lceil d/2 \rceil} + f^{\lfloor d/2 \rfloor} - 1$$

of section 12.3.1.

12.3 Discuss the following straightforward approach to implementing the alpha–beta algorithm in parallel: A process is created for each offspring of the root whose purpose is to search that offspring's subtree using the alpha–beta algorithm. If enough processors are available, then all processes are carried out simultaneously.

12.4 In procedure MIMD ALPHA BETA, an individual score table is assigned to each node when a process is generated to search the subtree containing that node. This table is initialized to the values in the score table of the node's parent. As a result, the information necessary for a deep cutoff to occur is not available in general. In practice, however, a node is not given a complete score table but rather just a small table containing the scores for the two previous plies and the node itself. This means that the complete score table for a node is actually distributed throughout the tree along the path from the root to the node. With this structure it would be possible to obtain deep cutoffs as follows. Suppose that during a search of the tree in Fig. 12.16 the following sequence occurs:
  (a) the search of the left subtree of the root begins,
  (b) the search of the right subtree begins, and
  (c) the search of the left subtree completes, backing up a temporary score to the root.
At this point searching along some paths in the right subtree could be cut off, the information indicating this being available in the score table of the root node. However, in order to effect this deep cutoff, the information must be propagated down the right subtree. Extend procedure MIMD ALPHA BETA to deal with this circumstance.

12.5 The alpha–beta algorithm owes its name to the fact that at any point during the tree search the final value of the root lies between two values that are continually updated. These two values are arbitrarily called *alpha* and *beta*. Consequently, the problem of finding the principal continuation can be viewed as the problem of locating the root of a monotonic function over some interval. This leads to the following alternative parallel implementation of the alpha–beta algorithm. The interval $(-\infty, +\infty)$ is divided into a number of disjoint subintervals. A process is created for each subinterval whose purpose is to search the game tree for the solution over its associated subinterval. If enough processors are available, then each process can be assigned to a processor, and hence all processes can be carried out independently and in parallel. Describe this algorithm formally.

12.6 Discuss the merits of each of the following approaches to speed up game tree search:
  (i) Computing the terminal node evaluation function in parallel.
  (ii) Storing the scores of some terminal nodes in a special *hash table* to avoid having to recompute them should these positions reoccur.
  (iii) Storing moves that created cutoffs in a special table: If any of these moves occurs at a later stage of the game, it is given priority by the search algorithm over other moves from the same node.

12.7 Can you think of other models of parallel computation, besides the SM MIMD computer, that can be used profitably to implement the alpha–beta algorithm in parallel? For example, how can a *tree of processors* be used to search a *game tree*?

12.8 Assume that a sequential algorithm can traverse a game tree up to a depth *d*. Argue for or against each of the following statements:
  (i) A parallel algorithm allows that tree to be traversed in a shorter amount of time.
  (ii) A parallel algorithm allows a tree of depth larger than *d* to be traversed in the same amount of time.

12.9 The subset sum problem of example 12.1 is a representative of the class of *decision problems*, where it is required to determine whether a solution satisfying a number of constraints exists. Another example is the *traveling salesman problem* of problem 10.50. Decision problems can sometimes be turned into *optimization problems*. The optimization version of the traveling salesman problem calls for finding the Hamilton cycle of *smallest weight* in a given weighted graph. Propose a parallel algorithm for solving this problem based on the branch-and-bound approach (problem 1.13).

12.10 Suggest other problems that can be solved through state-space traversal and design parallel algorithms for their solution.

12.7 BIBLIOGRAPHICAL REMARKS

State-space traversal has been used to solve decision and optimization problems. Both kinds of problems arise in a branch of computer science known as *artificial intelligence* (AI). This is a field of study concerned with programming computers to perform tasks normally requiring human "intelligence." Since our understanding of the essence of intelligence is at best vague, AI is largely defined by the kind of problems researchers and practitioners in that field choose to work on. Examples of such problems include making computers understand natural languages, prove mathematical theorems, play games of strategy, solve puzzles, and learn from previous experience ([Shapiro]). Parallel algorithms for AI problems are described in [Deering], [Feldman], [Fennell], [Forgy], [Miura], [Reddy], [Rumelhart], [Stanfill], [Uhr], [Ullman], and [Wah 1].

Programming computers to play games was one of the earliest areas of AI. As it did in the past, this activity continues today to attract researchers for a number of reasons. The first and most obvious of these is that the ability to play complex games appears to be the province of the human intellect. It is therefore challenging to write programs that match or surpass the skills humans have in planning, reasoning, and choosing among several options in order to reach their goal. Another motivation for this research is that the techniques developed while programming computers to play games may be used to solve other complex problems in real life, for which games serve as models. Finally, games provide researchers in AI in particular and computer scientists in general with a medium for testing their theories on various topics ranging from knowledge representation and the process of learning to searching algorithms and parallel processing. Procedure MIMD ALPHA BETA is from [Akl 1]. A number of parallel algorithms for traversing game trees, along with their empirical analyses, are described in [Akl 1], [Akl 2], [Baudet], [Finkel 1], [Finkel 2], [Fishburn], [Marsland 1], [Marsland 2], and [Stockman].

Various parallel implementations of the branch-and-bound approach to solving optimization problems and analyses of the properties of these implementations can be found in [Imai], [Kindervater], [Kumar], [Lai], [Li 1], [Li 2], [Li 3], [Mohan], [Quinn], [Wah 2], [Wah 3], and [Wah 4].

12.8 REFERENCES

[AKL 1]
Akl, S. G., Barnard, D. T., and Doran, R. J., Design, analysis, and implementation of a parallel tree search algorithm, *IEEE Transactions on Pattern Analysis and Machine Intelligence*, Vol. PAMI-4, No. 2, March 1982, pp. 192–203.

[AKL 2]
Akl, S. G., and Doran, R. J., A comparison of parallel implementations of the Alpha–Beta and Scout trees search algorithms using the game of checkers, in Bramer, M. A., Ed., *Computer Game Playing*, Wiley, Chichester, England, 1983, pp. 290–303.

[BAUDET]
Baudet, G. M., The design and analysis of algorithms for asynchronous multiprocessors, Ph.D. thesis, Department of Computer Science, Carnegie-Mellon University, Pittsburgh, April 1978.

[DEERING]
Deering, M. F., Architectures for AI, *Byte*, Vol. 10, No. 4, April 1985, pp. 193–206.

[FELDMAN]
Feldman, J. A., Connections, *Byte*, Vol. 10, No. 4, April 1985, pp. 277–284.

[FENNELL]
Fennell, R. D., and Lesser, V. R., Parallelism in artificial intelligence problem solving: A case study of Hearsay II, *IEEE Transactions on Computers*, Vol. C-26, No. 2, February 1977, pp. 98–111.

[FINKEL 1]
Finkel, R. A., and Fishburn, J. P., Parallelism in alpha–beta search, *Artificial Intelligence*, Vol. 19, 1982, pp. 89–106.

[FINKEL 2]
Finkel, R. A., and Fishburn, J. P., Improved speedup bounds for parallel alpha–beta search, *IEEE Transactions on Pattern Analysis and Machine Intelligence*, Vol. PAMI-5, No. 1, January 1983, pp. 89–92.

[FISHBURN]
Fishburn, J. P., An analysis of speedup in distributed algorithms, Ph.D. thesis, Computer Sciences Department, University of Wisconsin–Madison, Madison, May 1981.

[FORGY]
Forgy, C. L., Note on production systems and Illiac IV, Technical Report CMU-CS-80-130, Department of Computer Science, Carnegie-Mellon University, Pittsburgh, July 1980.

[IMAI]
Imai, M., Fukumara, T., and Yoshida, Y., A parallelized branch-and-bound algorithm: Implementation and efficiency, *Systems-Computers-Control*, Vol. 10, No. 3, 1979, pp. 62–70.

[KINDERVATER]

Kindervater, G. A. P., and Trienekens, H. W. J. M., Experiments with parallel algorithms for combinatorial problems, *European Journal of Operational Research*, Vol. 33, 1988, pp. 65–81.

[KUMAR]

Kumar, V., and Kanal, L., Parallel branch-and-bound formulations for AND/OR tree search, *IEEE Transactions on Pattern Analysis and Machine Intelligence*, Vol. PAMI-6, No. 6, November 1984, pp. 768–778.

[LAI]

Lai, T.-H., and Sahni, S., Anomalies in parallel branch-and-bound algorithms, *Communications of the ACM*, Vol. 27, No. 6, June 1984, pp. 594–602.

[LI 1]

Li, G.-J., and Wah, B. W., How to cope with anomalies in parallel approximate branch-and-bound algorithms, Proceedings of the National Conference on Artificial Intelligence, Austin, Texas, August 1984, pp. 212–215, Association for Computing Machinery, New York, N.Y., 1984.

[LI 2]

Li, G.-J., and Wah, B. W., Computational efficiency of parallel approximate branch-and-bound algorithms, Proceedings of the 1984 International Conference on Parallel Processing, Bellaire, Michigan, August 1984, pp. 473–480, IEEE Computer Society, Washington, D.C., 1984.

[LI 3]

Li, G.-J., and Wah, B. W., MANIP-2: A multicomputer architecture for solving logic programming problems, Proceedings of the 1985 International Conference on Parallel Processing, St. Charles, Illinois, August 1985, pp. 123–130, IEEE Computer Society, Washington, D.C., 1985.

[MARSLAND 1]

Marsland, T. A., and Campbell, M., Parallel search of strongly ordered game trees, *Computing Surveys*, Vol. 14, No. 4, December 1982, pp. 533–551.

[MARSLAND 2]

Marsland, T. A., and Popowich, F., Parallel game-tree search, *IEEE Transactions on Pattern Analysis and Machine Intelligence*, Vol. PAMI-7, No. 4, July 1985, pp. 442–452.

[MIURA]

Miura, H., Imai, M., Yamashita, M., and Ibaraki, T., Implementation of parallel Prolog on tree machines, Proceedings of the 1986 Fall Joint Computer Conference, Dallas, Texas, November 1986, pp. 287–296, IEEE Computer Society, Washington, D.C., 1986.

[MOHAN]

Mohan, J., Experience with two parallel programs solving the traveling salesman problem, Proceedings of the 1983 International Conference on Parallel Processing, Bellaire, Michigan, August 1983, pp. 191–193, IEEE Computer Society, Washington, D.C., 1983.

[QUINN]

Quinn, M. J., and Deo, N., An upper bound for the speedup of parallel branch-and-bound algorithms, Proceedings of the 3rd Conference on Foundations of Software Technology and Theoretical Computer Science, Bangalore, India, December 1983, pp. 488–504.

[REDDY]

Reddy, D. R., Some numerical problems in artificial intelligence: Implications for complexity and machine architecture, in Traub, J. F., Ed., *Parallel Numerical Algorithms*, Academic, New York, 1973.

[RUMELHART]

Rumelhart, D. E., and McClelland, J. L., *Parallel Distributed Processing*, Vols. 1 and 2, MIT Press, Cambridge, Mass., 1986.

[SHAPIRO]

Shapiro, S. C., Ed., *Encyclopedia of Artificial Intelligence*, Vols. 1 and 2, Wiley, New York, 1987.

[STANFILL]

Stanfill, C., and Waltz, D., Toward memory-based reasoning, *Communications of the ACM*, Vol. 29, No. 12, December 1986, pp. 1213–1228.

[STOCKMAN]

Stockman, G. C., A minimax algorithm better than alpha–beta? *Artificial Intelligence*, Vol. 12, 1979, pp. 179–196.

[UHR]

Uhr, L., *Multi-Computer Architectures for Artificial Intelligence*, Wiley, New York, 1987.

[ULLMAN]

Ullman, J. D., Flux, sorting, and supercomputer organization for AI applications, *Journal of Parallel and Distributed Computing*, Vol. 1, No. 2, November 1984, pp. 133–151.

[WAH 1]

Wah, B. W., Ed., Special Issue on New Computers for Artificial Intelligence Processing, *Computer*, Vol. 20, No. 1, January 1987.

[WAH 2]

Wah, B. W., Li, G.-J., and Yu, C. F., The status of MANIP—a multicomputer architecture for solving combinatorial extremum-search problems, Proceedings of the 11th Annual ACM International Symposium on Computer Architecture, Ann Arbor, Michigan, June 1984, pp. 56–63, Association for Computing Machinery, New York, N.Y., 1984.

[WAH 3]

Wah, B. W., Li, G.-J., and Yu, C. F., Multiprocessing of combinatorial search problems, *Computer*, Vol. 18, No. 6, June 1985, pp. 93–108.

[WAH 4]

Wah, B. W., and Ma, Y. W. E., MANIP—a multicomputer architecture for solving combinatorial extremum search problems, *IEEE Transactions on Computers*, Vol. C-33, No. 5, May 1984, pp. 377–390.

13

Decision and Optimization

13.1 INTRODUCTION

In the previous chapter we saw how state-space traversal techniques can be used to solve various decision and optimization problems. Recall that a decision problem asks whether a solution satisfying some constraints *exists*. Also, given an objective function, an optimization problem calls for finding an *optimal* solution, that is, one that maximizes or minimizes the objective function. Our purpose in this chapter is to present other ways to approach such problems. For illustration we use the problems of job sequencing with deadlines and the knapsack problem. Our parallel solutions to these problems rely on the ability to efficiently *sort* a sequence and *compute its prefix sums*. The first of these operations was covered in detail in chapter 4. We devote a large part of this chapter to a thorough study of the second operation first encountered in chapter 2.

In section 13.2 it is shown how a number of different models can be used to compute the prefix sums of a sequence. A decision problem (job sequencing with deadlines) and an optimization problem (the knapsack problem) are addressed in section 13.3.

13.2 COMPUTING PREFIX SUMS

A sequence of n numbers $X = \{x_0, x_1, \ldots, x_{n-1}\}$, where $n \geq 1$, is given. We assume throughout this chapter that n is a power of 2; in case it is not, then the sequence can be padded with elements equal to zero in order to bring its size to a power of 2. It is required to compute all n initial sums $S = \{s_0, s_1, \ldots, s_{n-1}\}$, where $s_i = x_0 + x_1 + \cdots + x_i$ for $i = 0, 1, \ldots, n-1$. These sums are often referred to as the *prefix sums* of X. Indeed, if the elements of X are thought of as forming a string $w = x_0 x_1 \ldots x_{n-1}$, then each s_i is the sum of those elements forming a *prefix* of length i.

Sequentially, the n prefix sums can be computed in $O(n)$ time by the following procedure.

procedure SEQUENTIAL SUMS (X, S)

Step 1: $s_0 \leftarrow x_0$.

Step 2: **for** $i = 1$ **to** $n - 1$ **do**
$$s_i \leftarrow s_{i-1} + x_i$$
end for. □

This running time is optimal since $\Omega(n)$ steps are needed simply to read the input.

By contrast, when several processors are available, each capable of performing the addition operation, it is possible to obtain the sequence $S = \{s_0, s_1, \ldots, s_{n-1}\}$ significantly faster. Procedure PARALLEL SUMS shows how this is done.

procedure PARALLEL SUMS (X, S)

Step 1: **for** $i = 0$ **to** $n - 1$ **do in parallel**
$$s_i \leftarrow x_i$$
end for.

Step 2: **for** $j = 0$ **to** $(\log n) - 1$ **do**
         for $i = 2^j$ **to** $n - 1$ **do in parallel**
$$s_i \leftarrow s_{i-2^j} + s_i$$
         end for
end for. □

This procedure uses a scheme known as *recursive doubling*. In chapter 2 we saw how this scheme can be implemented on a shared-memory SIMD computer. Procedure ALLSUMS of section 2.5.2 requires n processors $P_0, P_1, \ldots, P_{n-1}$. Initially, P_i holds x_i; when the procedure terminates, P_i holds s_i. The procedure runs in $O(\log n)$ time for a cost of $O(n \log n)$. This cost is not optimal in view of the $O(n)$ sequential operations sufficient to compute the prefix sums.

13.2.1 A Specialized Network

The first question that comes to mind is: Do we really need the power of the shared-memory model to implement procedure PARALLEL SUMS? A partial answer to this question is provided in section 2.8. There it is suggested that recursive doubling can be implemented on a special-purpose network of processors, as illustrated in Fig. 13.1 for $n = 8$. Here each square represents a processor. There are $1 + \log n$ rows, each with n processors, that is, $n + n \log n$ processors in all. Assume that the processors in each row are numbered from 0 to $n - 1$ and that the rows are numbered from 0 to $\log n$. Processor i in row $j + 1$ receives input from

   (i) processor i in row j, and
   (ii) processor $i - 2^j$ in row j, if $i \geqslant 2^j$.

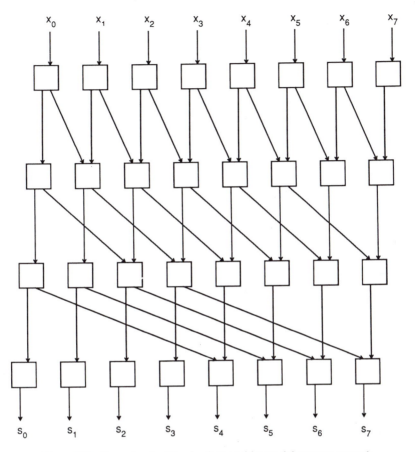

Figure 13.1   Recursive doubling implemented by special-purpose network.

Each processor is capable of computing the sum of its two inputs and of sending the result to the next row of processors using the connections indicated. A processor receiving only one input simply passes that input to the next row. The elements of X enter the network from one end (one element per processor), and the outputs are received at the other end. All prefix sums are computed in $O(\log n)$ time. This running time is the best possible in view of the $\Omega(\log n)$ lower bound derived in section 7.3.2. The network's cost is $O(n \log^2 n)$. In other words, a model of computation weaker than the shared memory is capable of achieving the same running time as procedure ALLSUMS using a larger number of processors.

13.2.2 Using the Unshuffle Connection

It is possible to reduce the number of processors in the network to $O(n)$ while preserving the $O(\log n)$ running time. The idea, hinted at in problem 2.2, is to use a

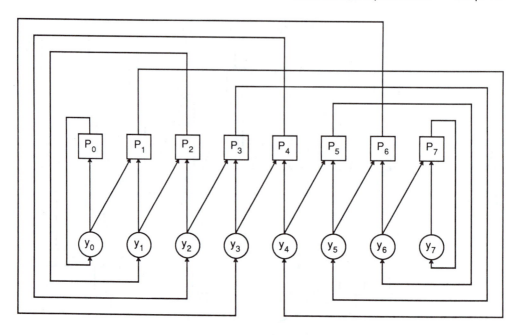

Figure 13.2 Unshuffle connection for computing prefix sums.

parallel computer with *one* row of processors and have it *simulate* the network of Fig. 13.1. All processors operate synchronously. At each step, the results of the computation are *fed back* to the processors as input. Depending on the value of a *mask variable* computed locally, a processor may produce as output the sum of its two inputs (if mask = 1) or simply propagate one of them unchanged (if mask = 0). Such a scheme is illustrated in Fig. 13.2, again for $n = 8$.

There are two kinds of nodes in Fig. 13.2:

 (i) the square nodes represent processors $P_0, P_1, \ldots, P_{n-1}$ capable of computing the mask variable and the addition operation and

 (ii) the circle nodes represent very simple processors capable of producing as output two copies of their input; we denote the contents of these processors by $y_0, y_1, \ldots, y_{n-1}$.

The square processors send their outputs to the circle processors via a *perfect unshuffle* interconnection. (The latter is obtained by reversing the orientation of the arrows in a perfect shuffle mapping, as explained in problem 2.2.) Initially, $y_i = x_i$ for $i = 0, 1, \ldots, n - 1$. During each iteration P_i receives y_i and y_{i-1} as input, except for P_0, which receives y_0 only. Now P_i computes the value of mask to determine whether to produce $y_i + y_{i-1}$ or y_i as output. Referring to Fig. 13.2, mask = 1 during the first iteration for all P_i, except P_0, for which mask $= 0$. Once the P_i produce their outputs, the new values of the y_i are as follows:

$$y_0 = x_0$$
$$y_1 = x_1 + x_2$$
$$y_2 = x_3 + x_4$$
$$y_3 = x_5 + x_6$$
$$y_4 = x_0 + x_1$$
$$y_5 = x_2 + x_3$$
$$y_6 = x_4 + x_5$$
$$y_7 = x_6 + x_7.$$

During the second iteration, mask $= 1$ for all P_i except where i is a multiple of 4 and the new values of the y_i are

$$y_0 = x_0$$
$$y_1 = x_1 + x_2 + x_3 + x_4$$
$$y_2 = x_0 + x_1$$
$$y_3 = x_2 + x_3 + x_4 + x_5$$
$$y_4 = x_0 + x_1 + x_2$$
$$y_5 = x_3 + x_4 + x_5 + x_6$$
$$y_6 = x_0 + x_1 + x_2 + x_3$$
$$y_7 = x_4 + x_5 + x_6 + x_7.$$

During the third and final iteration, mask $= 0$ for those P_i where i is a multiple of 2 and mask $= 1$ for the rest. Following the computation by the P_i, $y_i = s_i$ for all i. All prefix sums are therefore computed in $O(\log n)$ time using $O(n)$ processors for a cost of $O(n \log n)$, which is not optimal.

It should be noted that the parallel computer just described is clearly weaker than one with a shared memory. The comparison with the network of section 13.2.1, however, is more difficult:

1. On the one hand, the present model may be considered *weaker* since the interconnection it uses is not as specialized as the one in Fig. 13.1.

2. On the other hand, it may be considered *stronger* as it comprises more powerful processors, having to compute the mask variable locally at each iteration and behave according to its value.

13.2.3 Prefix Sums on a Tree

We now describe a parallel algorithm for computing the prefix sums that combines the advantages of those in the previous two sections without their disadvantages. First, the algorithm is designed to run on a (binary) tree of processors operating synchronously: A tree is not only less specialized than the network in section 13.2.1, but in addition is a simpler interconnection than the perfect unshuffle. Second, the algorithm involves no mask computation and hence requires very simple processors.

Let the inputs $x_0, x_1, \ldots, x_{n-1}$ reside in the n leaf processors $P_0, P_1, \ldots, P_{n-1}$ of a binary tree, one input to a leaf. When the algorithm terminates, it is required that P_i hold s_i. During the algorithm, the root, intermediate, and leaf processors are required to perform very simple operations. These are described for each processor type.

Root Processor

(1) **if** an input is received from the left child
   then send it to the right child
   end if.
(2) **if** an input is received from the right child
   then discard it
   end if. □

Intermediate Processor

(1) **if** an input is received from the left and right children
   then (i) send the sum of the two inputs to the parent
          (ii) send the left input to the right child
   end if.
(2) **if** an input is received from the parent
   then send it to the left and right children
   end if. □

Leaf Processor P_i

(1) $s_i \leftarrow x_i$.
(2) send the value of x_i to the parent.
(3) **if** an input is received from the parent
   then add it to s_i
   end if. □

Note that the root and intermediate processors are triggered to action when they receive an input. Similarly, after having assigned x_i to s_i and sent s_i to its parent, a leaf processor is also triggered to action by an input received from its parent. After the rightmost leaf processor has received $\log n$ inputs, the values of $s_0, s_1, \ldots, s_{n-1}$ are the prefix sums of $x_0, x_1, \ldots, x_{n-1}$.

Example 13.1

The algorithm is illustrated in Fig. 13.3 for the input sequence $X = \{1, 2, 3, 4\}$. □

Analysis.   The number of steps required by the algorithm is the distance between the leftmost and rightmost leaves, which is $2 \log n$. Thus $t(n) = O(\log n)$. Since $p(n) = 2n - 1$, $c(n) = O(n \log n)$. This cost is not optimal. It is not difficult, however, to obtain a cost-optimal algorithm by increasing the capabilities of the leaf processors.

Let a processor tree with N leaves $P_0, P_1, \ldots, P_{N-1}$ be available, where $n \geqslant N$. We assume for simplicity that n is a multiple of N, although the algorithm can easily be adapted to work for all values of n. Given the input sequence $X = \{x_0, x_1, \ldots, x_{n-1}\}$, leaf processor P_i initially contains the elements $x_{i(n/N)}$, $x_{i(n/N)+1}, \ldots, x_{i(n/N)+(n/N)-1}$. The root and intermediate processors behave exactly as before, whereas the leaves now execute the steps given in the next procedure. In what follows, v_i denotes the number of 1 bits in the binary representation of i, that is,

$$v_0 = 0$$

$$v_i = 1 + v_{i \bmod 2^{\lfloor \log i \rfloor}},$$

and $m = n/N$.

Leaf Processor P_i

(1) Compute all prefix sums of $x_{im}, x_{im+1}, \ldots, x_{im+m-1}$, store the results in s_{im}, $s_{im+1}, \ldots, s_{im+m-1}$, and send s_{im+m-1} to the parent processor.

(2) Set a temporary sum r_i to zero.

(3) **if** an input is received from the parent
   then add it to r_i
   end if.

(4) **if** r_i is the sum of exactly v_i inputs received from the parent
   then add r_i to each of $s_{im}, s_{im+1}, \ldots, s_{im+m-1}$
   end if. □

In order to understand the termination condition in 4, note that v_i is precisely the number of roots of subtrees to the left of P_i that will send input to P_i.

Analysis.   The number of data that are required by the algorithm to travel up and down the tree is independent of the number of elements stored in each leaf processor. It follows that the running time of the algorithm is the sum of

1. the time required by leaf P_i to compute $s_{im}, s_{im+1}, \ldots, s_{im+m-1}$ and then send s_{im+m-1} to its parent [i.e., $O(n/N)$ time] since all leaves execute this step simultaneously;

2. the time required by the rightmost leaf P_{N-1} to receive its final input [i.e., $O(\log N)$ time]; and

3. the time required by the rightmost leaf P_{N-1} (the last processor to terminate) to add r_{N-1} to each of the sums it contains [i.e., $O(n/N)$ time].

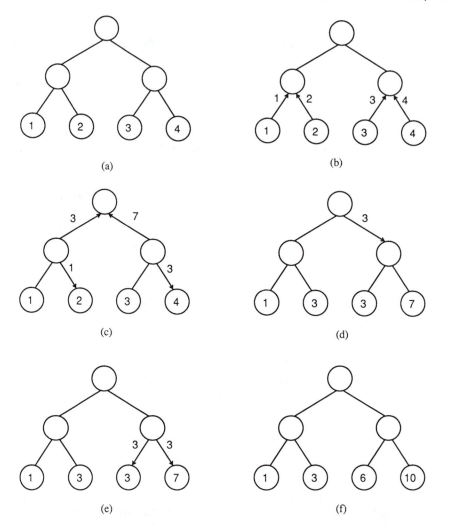

Figure 13.3 Computing prefix sums on tree of processors.

Thus $t(n) = O(n/N) + O(\log N)$. Since $p(n) = 2N - 1$, $c(n) = O(n + N \log N)$. It follows that the algorithm is cost optimal if $N \log N = O(n)$. For example, $N = O(n/\log n)$ will suffice to achieve cost optimality.

It should be noted here that the algorithm's cost optimality is due primarily to the fact that the time taken by computations within the leaves dominates the time required by the processors to communicate among themselves. This was achieved by partitioning the prefix sum problem into disjoint subproblems that require only a small amount of communication. As a result, the model's limited communication ability (subtrees are connected only through their roots) is overcome.

13.2.4 Prefix Sums on a Mesh

We conclude this section by showing how the prefix sums of a sequence can be computed on a mesh-connected array of processors. Our motivation to study a parallel algorithm to solve the problem on this model is due to two reasons:

1. As shown in the conclusion of section 5.3.2, when the time taken by a signal to travel along a wire is proportional to the length of that wire, the mesh is preferable to the tree for solving a number of problems. These problems are characterized by the fact that their solution time is proportional to the distance (i) from root to leaf in the tree and (ii) from top row to bottom row in the mesh. The problem of computing the prefix sums of an input sequence is one such problem.

2. As indicated in section 4.8, a mesh with n processors can sort a sequence of n inputs faster than a tree with n leaves regardless of any assumptions we make about the signal propagation time along the wires. This is particularly relevant since sorting is an important component of our solution to the problems described in the next section.

For ease of presentation, we assume in what follows that n is a perfect square and let $m = n^{1/2}$. The prefix sums of $X = \{x_0, x_1, \ldots, x_{n-1}\}$ can be computed on an $m \times m$ mesh-connected computer as follows. Let the n processors $P_0, P_1, \ldots, P_{n-1}$ be arranged in row-major order. Initially, P_i contains x_i. When the algorithm terminates, P_i contains s_i. The algorithm consists of three steps. In the first step, with all rows operating in parallel, the prefix sums for the elements in each row are computed *sequentially*: Each processor adds to its contents the contents of its left neighbor. In the second step, the prefix sums of the contents in the rightmost column are computed. Finally, again with all rows operating in parallel, the contents of the rightmost processor in row $k - 1$ are added to those of all the processors in row k (except the rightmost). The algorithm is given in what follows as procedure MESH PREFIX SUMS. In it we denote the contents of the processor in row k and column j by u_{kj}, where $0 \leqslant k \leqslant m - 1$ and $0 \leqslant j \leqslant m - 1$.

procedure MESH PREFIX SUMS (X, S)

Step 1:   **for** $k = 0$ **to** $m - 1$ **do in parallel**
      for $j = 1$ **to** $m - 1$ **do**
         $u_{kj} \leftarrow u_{kj} + u_{k,j-1}$
      end for
   end for.

Step 2:   **for** $k = 1$ **to** $m - 1$ **do**
      $u_{k,m-1} \leftarrow u_{k,m-1} + u_{k-1,m-1}$
   end for.

Step 3: **for** $k = 1$ **to** $m - 1$ **do in parallel**
      for $j = m - 2$ **downto** 0 **do**
        $u_{kj} \leftarrow u_{kj} + u_{k-1,m-1}$
      end for
    end for. $\square$

Note that in step 3, $u_{k-1,m-1}$ is propagated along row k from the processor in column $m - 1$ to that in column 0, each processor adding it to its contents and passing it to its left neighbor.

Analysis.   Each step requires $O(m)$ time. Therefore, $t(n) = O(n^{1/2})$. Since $p(n) = n$, $c(n) = O(n^{3/2})$, which is not optimal.

Example 13.2

Let $n = 16$. The behavior of procedure MESH PREFIX SUMS is illustrated in Fig. 13.4. In the figure, $A_{ij} = x_i + x_{i+1} + \cdots + x_j$. $\square$

Now assume that an $N^{1/2} \times N^{1/2}$ mesh of processors is available, where $N < n$. To compute the prefix sums of $X = \{x_0, x_1, \ldots, x_{n-1}\}$, each processor initially receives n/N elements from X and computes their prefix sums. Procedure MESH

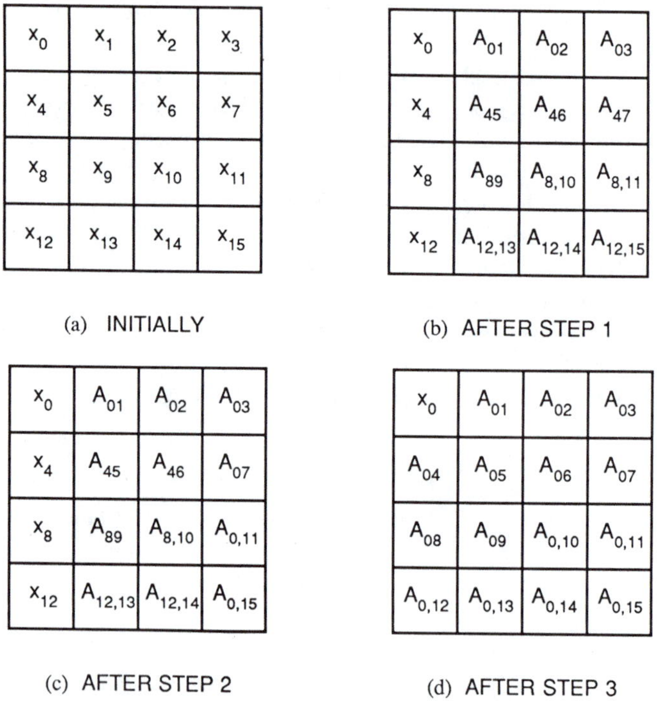

(a) INITIALLY

(b) AFTER STEP 1

(c) AFTER STEP 2

(d) AFTER STEP 3

Figure 13.4   Computing prefix sums using procedure MESH PREFIX SUMS.

PREFIX SUMS can now be modified, in the same way as the tree algorithm in the previous section, so that when it terminates, each processor contains n/N prefix sums of X. The modified procedure has a running time of $O(n/N) + O(N^{1/2})$ and a cost of $O(n) + O(N^{3/2})$. This cost is optimal when $N = O(n^{2/3})$.

13.3 APPLICATIONS

In this section we show how an efficient algorithm for computing the prefix sums of a sequence can be used to solve decision and optimization problems. Two problems are chosen for illustration: a decision problem, namely, *job sequencing with deadlines*, and an optimization problem, namely, the *knapsack problem*. For each of these problems we give an algorithm that runs on a tree-connected parallel computer. A crucial step in both algorithms is the computation of the prefix sums of a sequence as described in section 13.2.3. We conclude this section by showing that despite their simplicity the tree solutions to the two optimization problems are not as efficient as their mesh counterparts.

13.3.1 Job Sequencing with Deadlines

A set of n jobs $J = \{j_0, j_1, \ldots, j_{n-1}\}$ is given to be processed on a single machine. The machine can execute one job at a time, and when it is assigned a job, it must complete it before the next job can be processed. With each job j_i is associated

(i) a *processing time t_i* and
(ii) a *deadline d_i* by which it must be completed.

A *schedule* is a permutation of the jobs in J that determines the order of their execution. A schedule is said to be *feasible* if each job finishes by its deadline. The question is: Given n jobs $\{j_0, j_1, \ldots, j_{n-1}\}$, with processing times $\{t_0, t_1, \ldots, t_{n-1}\}$ and deadlines $\{d_0, d_1, \ldots, d_{n-1}\}$, does a feasible schedule exist? It turns out that this question can be answered in the affirmative if and only if any schedule where the jobs are executed in nondecreasing order of deadlines is feasible. Therefore, to solve the problem, it suffices to arrange the jobs in order of nondecreasing deadlines and test whether this yields a feasible schedule. In case it does, we know that the answer to the question is yes, otherwise the answer is no. Sequentially, this algorithm requires $O(n \log n)$ time to sort the jobs and then $O(n)$ time to test whether each job can be completed by its deadline.

We are now ready to present our parallel algorithm for solving the sequencing problem based on the preceding idea. The algorithm runs on a tree-connected parallel computer with leaf processors $P_0, P_1, \ldots, P_{n-1}$. We assume for notational simplicity that in the original statement of the problem, the jobs are already arranged in order of nondecreasing deadlines; in other words,

$$d_0 \leqslant d_1 \leqslant \cdots \leqslant d_{n-1}.$$

Initially, leaf processor P_i contains t_i and d_i. The algorithm is given as procedure TREE SEQUENCING.

procedure TREE SEQUENCING $(J$, answer$)$

Step 1:   Compute $s_0, s_1, \ldots, s_{n-1}$, the prefix sums of $t_0, t_1, \ldots, t_{n-1}$.

Step 2:   (i) leaf processor P_i
           if $s_i \leqslant d_i$
           then send "yes" to parent
           else send "no" to parent
           end if
       (ii) intermediate processor
           if inputs from both children are "yes"
           then send "yes" to parent
           else send "no" to parent
           end if
       (iii) root processor
           if inputs from both children are "yes"
           then answer ← "feasible schedule exists"
           else answer ← "no feasible schedule"
           end if. □

Example 13.3

Let $n = 4$ with $\{t_0, t_1, t_2, t_3\} = \{1, 3, 3, 4\}$ and $\{d_0, d_1, d_2, d_3\} = \{3, 5, 7, 9\}$. Thus $\{s_0, s_1, s_2, s_3\} = \{1, 4, 7, 11\}$. We have $s_0 \leqslant d_0, s_1 \leqslant d_1$, and $s_2 \leqslant d_2$; however, $s_3 > d_3$ and a feasible schedule does not exist for this problem. □

Analysis. Both steps 1 and 2 require $O(\log n)$ operations. However, the running time of the algorithm is dominated by the time taken to initially sort the jobs in the leaves in order of nondecreasing deadlines. This time is known from section 4.8 to be $\Omega(n)$.

13.3.2 The Knapsack Problem

We are given a knapsack that can carry a maximum weight of W and a set of n objects $A = \{a_0, a_1, \ldots, a_{n-1}\}$ whose respective *weights* are $\{w_0, w_1, \ldots, w_{n-1}\}$. Associated with each object is a *profit*, the set of profits being denoted by $\{p_0, p_1, \ldots, p_{n-1}\}$. If we place in the knapsack a fraction z_i of the object whose weight is w_i, where $0 \leqslant z_i \leqslant 1$, then a profit of $z_i p_i$ is gained. Our purpose is to fill the knapsack with objects (or fractions thereof) such that

(i) the total weight of the selected objects does not exceed W and
(ii) the total profit gained is as large as possible.

Formally, given $2n + 1$ positive numbers $w_0, w_1, \ldots, w_{n-1}, W, p_0, p_1, \ldots, p_{n-1}$, it is required to maximize the quantity

$$Q = \sum_{i=0}^{n-1} z_i \times p_i$$

subject to the two conditions

1. $0 \leqslant z_i \leqslant 1$ for all i and
2. $\sum_{i=0}^{n-1} z_i \times w_i \leqslant W.$

An *optimal solution* is a sequence $Z = \{z_0, z_1, \ldots, z_{n-1}\}$ that maximizes Q while satisfying conditions 1 and 2. Such a solution is obtained if the objects are examined in nonincreasing order of the ratios p_i/w_i. If an object whose turn has come to be considered fits in the remaining portion of the knapsack, then the object is included; otherwise only a fraction of the object is placed in the knapsack. Sequentially, this requires $O(n \log n)$ time to sort the profits and weights and then $O(n)$ time to examine all the objects one at a time.

   Our parallel algorithm for finding the optimal sequence $\{z_0, z_1, \ldots, z_{n-1}\}$ uses this approach. It runs on a tree-connected parallel computer with leaf processors P_0, $P_1, \ldots, P_{n-1}$. We assume for notational simplicity that in the original statement of the problem, the objects are already sorted in order of nonincreasing profit to weight ratios, in other words,

$$p_0/w_0 \geqslant p_1/w_1 \geqslant \cdots \geqslant p_{n-1}/w_{n-1}.$$

Initially, leaf processor P_i contains w_i, p_i, and W. The algorithm is given in what follows as procedure TREE KNAPSACK. When the procedure terminates, the solution $\{z_0, z_1, \ldots, z_{n-1}\}$ resides in the leaves. Let $s_{-1} = 2W$.

procedure TREE KNAPSACK (A, W, Z)

   Step 1:   (1.1) Compute $s_0, s_1, \ldots, s_{n-1}$, the prefix sums of $w_0, w_1, \ldots, w_{n-1}$
              (1.2) **for** $i = 1$ **to** $n - 1$ **do in parallel**
                       P_i computes s_{i-1}
                    end for.

   Step 2:   **for** $i = 0$ **to** $n - 1$ **do in parallel**
                 if $s_i \leqslant W$
                 then $z_i \leftarrow 1$
                 else if $s_i > W$ and $s_{i-1} \leqslant W$
                       then $z_i \leftarrow (W - s_{i-1})/w_i$
                       else $z_i \leftarrow 0$
                       end if
                 end if
              end for. $\square$

Note that the total profit Q may be computed at the root as follows:

(i) Each leaf processor P_i computes

$$\text{profit}_i \leftarrow z_i \times p_i$$

and sends profit_i to its parent.

(ii) Each intermediate processor adds the two inputs received from its children and sends the result to its parent.

(iii) The root adds the two inputs received from its children; this is Q.

Example 13.4

Let $n = 4$ with $\{w_0, w_1, w_2, w_3\} = \{5, 9, 2, 4\}$, $\{p_0, p_1, p_2, p_3\} = \{100, 135, 26, 20\}$, and $W = 15$. Thus $\{s_0, s_1, s_2, s_3\} = \{5, 14, 16, 20\}$. Since $s_0 \leqslant W$ and $s_1 \leqslant W$, $z_0 = z_1 = 1$. Also $s_2 > W$ and therefore $z_2 = (15 - 14)/2 = 0.5$. Finally, $s_3 > W$ and hence $z_3 = 0$. ☐

Analysis. Steps 1 and 2 require $O(\log n)$ and $O(1)$ steps, respectively. However, the running time of the algorithm is dominated by the time taken to initially sort the profits and weights in the leaves in order of their nonincreasing ratios. This time is known from section 4.8 to be $\Omega(n)$.

13.3.3 Mesh Solutions

As we saw in the previous two sections, the tree solutions require at least $\Omega(n)$ time if the input sequences are not properly sorted. Our purpose here is to briefly show that in these circumstances a mesh-connected parallel computer is a more attractive model for solving these decision and optimization problems.

Assume that the inputs to the job sequencing and knapsack problems are not sorted initially, as required by procedures TREE SEQUENCING and TREE KNAPSACK, respectively. If an $n^{1/2} \times n^{1/2}$ mesh-connected computer is available, then

(i) an input sequence with n elements can be sorted on the mesh in $O(n^{1/2})$ time as indicated in section 4.8 and

(ii) each of the two procedures TREE SEQUENCING and TREE KNAPSACK can be easily modified to run on the mesh in $O(n^{1/2})$ time.

It follows that the overall running time required to solve each of the job sequencing and knapsack problems is

$$t(n) = O(n^{1/2}).$$

This is significantly faster than the time that would be required by the corresponding tree algorithms. Since $p(n) = n$, it follows that $c(n) = O(n^{3/2})$. This cost is not optimal in view of the $O(n \log n)$ running time sufficient to solve these two problems sequentially.

Assume now that an $N^{1/2} \times N^{1/2}$ mesh is available, where $N < \log^2 n$. We know from section 4.8 that a mesh with this many processors can sort an n-element sequence with optimal cost $O(n \log n)$. Since $\log^2 n < n^{2/3}$ for sufficiently large n, we also have from section 13.2.4 that the prefix sums of an n-element sequence can be computed on this $N^{1/2} \times N^{1/2}$ mesh with an optimal cost of $O(n)$. These two operations, namely, sorting and computing the prefix sums, dominate all others in solving the job sequencing and knapsack problems. It follows that these two problems can be solved optimally on a mesh of processors.

13.4 PROBLEMS

13.1   Are the "circle" processors in Fig. 13.2 really needed?

13.2   Do the computers described in sections 13.2 and 13.3 belong to the SIMD or MIMD class?

13.3   State formally the modified procedure MESH PREFIX SUMS described at the end of section 13.2.4 and whose cost is optimal.

13.4   A number s_0 and two sequences of numbers $\{a_1, a_2, \ldots, a_n\}$ and $\{b_1, b_2, \ldots, b_n\}$ are given. It is required to compute the sequence $\{s_1, s_2, \ldots, s_n\}$ from the recurrence

$$s_i = a_i s_{i-1} + b_i, \qquad i = 1, 2, \ldots, n.$$

Sequentially, this can be done in $O(n)$ time. Show how procedure PARALLEL SUMS can be modified to produce the desired sequence in $O(\log n)$ time on an n-processor parallel computer. Define your model of computation.

13.5   Repeat problem 13.4 for the following computations:
   (a) $s_i = s_{i-1} \times a_i$
   (b) $s_i = \min(s_{i-1}, a_i)$
   (c) $s_i = \max(s_{i-1}, a_i)$
   (d) $s_i = a_i s_{i-1} + b_i s_{i-2}$
   (e) $s_i = (a_i s_{i-1} + b_i)/(c_i s_{i-1} + d_i)$
   (f) $s_i = (s_{i-1}^2 + a_i^2)^{1/2}$

13.6   Let s_0 and $\{a_1, a_2, \ldots, a_n\}$ be logical variables taking the value **true** or **false**. Repeat problem 13.4 for the following computations:
   (a) $s_i = s_{i-1}$ **and** a_i
   (b) $s_i = s_{i-1}$ **or** a_i
   (c) $s_i = s_{i-1}$ **xor** a_i

13.7   Prove that a feasible schedule exists if and only if any schedule where the jobs are executed in nondecreasing order of deadlines is feasible.

13.8   Modify procedure TREE SEQUENCING for the case where $N = \log n$ processors are available to perform both the initial sorting as well as steps 1 and 2. Analyze the resulting procedure and discuss its cost optimality.

13.9   Consider the following variant of the job sequencing with deadlines problem. With each job j_i is associated a profit $p_i \geqslant 0$. Profit p_i is earned if and only if job j_i is completed by its deadline. It is required to find a subset of the jobs satisfying the following two conditions:
   (i) all jobs in the subset can be processed and completed by their deadlines and
   (ii) the sum of the profits earned is as large as possible.

Assuming that $t_i = 1$ for all i, describe a parallel algorithm for finding an optimal solution.

13.10 Prove that an optimal solution to the knapsack problem is obtained if the objects are examined in nonincreasing order of the profit-to-weight ratios.

13.11 Repeat problem 13.8 for procedure TREE KNAPSACK.

13.12 In a variant of the knapsack problem, the condition that $0 \leqslant z_i \leqslant 1$ is replaced with $z_i = 1$ or $z_i = 0$, that is, the ith object is either included in the knapsack or not included. Derive a parallel algorithm for this variant known as the 0–1 knapsack problem.

13.13 Consider the problem of maximizing the function of n variables

$$h(x_1, x_2, \ldots, x_n) = \sum_{i=1}^{n} g_i(x_i),$$

where $g_i(0) = 0$ and $g_i(x_i) \geqslant 0$ subject to the conditions
(i) $\sum_{i=1}^{n} x_i = x$ and
(ii) $x_i \geqslant 0$ for all i.
One method for solving this problem is *dynamic programming*. In it the sequence $f_1(x)$, $f_2(x), \ldots, f_n(x)$ is constructed from

$$f_i(x) = \max_{0 \leqslant x_i \leqslant x} [g_i(x_i) + f_{i-1}(x - x_i)],$$

where $f_0(x) = 0$. The sequence $x_1(x), x_2(x), \ldots, x_n(x)$ is obtained in this way, where $x_i(x)$ is the value that maximized $g_i(x_i) + f_{i-1}(x - x_i)$. Computationally, $x_i(x)$ is found by probing the range $[0, x]$ at equal subintervals. Derive a parallel version of this algorithm.

13.5 BIBLIOGRAPHICAL REMARKS

As mentioned in chapter 2, the problem of computing in parallel the prefix sums of a sequence has received considerable attention due to its many applications. The parallel computer in Fig. 13.2 was proposed in [Stone]. Other algorithms for a variety of models and their applications are described in [Akl 1], [Akl 2], [Dekel], [Fich], [Goldberg], [Kogge 1], [Kogge 2], [Kruskal 1], [Kruskal 2], [Ladner], [Meijer 1], [Reif], [Schwartz], and [Wagner]. The tree-based algorithm of section 13.2.3 is from [Meijer 2].

All these algorithms exploit the associativity of the addition operation in order to compute the prefix sums. It is shown in [Kogge 2] that given two sequences of inputs $\{a_0, a_1, \ldots, a_{n-1}\}$ and $\{b_0, b_1, \ldots, b_{n-1}\}$, a recursive doubling algorithm can be used to compute, in logarithmic parallel time, outputs $\{s_0, s_1, \ldots, s_{n-1}\}$ of the form

$$s_0 = b_0$$

$$s_i = f(b_i, g(a_i, s_{i-1})), \qquad 1 \leqslant i \leqslant n-1.$$

Here f and g are functions that have to satisfy the following restrictions:

1. f is associative, that is, $f(x, f(y, z)) = f(f(x, y), z)$;
2. g distributes over f, that is, $g(x, f(y, z)) = f(g(x, y), g(x, z))$; and
3. g is semiassociative, that is, there exists a function h such that $g(x, g(y, z)) = g(h(x, y), z)$.

For example, if f is *addition* and g is *multiplication*, the algorithm computes the first-order recurrences

$$s_0 = b_0$$

$$s_i = a_i s_{i-1} + b_i, \qquad 1 \leqslant i \leqslant n - 1.$$

If $a_i = 1$ for all i, the s_i's thus computed are the prefix sums of $\{b_0, b_1, \ldots, b_{n-1}\}$. The results in section 13.2 imply that all recurrences with functions f and g as described in the preceding can also be computed in $O(\log n)$ time on an n-leaf tree and $O(n^{1/2})$ time on an $n^{1/2} \times n^{1/2}$ mesh. In particular, any binary associative operation such as multiplication, computing the maximum, computing the minimum, **and**, **or**, **xor**, and so on, can replace addition in these algorithms. Several other examples are provided in [Stone].

The need to compute the s_i's for various functions f and g arises in many applications. Two such applications are described in [Meijer 2], on which section 13.3 is partly based. Other applications are mentioned in [Fich], [Kogge 1], [Kogge 2], [Kruskal 1], [Ladner], [Reif], and [Stone]. They include the evaluations of polynomials, general Horner expressions, and general arithmetic formulas; the solution of linear recurrences; carry look-ahead adder circuits; transforming sequential circuits into combinatorial circuits; the construction of fast Fourier transform circuits; ranking and packing problems; scheduling problems; and a number of graph-theoretic problems such as finding spanning forests, connected components, biconnected components, and minimum-weight spanning trees. Also of interest is the related work on computing the logical or of n bits ([Cook]), general arithmetic expressions ([Brent] and [Winograd]), linear recurrences ([Hyafil]), and rational expressions ([Kung]).

Decision and optimization problems are treated in [Horowitz], [Lawler], and [Papadimitriou]. Most decision problems such as the *traveling salesman problem* (problem 10.50) and the *subset sum problem* (example 12.1) are *NP-complete*. Their optimization counterparts (problems 12.9 and 13.12) are said to be *NP-hard*. We mentioned in section 10.8 that all *known* sequential algorithms for these problems run in exponential time, and all *known* parallel algorithms have exponential cost; see, for example [Karnin], [Kindervater], [Mead], and [Mohan]. However, because of their many applications, solutions to these problems are needed in practice. Fast *approximation algorithms* are therefore used in these cases, as illustrated in problem 1.14 and in [Horowitz] and [Papadimitriou]. There are many kinds of approximation algorithms. For example, an approximation algorithm may provide a solution that is guaranteed to be very close to the optimal solution. Alternatively, the solution may be guaranteed to be optimal with a certain probability. Or the solution may combine the preceding two properties, that is, contain at most a certain amount of error with a known probability. Parallel approximation algorithms are described in [Cole], [Felten], and [Peters]. Parallel implementations of dynamic programming are proposed in [Gilmore] and [Kindervater].

13.6 REFERENCES

[AKL 1]
  Akl, S. G., *Parallel Sorting Algorithms*, Academic, Orlando, Fl., 1985.
[AKL 2]
  Akl, S. G., and Meijer, H., On the bit complexity of parallel computations, *Integration: The VLSI Journal*, Vol. 6, No. 2, July 1988, pp. 201–212.

[BRENT]

Brent, R. P., The parallel evaluation of general arithmetic expressions, *Journal of the ACM*, Vol. 21, No. 2, April 1974, pp. 201–206.

[COLE]

Cole, R., and Vishkin, U., Approximate parallel scheduling Part I: The basic technique with applications to optimal parallel list ranking in logarithmic time, *SIAM Journal on Computing*, Vol. 17, No. 1, February 1988, pp. 128–142.

[COOK]

Cook, S., and Dwork, C., Bounds on the time for parallel RAM's to compute simple functions, Proceedings of the 14th Annual ACM Symposium on Theory of Computing, San Francisco, California, May 1982, pp. 231–233, Association for Computing Machinery, New York, N.Y., 1982.

[DEKEL]

Dekel, E., and Sahni, S., Binary trees and parallel scheduling algorithms, *IEEE Transactions on Computers*, Vol. C-32, No. 3, March 1983, pp. 307–315.

[FELTEN]

Felten, E., Karlin, S., and Otto, S. W., The traveling salesman problem on a hypercubic MIMD computer, Proceedings of the 1985 International Conference on Parallel Processing, St. Charles, Illinois, August 1985, pp. 6–10, IEEE Computer Society, Washington, D.C., 1985.

[FICH]

Fich, F. E., New bounds for parallel prefix circuits, Proceedings of the 15th Annual ACM Symposium on Theory of Computing, Boston, Massachusetts, May 1983, pp. 100–109, Association for Computing Machinery, New York, N.Y., 1983.

[GILMORE]

Gilmore, P. A., Structuring of parallel algorithms, *Journal of the ACM*, Vol. 15, No. 2, April 1968, pp. 176–192.

[GOLDBERG]

Goldberg, A. V., Efficient graph algorithms for sequential and parallel computers, Ph.D. thesis, Department of Electrical Engineering and Computer Science, Massachusetts Institute of Technology, Cambridge, Mass., February 1987.

[HOROWITZ]

Horowitz, E., and Sahni, S., *Fundamentals of Computer Algorithms*, Computer Science Press, Rockville, Md., 1978.

[HYAFIL]

Hyafil, L., and Kung, H. T., The complexity of parallel evaluation of linear recurrences, *Journal of the ACM*, Vol. 24, No. 3, July 1977, pp. 513–521.

[KARNIN]

Karnin, E. D., A parallel algorithm for the knapsack problem, *IEEE Transactions on Computers*, Vol. C-33, No. 5, May 1984, pp. 404–408.

[KINDERVATER]

Kindervater, G. A. P., and Trienekens, H. W. J. M., Experiments with parallel algorithms for combinatorial problems, *European Journal of Operational Research*, Vol. 33, 1988, pp. 65–81.

[Kogge 1]

Kogge, P. M., Parallel solution of recurrence problems, *IBM Journal of Research and Development*, March 1974, pp. 138–148.

[Kogge 2]

Kogge, P. M., and Stone, H. S., A parallel algorithm for the efficient solution of a general class of recurrence equations, *IEEE Transactions on Computers*, Vol. C-22, No. 8, August 1973, pp. 786–792.

[Kruskal 1]

Kruskal, C. P., Rudolph, L., and Snir, M., The power of parallel prefix, *IEEE Transactions on Computers*, Vol. C-34, No. 10, October 1985, pp. 965–968.

[Kruskal 2]

Kruskal, C. P., Madej, T., and Rudolph, L., Parallel prefix on fully connected direct connection machines, Proceedings of the 1986 International Conference on Parallel Processing, St. Charles, Illinois, August 1986, pp. 278–283, IEEE Computer Society, Washington, D.C., 1986.

[Kung]

Kung, H. T., New algorithms and lower bounds for the parallel evaluation of certain rational expressions and recurrences, *Journal of the ACM*, Vol. 23, No. 2, April 1976, pp. 252–261.

[Ladner]

Ladner, R. E., and Fischer, M. J., Parallel prefix computation, *Journal of the ACM*, Vol. 27, No. 4, October 1980, pp. 831–838.

[Lawler]

Lawler, E. L., *Combinatorial Optimization: Networks and Matroids*, Holt, Rinehart & Winston, New York, 1976.

[Mead]

Mead, C. A., and Conway, L. A., *Introduction to VLSI Systems*, Addison-Wesley, Reading, Mass., 1980.

[Meijer 1]

Meijer, H., and Akl, S. G., Bit serial addition trees and their applications, *Computing*, Vol. 40, 1988, pp. 9–17.

[Meijer 2]

Meijer, H., and Akl, S. G., Optimal computation of prefix sums on a binary tree of processors, *International Journal of Parallel Programming*, Vol. 16, No. 2, April 1987, pp. 127–136.

[Mohan]

Mohan, J., Experience with two parallel programs solving the traveling salesman problem, Proceedings of the 1983 International Conference on Parallel Processing, Bellaire, Michigan, August 1983, pp. 191–193, IEEE Computer Society, Washington, D.C., 1983.

[Papadimitriou]

Papadimitriou, C. H., and Steiglitz, K., *Combinatorial Optimization*, Prentice-Hall, Englewood Cliffs, N.J., 1982.

[Peters]

Peters, J., and Rudolph, L., Parallel approximation schemes for subset sum and knapsack problems, *Acta Informatica*, Vol. 24, 1987, pp. 417–432.

[REIF]

Reif, J. H., Probabilistic parallel prefix computation, Proceedings of the 1984 International Conference on Parallel Processing, Bellaire, Michigan, August 1984, pp. 291–298, IEEE Computer Society, Washington, D.C., 1984.

[SCHWARTZ]

Schwartz, J. T., Ultracomputers, *ACM Transactions on Programming Languages and Systems,* Vol. 2, No. 4, October 1980, pp. 484–521.

[STONE]

Stone, H. S., Ed., *Introduction to Computer Architecture,* Science Research Associates, Chicago, 1980.

[WAGNER]

Wagner, R., and Han, Y., Parallel algorithms for bucket sorting and the data dependent prefix problem, Proceedings of the 1986 International Conference on Parallel Processing, St. Charles, Illinois, August 1986, pp. 924–930, IEEE Computer Society, Washington, D.C., 1986.

[WINOGRAD]

Winograd, S., On the parallel evaluation of certain arithmetic expressions, *Journal of the ACM,* Vol. 22, No. 4, October 1975, pp. 477–492.

14

The Bit Complexity
of Parallel Computations

14.1 INTRODUCTION

The theoretical models of computation commonly used to design and analyze algorithms, whether sequential or parallel, are usually based on two important assumptions.

1. The first of these assumptions is that the size of the smallest addressable unit in memory, or *word*, is fixed. On a binary computer, for example, each word has length b bits for some constant b.

2. The second assumption is that the entire word is available at once. Again for a binary computer, this means that all b bits are accessible when needed.

As a result of these two assumptions, all fundamental operations on pairs of words, such as comparison, addition, and multiplication, take a constant amount of time on conventional models of computation. All previous chapters make assumptions 1 and 2.

The most obvious reason (and indeed a good one) for including these assumptions in the theoretical models is that they are a faithful reflection of reality. Existing digital computers have a fixed-size word, and all digits of a word can be reached simultaneously. This is not to say that there are no situations where the preceding two assumptions do not hold. For many applications, we may want to make the size of a word variable, and/or the digits forming a word may not all be available at the same time. In these cases, the theoretical models need to be modified to count *digit operations*, while in practice software is used to enhance the existing fixed-size hardware. The net effect—in both theory and practice—is that the time required by operations on pairs of words is no longer a constant but rather a function that grows at least linearly with the word size.

The purpose of this concluding chapter is to describe a number of architectures that are specifically designed to handle those situations where the conventional assumptions do not hold, that is, where

1. the word size is variable and/or
2. the digits forming a word arrive serially, that is, one digit every time unit.

Although the concepts presented henceforth are applicable to all data types and numbering systems, we shall assume for concreteness that the data are *integers* expressed as strings of *bits*, and we shall take operations on bits as the basic operations.

The following problems are considered:

1. adding n b-bit integers;
2. multiplying two b-bit integers;
3. computing the prefix sums of a sequence of n b-bit integers;
4. multiplying two $n \times n$ matrices of b-bit integers;
5. determining the kth smallest of a sequence of n b-bit integers; and
6. sorting n b-bit integers into nondecreasing order.

The solutions to these problems are all based on the concept of "on-the-fly" use of the input and intermediate bits. To be specific, for each problem we describe a special-purpose architecture, or *network*, that processes bits as they arrive at the interface with the outside world. The concept is also applied within the network through *pipelining* until the output is produced. This is illustrated in Fig. 14.1. The networks are obtained by interconnecting a collection of simple devices known as *gates*. A gate receives two bits as input, computes a function of these two bits, and produces a single bit as output. This output may be one of another gate's two inputs. In analyzing these networks, we use the following measures:

1. *Number of processors used:* This is equal to the number of gates used to build the network.
2. *Solution time:* This is the time required by a network to produce its output, that is, the time elapsed from the moment the first input bit enters the network to the moment the last output bit leaves the network. The unit of time used in our analysis is the time required by a gate to produce its output.
3. *Cost:* This is the product of the previous two measures.

From the preceding description, it is clear that we view these networks as parallel algorithms. These algorithms receive their input words in parallel, each word being presented one bit every time unit (i.e., *bit serially*), hence the title of this chapter.

The remainder of this chapter is organized as follows. We begin in section 14.2 by describing a basic network that serves as a building block for most subsequent networks. Each of the following sections is devoted to one of the problems listed in the preceding.

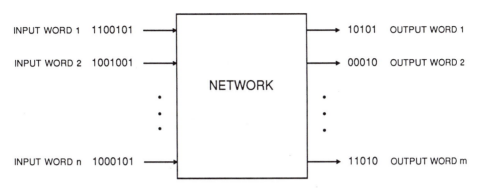

Figure 14.1   Network for processing variable-size input words arriving bit serially.

14.2 ADDING TWO INTEGERS

Assume that we want to add *two b*-bit integers x and y whose binary representations are

$$x(b-1)\, x(b-2)\ldots x(0) \quad \text{and} \quad y(b-1)\, y(b-2)\ldots y(0),$$

respectively. The addition can be performed by a network known as a *serial adder* (SA). This network consists of a number of gates that perform on pairs of bits the operations **and, or,** and **xor** defined as follows (the first two of these operations on bits were defined in chapters 5 and 10):

$$0 \textbf{ and } 0 = 0, \quad 0 \textbf{ and } 1 = 0, \quad 1 \textbf{ and } 0 = 0, \quad 1 \textbf{ and } 1 = 1,$$

$$0 \textbf{ or } 0 = 0, \quad 0 \textbf{ or } 1 = 1, \quad 1 \textbf{ or } 0 = 1, \quad 1 \textbf{ or } 1 = 1,$$

$$0 \textbf{ xor } 0 = 0, \quad 0 \textbf{ xor } 1 = 1, \quad 1 \textbf{ xor } 0 = 1, \quad 1 \textbf{ xor } 1 = 0.$$

The behavior of the serial adder network is explained with the help of Fig. 14.2. Integers x and y are fed into the network bit serially, least significant bit first. Denoting the bits available at time i at inputs u, v, and c and outputs s and r by u_i, v_i, c_i, s_i, and r_i, respectively, we have

$$u_i = x(i) \qquad\qquad\qquad\qquad\qquad\quad \text{for } i \geqslant 0,$$

$$v_i = y(i) \qquad\qquad\qquad\qquad\qquad\quad \text{for } i \geqslant 0,$$

$$s_i = (u_{i-1} \textbf{ xor } v_{i-1}) \textbf{ xor } c_{i-1} \qquad\quad \text{for } i \geqslant 1,$$

$$r_i = (u_{i-1} \textbf{ and } v_{i-1}) \textbf{ or } ((u_{i-1} \textbf{ or } v_{i-1}) \textbf{ and } c_{i-1}) \quad \text{for } i \geqslant 1,$$

$$c_i = r_i \qquad\qquad\qquad\qquad\qquad\qquad \text{for } i \geqslant 1,$$

$$c_0 = 0.$$

The network of Fig. 14.2 therefore behaves as required: The sum of x and y is produced one bit at a time at output s, starting with the least significant bit at time

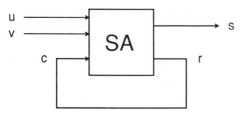

Figure 14.2 Serial adder.

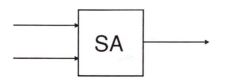

Figure 14.3 An SA-box.

$i = 1$. The network has the following properties:

1. It can be built using a constant number of gates.
2. Each gate has a fixed *fan-out*, that is, the number of other gates to which it needs to send an output signal is a constant.
3. The integers x and y can be arbitrarily large.
4. The bits of x and y arrive serially, and the sum of x and y is produced bit serially.
5. The sum is produced in $O(b)$ time.
6. Given that the running time is $O(b)$ and the number of processors is $O(1)$, the network's cost is $O(b)$. This cost is optimal since $\Omega(b)$ operations are needed to receive the input.

For simplicity, we shall represent the serial adder of Fig. 14.2 as shown in Fig. 14.3 (i.e., we omit input c and output r and the feedback line connecting them) and refer to it as an *SA-box*.

14.3 ADDING *n* INTEGERS

Suppose now that we want to compute the sum of n b-bit integers $a_0, a_1, \ldots, a_{n-1}$. Two solutions to this problem are described. Both solutions assume that b is a variable and that each of the integers arrives bit serially.

14.3.1 Addition Tree

The sum can be computed using a tree of SA-boxes with $n/2$ leaves (and $\log n$ levels), as shown in Fig. 14.4 for $n = 8$.

We call this network the *addition tree*. Starting at time $i = 0$, each one of the integers to be added is fed one bit every time unit, least significant bit first, into the u or

v input of a leaf. The sum of the n integers is produced on the s output of the root, beginning with the least significant bit at time $i = \log n$. Since each of the n integers has b bits, the time required by the addition tree to compute the sum is a function of both n and b and is given by

$$t(n, b) = O(\log n) + O(b).$$

Also, since the tree consists of $n - 1$ SA-boxes, each with a fixed number of gates, the number of processors, also a function of n and b, is given by

$$p(n, b) = O(n).$$

Finally, the tree's cost is

$$c(n, b) = O(n \log n + nb).$$

For $b \geqslant \log n$, this cost is optimal since $\Omega(nb)$ operations are needed to receive the input.

The foregoing analysis of the addition tree assumes that the time it takes a bit to propagate along a wire from one SA-box to the next is constant. If, on the other hand, the propagation time is assumed to be an increasing function of the length of the wire, then the preceding expression describing the addition time, namely, $O(\log n) + O(b)$, is no longer valid. Indeed, as pointed out in the conclusion of section 5.3.2, in any planar circuit layout of the addition tree, the edges in consecutive levels and hence the propagation time for a signal grow in length exponentially with the level number. In this case, a more regular structure is preferred where wires have constant length. Such a structure is provided by the mesh connection.

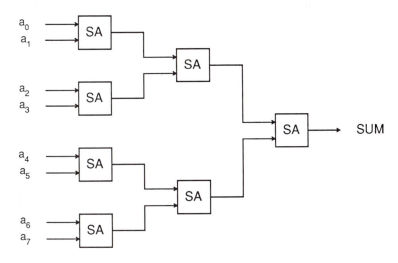

Figure 14.4   Addition tree.

14.3.2 Addition Mesh

An *addition mesh* consisting of SA-boxes is illustrated in Fig. 14.5 for adding twenty-six b-bit integers bit serially. The starting time for each SA-box, that is, the time i at which the box begins computing, is indicated below the box in the figure. Note that all wires have the same length regardless of the size of the mesh, and therefore the propagation time from one SA-box to the next is constant. It is easy to see that in general

$$t(n, b) = O(n^{1/2}) + O(b),$$

$$p(n, b) = O(n),$$

$$c(n, b) = O(n^{3/2} + nb).$$

For $b \geq n^{1/2}$, this cost is optimal in view of the $\Omega(nb)$ lower bound derived in the previous section. Furthermore, the period of the network (i.e., the time separating the last output bit of one input sequence and the first output bit of the following sequence) is constant. Therefore, the addition mesh represents a definite improvement over the addition tree assuming that the propagation time of a signal is an increasing function of the distance traveled.

14.4 MULTIPLYING TWO INTEGERS

We now turn to the problem of multiplying two b-bit integers

$$x = x(b-1)\, x(b-2)\ldots x(0) \quad \text{and} \quad y = y(b-1)\, y(b-2)\ldots y(0).$$

By the definition of multiplication, the product is obtained as follows:

$x(b-1)$	$x(b-2)$	$\cdots$	$\cdots$		$\cdots$	$x(2)$	$x(1)$	$x(0)$
								$\times$
$y(b-1)$	$y(b-2)$	$\cdots$	$\cdots$		$\cdots$	$y(2)$	$y(1)$	$y(0)$

		$\cdots$	z_{02}	z_{01}	z_{00}	
						$+$
	$\cdots$	z_{12}	z_{11}	z_{10}	0	
						$+$
$\cdots$	z_{22}	z_{21}	z_{20}	0	0	
	$\vdots$	$\ddots$	$\vdots$	$\vdots$	$\vdots$	$+$
$\cdots$ $z_{b-1,1}$	$z_{b-1,0}$	0	$\cdots$ $\cdots$ $\cdots$	0	0	0

$$\cdots \quad w(3) \quad w(2) \quad w(1) \quad w(0)$$

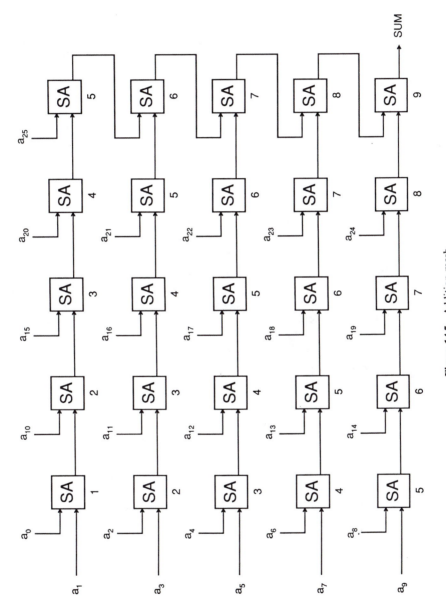

Figure 14.5 Addition mesh.

where $z_{ij} = y(i) \times x(j)$. In other words $x \times y = \sum_{i=0}^{b-1} r_i$, where r_i is a binary number given by

$$r_i = \cdots z_{i2}\, z_{i1}\, z_{i0}\, 0 \ldots 0 \quad \text{for } i = 0, 1, \ldots, b-1.$$

Note that r_i has exactly i zeros to the right of z_{i0}.

Since the product is expressed as the sum of a collection of binary integers, we can use our addition tree or addition mesh to perform the multiplication.

14.4.1 Multiplication Tree

We begin by considering the network in Fig. 14.6. For input integers arriving bit serially at a and g, the network behaves as follows:

$$h_i = a_i \text{ or } f_i,$$

$$d_i = h_{i-1} \text{ and } g_{i-1},$$

$$e_i = g_{i-1},$$

$$f_i = h_{i-1}.$$

This means that bit d at time i is the result of computing the **and** of two bits (h and g) available at time $i - 1$. One of these two bits (bit g) propagates down (as e) while the other (bit h) cycles back (as f). The **or** of a and f is now computed to produce a new value for h. If input a is 0 at all times, except for a single time unit where it is 1, then the left-hand side of the network serves to capture that 1 bit and maintain it as input to the right-hand side as long as needed. For simplicity, we represent the network of Fig. 14.6 as shown in Fig. 14.7 and refer to it as the *A-box*.

A *multiplication tree* for computing $x \times y$ consists of an array of *A*-boxes A_0,

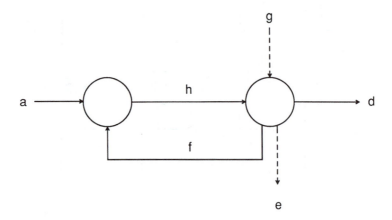

Figure 14.6 Special-purpose network for capturing 1-bit input.

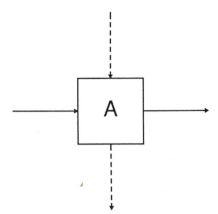

Figure 14.7 An A-box.

$A_1, \ldots, A_{b-1}$ followed by an addition tree with $b/2$ leaves. This is illustrated in Fig. 14.8 for $b = 8$.

Initially, all inputs are set to zero. Integer x is now fed into the g input of the top A-box, one bit per time unit; thus, bit $x(i)$ is made available to box A_0 at time i. Similarly, integer y is fed into the a inputs of all A-boxes one bit per box such that $y(i)$ is made available to A_i at time i. The first bit of the product emerges from the root after $1 + \log b$ time units. Therefore, for the multiplication tree we have

$$t(b) = O(\log b + b) = O(b),$$

$$p(b) = O(b),$$

$$c(b) = O(b^2).$$

14.4.2 Multiplication Mesh

Given that the two integers x and y to be multiplied arrive bit serially, we must ensure (as we did for the tree) that the strings r_i, whose sum gives the product, are properly formed and fed into the mesh at correct times. Let us reexamine the addition mesh. In Fig. 14.5, SA-boxes with the same starting time fall on the same diagonal. We can say that on diagonal j, the numbers to be added have to be fed into the network at time j. Now recall that

$$r_i = \cdots z_{i2} \, z_{i1} \, z_{i0} \, 0 \cdots 0.$$

If r_i is the input to an SA-box on diagonal j, then bit z_{i0} must arrive at time $i + j$ (since r_i has i zeros to the right of z_{i0}). In Fig. 14.9, the pair of indices (i, m) below the SA-boxes are interpreted as follows: bit z_{i0} of r_i must arrive at SA-box (i, m) on diagonal j at time $m = i + j$.

We are now ready to describe the *multiplication mesh*. It uses the A-box presented in the previous section as well as a delay network shown in Fig. 14.10. This

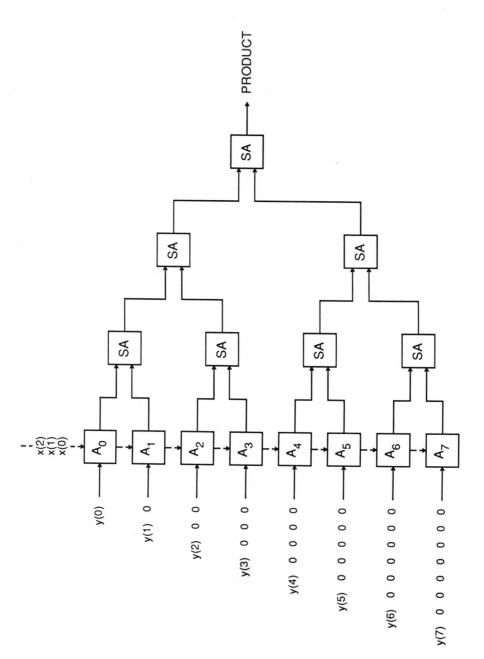

Figure 14.8 Multiplication tree.

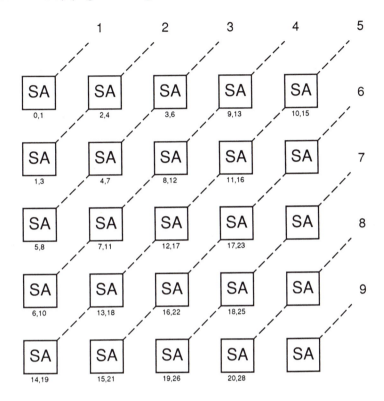

Figure 14.9   Transforming addition mesh into multiplication mesh.

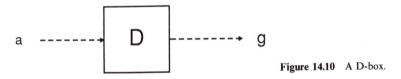

Figure 14.10   A D-box.

network, which we call a *D-box*, has the following behavior:

$$g_i = a_{i-1},$$

that is, the output at time i is equal to the input at time $i - 1$. A D-box may be built using an **and** gate (or an **or** gate) both of whose inputs equal the bit to be delayed.

A multiplication mesh for $b = 21$ is shown in Fig. 14.11. It consists of the addition mesh of Fig. 14.5 augmented with A- and D-boxes. The bits of x are fed, least significant bit first, into the top left corner. They circulate around the mesh in a snakelike fashion along the dashed lines. Bit $y(i)$ of y, on the other hand, is given as input to the A-box associated with SA-box (i, m) at time $m - 1$ [i.e., when $x(0)$ reaches that box]. For the network of Fig. 14.11, both $t(b)$ and $p(b)$ are $O(b)$. This means that the multiplication mesh has exactly the same requirements as the multiplication tree

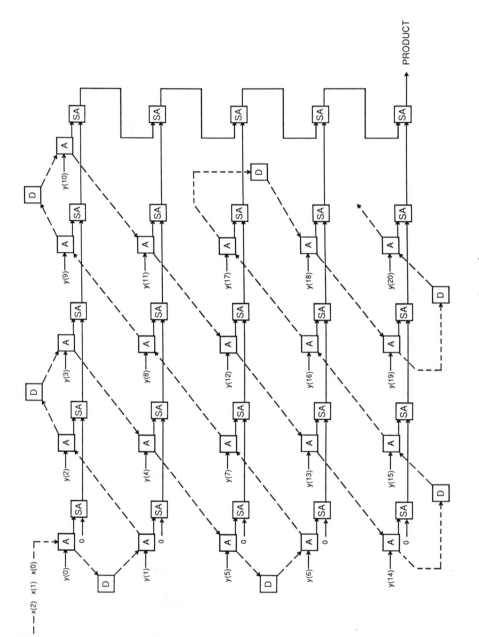

Figure 14.11 Multiplication mesh.

under the constant wire delay assumption. The multiplication mesh is, of course, faster when the signal propagation time along a wire grows as a function of the wire length.

We conclude this section by pointing out that the assumption made at the outset regarding the number of bits of x is really unnecessary. A b-bit multiplication tree or mesh will operate correctly for an x with any bit size provided y has b bits. Thus, if x has l bits, then

$$t(b, l) = O(b) + O(l) \quad \text{and} \quad p(b, l) = O(b)$$

for both multipliers.

14.5 COMPUTING PREFIX SUMS

Given a sequence $A = \{a_0, a_1, \ldots, a_{n-1}\}$ of n b-bit integers, it is required to compute the prefix sums $s_0, s_1, \ldots, s_{n-1}$, where $s_i = a_0 + a_1 + \cdots + a_i$. Solutions to this problem were described in chapters 2 and 13, assuming that b is a constant and all b bits of each integer a_i are available simultaneously. We now show how a collection of SA-boxes can be used to obtain all sums when the integers $a_0, a_1, \ldots, a_{n-1}$ have a variable size and arrive bit serially. Two solutions are described: The first uses variable fan-out gates; the second uses gates whose fan-out is constant. Both solutions are recursive in nature.

14.5.1 Variable Fan-out

The first solution is illustrated in Fig. 14.12 for $n = 8$.

In general, a network for $n = 2^m$ consists of two networks for $n = 2^{m-1}$ followed by $n/2$ D-boxes and $n/2$ SA-boxes. When $n = 2$, one D-box and one SA-box suffice. Let us define the *depth* $d(n)$ of a network with inputs as the longest path from input to output. For the network in Fig. 14.12,

$$d(2) = 1,$$

$$d(n) = d(n/2) + 1,$$

that is, $d(n) = \log n$. Therefore, the time requirement of the network in Fig. 14.12 is

$$t(n, b) = O(\log n) + O(b).$$

The number of processors used is

$$p(n, b) = 2p(n/2, b) + O(n)$$

$$= O(n \log n).$$

The fan-out of the gates used is $1 + n/2$. This can be seen from Fig. 14.12, where the value of s_3 has to be sent to one D-box and four SA-boxes.

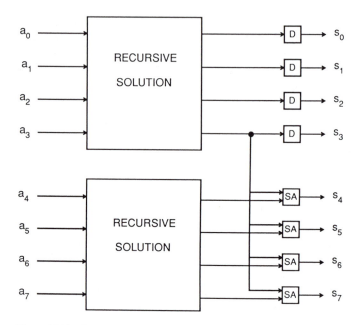

Figure 14.12 Computing prefix sums on network with variable fan-out.

14.5.2 Constant Fan-out

The second solution is illustrated in Fig. 14.13 for $n = 8$.

As mentioned in example 7.2 and section 13.2.2, the perfect shuffle connection (and its inverse, the perfect unshuffle) may be regarded as a mapping from a set of processors to itself or from a set of processors to another set of processors. The latter of these connections is used to construct the network in Fig. 14.13. As with the network in Fig. 14.12,

$$d(n) = \log n,$$

$$t(n, b) = O(\log n) + O(b),$$

$$p(n, b) = O(n \log n).$$

It is clear from Fig. 14.13 that the gate fan-out is 2.

14.6 MATRIX MULTIPLICATION

It is required to compute the product of two $n \times n$ matrices of b-bit integers. We begin by showing how the networks of the previous sections can be used for the computation of the *inner product* of two vectors of integers. A matrix multiplier is then viewed as a collection of networks for inner-product computation.

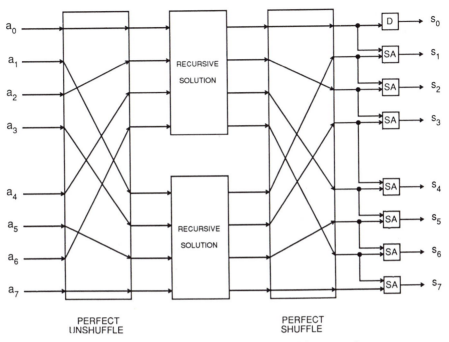

Figure 14.13   Computing prefix sums on network with constant fan-out.

Let $u = (u_0, u_1, \ldots, u_{n-1})$ and $v = (v_0, v_1, \ldots, v_{n-1})$ be two vectors of b-bit integers whose inner product, that is,

$$u_0 v_0 + u_1 v_1 + \cdots + u_{n-1} v_{n-1},$$

is to be computed. The n products $u_i v_i$, for $i = 0, 1, \ldots, n - 1$, can be computed in parallel using n multiplication trees. This requires $O(b)$ time and $O(nb)$ processors. These n products are now fed into an addition tree with $n/2$ leaves to obtain the final sum. This second stage runs in $O(\log n) + O(b)$ time on $O(n)$ processors. Consequently, the inner product requires $O(\log n) + O(b)$ time and $O(nb)$ processors. The inner-product network is illustrated in Fig. 14.14, where the small triangles represent multiplication trees and the large triangle an addition tree.

The product of two $n \times n$ matrices consists of n^2 inner vector products (each row of the first matrix is multiplied by each column of the second). Suppose that we have a multiplier for vectors that multiplies two vectors in q time units using p processors. Then n^2 copies of this multiplier can be used to multiply two $n \times n$ matrices in q time units using $n^2 p$ processors. In general, n^α copies, where $0 \leqslant \alpha \leqslant 2$, will do the job in $n^{2-\alpha} q$ time units and use $n^\alpha p$ processors.

Our vector multiplier of Fig. 14.14 has

$$q = O(\log n) + O(b),$$

$$p = O(nb).$$

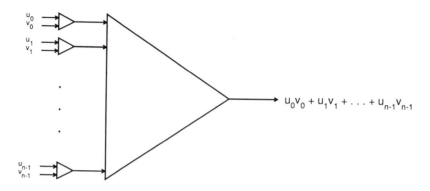

Figure 14.14   Inner-product network.

Thus n^α copies of this multiplier will compute the matrix product in time

$$t(n, b) = O(n^{2-\alpha}(\log n + b))$$

using $p(n, b) = O(n^{1+\alpha}b)$ processors.

14.7 SELECTION

Given a randomly ordered sequence $A = \{a_1, a_2, \ldots, a_n\}$ of n b-bit integers and an integer k, where $1 \leqslant k \leqslant n$, it is required to determine the kth smallest element of A. In chapter 2 we called this the *selection problem* and presented a parallel algorithm for its solution that runs on the EREW SM SIMD model, namely, procedure PARALLEL SELECT. Assuming that each integer fits in a *word* of fixed size b, the procedure uses n^{1-x} processors, where $0 < x < 1$, and runs in $O(n^x)$ time, when counting operations on words. When bit operations are counted, the procedure requires $O(bn^x)$ time for a cost of $O(bn)$. This cost is optimal in view of the $\Omega(bn)$ operations required to simply read the input.

We now describe an algorithm for the selection problem with the following properties:

1. The algorithm operates on b-bit integers where b is a variable, and the bits of each word arrive one every time unit.

2. It runs on a tree-connected parallel computer, which is significantly weaker than the SM SIMD model.

3. It matches the performance of procedure PARALLEL SELECT while being conceptually much simpler.

We begin by describing a simple version of the algorithm whose cost is not optimal. It is based on the following observation. If a set M consisting of the m largest members of

A can be found, then either

(i) the *k*th smallest is included in *M*, in which case we discard from further consideration those elements of *A* that are *not* in *M*, thus reducing the length of the sequence by $n - m$, or

(ii) the *k*th smallest is *not* in *M*, in which case the *m* elements of *M* are removed from *A*.

In order to determine *M*, we look at the most significant bit of the elements of *A*. If the binary representation of element a_i of *A*, where $1 \leqslant i \leqslant n$, is

$$a_i(b - 1) \, a_i(b - 2) \ldots a_i(0),$$

then a_i is in *M* if $a_i(b - 1) = 1$; otherwise a_i is not in *M* [i.e., when $a_i(b - 1) = 0$]. If this process is repeated, by considering successive bits and rejecting a portion of the original sequence each time, the *k*th smallest will be left. (Of course more than one integer may be left if all the elements of *A* are not distinct.)

For ease of presentation, we assume that *n*, the size of the input sequence, is a power of 2. The algorithm runs on a tree-connected network of simple processors with *n* leaves $P_1, P_2, \ldots, P_n$. Leaf processor P_i can

(i) receive the bits of a_i serially, most significant bit first, from some input medium;

(ii) send the bits of a_i to its parent serially;

(iii) send its own index *i* to its parent, if requested; and

(iv) switch itself "off" if told to do so.

Initially, all leaf processors are "on." Once a leaf has been switched off, it is excluded from the remainder of the algorithm's execution: It stops reading input and no longer sends or receives messages to and from its parent.

Each of the $n - 2$ intermediate processors can

(i) relay messages of fixed size from its two children to its parent and vice versa;

(ii) behave as an SA-box; and

(iii) compare two $O(\log n)$-bit values.

Finally, the root processor can

(i) send and receive messages of fixed size to and from its two children;

(ii) compare two $O(\log n)$-bit values;

(iii) behave as an SA-box; and

(iv) store and update three $O(\log n)$-bit values.

The algorithm is given in what follows as procedure TREE SELECTION. When the procedure terminates, the index of the *k*th smallest element of *A* is contained in the root. If several elements of A qualify for being the kth smallest, the one with the smallest index is selected.

procedure TREE SELECTION (A, k)

Step 1:   {Initialization}
    (1.1) The root processor reads n and k
    (1.2) $l \leftarrow n$ {l is the length of the sequence remaining}
    (1.3) $q \leftarrow k$ {the qth smallest element is to be selected}
    (1.4) finished $\leftarrow$ **false**.

Step 2:   **while not** finished **do**
    (2.1) **for** $i = 1$ **to** n **do in parallel**
             P_i reads the next bit of a_i
    end for
    (2.2) The sum s of the n bits just read is computed by the intermediate and root processors acting as an addition tree
    (2.3) **if** $l - q - s \geqslant 0$
    then {qth not in M}
      (i) $l \leftarrow l - s$
      (ii) the intermediate processors relay to all leaves the root's message:
           if latest bit read was 1
           then switch "off"
           end if
    else if $l - q - s = -1$ **and** $s = 1$
      then {qth element found}
        (i) the intermediate processors relay to all leaves the root's message:
             if latest bit read was 1
             then send index to root
             end if
        (ii) the intermediate processors relay to the root the index of the leaf containing the qth smallest element
        (iii) finished $\leftarrow$ **true**
      else {qth in M}
        (i) $q \leftarrow q - (l - s)$
        (ii) $l \leftarrow s$
        (iii) the intermediate processors relay to all leaves the root's message:
             if latest bit read was 0
             then switch "off"
             end if
      end if
    end if
    (2.4) **if** $l = 1$
    then (i) the intermediate processors relay to all leaves the root's message:
           if still "on"
           then send index to root
           end if

(ii) the intermediate processors relay to the root the index of the only remaining integer

(iii) finished ← **true**

end if

(2.5) **if** (there are no more input bits) **and** (**not** finished)

then (i) the intermediate processors relay to all leaves the root's message:

if still "on"

then send index to root

end if

(ii) the intermediate processors relay to the root the index of the smallest-numbered leaf that is still "on"

(iii) finished ← **true**

end if

end while. □

Note that none of the processors (root, intermediate, or leaf) is required at any stage of the algorithm's execution to store all b bits of an input integer. Therefore, the network's storage requirements are independent of b.

Example 14.1

Assume that we want to find the fourth smallest value in $\{10, 15, 12, 1, 3, 7, 6, 13\}$. Initially, $l = 8$ and $q = 4$. During the first iteration of step 2, the most significant bit of each input integer is read by one leaf, as shown in Fig. 14.15(a). The sum of these bits, $s = 4$, is computed at the root. Since $l - q - s = 0$, leaf processors P_1, P_2, P_3, and P_8 are switched off, and $l = 4$.

During the second iteration, the second most significant bits are read by the processors that are still on. This is shown in Fig. 14.15(b), where the processors that were switched off are marked with an $\times$. Since $s = 2$, $l - q - s = -2$, and processors P_4 and P_5 are switched off. Now $l = 2$ and $q = 2$.

In the third iteration, the sum of the third most significant bits, read by P_6 and P_7, is $s = 2$. Since $l - q - s = -2$ and both input bits were 1, no processor is switched off. Again, $l = 2$ and $q = 2$.

In the fourth (and last) iteration, $s = 1$ and $l - q - s = -1$: The index of processor P_6 is sent to the root, signifying that the fourth smallest value in the input sequence is 7. □

Analysis. Step 1 takes constant time. There are at most b iterations of step 2. During each iteration the sum s of n bits read by the leaves can be obtained by the root in $O(\log n)$ time by letting the $n - 2$ intermediate nodes and root simulate an addition tree with n one-bit numbers as input. Unlike the root of the addition tree, however, the root processor here retains the $\log n$ bits of the sum. Thus the time required is $O(b \log n)$. Since the number of processors is $2n - 1$, the algorithm's cost is $O(bn \log n)$, which is not optimal.

An algorithm with optimal cost can be obtained as follows. Let N be a power of 2 such that $N \log n \leqslant n$, and assume that $2N - 1$ processors are available to select the

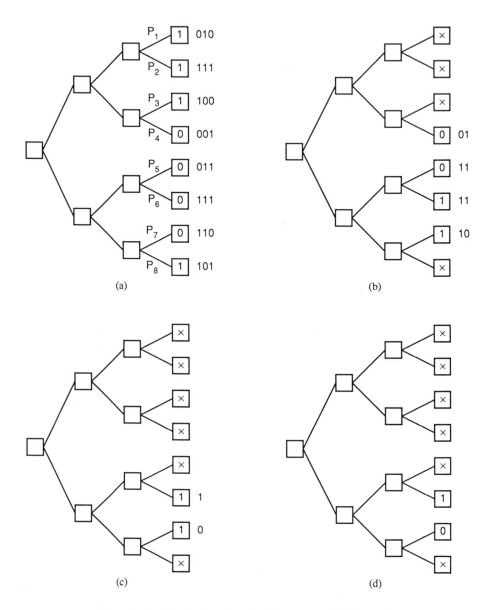

Figure 14.15 Selecting fourth smallest in sequence of eight numbers.

kth smallest element. These processors are arranged in a tree with N leaves. The leaf processors are required to be more powerful than the ones used by procedure TREE SELECTION: They should be able to compute the sum of n/N bits. Each leaf processor is "in charge" of n/N elements of the sequence A. These n/N integers arrive on n/N input media that the leaf examines sequentially. The parallel algorithm consists of b iterations. For $j = b - 1, b - 2, \ldots, 0$, iteration j consists of three stages.

(i) Every leaf processor finds the sum of the jth bits of (at most) n/N integers.

(ii) These sums are added by the remaining processors, and the root indicates which elements must be discarded.

(iii) Every leaf processor "marks" the discarded inputs.

Stages (i) and (iii) require $O(n/N)$ operations. There are $O(\log n)$ operations involved in stage (ii) to go up and down the tree. The time per iteration is $O(n/N)$, for a total running time of

$$t(n) = O(bn/N).$$

Since $p(n) = 2N - 1$, we have

$$c(n) = O(bn),$$

and this is optimal.

14.8 SORTING

Given a sequence of n b-bit integers $A = \{a_1, a_2, \ldots, a_n\}$, it is required to sort A in nondecreasing order. We assume that b is a variable and that the bits of each integer arrive one every time unit. The sequence can be sorted by adapting the odd–even sorting network of Fig. 4.1. The adapted network has two features:

1. Each integer a_i is fed into the network *most significant bit first*.

2. *Bit comparators* replace the *word comparators* in Fig. 4.1. A bit comparator has the same function as a word comparator: It compares two integers, producing the smaller on the *top* output line and the larger on the *bottom* output line. The only difference is that bit comparators perform their task bit serially. A bit comparator receives two bits as input and produces two bits as output in the following way. As long as the two input bits are equal, they are produced on the two output lines *unchanged*. As soon as the two input bits differ,

(i) the 0 bit, and all subsequent bits of that integer, are produced as output on the top output line of the comparator and

(ii) the 1 bit, and all subsequent bits of that integer, are produced as output on the bottom output line of the comparator.

As the odd–even network consists of $O(\log^2 n)$ stages, the modified network requires

$$t(n, b) = O(\log^2 n) + O(b)$$

time and

$$p(n, b) = O(n \log^2 n)$$

processors.

14.9 PROBLEMS

14.1 Let x and y be two b-bit integers, where b is a variable. Design a network for computing $x - y$.

14.2 A *full adder* for bits is a device that takes three bits as input and returns their sum as a two-bit binary number. A collection of full adders (arranged side by side) can take three b-bit integers x, y, and z as input and return two binary integers u and v as output such that $x + y + z = u + v$. Assume that b is a constant and all bits of x, y, and z are available at once. Each full adder receives one bit from each of x, y, and z and returns one bit of each of u and v. Thus u and v can be obtained from x, y, and z in constant time. Let us call this device a $(3, 2)$-*adder*. Show that a network of $(3, 2)$-adders reduces the problem of adding n numbers to the problem of adding *two* numbers. Analyze the running time, number of processors, and complexity of this network.

14.3 Discuss the cost optimality of the networks described in section 14.4.

14.4 Let x and y be two b-bit integers, where b is a power of 2. A *divide-and-conquer* algorithm can be used to multiply x and y. We first split each of x and y into two equal parts of $b/2$ bits each and write

$$x = u \times 2^{b/2} + v,$$

$$y = w \times 2^{b/2} + z.$$

Now $x \times y$ is computed from

$$(uw)2^b + (uz + vw)2^{b/2} + vz,$$

where the products uw, uz, vw, and vz are obtained by the same algorithm recursively. Let $q(b)$ be the number of bit operations required to compute $x \times y$ by the preceding algorithm. Since the algorithm involves four multiplications of two $(b/2)$-bit integers, three additions of integers with at most $2b$ bits, and two shifts (multiplications by 2^b and $2^{b/2}$), we have

$$q(1) = 1,$$

$$q(b) = 4q(b/2) + cb,$$

for some constant c. It follows that $q(b) = O(b^2)$.

(a) Can the algorithm be implemented in parallel? Can it be used in a setting where b is a variable and the bits of x and y arrive serially?

(b) Consider now the following modification to the algorithm. The quantity $uz + vw$ is obtained from $(u + v)(w + z) - uw - vz$. Only three multiplications of $(b/2)$-bit integers are now required, four additions, two subtractions, and two shifts.

Consequently,

$$q(1) = 1,$$

$$q(b) = 3q(b/2) + cb,$$

for some constant c. It follows that $q(b) = O(b^{\log_2 3}) = O(b^{1.59})$. Repeat part (a) for this new version.

14.5 Let x and y be b-bit integers. Design a network to compute the quotient and remainder of x divided by y.

14.6 Which of the two networks described in section 14.5 for computing the prefix sums of a sequence relies on the *commutativity* of the addition operation, that is, $a + b = b + a$?

14.7 The networks of section 14.5 have a cost of $O(n \log^2 n + bn \log n)$. This cost is clearly not optimal since a *single* SA-box can compute all prefix sums in $O(bn)$ time. Can a cost-optimal solution be obtained for the bit-serial version of the prefix sums problem?

14.8 The networks of section 14.5 produce, as one of their outputs, the sum of their n inputs. Compare this method of computing the sum of n integers to the one described in section 14.3.

14.9 Repeat problem 13.4 for the bit-serial case.

14.10 Repeat problem 13.5 for the bit-serial case.

14.11 Repeat problem 13.6 for the bit-serial case.

14.12 Discuss the cost of the matrix multiplier of section 14.6.

14.13 Describe formally the algorithm given at the end of section 14.7.

14.14 Adapt procedure TREE SELECTION to run on an $n^{1/2} \times n^{1/2}$ mesh-connected computer and analyze its running time.

14.15 Can the cost of the algorithm derived in 14.14 be made optimal?

14.16 Consider a linear array of processors $P_1, P_2, \ldots, P_n$ and the following algorithm for sorting a sequence of n b-bit integers that arrive one at a time at P_1. At every step, the contents of the entire array of processors are shifted to the right making room in P_1 for a new input item. This is followed by a *comparison–exchange*: For all odd i, the items in P_i and P_{i+1} are compared, with the smaller going to P_i and the larger to P_{i+1}. After n repetitions of these two steps, input is complete and output can start. The contents of the array are shifted left producing as output from P_1 the current smallest element in the array. This is followed by a comparison–exchange. After n repetitions of the preceding two steps output is complete. When several sequences are queued for sorting, this sorter has *period 2n*. The period can be reduced to n by allowing both P_1 and P_n to handle input and output. While P_1 is producing output, P_n can receive input and conversely. Sorted sequences are produced alternately in ascending order (through P_1) and in descending order (through P_n). Thus m sequences of n integers each are sorted in $(m + 1)n$ instead of $2mn$ steps. Obviously the time to compare two b-bit integers x and y, when b is not fixed, is a linear function of b. Thus, the preceding times are in reality $(m + 1)nb$ and $2mnb$. It is of course possible to compare two b-bit integers in fewer than b steps by using additional circuitry in each processor. This circuitry is in the form of a complete binary tree with b leaves. Assume that *bit-parallel* input is allowed, that is, all b bits of an integer arrive simultaneously. Each leaf compares one bit of x with the corresponding bit of y and sends the result upward. These results propagate up the tree, and in $\log b$ steps the larger of x and y is determined. This would make the running time $(m + 1)n \log b$ and $2mn \log b$.

Show that a network derived from the linear array whose processors use no special circuitry and operate at the bit level can sort in $(1 + m/2)n + b$ time. This would represent a significant improvement over the preceding approach.

14.17 Consider the following algorithm for sorting the sequence $A = \{a_1, a_2, \ldots, a_n\}$ of b-bit integers. Two arrays of n entries each are created in memory. These two arrays are called *bucket 0* and *bucket 1*. The algorithm consists of b iterations. At the beginning of each iteration, all positions of both buckets contain zeros. During iteration j, each element a_i of A, where

$$a_i = a_i(b-1)\, a_i(b-2) \ldots a_i(0),$$

is examined: A 1 is placed in position i of either bucket 0 or bucket 1 depending on whether $a_i(j)$ is 0 or 1, respectively. The values in bucket 0, followed by those in bucket 1, form a sequence of 0's and 1's of length $2n$. The prefix sums $\{s_1, s_2, \ldots, s_{2n}\}$ of this sequence are now computed. Finally element a_i is placed in position s_i or s_{i+n} of A (depending on whether bucket 0 or bucket 1 contains a 1 in position i), concluding this iteration. Show how this algorithm can be implemented in parallel and analyze its running time and cost.

14.18 The networks in sections 14.2–14.6 receive their inputs and produce their outputs *least significant bit first*. By contrast, the networks in sections 14.7 and 14.8 receive their inputs and produce their output's *most significant bit first*. This may be a problem if the output of one network (of the first type) is to serve as the input to another network (of the second type), or vice versa. Suggest ways to overcome this difficulty.

14.19 Let us define
   (i) *clock cycle* as the time elapsed from the moment one input bit arrives at a network to the moment the following bit arrives and
   (ii) *gate delay* as the time taken by a gate to produce its output.
   Show that, for the networks in this chapter to operate properly, it is important that

   clock cycle > gate delay.

14.20 Argue that the running time analyses in this chapter are correct provided that the ratio of clock cycle to gate delay is constant.

14.21 Show that the process of computing the majority of fundamental statistical quantities, such as the *mean, standard deviation*, and *moment*, can be speeded up using the networks described in this chapter.

14.22 Design a network for computing the *greatest common divisor* of two b-bit integers.

14.10 BIBLIOGRAPHICAL REMARKS

As mentioned in the introduction, most models of computation assume that the word size of the input data is fixed and that each data word is available in its entirety when needed; see, for example, [Aho], [Akl 1], [Horowitz], and [Knuth 1]. In this section, we briefly review some of the algorithms that were designed to solve the problems addressed in sections 14.2–14.8 based on these two assumptions. When comparing those algorithms to the networks of this chapter, one should keep in mind that the latter do not make the preceding two assumptions and can therefore be used (if needed) in situations where these assumptions apply (as well as in situations where they do not).

The fastest known algorithm for adding two b-bit integers is the *carry-look-ahead adder* [Kuck]. It runs in $O(\log b)$ time and uses $O(b \log b)$ gates with arbitrarily large fan-out. The algorithm's cost is therefore $O(b \log^2 b)$. This is to be contrasted with the $O(b)$ cost of the SA-box ([Baer]).

The sum of n b-bit integers can be computed by a tree of carry-look-ahead adders [Ullman]. This requires $O((\log n)(\log b))$ time and $O(nb \log b)$ gates for a cost of $O((n \log n)(b \log^2 b))$. By comparison, the tree of SA-boxes described in section 14.3 uses fewer gates, has a lower cost, and is faster for $b = O(\log n)$. Another algorithm superior to the tree of carry-look-ahead adders is described in problem 14.2.

Two solutions are given in [Kuck] to the problem of multiplying two b-bit integers. The first one uses carry-look-ahead adders and requires $O(\log^2 b)$ time and $O(b^2 \log b)$ gates. The second and more elaborate solution is based on a combination of *carry-save* and carry-look-ahead adders. It uses $O(b^2)$ gates and runs in $O(\log^2 b)$ time (when the fan-out of the gates is constant) and $O(\log b)$ time (when the fan-out is equal to b) for costs of $O(b^2 \log^2 b)$ and $O(b^2 \log b)$, respectively. Both of these costs are larger than the $O(b^2)$ cost of the multiplication tree and multiplication mesh of section 14.4.

If carry-look-ahead adders are used in section 13.2.3 for computing the prefix sums of a sequence of n integers, then the tree algorithm described therein would require $O((\log n)(\log b))$ time and $O(nb \log b)$ gates for a cost of $O((n \log n)(b \log^2 b))$. Assume for concreteness that $b = O(\log n)$. Then the preceding expressions describing the running time, number of gates, and cost become $O((\log n)(\log \log n))$, $O((n \log n)(\log \log n))$, and $O((n \log^2 n)(\log^2 \log n))$, respectively. The corresponding expressions for the networks of section 14.5 are $O(\log n)$, $O(n \log n)$, and $O(n \log^2 n)$.

Procedure CUBE MATRIX MULTIPLICATION of section 7.3.2 uses n^3 processors and runs in $O(\log n)$ time. If the processors are based on the integer multiplier given in [Kuck] and whose gate and time requirements are $O(b^2)$ and $O(\log^2 b)$, respectively, then the product of two $n \times n$ matrices of b-bit integers can be obtained in $O((\log n)(\log^2 b))$ time using $O(n^3 b^2)$ gates. This yields a cost of $O((n^3 \log n)(b^2 \log^2 b))$. Again, let $b = O(\log n)$. The cost of procedure CUBE MATRIX MULTIPLICATION in this case is $O(n^3 \log^3 n \log^2 \log n)$. This is larger than the $O(n^3 \log^2 n)$ cost of the network described in section 14.6. Note also that the product of the *solution time* by the *number of gates used* for any *sequential* matrix multiplication algorithm of the type described, for example, in [Coppersmith] and [Gonnet], can be improved from $O(n^x b^2 \log^2 b)$ where $x < 3$ (using the integer multiplier in [Kuck]) to $O(n^x b^2)$ (using the multiplication tree or mesh of section 14.4).

Many tree algorithms exist for selecting the kth smallest element of a sequence of n b-bit integers (assuming that all bits are available simultaneously). Some of these are reviewed in [Aggarwal 1]. The best such algorithm uses $O(n)$ processors and runs in $O(\log^2 n)$ time. Counting bit operations, this running time becomes $O(b \log^2 n)$. Unlike (the modified) procedure TREE SELECTION described in section 14.7, this algorithm is not cost optimal.

A cost-optimal algorithm for sorting n b-bit integers is described in [Leighton]. It uses $O(n)$ processors and runs in $O(b \log n)$ time (counting bit operations), for an optimal cost of $O(bn \log n)$. Using the bit comparators described in section 14.8 and in [Knuth 2], sorting can be performed in $O(b + \log n)$ time with $O(n)$ gates.

The networks in this chapter are mostly from [Akl 2], [Cooper], and [Meijer]. Other algorithms concerned with bit operations are described in [Aggarwal 2], [Akl 3], [Batcher], [Bini], [Brent], [Kannan], [Luk], [Reeves], [Siegel], and [Yu] for a variety of computational problems.

14.11 REFERENCES

[AGGARWAL 1]

Aggarwal, A., A comparative study of X-tree, pyramid and related machines, *Proceedings of the 25th Annual IEEE Symposium on Foundations of Computer Science*, Singer Island, Florida, October 1984, pp. 89–99, IEEE Computer Society, Washingon, D.C., 1984.

[AGGARWAL 2]

Aggarwal, A., and Kosaraju, S. R., Optimal tradeoffs for addition on systolic arrays, in Makedon, F., Mehlhorn, K., Papatheodorou, T., and Spirakis, P., Eds., *VLSI Algorithms and Architectures*, Lecture Notes in Computer Science, Vol. 227, Springer-Verlag, Berlin, 1986, pp. 57–69.

[AHO]

Aho, A. V., Hopcroft, J. E., and Ullman, J. D., *The Design and Analysis of Computer Algorithms*, Addison-Wesley, Reading, Mass., 1974.

[AKL 1]

Akl, S. G., *Parallel Sorting Algorithms*, Academic Press, Orlando Fl., 1985.

[AKL 2]

Akl, S. G., and Meijer, H., On the bit complexity of parallel computations, *Integration: The VLSI Journal*, Vol. 6, No. 2, July 1988, pp. 201–212.

[AKL 3]

Akl, S. G., and Schmeck, H., Systolic sorting in a sequential input/output environment, *Parallel Computing*, Vol. 3, No. 1, March 1986, pp. 11–23.

[BAER]

Baer, J.-L., *Computer Systems Architecture*, Computer Science Press, Rockville, Md., 1980.

[BATCHER]

Batcher, K. E., Bit-serial parallel processing systems, *IEEE Transactions on Computers*, Vol. C-31, No. 5, May 1982, pp. 377–384.

[BINI]

Bini, D., and Pan, V., A logarithmic boolean time algorithm for parallel polynomial division, in Makedon, F., Mehlhorn, K., Papatheodorou, T., and Spirakis, P., Eds., *VLSI Algorithms and Architectures*, Lecture Notes in Computer Science, Vol. 227, Springer-Verlag, Berlin, 1986, pp. 246–251.

[BRENT]

Brent, R. P., and Kung, H. T., The area-time complexity of binary multiplication, *Journal of the ACM*, Vol. 28, No. 3, July 1981, pp. 521–534.

[COOPER]

Cooper, J., and Akl, S. G., Efficient selection on a binary tree, *Information Processing Letters*, Vol. 23, No. 3, October 1986, pp. 123–126.

[COPPERSMITH]

Coppersmith, D., and Winograd, S., Matrix multiplication via arithmetic progressions, *Proceedings of the 19th Annual ACM Symposium on Theory of Computing*, New York, May 1987, pp. 1–6, Association for Computing Machinery, New York, N.Y., 1987.

[GONNET]

Gonnet, G. H., *Handbook of Algorithms and Data Structures*, Addison-Wesley, Reading, Mass., 1984.

[HOROWITZ]

Horowitz, E., and Sahni, S., *Fundamentals of Computer Algorithms*, Computer Science Press, Rockville, Md., 1978.

[KANNAN]

Kannan, R., Miller, G., and Rudolph, L., Sublinear parallel algorithm for computing the greatest common divisor of two integers, Proceedings of the 25th Annual IEEE Symposium on Foundations of Computer Science, Singer Island, Florida, October 1984, pp. 7–11, IEEE Computer Society, Washington, D.C., 1984.

[KNUTH 1]

Knuth, D. E., *The Art of Computer Programming*, Vol. 1, *Fundamental Algorithms*, Addison-Wesley, Reading, Mass., 1973.

[KNUTH 2]

Knuth, D. E., *The Art of Computer Programming*, Vol. 3, *Sorting and Searching*, Addison-Wesley, Reading, Mass., 1973.

[KUCK]

Kuck, D. J., *The Structure of Computers and Computations*, Vol. 1, Wiley, New York, 1978.

[LEIGHTON]

Leighton, F. T., Tight bounds on the complexity of parallel sorting, *IEEE Transactions on Computers*, Vol. C-34, No. 4, April 1985, pp. 344–354.

[LUK]

Luk, W. K., and Vuillemin, J. E., Recursive implementation of optimal time VLSI integer multipliers, in Anceau, F., and Aas, E. J., Eds., *VLSI '83*, North-Holland, Amsterdam, 1983, pp. 155–168.

[MEIJER]

Meijer, H., and Akl, S. G., Bit serial addition trees and their applications, *Computing*, Vol. 40, 1988, pp. 9–17.

[REEVES]

Reeves, A. P., and Bruner, J. D., Efficient function implementation for bit-serial parallel processors, *IEEE Transactions on Computers*, Vol. C-29, No. 9, September 1980, pp. 841–844.

[SIEGEL]

Siegel, A. R., Minimum storage sorting networks, *IEEE Transactions on Computers*, Vol. C-34, No. 4, April 1985, pp. 355–361.

[ULLMAN]

Ullman, J. D., *Computational Aspects of VLSI*, Computer Science Press, Rockville, Md., 1984.

[YU]

Yu, G.-S., and Muroga, S., Parallel multipliers with NOR gates based on G-minimum adders, *International Journal of Computer and Information Sciences*, Vol. 13, No. 2, 1984, pp. 111–121.

Author Index

Subject Index